OPERATION THUNDERBOLT

FLIGHT 139 AND THE RAID ON ENTEBBE AIRPORT, THE MOST AUDACIOUS HOSTAGE RESCUE MISSION IN HISTORY

SAUL DAVID

Little, Brown and Company

New York   Boston   London

Little, Brown and Company
Hachette Book Group
1290 Avenue of the Americas, New York, NY 10104
littlebrown.com

First North American edition: December 2015
Originally published in Great Britain by Hodder & Stoughton, July 2015

Little, Brown and Company is a division of Hachette Book Group, Inc.
The Little, Brown name and logo are trademarks of Hachette Book Group, Inc.

The publisher is not responsible for websites (or their content)
that are not owned by the publisher.

The Hachette Speakers Bureau provides a wide range of authors for speaking events.
To find out more, go to hachettespeakersbureau.com or call (866) 376-6591.

ISBN 978-0-316-24541-8
Library of Congress Control Number: 2015946917

10 9 8 7 6 5 4 3 2 1

RRD-C

Printed in the United States of America

For Stewart and Noreen.

*And in memory of Bruce McKenzie and the five Israelis
who lost their lives as a result of Operation Thunderbolt:
Dora Bloch, Ida Borochovich, Pasco Cohen, Jean-Jacques
Mimouni and Yoni Netanyahu.*

CONTENTS

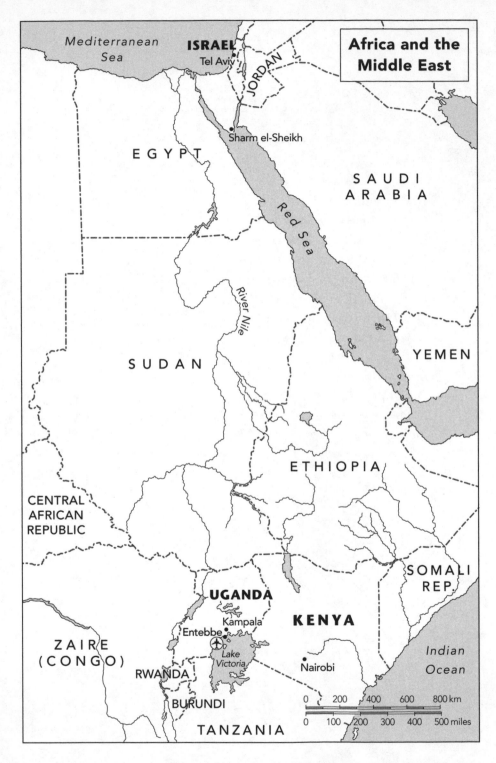

Country names and borders as they were at the time of the raid.

OPERATION THUNDERBOLT

DAY 1: SUNDAY 27 JUNE 1976

0500hrs GMT, Lod, Israel

A chaotic scene greeted Frenchman Michel Cojot and his twelve-year-old son Olivier as they entered the ground-floor check-in area of Ben-Gurion International Airport's Terminal 1, an unsightly four-storey concrete and glass construction that had replaced the original whitewashed terminal built by the British in the 1930s. The flow of people reminded Cojot of an Oriental bazaar as it 'tried to make a path among the baggage carts, the pillars, and the barriers under the watchful eyes of young women in khaki and young soldiers . . . the only persons there who were not bustling about'.

A spate of recent terrorist attacks against Israel – including the infamous massacre of twenty-six people, most of them Christian pilgrims from Puerto Rico, by three pro-Palestinian members of the militant communist Japanese Red Army at Ben-Gurion four years earlier – had left the country with the tightest airport security in the world. Anyone who could not convince the officials that he was harmless would have his alarm clock 'dismantled, the heels of his shoes probed, his camera opened, his can of shaving cream tested'. Despite the delay, most were happy to cooperate because they 'approved of the reasons for the controls'.

In truth the stringent checks were the final straw for young Olivier Cojot. His parents had recently separated and he had jumped at the chance to join his management-consultant father on a week-long business trip to Israel, leaving his mother and two younger siblings in France. He had hoped to bond with his father and learn more about his Jewish heritage. But apart from a 'pretty interesting' visit to a factory run by Negev Phosphates, the mining firm his father was advising, he had spent much of his time alone and sweltering in a Beersheba hotel and could not wait to get home.

Not that the temperature in France was any cooler. It, like the rest of Western Europe, was wilting in a heatwave that would prove to be the hottest on record. Olivier was just relieved that the queuing for the early-morning flight was at a comparatively cool time of day. He found the lengthy security checks at Ben-Gurion 'a pain in the arse' and the terminal's lack of air-conditioning did not help.

Finally reaching the Air France check-in desk, the Cojots were told their flight to Paris would be making an unscheduled stopover at Athens. The Greek capital's international airport was well known for the laxity of its transit security, and Olivier voiced his father's fears when he piped up: 'Hey Dad, if I were a terrorist I would get on at the stopover.'

Such fears of a terrorist attack – more specifically a plane hijacking – were far from unfounded. Since Israel's victory over the Arab states of Egypt, Jordan and Syria in the Six-Day War of 1967, various Palestinian and pro-Palestinian terror groups had used plane hijackings as a means of forcing concessions out of Israel and publicizing their cause to the world. Before the Six-Day War there had typically been five hijackings annually. By 1969 this had risen to eighty-two hijackings worldwide – the most in a single year – and, though the average had since fallen, it was still more than three a month.

Only too aware of the recent spate of hijackings, Cojot inquired about a direct flight to Paris on the Israeli airline El Al that, with its armed sky marshals, 'seemed to offer better security'. But hearing the flight was full, and unwilling to wait for another, he reluctantly returned to Air France, his concern only partly assuaged by the knowledge that his frequent-flyer status meant he qualified for 'service plus'.

Other travellers on Air France Flight 139 were just as alarmed by news of the stopover. Ilan Hartuv, forty-nine, a short-sighted and rotund former Israeli diplomat and now deputy director-general of a Jerusalem urban-regeneration company, was accompanying his seventy-three-year-old mother Dora Bloch on the first leg of her journey to New York for the wedding of his younger brother Daniel. Hartuv planned to part from her in Paris where he would meet his brother-in-law and their respective wives for a short holiday and, aware of the threat from terrorists, he had specifically instructed his travel agent to book non-stop tickets. So too had Sara Davidson, en route to the United States for a coast-to-coast tour with her husband Uzi and their two sons, seventeen-year-old Roni and Benny, thirteen. 'Let's not go on the plane,' she told Uzi when she heard it would stop in Greece. 'We don't know who's likely to get on in Athens.' They also tried to change to El Al without success.

Other passengers made late switches *to* Flight 139. Nineteen-year-old Jean-Jacques Mimouni, French-born but of Tunisian descent, had been booked on a Saturday flight to Paris. Tall and boyishly hand-some, with a moustache and fashionably long, dark-brown curly hair, a talented guitar player and artist, Jean-Jacques had just finished his matriculation exams and was planning to spend the summer in France with two elder sisters before either staying on – his father's preference – or returning to Israel for military service. But he was persuaded to delay his flight until Sunday by his best friend Thierry Sicard, the son of the French consul in Tel Aviv, so that they could fly together.

Belgians Gilbert and Helen Weill had just completed a short holiday in Israel and were due to take a later Air France flight to Paris. Their plan was to pick up their children in Metz and then return home to Antwerp. But when told that their original plane had been delayed in Iran and their best option was Flight 139, leaving in just an hour, they took it. Walking away from the Air France desk they met an acquaint-ance travelling on their original flight. 'Quick,' advised Mr Weill, 'get on the earlier flight before all the seats are taken. Who knows how long that other plane is going to be delayed.'

At 8.59 a.m. local time, Air France Flight 139 took off in perfect weather – a blazing sun and clear blue skies – and headed north-west across the Mediterranean for Athens. The plane was one of the recently introduced wide-bodied Airbus A300B4s, a comfortable twin-engined jetliner capable of carrying 272 passengers in a two-class layout: 24 first-class seats at the front of the plane in a 2:2:2 configuration; and a further 248 seats in two economy cabins to the rear, the seats divided 2:4:2 by two aisles. For the last six rows, as the fuselage tapered towards the tail, the middle row was just three seats. Possibly because of late cancellations, only 228 seats were occupied.

Captaining the plane was a dashing fifty-one-year-old father of three called Michel Bacos, a former naval pilot who had fought with de Gaulle's Free French forces in the Second World War. His eleven-man crew consisted of a co-pilot, flight engineer, chief steward, four stewards and four stewardesses. Apart from a Swedish stewardess called Ann-Carina Franking, all were French.

Sitting in the rear economy cabin, three rows from the front, Michel Cojot quickly forgot his fears as the Air France crew made a fuss of him and his son. 'After this heavy dose of the East it was a pleasure' for him 'to go back to the language, the elegant restraint of the stewardesses' uniforms, and even the food tray'. There was nothing in the way of in-flight entertainment on a 1970s airliner, and Cojot passed the two-and-a-half-hour flight time to Athens by writing 'a probably useless professional memorandum' and giving Olivier 'an exercise in spelling by dictating a vaguely humorous piece on the joys of air travel'. It was typical of the high-achieving Cojot to try and educate his son even when he was on holiday. For Olivier, a 'terrible speller', these regular dictations by his father were 'a huge pain in the behind'.

The only bleak spot for the thirty-seven-year-old Cojot was the proximity of unruly neighbours who included 'brawling brats, a woman who spilled over her seat on both sides, and a couple of retired Americans'.

0902hrs GMT, Athens, Greece

Just after noon local time, the Airbus touched down at Athens's Ellinikon International Airport, a few miles south of the Greek capital. As the stop was a brief one – just forty-five minutes – only the thirty-eight disembarking passengers were allowed to leave the plane. They included the retired Americans but not, to Michel Cojot's chagrin, the squabbling children.

In their place came fifty-six new passengers, bringing the total to 246, not far from capacity. The majority were still nationals of Israel and France, though more than twenty other nationalities were now present, including American, Australian, Belgian, Brazilian, Canadian, Colombian, Greek, Japanese, Jordanian, Lebanese, Moroccan, Romanian, Spanish and Turkish. Of the new arrivals, many had been holidaying in or around the Greek islands. Among them were British yachtsmen and old friends Tony Russell, a married fifty-five-year-old senior official for the Greater London Council, and George Good, sixty-five, a retired accountant and widower, who had been sailing round Ithaca and Paxos in the Ionian Sea; Frenchman Gérard Poignon and his English-born wife Isabella, twenty-eight, who had left their eighteen-month-old daughter in the care of Gérard's parents while they enjoyed a ten-day cruise; Colin and Nola Hardie from Christchurch in New Zealand, where Colin was general manager of the *Star* newspaper; Peter and Nancy Rabinowitz, two young Jewish American academics who were teaching literature at Kirkland College in New York State; and Claude Moufflet from Versailles in France.

The Rabinowitzes were in Europe to celebrate thirty-one-year-old Nancy's recent completion of her PhD in comparative literature (a degree that Peter, two years her senior, already possessed). Arriving in London from the US, they had asked if they could buy a return plane ticket to Athens with a stopover in Paris on the second leg. Informed that that was impossible, they bought a standard return with the intention of taking the boat-train over the Channel. But when they returned to Athens Airport after a two-week stay in Greece, they were told by their airline that they *could* trade in their Athens–London tickets for Athens–Paris–London at no extra cost. As a switch to another carrier was also possible, Peter chose Air France because he did not like Greek food and thought that airline cuisine on a French plane would be the best. Both Rabinowitzes were acutely aware of the danger of hijacking and would not have got on Flight 139 if they had known it was on a stopover from Tel Aviv. It never occurred to them to ask.

Claude Moufflet was returning from a work trip to Teheran in Iran, where his company owned a business, and had arrived at Ellinikon's East Terminal – an ugly single-storey concrete building designed by the celebrated Finnish architect Eero Saarinen in the 1960s – by taxi from Athens's original airport at 11.30 a.m. local time. Shortly after checking in his suitcases at the Air France desk, he was approached by a young Greek man who asked him if he was willing to post a very urgent letter in Paris. Satisfied that the envelope contained only paper, he put it in his briefcase.

Moufflet next passed through passport control and security, the latter a 'systematic and rigorous' series of checks. As his hand luggage went through a radar detection tunnel he could clearly see his electronic calculator, Dictaphone, camera, film and flash appear on the screen. Alarmed by this last unusual image, the policeman on duty stopped the conveyor belt and instructed Moufflet to open his briefcase so that he could check the authenticity of these objects. Once he was satisfied, he passed Moufflet on to his colleague for a body search. Finally convinced that the Frenchman was a harmless businessman, and that the cylindrical 1.5-volt batteries that appeared on the radar screen were for his Dictaphone and calculator, and not part of 'an elaborate explosive system', they let him continue.

Four of Flight 139's new passengers, however, were not subjected to the same level of security because they were in transit, having landed at 6.45 a.m. on Singapore Airlines Flight 763 from Bahrain. Two were travelling on South American passports: a tall blond-haired Peruvian called A. Garcia, wearing a natty brown corduroy suit and a green shirt; and a young Ecuadorian woman, Ortega, in a blue denim skirt and top, with shoulder-length dark hair and wire-rimmed glasses. The other pair were Middle Eastern in appearance and carrying Bahraini and Kuwaiti travel documents: one was tall with long fair hair and 'wild staring' blue eyes that put one of his fellow passengers in mind of Mick Jagger on drugs; the other short and stocky, with dark hair and a bushy moustache.

Despite the fact that all four were carrying large bags, none was particularly scrutinized because it was assumed they had been scanned at their airport of origin. It did not help that 'nobody was on duty at the metal detector in the passenger corridor, and the policeman at the fluoroscope was paying little attention to the screen at his side'.

At 12.15 p.m., Air France Flight 139 was announced. Clutching his briefcase and a Duty Free bag containing two bottles of ouzo, a bottle of Scotch and a carton of cigarettes, Claude Moufflet slowly made his way to Gate 2, 'through which passengers were flowing in dribs and drabs to board the shuttle bus'.

With an outside temperature of 90 degrees Fahrenheit, and no air-conditioning on the shuttle, the passengers were perspiring freely by the time they reached the waiting plane at 12.35 p.m. Moufflet had scanned his fellow travellers on the bus, but none particularly drew his attention. He was more interested in the type of plane and noted with satisfaction that it was a modern Airbus 'which, given the temperature, promised a comfortable, quick and cool flight'.

The two South Americans had first-class tickets and took their seats at the front of the plane. The other pair in transit had cheaper tickets and sat in the forward economy cabin where their Arab appearance, large bags and cans of stuffed dates caused some suspicion. Ilan Hartuv was looking out of the window when his mother whispered to him that she had seen two young people get on who looked like Arabs and had very big bags, and that she was afraid. Hartuv wanted to alert the crew, but as everyone had fastened seatbelts and the plane was about to depart, he decided not to.

Another alarmed by the new arrivals was Helen Weill, an Orthodox Jew from Antwerp in Belgium who was sitting with her husband Gilbert at the front of economy class. 'Arabs!' she hissed at him. 'Maybe we should find another flight.' But Gilbert was more concerned with picking up his children on time and told her to stop worrying. French-born Emma Rosenkovitch – en route with her husband Claude and their two children Noam and Ella to visit her parents in Paris – hardly noticed that two of the Athens passengers were Arabs: she and Claude were peace activists and had many Palestinian friends. Instead she was struck by their rudeness as they struggled up their aisle with their giant black bags, bumping into people. 'Why would an airline let people get on with such big bags anyway?' she wondered.

Meanwhile Claude Moufflet, having stowed his briefcase and Duty

Free in the overhead locker, had settled down in the row behind the Weills. With his seatbelt fastened, he began reading a newspaper. So too did Gilbert Weill, noticing as he flicked through his paper an article about Idi Amin Dada, Uganda's eccentric, erratic, flamboyant and ruthless dictator who, just two days earlier, had been declared 'President for Life' by the Ugandan parliament. A few minutes later, as the plane was about to take off, Weill heard a young boy a few rows behind him asking one of the Arabs what was in the large bag he was carrying. 'Dates for you,' the Arab replied, 'and grenades for your parents.'

As if to show his comment was harmless, the Arab offered a stuffed date to his neighbour, a forty-eight-year-old Tunis-born Israeli called Joseph Abougedir who took and ate it. But not before noting the place of origin on the box's Arabic label: Iraq.

1010hrs GMT, Greek airspace above the Gulf of Corinth

Barely eight minutes after takeoff, with the plane still climbing towards its cruising height of 31,000 feet, and the stewards and stewardesses 'already busy in the galleys preparing lunch', the two South American transit passengers in first class sprang to their feet, both holding a pistol and a grenade. While the female Ortega stood guard, Garcia made straight for the door leading to the flight deck. Nearby passengers screamed in alarm.

Inside the cockpit was Bacos, his co-pilot Daniel Lom and flight engineer Jacques Lemoine. Hearing shouting in the first-class cabin, and thinking that a fire had broken out, Bacos told his flight engineer to check. But no sooner had Lemoine opened the door than he came face to face with a man holding a pistol and a grenade. The engineer was forced to the ground, the gun pressed to his temple, as Bacos begged: 'Please don't kill him!'

Convinced as he was that Lemoine was about to be executed, those first few minutes seemed endless to Bacos. But the crisis passed and, having confiscated Bacos' oxygen mask and microphone, Garcia told the occupants of the flight deck that the plane had been taken over by a commando of the Popular Front for the Liberation of Palestine, and that the captain should set a course for Benghazi in Libya. If he and his crew cooperated, no harm would come to them. By now the terrorist's gun was pointed at Bacos' head; if he tried to turn round, the muzzle was prodded in his neck to discourage him.

Back in economy class, the two Arabs had leapt out of their seats to join in the hijacking. Moshe Peretz, a twenty-six-year-old Israeli medical student, noted in an improvised diary that one was 'a long-haired youth wearing a red shirt, gray trousers, and a beige pullover' and the other had 'a thick mustache, wears long trousers and a yellow shirt'. They were 'running towards the first-class compartment'. Soon after 'frightened and hysterical stewardesses' emerged from there and, with 'trembling arms', tried to calm the agitated passengers.

In the aisle to the left of Claude Moufflet appeared a 'livid, flustered' stewardess who kept saying: 'Stay calm. Sit down. Stay calm.' Moufflet repeated the instructions 'without knowing the reason, in English and French', to the passengers on his right until he noticed the barrel of a pistol 'resting on the backrest of the first seat in [economy] class, approximately 20 centimetres' from his face. The man holding it was 'about 25 years old, average height, stocky, Mediterranean looking, his tanned faced sporting a very black moustache'. In his left hand he was holding a 'fragmentation grenade' that was clearly unpinned because Moufflet could see the pin 'passed like a ring' around the hijacker's middle finger.

Then to his left Moufflet saw the second Arab – 'small, very thin, with a pale, angular face, blue eyes and long straight hair' – herding two stewards at the point of a gun. He and his comrade kept shouting in bad English: 'Don't move! Put your hands on your head! Don't move! Keep quiet! Don't move!'

Back in the rear economy cabin, the passengers thought the plane was on fire. Michel Cojot heard a shout 'and saw a man, bent over, running towards the front of the plane'. The rumour quickly spread that the plane was on fire, though there was no sign of smoke or flame. Cojot's son Olivier felt more excited than afraid, and was 'already thinking this is going to be a good story to tell at school'. As he kept glancing back, half expecting to see smoke, he heard his father curse, 'something he never did, and it was a bad curse, so I know something bad has happened'.

He turned to see a steady stream of passengers, stewards and stewardesses coming from the front of the plane with their arms raised. Some were screaming but most were mute with shock. They were the occupants of first class and the first fifteen rows of the forward economy tourist cabin – among them Claude Moufflet, Moshe Peretz and the Weills – and had been moved to create a cordon sanitaire between the cockpit and the passengers in case anyone tried to intervene. Herding the crowd were three hijackers: two Arabs and one young Western woman who kept shouting in heavily accented English: 'Sitonzeflor! Sitonzeflor!'

She was, thought Moufflet, 'about 25 years old with straight dark black hair that came down to her collar, a fringe at the front, dark eyes and a very pale face that reminded me of a prison guard. She wore little round glasses with steel rims and was dressed in an outfit of navy and petrol blue, black shoes with wedged soles and holding in her right hand an automatic pistol and in her left a grenade. I couldn't see from where I was whether or not it had the pin taken out.'

Shortly after the appearance of the female hijacker, who sounded German, 'a short bearded man, about five feet three, who spoke French with a heavy Yiddish accent, tried to resist'. Julie Aouzerate, a sixty-two-year-old Algerian-born French Jewish grandmother, watched on in horror as the hijackers 'knocked him to the floor and beat him severely – the German woman doing most of the punching'. As everyone froze, chief steward Daniel Courtial tried to calm the situation by saying: 'There's nothing to worry about. Don't be frightened.'

Yet even he was shaking like a leaf.

The intercom crackled into life. 'This plane has been hijacked,' said a male voice with a German accent, 'and is now under the control of the Basil al-Kubaisi* Commando of the Che Guevara of Gaza Group of the Popular Front for the Liberation of Palestine. The plane has been renamed "Haifa" and only that name will get a response. I'm your new captain. As long as you obey our orders and do exactly as we ask you, you will not be harmed.'

Moments later the message was repeated in French by a stewardess's trembling voice. It was now clear to many of the 246 passengers – most of whom were Jews – that their greatest fears had come to pass: the plane had been hijacked by the PFLP, a Palestinian guerilla organization that was committed to the destruction of the Israeli state. The threat to the Israelis on board was obvious, and on hearing mention of the dreaded PFLP many of them began 'ripping off their Jewish star necklaces and throwing them on the floor'.

Every Israeli knew and feared the Popular Front for the Liberation of Palestine. Formed by Dr George Habash, a Palestinian Christian, in the wake of the Six-Day War of 1967, it was the second largest faction in the Palestine Liberation Organisation (PLO) after Yasser Arafat's Fatah. Yet it quickly became the best known after it pioneered the use of plane hijackings to strike back at Israel. The architect of this strategy was Habash's forty-nine-year-old deputy Dr Wadie Haddad, another Palestinian Christian from Safed in northern Israel, who realized that the initial tactic of cross-border raids from the PLO's bases in Jordan would 'never achieve the liberation of Palestine'. In 1967 he told the PFLP leadership that it was impossible to fight the Israelis 'plane for plane, tank for tank, soldier for soldier'. Instead they had to concentrate on the Israelis' 'weak points' by using 'spectacular, one-off operations' that would help to focus the world's attention on Palestine. This would cause people to ask: 'What the hell is the problem in Palestine? Who are these Palestinians? Why are they doing these things?' In the end the world would 'get fed up' and

---

* Dr Basil al-Kubaisi, the PFLP's logistics chief, had been assassinated by Israeli agents in Paris in April 1973 as part of the Wrath of God operation to avenge the deaths of eleven Israeli athletes at the Munich Olympics a year earlier. Naming commandos after martyred comrades was common practice in the PFLP.

decide it had to do something about Palestine. It would be forced to give the Palestinians 'justice'.

Bassam Abu-Sharif, the public face of the PFLP and a member of its Central Committee, thought Haddad's speech electrifying. Once it was over, he 'felt like standing up and applauding', and could tell others felt the same way. It was as if the world had tilted on its axis in favour of the Palestinians. Here, at last, thought Bassam, 'was a new way forward – a chance to get the Israeli boot off the back of the Arab neck'. Henceforward they 'would carry the attack to Israel'; they 'would take – and keep – the initiative'. From this moment on, Haddad became known as 'the Master'.

With his strategy duly endorsed by Habash and the Central Committee, Haddad went to work training selected guerillas to hijack planes in mid-air. Most of the early volunteers came from within the PFLP. Talent spotters in the camps would refer the best recruits for further training, and 'from this second, much smaller pool, Haddad would select the best again, looking for intelligence, persistence, strength of character, resourcefulness and physical toughness'. Their final training, according to Bassam Abu-Sharif, 'went far beyond such things as proficiency with weapons and explosives'. They were trained to fly 'even the biggest and [most] modern airliners' so they knew exactly what the pilots were doing, and 'couldn't be bluffed'. If a pilot needed to be killed, they would take control. They also practised exchanging gunfire in confined spaces, and learned not only how to defeat airport security checks but what local laws applied to them if they were captured.

The first hijacking planned by Haddad – the takeover of an Israeli El Al plane en route from Paris to Tel Aviv in July 1968 – was a spectacular success. Forced to land in Algiers, the plane and its twenty-two Israeli passengers and crew were kept for forty days until Israel finally agreed to the terrorists' terms: the release of sixteen convicted Arab terrorists in return for the Israeli hostages (the non-Israelis had been returned to France at the start of the ordeal).

Other Palestinian terror groups such as Black September began to copy the PFLP's hijacking strategy. They mostly targeted Israeli and Western airlines like El Al, BOAC, Lufthansa, TWA, Pan Am and Swissair, and it seemed to many at the time as if the West's security forces were powerless to stop the hijackings. The one consolation for Israeli citizens was that, thanks to the tight security at Ben-Gurion, no plane flying direct from Israel had ever been skyjacked. That did not, of course, prevent terrorists joining the plane during a stopover en route to or away from a non-Israeli airport: just such a tactic had been used in the Sabena hijacking of 1972 when four Black September guerillas got on the Paris-to-Tel Aviv flight after a stop in Rome.

The most ambitious early PFLP operation was the coordinated hijacking of three planes bound for New York in September 1970. The plan was to force all three to land at Dawson's Field, a disused former British air base in Jordan, where the hostages would remain until the PFLP's demands had been met. But only two of the three hijackings were successful: that of a TWA Boeing 707 and a Swissair Douglas DC-8 from Frankfurt and Zurich respectively. The third was foiled when two of the four hijackers were removed from an El Al Boeing 707 out of Amsterdam, and the remaining pair – Palestinian Leila Khaled and her Nicaraguan accomplice Patrick Argüello – were overpowered during the flight.* This did not prevent the other two thwarted terrorists from opportunistically hijacking a Pan Am Boeing 747, but it was blown up on the ground at Cairo because Haddad feared it was too heavy for the packed-sand runway at Dawson's Field. A third plane – a BOAC Vickers VC-10 out of Bahrain – eventually joined the others in Jordan after it had been hijacked by a PFLP sympathizer keen to secure Khaled's release.

The PFLP might have achieved all its demands had its actions not alienated its Jordanian hosts. On 16 September, four days after the three planes at Dawson's Field had also been blown up by the PFLP, King Hussein of Jordan turned on his former Palestinian allies. He was forced to do so by the United States who 'made it very clear to him that unless he got rid of the Palestinian "terrorists" operating from his country, they would come in and do it themselves'. Faced with this ultimatum, Hussein ordered his tanks and loyal Bedu infantry

---

* Argüello and a steward were killed in the struggle, the former shot by a sky marshal.

into the Palestinians' camps and training bases. Hundreds were killed in the fighting: all of them Arabs. Bassam Abu-Sharif wrote later: 'Our own Arab brothers had taken up arms against us: a catastrophe for the Palestinian cause. We called it "Black September".'

The one tiny consolation for the PFLP was that Leila Khaled and three Palestinian terrorists in a Swiss prison were exchanged for the remaining Israeli hostages. But the loss of Jordan as a base for terrorist operations against Israel was a disaster for the PLO leadership and, blaming the PFLP, they ordered Haddad to stop attacking targets outside Israel. He refused and was eventually expelled from the PFLP by Habash in 1973. Yet he continued to operate under the banner of the Popular Front for the Liberation of Palestine–External Operations (PFLP–EO), and it was this rogue group, with its headquarters in Baghdad, that was behind the hijacking of Air France Flight 139.

With the first stage of the hijacking accomplished, the terrorists – who referred to themselves as Number 1 (Garcia), 10 (Ortega), 39 (red shirt) and 54 (yellow shirt) – decided to separate those who were potentially dangerous from the others by moving mothers with infants and all children to the first-class buffer zone in the front of the plane. This meant a few kids, like Olivier Cojot and a young Dutch boy of about the same age, were taken from their fathers.

The look of distress on young Olivier's face as he was led away was a heart-rending moment for Michel Cojot. His son had 'become a little boy again, my little boy', and he was sorry for dragging him into 'an adventure which could cost him his life'. On the other hand he was happy he was not alone, as his own father Joseph Goldberg, a Polish-born Jew, had been when facing a similarly lethal situation.

Four years after fighting for France in the ill-fated 1940 campaign against the Germans, Goldberg had wanted to take the then five-year-old Michel with him as he travelled in to Lyons on a cold winter day to donate his French-Jewish passport – he had acquired a forged non-Jewish replacement – to a foreign Jew. But Michel's mother had refused to let him go because his boots were being repaired and it had saved his life. On arrival in Lyons Goldberg had been arrested with his two passports in a roundup organized by Klaus Barbie, the

Gestapo chief, and was eventually sent to his death in Auschwitz. Michel and his mother survived the German occupation by hiding their Jewishness and using the name Collenot (courtesy of a Gentile neighbour of that name who risked his life to give them a new identity, and was later honoured as one of the Righteous Among the Nations in Jerusalem's Mount of Remembrance). This, in turn, became Cojot when Michel's mother remarried after the war. But, ever since, Michel had been burdened with the guilt of not accompanying his father that day. Which is why he was now glad that, come what may, he and his son would face the danger of the hijacking together.

Not all the passengers were so sanguine. One Israeli mother hid her son under her skirts, ignoring the hijackers' threats of 'severe' punishment for anyone who did not send or accompany their children to first class. There he remained – 'crouched noiselessly' – for more than an hour, only emerging when it was 'clear that children would not be harmed'.

Other passengers were finding it hard to cope with the ever-present threat of injury or death. Tony Russell and his friend George Good were just two rows back from the German girl, who was chain-smoking with her right hand while in her left she held a pistol that was 'pointed for a large part of the time straight at them'.

Sitting in the aisle on Claude Moufflet's right was a well-dressed, heavily made-up 'official-looking' Israeli woman in her fifties who was on the verge of a nervous breakdown. She lit cigarette after cigarette 'in a feverish way with trembling hands', her face 'consumed with tics as she sobbed pleas to everyone in general and no one in particular'.

When Moufflet tried to reassure her, she put her hand protectively on the head of a brown-haired girl of about seventeen who was accompanying her. The girl, who was the woman's niece, was much calmer and spoke better English. It was the first sign of a marked difference in attitude between the various age groups – the young coping better than their elders – that surprised Moufflet. 'Where do you think we are going?' the girl asked Moufflet.

'I don't know, maybe Libya,' he replied. 'Gaddafi is very pro-Palestinian.'

A young dark-haired woman, sitting to Moufflet's left, interrupted them. 'Please tell my husband to stay calm,' she begged Moufflet in almost faultless French, indicating a dark-skinned man around thirty-five, wearing a garish shirt with vertical brown and yellow stripes. 'He wants to jump on top of them and is going to get himself killed.'

Moufflet asked the man what he wanted to do.

'I don't know,' the man replied, his gaze darting back and forth. 'But there are many of us and only a few of them. If we jump them we should be able to disarm them.'

The man's neighbour, a well-built teenager with curly hair, agreed: 'It's true. We've only got to jump on them. There's no reason not to.'

Moufflet brought them back to reality. 'Listen,' he said quietly, 'just think about it. Even if we could do it, the first to get up will be shot and even killed. And then what? What about the grenades?'

'They still have their pins in,' said the husband, pointing to his neighbour: 'He told me that.'

Moufflet shook his head in exasperation. 'Look at the metallic ring round his finger. It's the ring from the grenade's pin. If that grenade falls there will be no way to stop it exploding.'

The husband was not convinced, insisting that there was time to put the pin back in the grenade, and that the other passengers would help with the remaining terrorists. Genuinely worried that the husband's recklessness would get them all killed, Moufflet played his last card. 'Do you have children?' he asked the wife.

'Yes, three.'

'Are they on the plane?'

'No, they're with my parents.'

He turned to the husband. 'Would you like to see your children again? If yes, stay calm and see what happens.'

Before the husband could respond, the voice of the terrorist leader sounded on the intercom. 'This is your new captain speaking. We are going to body-search you because we want to assure ourselves that you aren't armed. If you have a weapon, throw it immediately into the aisle. If you have anything that could be used as a weapon, throw that also. Don't try to fool us, or you'll be sorry. We are going to frisk you and if you have anything hidden that you haven't given up it will be very serious for you.'

After a steward had repeated the message in French, the two young Arab hijackers began searching the passengers and collecting 'weapons'. Moufflet handed over his pipe cleaner, but young Olivier Cojot was less keen to surrender the 'beloved' Swiss army knife that he always wore chained to his trousers. He eventually added it to 'the little pile of pocket knives, nail files, knitting needles and other engines of death that had escaped Israeli vigilance'.

One by one the passengers were called and searched 'in all the intimate parts of their bodies'. But the longer the searches went on, the more superficial they became. Sara Davidson was dreading the experience, not least because she had had what she coyly termed 'special surgery' and did not want the hijackers to know about it. To her great relief she was overlooked.

1030hrs GMT, Jerusalem, Israel

Israeli Prime Minister Yitzhak Rabin was chairing the government's weekly midday Cabinet meeting in his office complex at 3 Kaplan Street in the official district of Givat Ram in west Jerusalem when his military aide, Brigadier-General Ephraim 'Freuka' Poran, entered the room and handed him a note. It read: 'An Air France plane, Flight 139 from Tel Aviv to Paris, has been hijacked after taking off from a stopover in Athens.'

Small and dapper, with a receding hairline that had gone grey at the temples, Rabin was a former head of the Israeli Defense Forces (IDF) and ambassador to the United States who possessed a keen analytical mind and ample reserves of physical and moral courage. But he did not always react well to a crisis – as his temporary nervous breakdown at the start of the Six-Day War in 1967 had demonstrated – and this news startled him. He stared at the papers in front of him, trying to decide what to do. Eventually he turned Poran's note over and wrote: 'Freuka – find out: 1) How many Israelis are on board. 2) How many hijackers are on board. 3) Where the plane is heading.'

As Poran left the room, Rabin 'banged his gavel to silence a minister who was working himself up over the price of bread, and informed his Cabinet of the shocking news'. He then announced that after the Cabinet had adjourned a special task force of relevant ministers – himself, Foreign Minister and Deputy Prime Minister Yigal Allon, Defense Minister Shimon Peres, Transport Minister Gad Yaacobi, Justice Minister Chaim Zadok and Minister without Portfolio Yisrael Galili – would meet in the downstairs conference room to consider the government's response.

On the way to the meeting he told Yaacobi to warn Ben-Gurion Airport that 'the hijackers might want to do another Sabena'. He was referring to the 1972 hijacking by Black September* terrorists of a Boeing 707 operated by the Belgian national airline Sabena en route from Rome to Tel Aviv. Having landed at Ben-Gurion Airport (then known as Lod), the hijackers threatened to blow up the plane unless more than 300 Palestinian terrorists were released from Israeli jails. But while negotiations were ongoing, commandos from the IDF's elite anti-terrorist force Sayeret Matkal (known simply as 'the Unit') stormed the plane dressed as mechanics, killing both male hijackers and capturing the two women. Though one of the hostages was mortally wounded in the crossfire, the operation was considered a success and Rabin wanted the airport to be ready for a repeat performance if the latest hijacked plane returned to Ben-Gurion.

1055hrs GMT, Tel Aviv, Israel

Deep in the bowels of the Kirya, the complex of government buildings in central Tel Aviv that since 1948 had housed the Ministry of Defense, was a concrete warren of bomb-proof tunnels and cinderblock offices known as the 'Pit'. Operating day and night, this

---

* The Black September Organization (BSO) was a Palestinian terrorist group formed in 1970 by Fatah extremists in the wake of the PLO's expulsion from Jordan. In September 1972, three months after the Sabena hijacking, it kidnapped and murdered eleven Israeli athletes at the Munich Olympic Games. All five Black September terrorists were also killed.

'windowless, fluorescent-lit complex' was the nerve centre of the Israeli Defense Forces.

Meeting in one of the Pit's small offices with colleagues from operations, intelligence and the air force was Major Moshe 'Muki' Betser, the thirty-year-old reserve commander of the Unit and one of Israel's most experienced combat soldiers. Just before 1 p.m. local time, their discussion about a potential special-forces mission unconnected to the hijacking was interrupted by a knock at the door. 'We have a hijacking,' said an IDF major. 'An Air France plane out of Greece. It took off from Tel Aviv earlier this morning.'

With the Unit's commander Yoni Netanyahu and deputy Yiftach Reicher away in the Sinai on an exercise, Betser was the duty officer in the event of an emergency. He reached for the phone and put in a call to the Unit's base. It was answered by the operations officer. 'They just called from Operations,' said the officer, pre-empting the news.

'Good. Get the team to the airport on the double. I'll meet you there.'

The Israeli Army has many reconnaissance units – or sayerets – for special operations: Sayeret Golani, scouts for the crack Golani Infantry Brigade of northern command; Sayeret Shaked, scouts for the southern command; and a Sayeret Tzanchanim for the paratroops. But the best of the best is Sayeret Matkal – or General Staff Reconnaissance Unit – the brainchild of the legendary Jewish fighter Avraham Arnan who in the late 1950s petitioned the chief of staff to create a force that could carry out top-secret missions behind enemy lines. Backed by David Ben-Gurion and Yitzhak Rabin, Arnan got his way and the new unit began independent operations under the direct authority of the IDF's General Staff in 1958.

Modelled on the British Army's SAS – and with the same 'Who Dares Wins' motto – the Unit was, and still is, recruited from the cream of Israeli youth and at first specialized in strategic intelligence gathering. But by the late 1960s, with the emergence of the PFLP and other Palestinian terror groups, the Unit began to develop the world's first hostage-rescue and counter-terrorism techniques. It was soon called upon for the tasks inside and outside Israel that demanded brains as well as brawn, including assassination, kidnapping and demolition. So secret was its work, however, that few outside the General Staff even knew its name until the late 1980s.

It was shortly after the Unit's most conspicuous anti-terrorist operation – the storming of Sabena Flight 571 at Lod Airport in 1972, known as Operation Isotope – that Muki Betser joined its ranks. The grandson of Russian immigrants, Betser had grown up on Israel's first moshav* in the Jezreel Valley near Galilee where the constant threat of Arab incursion from neighbouring Syria meant he was taught to shoot at a young age. By sixteen he was six foot three, a fine athlete and an expert field navigator using only a map and the stars. Yet he had no interest in becoming a career soldier and assumed that the thirty-month compulsory military service expected of all Israeli nineteen-year-olds irrespective of gender would be a 'rankling' experience.

He was wrong. Supremely fit, he sailed through basic training and the brutal paratroop course – with its dropout rate of more than 50 per cent – to gain entry to the Sayeret Tzanchanim, known at the time as 'the tip of the IDF's spear'. It was during his time as a paratroop scout that he first used a Russian-made Kalashnikov assault rifle that had been captured from Arab troops in the Six-Day War. It was, he soon discovered, the best and most reliable 'all-round assault weapon available', and was his constant companion for the next eighteen years of active and reserve service.

No admirer of authority for authority's sake, Betser appreciated the democratic nature of service in a sayeret where even new recruits were 'encouraged to speak their minds about ways to improve the unit's performance, even if it means challenging the commanding officer'. All officers had to earn the respect of their men by leading by example and 'combining distance and friendship, an aloofness with intimacy'. Most ranks, like Betser, hailed from the kibbutz and moshav farms of Israel where 'the

---

* An experimental farming community that gave each family an equal share of land. In a communal kibbutz, by contrast, the land belongs to everyone and private possessions were absent.

values of settling the land' were 'inseparable from the values of defending it'. City boys made good fighters, but were less patient and more averse to hard work.

A natural leader, Betser was persuaded to train as an officer and stay on an extra six months when his compulsory period of military service came to an end in late 1966. His first posting was to Sayeret Shaked, commanded by the Bedouin Amos Yarkoni (born Abed al-Majid), and chiefly involved tracking Egyptian spies and Palestinian *fedayeen* in the Negev Desert. It was now that he married his childhood sweetheart Nurit, a niece of Moshe Dayan, the former IDF chief of staff who lost an eye fighting for the Allies against the Vichy French in 1941 and would shortly be appointed minister of defense. Betser's intention was to finish his final six months and return to the Jezreel Valley to farm. But the Six-Day War intervened – a decisive pre-emptive strike by Israel against its Arab enemies that was prompted by Egypt's provocative blockade of the Red Sea and massing of troops in the Sinai Desert – and Betser played his part by leading the first Israeli troops on to Egyptian territory.

With the war over, and a new attritional struggle against Egyptians and Palestinian terrorists just beginning, Betser again extended his military service by returning to the paratroop scouts as deputy commander. But he was seriously wounded in the jaw during the IDF's flawed and costly attempt to destroy a PLO camp at Karameh in Jordan in 1968, and spent the next six months recuperating.

A succession of civilian and military jobs followed – including eighteen uneventful months as an El Al sky marshal, and a year as a staff officer with Sayeret Egoz (the northern command's new scout force) – until in January 1971 word came from Uganda, an East African country with close commercial and military ties to Israel, that President Milton Obote had been ousted in a coup led by his former chief of staff, General Idi Amin. A graduate of the IDF paratroop course and on good terms with Golda Meir and Moshe Dayan – respectively Israeli prime minister and defense minister – Amin was seen as a friend of Israel. Would Betser consider going to the Ugandan town of Jinja to form a battalion of paratroopers on Israeli principles? asked Baruch 'Burka' Bar-Lev, the IDF colonel who headed Israel's military mission to Uganda. The answer was yes, and Betser and his wife and young son left for Uganda soon afterwards.

Betser enjoyed his time at Jinja, situated fifty miles north of the capital Kampala on the banks of the White Nile: the perks of the job included a house with servants and a brand-new Peugeot 404; and he found the Ugandans eager to learn, though the distance the officers kept from their soldiers and their aversion to hard work was difficult for him to accept. But the training progressed smoothly enough until he received word from Bar-Lev, in March 1972, that all non-military Israeli organizations and companies had twenty-four hours to leave the country. A second ultimatum, two days later, ordered Betser and other military personnel to follow them. Frustrated by Israel's refusal to give him the latest Phantom jets, the fickle Amin had turned instead to Gaddafi's Libya and the Soviet Union for military support: their price for MiG jet fighters and other hardware was Israel's expulsion. As Betser took off from the country's international airport at Entebbe, near Kampala, he 'mourned for the beautiful country' he would miss, for its people 'who deserved better than Amin', and lastly for his own country Israel, 'humiliated by a tin-pot dictator'. He did not expect to return.

Arriving back in Israel, he was offered and accepted a post in a paratroop battalion. But when Lieutenant-Colonel Ehud Barak, commander of the Unit, heard of his availability, he made him a counter-offer. If he only came for a year or two, said Barak, a short and stocky kibbutznik who exuded energy and confidence, he would have a 'great time' and then he could join the reserves. But if he wanted an army career, time with the Unit would give him 'ideas' and 'something for the road to bring to other jobs'.

The chance to serve under the man who had commanded the Sabena operation was too good to refuse. Nor would Betser regret his decision as, during the next four years, he was at the heart of all the Unit's major operations: the 1972 kidnap of high-ranking Syrian intelligence officers in Lebanon (later exchanged for Israeli POWs); the 1973 assassination in Beirut of senior PLO leaders implicated in the Munich massacre (Operation Spring of Youth, a mission Barak took part in dressed as a woman); and the recapture of Mount

Hermon from Syrian commandos during the Yom Kippur War in 1973.

But there was one mission he did not remember with any pride: Ma'alot. It began in late May 1974 when three Palestinian terrorists crossed from Lebanon into northern Israel and killed two Israeli Arab women in a van before heading for the town of Ma'alot, where they shot another four people: a city worker, a couple and their three-year-old son. Then they made for the local elementary school and took hostage more than a hundred high-school students and their teachers.

For most of the following day Betser and his comrades waited for the Israeli government to make a decision: either agree to the terrorists' demands – the students' lives for the release of twenty-three Palestinian militants from Israeli jails – or let the Unit off the leash. When the green light was finally given at 5 p.m., dusk was falling. But the assault took place anyway and it was a disaster. 'Without any formal doctrine', commented Betser, 'regarding an adequate number of break-in points, optimum firepower, the use of grenades, small caliber or large caliber weapons, we improvised.' This meant setting up a net of snipers round the school in the hope that all three terrorists would appear in their sights at the same time. Their coordinated shots were the signal for the assault. Yet they only managed to wound two terrorists rather than kill them, and before Betser and the other assaulters could break in the Palestinians had turned their Kalashnikovs and grenades on the students. In the first classroom Betser found a scene from his 'worst nightmare': dozens 'lay on the floor, piled on top of each other where they fell, wounded or dead'. Only a handful of students were unscathed.

Betser knew that he and his comrades had made mistakes, and vowed to learn from them. 'Into our new doctrine for hostage situations,' he wrote, 'went a string of lessons for future incidents.' But the greatest failing in his opinion was the government's hesitation: 'Their policy said no negotiations with terrorists, but their hesitation in fulfilling that policy proved costly.'

In the wake of Ma'alot, the Unit rethought its tactics and training. New recruits 'learned how to break into a room crowded with hostages, identify the terrorists, and [practise] selective shooting to kill terrorists and avoid hostages'. They rehearsed assaulting 'houses, apartment buildings, ships, trains, planes, buses – any target the terrorists might capture'. They designed a different doctrine for every type of structure 'regarding entry, firepower, adequate number of teams'. They were determined never to witness another Ma'alot.

Swerving through traffic and running the occasional red light on his way to the airport, Muki Betser thought about the best tactic to use on the hijacked Air France plane if it returned to Israel. Since the Sabena rescue in 1972, the Unit had devised a number of different doctrines and methods for a plane on the ground. It never used the same ploy twice.

By the time he reached the airport perimeter, he had made up his mind. They would use the latest method they had demonstrated to the General Staff just a few weeks earlier. Flashing his ID to the guard on the main gates, he drove towards the small hangar on the landing field where he could see the Unit's crews readying their gear. But as he got out of the car he was told the plane was heading not for Israel but for Libya. It was no surprise. 'Gaddafi's oil-financed support for international terrorism, especially Palestinian terror against Israeli targets, was well known.' There was still a possibility, however, that the plane would fly on to Israel. And until that was ruled out, Betser and his team would remain at Ben-Gurion.

1130hrs GMT, International airspace above the Mediterranean

As the minutes ticked by, several passengers on hijacked Flight 139 asked for and got permission to go to the toilet. At first it was just one or two people going to the facilities at the front of the plane, and the same number to those at the back. But as people realized these brave souls were coming back unharmed, more got up. The terrorists let them get on with it 'until some fairly long queues started forming'. This caused even more people to join them until it was almost impossible to walk down either aisle. Observing the chaos, the female terrorist screamed: 'Sit down! Sit down! You can't all go in there. Sit down and be quiet.'

When certain passengers did not react quickly enough, the woman abused them in such shrill tones that Moufflet could tell she was compensating for her nervousness. But it had the desired effect as passengers pushed and shoved each other in their panic to sit down.

Again the voice of the chief terrorist came over the intercom: 'Here is your new captain. Stay calm and seated. We will let you go to the toilets but you must realize that we have revolvers and explosives and that you cannot do anything about that. Respect our orders and do what we ask. As the explosives are here in the front of the plane, you can only go to the toilets at the back. We will not do you any harm and we will not kill you. Do what we say. Obey our orders. I will give you more instructions later.'

The tension was relieved by a brief moment of farce when Michel Cojot noticed that two buttons on the female terrorist's blouse had come undone, 'allowing a glimpse of breasts primly encased in a rather feminine brassiere'. This glimpse of vulnerability contrasted starkly with the woman's aggressive actions and stern appearance – she had, thought Cojot, the 'unappealing face of a bookworm' with her metal-rimmed glasses, plain suit and blue stockings – and he was about to say something. But another passenger tapped her on the hip as she was passing, and 'indicated with his finger that her blouse was gaping'.

She smiled thinly and tried to adjust her blouse without putting down her weapons, causing Cojot to speculate on the irony of her dropping the fragmentation grenade and 'no one ever knowing that we had died for modesty'. Unable to accomplish the task with her hands full, she used a hairpin borrowed from a passenger to lock the grenade's handle. She then placed it on the floor and did up her buttons.

Soon afterwards, at the terrorists' bidding, two stewardesses and a steward distributed water, fizzy drinks and pieces of bread to the thirsty and hungry passengers. But this only prompted more visits to the toilet and, within minutes, the same disorderly queues had formed outside the two cubicles at the back of the plane. 'Sit down and stay there!' shouted the exasperated female terrorist. 'You are not children, and yet you behave worse than them. You're all mad. Sit down and stay there.'

The Rabinowitzes thought the woman hijacker was 'less like a commando than a frustrated substitute teacher beset by an unexpected problem'. Another passenger agreed. 'Some hijackers!' he grunted. 'More like glorified toilet monitors.'

By now tempers among the passengers were also fraying with some joining the terrorists in exhorting their fellows to stay seated. Others took advantage of the absentees by stealing their seats. Among the squatters was a large bald man in his sixties wearing glasses and a grey suit. When the occupant returned, he refused to move. 'I didn't ask to come here,' he said in French. 'I'm a passenger from first class. I have a right to a seat and I'm taking this one.'

Claude Moufflet gave up his place to accommodate the interloper, and instead shared a pair of seats with two 'nice' young French girls called Agnès and Maggy. Short and chubby, Agnès had her long black hair in a ponytail and was wearing glasses too big for her face. Her unusual accent, she later explained, was because she came from Bône in Algeria. A little taller, Maggy had very curly hair and was dressed in jeans and a blue cotton jumper. They told Moufflet they both worked in information services and were returning from a holiday to their homes in Paris. It seemed to him they were 'controlling their emotions really well', and he was happy to keep them distracted by taking part in their 'best legs on the plane' competition that they eventually awarded to one of the stewardesses. Their lighthearted banter was interrupted by yet another intercom announcement.

'Ladies and gentlemen,' said the terrorist chief, 'the members of the commando are going to come amongst you to collect up your identity cards. It's important that you give them *all* up, particularly if you are of dual nationality and have an Israeli identity card or passport. Any attempt to hide anything will be severely punished.'

Moufflet put everything into the plastic bag held open by the Arab with the moustache: his passport, identity papers and driving licence. His two young neighbours followed suit, handing over all their pieces of photo identity. But some on board, particularly those of dual nationality, tried to hide or destroy their Israeli identity cards because they knew that in previous pro-Palestinian hijackings the Israeli hostages had often been kept after others were released. The most at risk were the many Israeli men with connections to the military like Sara Davidson's husband Uzi who was a reserve colonel with the Israeli Air Force (IAF). Aware that Uzi's ID card would give him away, they both chewed part of it and squeezed the pieces into a used cola can with just 'seconds to spare'.

But most chose not to defy the terrorists. Mindful of their young children, Claude and Emma Rosenkovitch handed over their French *and* Israeli passports, as did young Jean-Jacques Mimouni, while reserve soldier Moshe Peretz gave up his army card.

'What will they do with our passports?' one of the French girls asked Moufflet, a question on countless minds as the bags containing them were taken to the front of the plane.

'Well, first they'll use them to establish a list of who is on the plane,' he replied. 'Then I don't know.'

To further 'reduce tension and free the aisles', the terrorists allowed some more 'passengers they considered harmless' up to the front of the plane. They included Michel Cojot who, as a single parent travelling with a child, was able to rejoin his son Olivier. 'I thus reaped,' noted Cojot, "an unexpected dividend from the solidarity of two liberation movements": the women's and the Palestinians.'

It was around this time that one of the hijackers told some of the passengers their aims: the release of 'dozens of Palestinian prisoners and Kozo Okamoto' – the sole survivor of the Japanese Red Army's deadly terrorist attack at Lod Airport in 1972. 'If Israel acceded to these demands,' noted Emma Rosenkovitch, 'no one would be harmed, they said.'

1200hrs GMT, Tel Aviv, Israel

Twenty-two-year-old Martine Mimouni-Arnold had just returned from work to her Tel Aviv apartment when the phone rang. It was a friend with the alarming news that Martine's parents had failed to pick up her two-year-old daughter Aurelia from kindergarten, as they did each weekday, and so the friend had collected her instead.

Martine was perplexed. Her father Robert, a Tunisian Jew who had worked for fifteen years as a policeman in France before moving his family to Israel in 1971, was not the type to forget his granddaughter. His only appointment that day had been to drop off his son Jean-Jacques – Martine's younger brother – at Ben-Gurion for his flight to Paris. Something serious must have happened. She hurried round to her parents' house but no one answered the door, so she returned home and, in an attempt to keep busy, took out the rubbish. As she did so she overheard two people in the street talking about the hijacking of an Air France plane. Shocked by the news, and fearful for her brother's safety, she ran back up the steps to phone for confirmation. But as she did so she tripped and felt a stabbing pain in her ankle. It was fractured.

Only later, in hospital, did she learn that her parents' had returned to Ben-Gurion as soon as they heard of the hijacking, all thoughts of their granddaughter far from their minds; and there they remained, waiting in vain for news that their precious only son – conceived after five daughters – was safe.

1215hrs GMT, International airspace above the Mediterranean

The confiscation of the passengers' identity papers was followed by an even more alarming development as the two Arab hijackers reappeared from the front of the plane with huge boxes that looked to Claude Moufflet as if they might once have held sweets and cakes. Protruding from them, however, were long pink fuses – a quarter of an inch in diameter to eight inches in length – that left most passengers in no doubt they now contained explosives.

To free up space for the boxes, the passengers in the two seats next to the central emergency exits were moved to the central block where armrests were lifted so that five people could sit on four seats. Then a terrorist came back and placed what appeared to be small white packages between the doors of the plane and the boxes of explosives. Moufflet assumed this 'was a system of detonation that would go off if the exit doors were opened'.

Not all the passengers nearby drew the same conclusion. Once the terrorists had left, a small well-dressed lady of around sixty-five years of age, wearing her hair in a chignon, declared her determination to return to her confiscated seat. 'Madam, you can't,' advised Moufflet. 'They have just blocked the exits.'

When she continued to complain, saying that to expect five people to share four seats was unfair because not everyone was thin, he lost his temper. 'Listen, madam,' he said harshly, 'it is dynamite that they have put under your seat. Would you really like to go and sit on top of it?'

This brought her to her senses, and confirmation, if it was needed, came with the chief terrorist's next announcement: 'Sit down please. Put your seatbelts on and stop smoking. We will soon land at Benghazi. You should know that the emergency exits have been wired with explosives. It is strictly forbidden to go near them or to sit on the seats next to them. Any attempt to open them will set off the charge. Therefore you have been warned. Be careful. Remain in your seats and, above all, do not smoke any more.'

Up in the cockpit, after circling the airport a number of times, Michel Bacos was finally given permission to land by Benghazi airport's control tower. 'Land it gently,' he was warned by the gun-wielding chief terrorist. 'We don't want the explosives to ignite.'

1258hrs GMT, Benghazi, Libya

The screech of wheels on tarmac caused many of the passengers to flinch as Bacos landed the plane as softly as he could on the single rudimentary airstrip at Benina International Airport near Benghazi, the second-largest city in Libya and capital of the eastern province of Cyrenaica. It was just before 3 p.m. local time.

For the many Israelis and Jews on board this was a worrying time. Colonel Muammar Gaddafi, dictator of Libya since his successful military coup in 1969, was an ardent Arab nationalist and an inveterate enemy of Israel. 'We knew, my neighbours and I,' recalled Julie Aouzerate, 'that our "visit" to an Arab country dedicated to destroy Israel was not good news. This was certainly not a safe haven for us.' But was Libya the terrorists' final destination, they wondered, or simply a stop along the way?

After taxiing for fifteen minutes, the plane came to a halt in a secluded section of the airport and the engines were shut down. The blinds were closed but a few passengers risked the terrorists' anger to sneak a look outside. Moshe Peretz could see 'arid landscape, four bored soldiers sitting on the runway' and fire brigade trucks nearby. The majority of passengers sat patiently, unable even to see beyond the drawn curtain between first and economy class. For Claude Moufflet, time seemed to crawl as passengers 'read or spoke in a low voice'. They were waiting, the two Palestinian hijackers announced, 'for the arrival of the representative of the Libyan government'. Some passengers lit cigarettes, in spite of many protests, but were ordered to put them out by the hijackers.

Eventually a steward opened the front-left exit door, and Olivier Cojot could see a cordon of soldiers on the tarmac and the chief terrorist being greeted by a 'welcoming committee' of civilian handshakes and hugs. He assumed they were comrades from the PFLP. Then a Libyan official climbed the stairs and came on board, greeting the passengers 'not without humour' in 'guttural English'. He welcomed them to the Arab Republic of Libya, but regretted the circumstances of their arrival. He then asked for and was given the bags with the identity documents, and took them back down the stairs to where another official was waiting behind a table with a rubber stamp. Olivier could hardly believe his eyes. They were issuing visas to each passport as if the hijacking had never happened. 'What the hell,' he wondered, 'is going on?'

1330hrs GMT, Lod, Israel

Major Muki Betser was still at Ben-Gurion International Airport with the Unit's specialist anti-hijacking team when word reached him from the Pit that the terrorists had radioed ahead to

Benghazi with two demands: that they be given enough fuel for four hours' onward flight; and that the local representative of Wadie Haddad's branch of the PFLP be summoned to the airport to meet them.

The news that the terrorists wanted more fuel was a clear indication that Benghazi was not their final destination, and that, as Betser put it, they might still want 'to try landing in Israel'. His men, as a result, would remain at Ben-Gurion until the picture was clearer. But any possible operation would not be for some time, and in the interval he put a radio call through to the Unit's commanding officer, Yoni Netanyahu, on an exercise at Umm Hashiba in the Sinai Peninsula.

A few months younger than Betser, Netanyahu came from a very different political and social milieu: that of right-wing urban intellectuals. The grandson of a prominent Lithuanian Zionist who had emigrated to Palestine in the 1920s, Netanyahu was born on 13 March 1946 in New York City where his right-wing and pro-Revisionist* father Benzion was studying for a history doctorate. The family returned to the Middle East after Israel's creation in 1948, and Netanyahu's early years were spent in Talpiot, the idyllic south Jerusalem suburb much favoured by scholars and professionals. Though not religious, he nevertheless 'preserved a deep affection for Jewish ritual and tradition'.

He was educated at Jerusalem's Gymnasium Elementary School and later the Darom School and, like Betser, enjoyed athletics and games of any kind. He was a 'natural leader, a boy whom other children deferred to and wanted to follow, and from his mid teens one to whom girls were immediately attracted' by his impish, mischievous grin and remorseless energy.

From the age of eleven to thirteen, and again from sixteen to eighteen, Yoni lived with his parents and two younger brothers – Binyamin

---

* In the 1930s, as the rest of the Zionist movement tried to build bridges with Palestinian Arabs and negotiated with the British for increased Jewish immigration, Ze'ev Jabotinsky's Revisionist Party demanded an independent Jewish state that included the whole of Palestine and Transjordan. Its paramilitary wing, led by Menachem Begin, was known as Irgun.

('Bibi') and Iddo – on the east coast of the United States while his father taught Hebrew studies at Dropsie College in Philadelphia. During the latter sojourn he was a model student, but deeply unhappy. 'I feel I belong to a different world,' he wrote to an Israeli friend. 'I am remote from them and the distance does not diminish as time passes but quite the reverse . . . There isn't a moment here that I would not sacrifice at once for my immediate return to Israel. My friends in Israel, my social life and, above all, the land itself – I miss very much.'

Conscript service gave him the opportunity to return to Israel in 1964. Like Betser, he joined a paratroop unit (though not the elite Sayeret) and was quickly marked down as a natural soldier. His 'physical toughness and fierce determination carried him through every exercise. He absorbed with ease the principles of navigation, tactics, weapon-training.' Promotion followed rapidly, and by early 1966 he had passed out of officer school as the prize cadet.

In 1967, having left the army to resume his academic studies, he was mobilized for the Six-Day War and fought in both the Sinai and on the Golan Heights, receiving a bullet wound in the arm during the latter battle. Once he had recovered he married his girlfriend Tutti and took up a place at Harvard in the United States to study philosophy, physics and mathematics. But though he thrived academically, he soon tired of the anti-Vietnam War atmosphere of the Cambridge campus – the 'shaggy young men and beaded girls' – and yearned to take part in Israel's struggle against Fatah and the other Palestinian *fedayeen*. 'I hope with all my heart,' he wrote to his brother Bibi, 'that my hand will improve enough for me to be able to go back to reserve duty. It's important because it's the duty of every good Jew . . . Each terror operation in Israel strengthens my conviction that the sooner I come back the better . . . I know I must. If Fatah come to fight, then my responsibility is many times greater. One thing is certain: I am a better soldier than any of them, and my national consciousness is stronger than theirs. If they want war – we have no choice but to fight for our existence.'

He and Tutti returned to Israel in 1968. The following spring he was fortunate to be passed fit by an army medical board. The army doctor, a recent immigrant, had only a flimsy grasp of Hebrew and mistakenly examined Netanyahu's leg rather than his damaged arm, thus failing to notice that the muscles were still badly wasted and the hand could not be fully straightened. With his new bill of health, Netanyahu joined his younger brother Bibi as a junior officer in the IDF's finest fighting force: the Unit. At first his men 'were a little suspicious of his incessant reading, his solitariness, his almost inhumanly high standards'. Yet they gradually came to appreciate his exceptional qualities. 'They had always sensed his inner strength, his iron resolution. But in the field they began to see this translated into the spirit of a superb fighting commander.'

The initial training of Yoni's team was thorough and relentless. They 'began months of navigation practice, route marches, fire exercises and team attacks'. They learned to shoot at figure targets while running, and were taught to close the range at all costs, and never to fight a long-range duel. They practised house clearing in abandoned Golan villages, crawling from stone to stone across open country, and to fire single aimed shots rather than bursts. They acquired specialist skills like first aid, communications, photography and demolition. And they were reminded that every member of the Unit had to act both as a member of a team and as a self-contained soldier who could think for himself.

After a seven-month break from the Unit, commanding a company of the Sayeret Haruv in the Jordan Valley, Yoni returned as a captain in July 1971 and was furious to be barred from the Sabena operation because his younger brother Bibi was taking part. The IDF have a rule that two members of the same family cannot go together on an operation in case both are killed. In the event, Bibi was wounded by friendly fire.

Yoni did, however, take part with Betser in many of the Unit's subsequent operations: the kidnap of the Syrian intelligence officers from Lebanon in 1972; Operation Spring of Youth and the fighting on the Golan Heights during the Yom Kippur War in 1973 (for which latter action he was awarded the Distinguished Conduct Medal).

By now a single man – his marriage having failed a year earlier – Yoni chose to further his military education, and ease promotion to senior rank, by leaving the Unit in late 1973 to command a tank battalion. There he began a relationship with a pretty young female conscript called Bruria that continued after he was appointed to command the Unit in the summer of 1975. A friend, on hearing he was going back, asked: 'Why do it? If you stay alive, you're going to be a general. But if you go on like this, you're going to be killed. Why push in the queue for hell?'

Yoni's chief concern was not that he might die in action, but that he would struggle to lead one of the most sensitive, highly bred groups of men in the IDF. It did not help that his predecessor, Giora Zorea, was everything he was not: compulsively frank, open and easy-going, every soldier's friend. Yoni, on the other hand, was viewed by some members of the Unit as off-hand and tyrannical in his ruthless drive to raise standards.

The tension had still not been properly resolved by the time Yoni received Betser's call from Ben-Gurion on 28 June 1976. 'You need us?' asked Yoni, his voice hard to make out over the patchy radio connection.

'No, I don't think so,' said Betser. 'It's pretty straightforward. I'm planning to use the new method.'

Thorough as ever, Yoni checked that certain key officers, men and matériel were at the airport. Betser said they were.

'Keep me posted.'

'Of course.'

1400hrs GMT, Jerusalem, Israel

Yitzhak Rabin opened the 4 p.m. meeting of the ministerial task force in the downstairs conference room of his Kaplan Street office: 'The only thing we know for sure right now is that the hijacked plane is Air France.'

He then turned to Justice Minister Chaim Zadok, a portly round-shouldered man with an encyclopaedic legal brain, and asked: 'What exactly is the legal status of passengers on board that plane?'

'By law,' responded Zadok without a pause, 'the passengers are under French sovereign protection. The French government is responsible for the fate of them all.'

Rabin seemed relieved. 'Yigal,' he said to his foreign minister, 'have your people inform the French government, and tell them we're issuing a public statement to that effect. Ask Paris to keep us informed of their actions.'

As Allon left the room to telephone his officials, Zadok called after him: 'And tell them they must make no distinction between the Israeli passengers and the rest.'

'That goes without saying,' muttered a huffy Allon.

Moments later Poran returned with a new note that Rabin read out loud: 'There are 230 passengers* on board, 83 of them Israeli, and 12 crew members. The Libyans have allowed the plane to land at Benghazi.'

The prime minister lit a cigarette. 'So now at least we know where the passengers are,' he said frowning. 'But there are three crucial things we don't know. We don't know whether Benghazi will be their final stop. We don't know who the hijackers are. And we don't know what their demands will be.'

For the next thirty minutes the ministers discussed these unknowns, including the possibility that the plane would return to Ben-Gurion. They also agreed that Yaacobi, the transport minister, would deal with the media and liaise with the hostages' families, though he himself thought an Air France representative at Ben-Gurion should be the one to tell them the bad news. This prompted Allon to blurt out: 'We are in deep trouble.'

'Yes we are,' agreed Rabin.

They were interrupted by a message for Allon from Jean Herly, the French ambassador to Israel, which was read to the room. It confirmed that the French government of Jacques Chirac was prepared to take 'full responsibility for the safety of all the passengers without distinction on Air France Flight 139', and that it would keep Israel 'apprised of its actions in this regard'.

---

* An underestimate that was close to the 228 passengers who had departed Ben-Gurion on Flight 139 that morning.

Satisfied by this response, Rabin adjourned the meeting but warned the ministers to stay close to their phones. His office then issued an official statement giving a bare outline of the hijacking that recognized France's assumption of responsibility for the passengers' wellbeing, and declared that, as Shimon Peres later put it, 'Israel would not submit to blackmail on the part of the hijackers'.

1430hrs GMT, Benghazi, Libya

After a message from the terrorist chief had invited 'any other women and children' to move to the comfort of first class, a steady trickle of hostages made their way to the front of the parked plane at Benina International Airport. Of the vacated seats they left behind, one was occupied by Claude Moufflet on the left side of the central block, a little in front of the wings, next to two young Canadian women: twenty-year-old Louise Kourtis and her friend Jo-Anne Rethmetakis, eighteen, both from Montreal. Kourtis, a small pretty girl with chestnut hair and very long varnished nails, was sitting cross-legged on her seat. The slightly taller Rethmetakis, next to the window, wore her brown hair in a ponytail and reminded Moufflet of a 'Red Indian', with her 'great big dark sloping eyes', 'slightly hooked nose' and white even teeth.

They told Moufflet that they were on the plane only because they had got tired and had decided to cut short their tour of Europe by a few days. 'Our parents aren't even expecting us until 1 July,' said Kourtis. 'So as of now they won't be worried. They don't even know we're on this plane.'

'Well,' said Moufflet, trying to reassure them, 'with a little bit of luck it's you who will be able to let them know about your adventure, and then they can find out at the same moment about your hijacking as well as your liberation.'

The thought amused the girls, and Kourtis pretended to sulk. 'Ah yes, but if it did happen like that nobody would believe us.'

Suddenly Rethmetakis became more serious. 'If it finishes that way,' she said quietly, 'then I don't care if they don't believe us.'

To Moufflet's right sat two Moroccan men whispering in heated tones. Eventually the older one turned to him and asked: 'Shouldn't we do something?'

This was the second time Moufflet had been forewarned of a potential mutiny and, conscious of the danger, his answer was cautious. 'Well, perhaps, but what?'

'I don't know. Jump on them? Disarm them?'

'What are you going to do with their pistols and their grenades?'

The younger one responded by saying the grenades had not had their pins taken out.

Moufflet gasped in exasperation. 'Look,' he said, pointing to the ring of the pin which each terrorist had around a finger, 'you can see very well they've had the pins taken out.'

'Well,' persisted the older Moroccan, 'I doubt the guns are loaded.'

'Well, there is no way we can be certain there are bullets inside. But I, for one, am not going to give them the opportunity to prove it. Are you?'

Seeing the Moroccan hesitate, Moufflet continued: 'In any case, you've already seen that they're very organized and are part of the Popular Front for the Liberation of Palestine. You know as well as I do that these people can obtain all kinds of weapons and that there is no chance they're bluffing.'

'It's true,' said the younger one.

'So you really think there's nothing to do?'

'Certainly not for the moment.'

Up at the front of the plane, where the terrorists had left two big bags of weapons unattended on the seats of Row 1, Michel Cojot was having similar thoughts of rebellion. 'It was tempting,' he wrote later. 'But the terrorists were always well distributed in the plane, and one couldn't predict what the reaction of the Libyan soldiers would be.'

1459hrs GMT, San Juan, Puerto Rico

British Foreign Secretary Tony Crosland was attending a morning session of the second G7 economic conference at the Dorado

Beach Resort near San Juan in Puerto Rico with Prime Minister Jim Callaghan when he received a cipher telegram from the Foreign and Commonwealth Office (FCO) in London: Reuters had reported the 'hijacking, and landing at Benghazi, of Air France Flight en route for Paris from Athens (having originated at Lydda [Lod])'.

A public-school- and Oxford-educated socialist who had served as a paratrooper during the Second World War, Crosland began as a university lecturer in economics. But after entering Parliament as a Labour MP in 1950, he wrote the influential *The Future of Socialism* and became the chief intellectual force behind left-wing 'revisionism'. For the first two years of Harold Wilson's second Labour government, Crosland served in the Cabinet as environment secretary. When Wilson resigned as prime minister on 5 April 1976, Crosland threw his hat into the ring in the leadership contest of the ruling Labour Party. But on falling at the first hurdle, he supported the eventual winner and new prime minister James Callaghan, and the vital portfolio of foreign affairs, for which he had no experience, was his reward.

His first couple of months in the job were dominated by two main issues: the 'Cod War' between British and Icelandic fishermen which Crosland defused with some canny diplomacy; and the long-term future of Rhodesia which, since Ian Smith's unilateral declaration of independence (UDI) in 1965, had been ravaged by a guerilla war between the white government and black rebels. Crosland's attempts to broker a deal between the two sides that would usher in majority rule had already, he felt, been undermined by some clumsy interventions by Dr Henry Kissinger, the US secretary of state.

The news that an Air France plane had been hijacked was, by contrast, a relatively minor matter. Concerned that British citizens might be involved, Crosland wired the British ambassador in Tripoli: 'Grateful for any details you or Athens or Tel Aviv can obtain of (A) British subjects among passengers (B) Present situation of aircraft and passengers (C) Identity and motives of hijackers.'

1500hrs GMT, Benghazi, Libya

At about the same time that the British government was trying to find out if any of its nationals were on the hijacked plane still parked at Benina International Airport, one of them was making an audacious bid for freedom. Her name was Patricia Martell, a thirty-year-old nurse from Manchester who had recently emigrated to Israel with her Leeds-born husband Howard. She was returning to Britain to attend the funeral of her mother when the hijacking intervened. Determined not to miss the service, she was prepared to do almost anything to escape. 'I had to get off that plane,' she remembered, 'and that's all there was to it. I wasn't scared.'

Her first thought was to feign a heart or asthma attack. But eventually she decided on a fake miscarriage, though not pregnant. She 'screwed up her face in simulated agony', blanched, perspired and 'began to twist and turn with pain'. Then she called to the female terrorist: 'I'm pregnant . . . second month . . . I think something's happening to me . . .'

'I'll call a doctor,' the girl said, before moving Martell up the plane to a bigger seat in first class. A minute or two later a doctor appeared: David Bass, forty, a US-born surgeon who had emigrated to Israel in 1972 and was working as head of gastroenterology at Kaplan Hospital in Rehovot, south of Tel Aviv. The hijackers had checked, soon after taking control of the aircraft, if any of the hostages had medical training. 'I'm bluffing,' murmured Martell. 'I must get out of here.'

Bass was aghast. 'You're better off on the plane than in Libya,' he insisted.

But Martell would not be deterred and a second opinion was sought from a Libyan doctor who, when he first came on board, pronounced her a fraud. 'There's nothing wrong with her,' he said. 'Just frightened that's all.'

He changed his mind when Martell showed him her menstrual blood as 'proof' she was about to miscarry. He needed to take her with him for emergency treatment, he told the terrorists, or she might lose her child. After some debate, they decided to let her go. It was the start of the hijacking, recalled Martell, and the terrorists were 'very uptight and very nervous. The woman hijacker realized that if I miscarried there would be a hell of a mess. It wasn't worth their while. I wasn't that important.'

The terrorists were not the only ones who were duped. Sitting across from Martell in first class were Olivier Cojot and his father. 'All of a sudden,' remembered Olivier, 'I see she's bleeding. I was convinced she was having a miscarriage.'

As she was led off the plane, Martell turned to the Cojots and whispered: 'Good luck.'

1600hrs GMT, Tel Aviv, Israel

While the other members of the Cabinet committee remained in Jerusalem to await news of the plane, Defense Minister Shimon Peres hurried back to his office in the Kirya complex in Tel Aviv to consult with the IDF chief of staff, Mordechai 'Motta' Gur.

Born Szymon Perski in 1923, the son of a Polish lumber merchant, Peres had played a key role in the security of the Israeli state since its creation in 1948. Having emigrated to the then British Mandate of Palestine with his family at the age of eleven, he had lived for a time on a kibbutz and was later elected secretary of a Labour Zionist youth movement. His route into politics, however, was via the Haganah – the Jewish defence organization that later became the core of the IDF – which he joined in 1947 on the advice of David Ben-Gurion, the de facto leader of the Jewish community in Palestine and soon to become Israel's first prime minister. Peres's job was to mobilize new manpower and procure arms for the Haganah/IDF. Though he did not fight on the front line, he played a significant part in Israel's hard-fought victory in the eighteen-month First War of Independence (1948–9). This paved the way for his meteoric rise in Israel's Ministry of Defense, culminating in his appointment in 1953 as director-general, or senior permanent official, at the age of just twenty-nine.

As the Defense Ministry's top official, Peres was responsible for arms purchases and establishing strategic alliances. The most important was with France, enabling Israel to acquire the latest weapons – including the modern Dassault Mirage III jet fighter – and the Dimona nuclear reactor that had become active in 1963. He was elected to Israel's unicameral parliament, the Knesset, in 1959 and eight years later joined the Labor Party – a social democrat and Zionist organization that had been formed out of various left-wing parties. From 1970 to 1974 he served in Golda Meir's Labor government as minister of transport. When Meir was forced to resign as both prime minister and leader of the Labor Party in 1974, bowing to mounting criticism that her government had failed to anticipate the Yom Kippur War – when Israel's intelligence services and the IDF was caught badly off guard by sudden and coordinated Arab attacks – Peres stood as her successor. But he was narrowly defeated by his politically inexperienced rival Yitzhak Rabin and had to make do with the post of minister of defense.

It was not an appointment Rabin wanted to make. 'I did not consider Shimon Peres suitable,' he explained, 'since he had never fought in the IDF and his expertise in arms purchasing did not make up for that lack of experience.' But as other members of the Labor Party wanted Peres to receive the defense portfolio, and Rabin was loath to split the party, he approved the appointment 'with a heavy heart'. It was an error he would later 'regret'.

Their political alliance, as a result, was one of expediency rather than shared convictions, and Rabin always suspected Peres of trying to undermine his premiership. Peres denied the charge, insisting that he 'served the 1974–77 government, and the man who led it, loyally, fully shouldering the collective responsibility of a cabinet minister'. Short and stocky, with swept-back greying hair and a handsome, heavily lined face, Peres looked every inch the soldier he had never been. Instead he was a consummate politician who resented the fact that Rabin, militarily experienced but a political neophyte, had beaten him to the premiership.

Peres's main priority on hearing of the Air France hijacking was to prevent the Israeli government from caving in to blackmail. It was to that end that he rushed back to Tel Aviv during the late afternoon of 27 June to talk to the IDF chief of staff Motta Gur, a man he had known since the 1950s and who had always impressed him 'as a straight talker with a firm grasp of strategy'. Seven years Peres's junior, Gur had fought with the elite Palmach branch of the Haganah before joining the IDF. He had since commanded the Golani Brigade and served for a time as the IDF's chief of operations. But he came to national prominence as the commander of the paratroop brigade that 'liberated' the Old City of Jerusalem in 1967, and was the choice of both Moshe Dayan and Peres to succeed David Elazar when the latter stepped down as IDF chief of staff in the wake of the Yom Kippur War.

Since their respective appointments, Peres and Gur had striven to rebuild and strengthen the Israeli army. They 'worked well together', Peres wrote later, often 'as many as eighteen or twenty hours a day'. The 'general mood of aftershock and depression that pervaded the nation' after the Yom Kippur War had made them 'doubly aware' of their 'responsibilities at the head of the nation's defenses'. Peres had 'full confidence' in Gur and gave him his 'total political support'. Together they groomed 'a new generation of promising officers, among them Dan Shomron and Ehud Barak', to lay 'the groundwork for what came to be called the "long-arm option" – a capacity to strike hard and fast at targets far beyond our immediate frontiers'.

When Peres met with Gur and his aides on 27 June, however, their discussion centred on the possibility that the hijackers might bring the Air France plane back to Ben-Gurion. If they did, their preferred option was to use the Unit to storm the plane as it had during the Sabena hijacking in 1972 when Peres, as minister of transport, worked alongside Moshe Dayan, the defense minister, 'during a long night of negotiation and preparation'. Once again, Peres intended to be at the centre of the action and was only awaiting news of the plane's departure from Benghazi before he made his way to the airport.

1708hrs GMT, London, UK

Barely an hour after Foreign Secretary Tony Crosland's request for information on the Air France hijacking, a cipher telegram from the British Embassy in Athens was decoded in the FCO's imposing George Gilbert Scott-designed Italianate headquarters in King Charles Street. It read: 'Air France Office here say that 2 British subjects embarked at Athens: A Mr G. Good and a Mr C. Russell . . . They say the aircraft is still at Benghazi. Nationality of hijackers unknown.' It then confirmed Good's and Russell's passport numbers, year of birth (1911 and 1921 respectively) and the fact that both had entered Greece on 17 June.

The news that at least two of the Air France passengers were British prompted Crosland, still in Puerto Rico, to cable his embassies in Tripoli (the capital of Libya) and Paris with an exhortation for the former to 'keep in close touch with your French colleague' who, it was assumed, would be leading the negotiations to free the hostages. He added: 'We should be grateful if Paris could likewise liaise closely with appropriate French authorities and . . . keep us and Tripoli informed of French plans to secure release of passengers and aircraft.'

The response from Sir Donald Murray, the British ambassador to Libya and a former Royal Marine commando, was that the Embassy at Tripoli was 'keeping in close touch' with its French colleagues and had passed them Good's and Russell's details. 'We have also,' he continued, 'told them that we understand from BBC reports that there are a number of Commonwealth citizens aboard as well. They have undertaken to pass this information to French consul in Benghazi, who is at Benghazi Airport, when they next speak to him. Second Secretary (R. D. Lamb), who happened to be visiting Benghazi, has been instructed to liaise closely with French Consulate there.'

Murray had yet to be informed that the dual Israeli–British national Mrs Patricia Martell (née Hayman) had been released, and that Lamb had spoken to her. That news would reach London later that evening.

1715hrs GMT, Benghazi, Libya

Four hours after their arrival at Benina International Airport, while many passengers were stretching their legs in the aisles, the terrorist chief gave the first hint of Flight 139's future destination. 'Sit down,' he instructed over the intercom. 'We are preparing for a flight of about three hours. We will serve you something to eat in a short while. It is still forbidden to smoke and we will let you know when you can.'

The news prompted Claude Moufflet to check on the map in his diary the possible airports that were within the requisite flying time from Libya. Eliminating anything to the south, he settled on Baghdad in Iraq as the most likely objective and said as much to his neighbours. This prompted a flurry of questions from the two young Canadians: 'Where is it?' 'Is it an Arab country?' 'Is the government an ally of the terrorists?' 'Will they put us in prison?'

To stop the girls from worrying unnecessarily, Moufflet replied 'as vaguely as possible' before immersing himself in a crossword puzzle.

Moments later, perhaps regretting his earlier decision to allow Mrs Martell to leave the plane, the terrorist chief issued a warning over the intercom. 'Listen,' he said, 'we don't want all of you to start inventing illnesses so that you can get off the plane. You have been warned. We have a doctor here. Do not try to trick us. If you do you'll be severely punished.'

To relieve the tension, the terrorists told the crew to serve the food that had been intended as lunch on the original flight, complete with plastic trays and cake as pudding. Akiva Laxer, a thirty-year-old Tel Aviv lawyer who had been en route to the Montreal Olympic Games, was astonished to be given the same gefilte fish he had pre-ordered for the flight in Israel. As he ate it he mused on the irony of an Orthodox Jew 'sitting on a hijacked plane in Benghazi eating kosher fish from Israel'. He also cursed his bad luck at having been present at two of Israel's most infamous terrorist atrocities – the Lod Massacre in 1972 followed a few months later by the murder of Israeli athletes at the Munich Olympic Games – and now this hijacking. Was he the common denominator?

Claude Moufflet decided to keep his cake, orange juice and a little water for the long night ahead. A can of Schweppes fizzy drink he gave to the grateful young Canadians. Medical student Moshe Peretz thought the cold supper was 'not bad'. He noted in his makeshift diary that 'the stewards serve cans of juice, with Arab inscriptions' and that the female German terrorist was 'the sort who gets things together fast'. If anyone wanted to go to the toilet, they had to raise their hand and she would shout an order for them to go. But when two passengers got up at the same time she screamed 'like a veritable animal'.

An hour later a new message came over the intercom, informing the passengers that despite a few technical difficulties the preparations for the onward flight were almost complete. Already 5,500 gallons of kerosene had been added to the fuel tanks; only another 2,000 gallons were needed. 'The aeroplane has been checked,' said the chief terrorist. 'It's in good condition and our departure is now estimated at 2100hrs local time.'

That time came and went. But shortly before 9.30 p.m. Libyan time (GMT + 2 hours) the passengers were told to sit down and buckle their seatbelts for takeoff. A few minutes later the two General Electric CF6-50 engines roared into life and the plane began its long taxi to the main runway. At 9.50 p.m., the Airbus rose into the night sky and headed south.

Peretz scribbled: 'At long last, in the air. Unbelievable. After 6½ hours on the ground. Our treatment is fairly good. But where are we flying? To Damascus? Baghdad? Beirut? Tel Aviv? Or Paris? The passengers conduct a kind of lottery about the destination of our flight. We speak freely to one another, with the unknown factors being our destination and the hijackers' demands.'

2005hrs GMT, Tel Aviv, Israel

Major Muki Betser was still at Ben-Gurion International Airport with the Unit's anti-terrorist team when word reached him that the hijacked Air France plane had taken off from Benghazi. Aware that the plane was just three hours' flying time from Ben-Gurion, he called his men into the briefing room and conducted a final review

45

of the assault plan for the benefit of Major-General Yekutiel 'Kuti' Adam, the IDF's chief of operations and deputy chief of staff.

Born near Tel Aviv in 1919, and therefore a Sabra Israeli – literally a 'prickly pair' or native Jew – who spoke Hebrew as his native tongue, Adam had joined the Haganah at the age of fifteen and later transferred to the IDF. A soldier's soldier with an extravagant Zapata mustache and extensive combat experience to match, he also possessed a keen analytical mind that had been honed by two years' study at France's War Academy in the 1960s. He, like his political master Peres, regarded military action as the *only* response to terrorism, and was convinced that the men of the Unit were up to the task if the plane returned.

With the briefing over, Adam gave his authorization for an assault. Now there was nothing more that Betser and his men could do but wait.

2012hrs GMT, London, UK

While Betser was still briefing Adam, word finally reached the Foreign and Commonwealth Office in London that 'a British subject, a Mrs Neman (They are not sure of the exact spelling), has been allowed to leave the plane'. The cipher telegram from the British Embassy in Paris added: 'She is, as far as the Quai [d'Orsay, the French foreign office] know, the only person allowed to do so.'

More detailed and up-to-date information was provided twenty minutes later by a cable from Sir Donald Murray at Tripoli:

> Aircraft left Benghazi at 2149hrs local time (GMT Plus 2).
>
> Heading South. Beyond taking on food, water and fuel, hijackers made no requests at Benghazi. The aircraft is said to have four and one half hours endurance.
>
> One sick passenger, a British nurse, Miss Patricia Suzanne Hayman (Passport No. L989499, issued April 1975), was allowed to disembark at Benghazi. She will travel to Tripoli and on to London tomorrow.

Hayman saw 2 Arab and 2 non Arab hijackers, whom she described as very nervous. They have placed explosives in the aircraft. She said the morale of the passengers was holding up excellently.

Please try and inform Hayman's next of kin (her mother has just died). Second Secretary [R. D. Lamb] was unable to obtain her home address before she was whisked away by the Libyan authorities.

The confusion over Mrs Martell's name was down to the fact that she had only married a few weeks earlier and still possessed a passport in the name of Miss Hayman. Met in Tripoli a day later by Sir Donald Murray, she was described as 'well but still somewhat shaken'. She later admitted that her ruse to get off the plane was 'pretty stupid'. She added: 'It could have gone very wrong, but it didn't and it paid off.'

Mrs Martell arrived back at Heathrow on a scheduled Libyan Airways flight in the early afternoon of Monday 28 June and was met by Scotland Yard and a member of the Mossad – Israel's highly effective foreign intelligence service – who was attached to the Israeli Embassy. In her subsequent interview she confirmed there were four terrorists: two Arabs from the PFLP and two that sounded German. They were later identified as members of a little-known radical left-wing terrorist organization known as the Revolutionary Cells (RC, or Revolutionäre Zellen in German). Their names: Wilfried Böse and Brigitte Kuhlmann.

Born in 1949 in the beautiful historic Bavarian town of Bamberg, Wilfried Bonifatius ('Boni') Böse was a warm-hearted and jovial young man who liked to relax by drinking the local Franconian wine and eating bratwurst. But the former sociology student at Frankfurt University was also a committed political activist who, like many founding members of both the RC and the more notorious Red Army Faktion* (RAF, better known as the Baader–Meinhof Gang), had

---

* Rote Armee Fraktion (in German). Founded in 1970 by Andreas Baader, Gudrun Ensslin, Horst Mahler and Ulrike Meinhof, the RAF described itself as a communist and anti-imperialist urban guerilla group engaged in armed resistance to a fascist state.

played a leading role 'in the student and protest movement in the late 1960s and had been involved in a range of leftist groups and local initiatives'. They included the Black Panther Solidarity Committee (Black-Panther-Solidaritätskomitee) – modelled on the revolutionary Marxist Black Panther Party in the US – that 'sought to organize educational work about and active support for the Black Panthers in Germany'. This 'identification with the countercultural style, the readiness to use violence, and the radical anti-imperialist stance of the Black Panthers played a decisive role in the radicalization' of Böse and other founding members of the RC and RAF.

Another common denominator among many early members of the RC – including Böse, Johannes Weinrich and Gerd Schnepel – is that they either sold or published leftist literature before joining the armed struggle. In Frankfurt in 1970, Böse and Weinrich founded the left-wing publishing house Red Star (Roter Stern), producing many books on revolutionary struggle and armed rebellion. Schnepel was running a leftist bookstore and publishing house when he decided that 'political literature and legal forms of protest alone' were not enough to force through fundamental political change. Aware of the 'cruelties' done in the name of capitalism, he felt duty bound to act. Yet it was Böse, a 'bustling organizational talent and key actor in the radical leftist scene', who seems to have been the 'driving force' behind the formation of the Revolutionary Cells in 1973.

Brigitte Kuhlmann, co-founder of the RC and the female terrorist on Flight 139, was two years older than Böse. A plain serious-looking woman of medium height – her mother once said to her, 'You are not pretty, this is sure, but you are interesting' – she was born in the north German city of Hanover in Lower Saxony and studied pedagogy (the science of teaching) before moving to Frankfurt where she worked with handicapped children. Like Böse, she 'moved within radical leftist circles and knew leading members of the RAF'. She was also 'a feminist who enjoyed life but had a strong sense of social and pedagogical responsibility'. She had been in a relationship with Böse, but was sleeping with Schnepel prior to the Air France operation. Schnepel thought she was 'women's lib, anti-authoritarian, resolute and honest', a 'friendly, caring person with social commitment'.

Kuhlmann formed the original Revolutionary Cell with Böse and Weinrich in Frankfurt in 1973; Schnepel was recruited soon afterwards. Within five years there were eleven cells across West Germany: four in Frankfurt and its environs, and others in Berlin, the Ruhr and south Germany. Each cell was composed of three to five members and acted autonomously of the others; no RC member used their real name, and to reduce the risk of betrayal only one person in each cell communicated with the other groups. Often the members of local groups were – like Böse, Kuhlmann and Schnepel – 'friends or lovers and lived or worked together'. Moreover they divided tasks equally, sharing domestic chores like cooking and washing up, with only 'occasional relapses in "typical" [gender-specific] behaviour'.

The core beliefs of the RC were a mixture of left-wing anti-imperialist liberation doctrine with strong anti-Zionist, anti-patriarchal and anti-racist elements. Rejecting 'the dogmatism and elitism of the RAF', they wanted to 'create small nuclei of resistance, who work autonomously in different spheres of society, and who fight, intervene . . . [and] form a part of the political mass movement'. They believed that members should remain part of mainstream German society, in contrast to the more elitist RAF which thought that revolutionaries should be wholly 'underground' (outside the mainstream socio-political system). Many members of the RC 'led a double life for years without arousing suspicion' and, as a result, were sometimes referred to as *Feierabendterroristen* ('after-work terrorists').

The RC's early terror attacks were mostly bombings of foreign (chiefly US) businesses, courts and railway ticket machines using homemade explosives that resulted in few casualties. There was even one with an openly feminist agenda when female RC members – including, most likely, Kuhlmann – bombed the Federal Court of Justice in Karlsruhe in March 1975 to protest against the court's recent decision to block the decriminalization of abortion. But soon Kuhlmann, Böse and Weinrich began to forge links with various international terror groups like the IRA, the Red Brigades in Italy and especially Wadie Haddad's offshoot of the PFLP. They did this, according to Schnepel, because they were keen to 'strengthen the group' by cooperating with other terror organizations that shared their basic left-wing political philosophy. They saw the Palestinians' anti-Zionist cause as part of a wider anti-imperialist and anti-capitalist struggle that was loosely characterized as 'world revolution'.

But there was also a practical reason: if they were part of the international hostage-taking process they could force the German government to release some of its political prisoners. 'There were a lot of differences with the Red Army Faktion,' said Schnepel, 'but we felt it was an obligation on all of us to do anything that we could to free them. And so the connection with Wadie Haddad seemed to be a promising way to succeed in this idea.'

No one felt this obligation more than Kuhlmann. She blamed herself for Ulrike Meinhof's arrest in 1972 because she had recommended a safe house in Langenhagen. Unfortunately the owner, a teacher, became suspicious that he was harbouring a member of the RAF and called the police. By 1974, many of the other RAF leaders – Baader, Ensslin and Raspe – were also behind bars and Kuhlmann and her comrades were determined to free them.

The first joint operation with Wadie Haddad's PFLP was at Paris's Orly Airport in January 1975 when Johannes Weinrich and Venezuelan-born Ilich Ramírez Sánchez (better known as 'Carlos the Jackal') tried to shoot down an El Al plane with a Russian-made RPG-7 (rocket-propelled grenade launcher). But Weinrich missed with both shots and was later arrested in Frankfurt for providing the cars used in the attack. He jumped bail while awaiting trial and in 1977 became Carlos's right-hand man.

With Weinrich on the run, a second RC terrorist called Hans-Joachim Klein teamed up with Carlos for an even more spectacular Haddad operation: an attack on the OPEC (oil producers) Conference in Vienna in December 1975. Their intention was to kidnap the oil ministers, fly them out of Vienna to a 'friendly' destination and release them only on receipt of a ransom and a pro-Palestine statement by their governments. If the demands were not met, the ministers were to be executed.

As well as Klein, the Jackal's commando included a second German terrorist, Gabriele Kröcher-Tiedemann of the anarchist Movement

2 June (J2M), a Palestinian and two Libyans. On 21 December they stormed the building hosting the conference, killing three people and taking sixty-two hostages (including eleven oil ministers). In the ensuing gun battle with police, Klein was wounded in the stomach. But after treatment in a Vienna hospital he was allowed to rejoin the terrorists and the bulk of their hostages for a flight to Algeria. After a short detour to Libya, the plane returned to Algeria and the hostages were released in return for an unspecified ransom of up to $20 million (allegedly paid by Saudi Arabia) and safe passage out of the country.

Wadie Haddad, however, was unimpressed. According to Bassam Abu-Sharif of the PFLP, 'none of the financial and political objectives of this immensely complex operation' had been met and Haddad considered it to be 'a complete failure'. Carlos had 'missed a fabulous opportunity'. On the Jackal's return to the PFLP's training camp in the South Yemen, Haddad told him he had developed a 'star complex' and that there was 'no room for stars in my operational teams'. He was ordered to go.

And so the Jackal left Haddad's PFLP to strike out on his own, telling Bassam that he was thinking of setting up a direct-action group in South America where there were 'plenty of fascists who needed sorting out'. Bassam was not convinced. He felt the Jackal did not have the organizational ability to run a terrorist group. He was an 'executioner' rather than a 'mastermind', and 'for once he had failed to execute'.

Undeterred by the Jackal's failure, Haddad began plotting a new operation with the RC: the hijacking of a plane carrying Israeli passengers to France. His PFLP would provide two of the four-man commando, Khaled al-Khalili and Ali al-Ma'ati, both young Palestinians on their first mission (and wearing, respectively, yellow and red shirts during the hijacking); the RC leaders Boni Böse and Brigitte Kuhlmann would make up the balance, with Böse in overall command.

Böse had already trained at Haddad's camp in the desert of South Yemen. Now it was Kuhlmann's turn, along with her boyfriend Gerd Schnepel, who was preparing for future missions. As well as cleaning, repairing and firing weapons – including pistols, automatic rifles and even bazookas – they learned how to handle and prime grenades and explosives. But their most effective training was psychological: how to control and speak to hostages. Kuhlmann, in particular, was told by Haddad to keep her distance and not feel sorry for them. 'We were told to treat it as a military action,' remembered Schnepel, 'and not go round offering tea to the hostages.'

Schnepel is convinced that a combination of this training and the fact that Kuhlmann might have felt that as a woman she had to be 'tougher' than the men of the commando is the reason why some of the Jewish hostages from Air France Flight 139 later claimed she had behaved like a 'Nazi'. In reality, he says, 'Brigitte was very kind, very caring . . . She was normally a soft person, but at the same time she was very disciplined.'

Kuhlmann did not give Schnepel any details about her and Böse's mission. Instead she simply told him that he wouldn't hear from her for some time, adding: 'Then hopefully I'll come back. But it's a dangerous operation.' When he asked if he could go with her, she refused to answer.

2020hrs GMT, Jerusalem, Israel

In possession of the latest intelligence from Benghazi, Yitzhak Rabin called a second meeting of the ministerial committee in his office in Jerusalem at 10.20 p.m. Present were Allon, Yaacobi, Zadok and Galili, but not Peres who was still in the Kirya in Tel Aviv conferring with Chief of Staff Gur.

'Here is the new information,' said Rabin, scanning a dossier in front of him. 'The plane was seven hours on the ground at Benghazi, for refuelling. One passenger, a pregnant woman, was released. The plane took off . . . We have no idea where the plane is heading now. Meanwhile, Ben-Gurion Airport is on the highest alert. As for the identity of the attackers, it seems there are four – two Arabs from the Popular Front for the Liberation of Palestine, and two Germans from a terrorist splinter group calling itself the "Revolutionary Cells". That's as much as we know.'

As the subsequent 'anxious' discussion added nothing to the 'sum total of knowledge or ideas', Rabin brought the meeting to a close and left for his private residence. He was to be contacted immediately if there was any news.

2100hrs GMT, Libyan airspace

Still unaware of the plane's final destination, though vaguely conscious that it was heading south, the passengers tried to sleep. But for some it was impossible. There were loud squabbles over seats and then, from the front of the plane, a woman's anguished screams as she contemplated the full gravity of her predicament. She fell silent only when the female terrorist Brigitte Kuhlmann, her face 'mean and full of hate', threatened to shoot her.

As the plane flew on, Michel Cojot noticed that the new 'captain' – Wilfried Böse, a man he described as 'a blond, chubby German about thirty years-old' – 'began to spend more time with the passengers, trying to smile and even to joke'. He went to 'great lengths to calm his companions, especially the two young Arabs, who were still very nervous'. Gradually they became 'less tense and some passengers went to sleep'. Even young Olivier 'stopped asking questions and dozed off' on his father's shoulder. 'I thought about possible landing places,' recorded Cojot. 'I was very much afraid of the south of the Arabian Peninsula: South Yemen or, worse, the Dofar Province in rebellion. I preferred a well-established sovereign state with a seat in the United Nations and numerous diplomatic ties.'

2330hrs GMT, Lod, Israel

More than three hours after the hijacked plane had left Benghazi – about the time it would take to fly from there to Israel – Muki Betser and the Unit's anti-terrorist team were on high alert in a small hangar at Ben-Gurion International Airport when General Adam walked in with Defense Minister Shimon Peres. 'Several of the soldiers were inside,' recorded Peres, 'looking serious and businesslike. They showed no signs of tension.'

Asked by Adam to go over the plan's essentials once again for Peres, Betser did so, 'tapping at the airport map' on the wall behind him, and 'counting off "Positions One, Two, Three, and Four" for each of the squads'.

He continued: 'Here's the runway, the control tower will direct the plane to here.' He pointed at a runway marked on the map. 'And as always,' he concluded, 'if we take the initiative, we can control the events. Any questions?'

A few soldiers asked some technical questions and then the room fell silent. 'Does anyone here want to comment?' asked Peres from the rear of the hangar.

Nobody spoke.

'Anyone here take part in the Sabena operation?' persisted Peres.

A soldier named Danny raised his hand.

'Do you want to comment on the plan?'

'No.'

'Well then,' said Peres. 'I wish you all luck.'

But, instead of leaving, Peres called Betser, Adam, the latter's assistant Colonel Avigdor 'Yanosh' Ben-Gal and Colonel Ran Bag, the head of counter-terrorism in the Infantry and Paratroop Command (who had spent the day refining details of the plan with Betser), into a side room. As the door closed behind them, Peres asked: 'Why this way and not the Sabena method?'

Because, explained an exasperated Betser, it was a mistake to use the same method twice.

Adam backed him up. 'They demonstrated it last week to the General Staff,' he told Peres. 'It works.'

'Okay,' said Peres. 'Approved.'

Peres departed, leaving Betser and his men 'to wait for the plane's appearance'. As the night wore on, reports came in that the plane had headed south, not east, 'over the Sahara, into Africa, and far from our purview'. Betser had still not ruled out the possibility of the plane appearing 'on a surprise route over southern Egypt and then up the Red Sea'. But by dawn the plane had 'disappeared into central Africa', and Betser finally called off the alert at the airport and headed back to base.

DAY 2: MONDAY 28 JUNE 1976

0002hrs GMT, Ugandan airspace, East Africa

The first that Captain Michel Bacos knew of the plane's final destination was more than five hours into the flight when he was told by a pistol-wielding Wilfried Böse to prepare for a landing at Entebbe, the international airport for the Ugandan capital of Kampala.

At around the same time Claude Moufflet woke from a fitful two-hour sleep to find the Canadian girls 'chatting in low voices' and other passengers praying and sleeping. The terrorists were in their usual positions: one at the back of economy class and one at the front, with the German girl sitting in first class. He began to leaf through a copy of *Cosmopolitan* magazine when Böse's voice came over the intercom: 'We are getting ready to land at Kampala. Close the blinds and fasten your seatbelts.'

The news caused general astonishment in Moufflet's vicinity of the plane because practically no one knew that Kampala was the capital of Uganda, still less that Uganda was a black African country, a former British colony, and that the country's head of state was Field Marshal Dr Idi Amin Dada, an ex-NCO of the British Army. Moufflet doubted he would have known had his cousin not been working in neighbouring Rwanda, and had he himself not recently seen a 'fascinating' film in Paris about Amin and the Organization of African Unity (OAU).

On telling his neighbours, he circulated the little map in his diary so that they could see the location of Kampala on the edge of Lake Victoria, just above the Equator in East Africa. To the north lay the Sudan, to the west Zaire, to the south Rwanda and Tanzania, and to the east Kenya. As they were scanning the map, the two Palestinian terrorists stationed themselves next to the emergency exits in the middle and rear of the plane. Kuhlmann did the same in first class.

Just after 3.20 a.m. local time (GMT + 3 hours), following a circuit of the airport, the plane touched down on the main runway of Entebbe and came to a halt at its far end. It was still dark, but through a half-open blind Moufflet could see the lights of two vehicles approaching the plane.

Up in first class a French woman sitting with her two-year-old infant in the row of seats in front of Michel and Olivier Cojot suddenly started screaming. It seemed to Olivier as if she had 'totally lost her mind'. Worried that she might harm her child, he and his father held her arms 'to restrain her'. She had clearly been under a lot of stress and the arrival at 'Entebbe caused her to break down a little bit'. Eventually, with the help of the crew, they managed to calm her down. Fortunately her young daughter, 'dumbfounded at the sight of Mama stamping both her feet', had 'remained quiet'. But she had left her mark on Michel Cojot in the form of deep scratches on both his hands.

An hour later Böse announced that soon they would open one of the plane's exits so that he could speak to President Idi Amin Dada, either in person or by radio. But nothing happened, and the passengers continued their 'interminable coming and going to the toilets', amid shouts of 'Sit down!', 'Don't smoke!', 'Where is Uganda?', 'You think we're going to see Idi Amin Dada?' and 'Oh, shut up!'

Any mention of Amin was enough to terrify Algerian-born Julie Aouzerate, who recalled the African dictator boasting how much he admired Adolf Hitler. 'First the German woman was screaming out orders,' she noted, 'and casting terrifying glances – and now: the country of Idi Amin. During those moments I fancied that I had entered a terrible nightmare world – the world of the concentration camps of World War II.'

This fear of what awaited the hostages in Uganda was only to be expected. The country's lifelong president and effective dictator Idi Amin had, since taking power in 1971, cut off ties with his former ally Israel, ordered the expulsion of non-citizen Asians, and executed tens of thousands of political opponents. He had further alienated the West by courting rogue Arab countries like Libya and the Soviet Union;

moreover it was Amin who had helped to persuade almost all African countries to break off diplomatic relations with Israel in the wake of the 1973 Yom Kippur War.

A former heavyweight boxer – six feet four inches tall and stout – Amin was a larger-than-life figure who divided opinion: in the eyes of many black Africans, his willingness to stand up to his former colonial overlords made him a hero; to those in Israel and the West, on the other hand, he was seen as a political loose cannon with a huge sexual appetite – he had had five wives, countless mistresses and numerous brief sexual encounters, not all of them consensual – and a penchant, so it was rumoured, for eating human flesh. The charge of cannibalism was never proven. What is not in doubt, however, is that Amin was a man of extremes. One of his former Cabinet ministers described him on the one hand as 'nearly illiterate', 'politically naïve', 'violently unpredictable' and 'utterly ruthless', and on the other as 'jovial and generous' and with 'extraordinary talents – for practical short-term action, for turning apparent weaknesses to his own advantage, and for asserting his leadership among a gang of thugs'.

Small wonder that the hostages – particularly the Israelis – were nervous.

0200hrs GMT, Jerusalem, Israel

Yitzhak Rabin was sleeping soundly at Beit Aghion, his official residence at 9 Smolenskin Street in the upmarket west Jerusalem district of Rehavia, when his bedside phone rang. 'Who is this?' he said, half awake.

'Freuka.'

'What time is it?'

'Four in the morning. Sorry for waking you. The plane has landed in Entebbe, Uganda.'

Rabin was relieved. 'Better there than an Arab country,' he told his military aide, Brigadier-General Freuka Poran. 'We know the Ugandan president, Idi Amin.'

'Didn't he do his parachute training here?' asked Poran.

'He did. And during the heyday of Golda Meir's African aid programme quite a few of our specialists worked in Uganda. Some should know him personally so, hopefully, we can straighten this thing out soon. Try and find out who knows him. Any word yet of the hijackers' demands?'

'None.'

'Convene a meeting first thing.'

'I will. Try and get back to sleep.'

0340hrs GMT, Entebbe International Airport, Uganda

At dawn – 6.40 a.m. local time – the more daring passengers raised their blinds and looked out of the plane. Through the window to his right, Claude Moufflet could see Lake Victoria and 'armed soldiers in leopard uniforms who, hidden slightly by long grass', were 'cautiously approaching the plane'.

On his left side he could see a Jeep carrying more Ugandan soldiers and a civilian, and beyond them a road on which were passing 'cars, a lorry and a coach, and several people on foot'. Along the edge of a ditch, just fifteen yards from the plane, were posted a ring of armed Ugandan soldiers in camouflage uniforms and red berets (denoting, though Moufflet was not aware of this, elite paratroopers). The plane, Moufflet realized, was 'completely surrounded'.

Michel Cojot, who had spent many happy years working in Africa, looked with nostalgic fondness on 'the savannah, the groves of tall leafy trees' and the 'large El Greco clouds'. He knew that Kampala was several thousand feet above sea level, and that on its 'high plateau' they 'would not suffer from the heat'. Yet it was ironic 'to land in the country' that Britain had 'offered to the Jews for their state at the start of the century!' If 'they had not refused', he mused, 'perhaps today we would be in the hands of Ugandan terrorists', rather than Palestinians and Germans.

Desperate for any information he could glean, Moshe Peretz asked 'the yellow-shirted terrorist' in Arabic how many days they planned to stay in Entebbe. A 'long time', came the reply.

'Where are you from?'

'I was born in Haifa,' said the terrorist, confirming Peretz's suspicion that he was a Palestinian.

Just after 8 a.m., the exit door at the front of the plane was opened. Wilfried Böse informed the passengers that a delegation from the Ugandan government had arrived and negotiations were about to begin. Moufflet could see through the window a Jeep arrive with two Ugandan officials. One was tall and thin, and dressed in a navy-blue uniform with three stars on the shoulders; the other was even taller and more thickset, wearing a khaki uniform with gold epaulettes and a chest full of medals. This second officer – assumed at first by Moufflet to be Amin – was deep in conversation with 'a little guy wearing glasses, a blue suit and a green cap' who resembled Yasser Arafat.

The Arafat lookalike was, in fact, a senior member of Wadie Haddad's PFLP called Jayel Naji al-Arjam – who, with two comrades, had come to join the original four hijackers. The Ugandan officer was not President Idi Amin but one of his generals. They were discussing what to do with the hostages. The fact that the PFLP reinforcements, armed with assault rifles, were able to move 'freely about the airport in diplomatic vehicles', and were not prevented by the Ugandans from assisting their hijacker comrades, was confirmation for Michel Cojot and many other passengers that Amin was colluding with the terrorists and had known about their plans in advance. This link between the Ugandan dictator and the hijackers was later confirmed by Gerd Schnepel, the colleague of Böse and Kuhlmann, who stated: 'Amin was cooperating with the PFLP. The [Ugandan] soldiers who defended the airport didn't know. But the government of Idi Amin itself was helping Wadie Haddad, because of his history with Israel.'

While al-Arjam's discussion with the Ugandan general continued, Böse tried to reassure the passengers that the soldiers around the plane were there for their security and not to harm them. He had, he continued, asked the airport director 'for a little breakfast for everyone' and was certain that he would soon be able to speak to President Amin.

As the waiting continued, the temperature rose and the stench from the overflowing toilets became almost unbearable. Sara Davidson was convinced that the Israelis would be 'separated from the other passengers', as had happened in previous hijackings, and was terrified that her family would be split up too. 'Take my husband away from my children and myself?' she scrawled in her diary. 'We'll never be able to stand it.' Yet simply being on terra firma was a relief to her and 'less dangerous than to fly through the air with a band of hijackers pointing revolvers at the heads of the pilots'.

The young Canadian Louise Kourtis, on the other hand, was certain the end was near. 'They're going to kill us,' she told her friend Jo-Anne Rethmetakis. 'They're going to blow up the plane.'

'Certainly not,' interjected Claude Moufflet. 'They're hardly likely to blow up the plane at the start of negotiations. Be patient, stay calm and make yourself as comfortable as possible.'

Rethmetakis backed him up, and Kourtis, though far from convinced, fell silent.

At around 10 a.m. Böse made another announcement: 'Please sit down. You are going to be served breakfast and it is necessary for you to remain in your seats. I am very satisfied with the negotiations at the moment. I still haven't told you the reasons for this hijacking because I haven't had lots of time. But I will communicate to you our objectives as soon as I can.'

Soon afterwards, breakfast was brought on board the plane. It consisted of a fried egg accompanied by either mushrooms from a tin, potatoes or a piece of bread, served on little plastic pink plates and eaten with either a fork, a knife or a spoon, one piece of cutlery per passenger. This prompted the usual complaints from the passengers, but a steward responded calmly: 'It's bread *or* potatoes. There's not a lot and everyone must have something to eat.'

Eventually more food was brought on board – tiny cuts of meat in sauce and some slices of bread – and the crew decided to take it straight to the back of the plane so that the passengers could serve themselves. 'They'll see soon enough,' said one steward to another, 'if it's easy to make each portion equal'.

Moufflet overheard this comment and thought it was 'the only demonstration of bad humour on the part of the crew' since they had left Athens.

At 10.30 a.m., in an attempt to get some air into the sweltering plane, the terrorists opened the rear exit door and roped off the opening with the stewards' neckties. Through it Moshe Peretz was certain he could see 'Idi Amin negotiating with the Guerillas'.

0600hrs GMT, Kampala, Uganda

The first that Henry Kyemba, Uganda's thirty-six-year-old minister of health, knew of the Airbus's arrival at Entebbe was when he heard a BBC World Service broadcast at 6 a.m. Not a member of Idi Amin's inner circle – and a man increasingly disillusioned with his president's unpredictable and psychotic style of rule – Kyemba had been excluded from the plotting with Wadie Haddad. But after hearing the BBC report, he realized that his ministry 'would be closely involved in any operations connected with the hostages and crew', and went straight from his house in Kampala to the ministry headquarters in Entebbe, next door to Amin's State House and just two miles from the airport.

At 9 a.m. he got a call from Amin. 'Kyemba,' said the president, 'Palestinians have hijacked this plane from Israel and brought it to Entebbe.' He had, he said, already been in touch with them. Now he wanted Kyemba to arrange for a doctor and nurse 'to assist with any medical treatment required'. As secrecy was paramount, he wanted just a small, sympathetic team and specified 'a particular Nubian nurse for the job'. The choice of a doctor 'acceptable to the Palestinians' he left to his health minister. Kyemba duly contacted an Egyptian, Dr Ayad, and asked him to stand by at Entebbe hospital with the nurse 'for emergency duty'.

0600hrs GMT, Tel Aviv, Israel

Waking early from just a few hours of sleep, Shimon Peres phoned Prime Minister Rabin 'to report on the night's events'. Then he showered and made coffee before heading back to his office in downtown Tel Aviv, 'where a ceaseless flow of reports' about the hijacking 'was being monitored'. To Peres 'some appeared fanciful, others just plain contradictory', and it 'was hard to sift fact from fiction'.

According to one, the hijacked passengers included a group of senior Israel Defense Forces officers. But Peres knew this was false because by this time the ministry had 'obtained a complete and accurate' list of passengers and crew from Air France – confirming their number as 246, and not 230 as first thought – and it did not include any IDF brass.

0715hrs GMT, Entebbe International Airport, Uganda

With breakfast cleared away, two young Ugandans came down the aisle of the Airbus with huge basins of water on their shoulders. Their job, explained Wilfried Böse through the intercom, was to clean the toilets and then provide fresh basins of water for the hostages to wash in. At the same time the stewards and stewardesses moved down the aisles with big plastic bags collecting any 'old papers, empty bottles, plates, cutlery, and any remains of food'.

The relaxed atmosphere – which Claude Moufflet likened to people 'in a charter plane going on holiday' – meant that many hostages were laughing and talking in loud voices 'as if everything was over'.

Böse added his own words of reassurance. 'You probably know,' he told the hostages, 'that the history of aircraft hijackings has shown that none of the captives have ever been killed. We'll conduct negotiations. We have claims. If our claims are accepted, we shall release you and send you back soon to your homes and families.' For those like Michel Cojot who knew the truth – that hostages had been killed by hijackers, most recently a German banker during the takeover of a British Airways VC-10 by Palestinians at Tunis in 1974 – this assertion was far from comforting.

Böse continued: 'I have not yet had the time to explain the reasons for this hijacking. People are often told that Air France planes cannot be the target of hijackings because France has a very pro-Arab policy.

This is not true. France is one of the first countries in the rank of Palestinian enemies.'

The German then read from a typed PFLP–EA communiqué that was, in effect, a justification of the hijacking. They had chosen a French plane, he said, 'to declare to the world that the French State is an historic enemy of the Arab Nation'. It was 'no more than a junior partner prostrate in front of United States imperialism', and yet it was 'an important executor of neo-colonialism in the Mediterranean'. Proof of this was its collusion with the United Kingdom and Israel in the invasion of Egypt in the Suez Crisis of 1956, its supply of Mirage jets and other military hardware to Israel that enabled the latter to achieve a 'decisive victory' in the Six-Day War, and its role in Israel becoming an atomic power.

Israel itself, the communiqué continued, had 'exploited the human-istic sentiments of its people to inhuman ends' by expelling the Palestinians 'from their homeland' and importing 'alien people to replace them under the slogan of rescuing the Jews from the Nazi-planned . . . European barbarity'. Israel had become, as a result, the 'heir of Nazism'. The aim of the PFLP, said Böse, was to liberate the whole of Palestine, expel the Jews and establish 'a socialist secularist democracy'.

After turning on President Anwar Sadat's Egypt for signing a provisional agreement with Israel over the future of the Sinai, and President Hafaz Assad's Syria for promoting civil war in the Lebanon (the new home of the PLO), the communiqué then declared the PFLP's support for anti-government rebels in Eritrea, Morocco, South Africa, Angola and French-controlled Djibouti. It ended with a call for 'revolutionaries everywhere' to 'represent the oppressed' and 'come together and create a world revolutionary front and defeat imperialism everywhere'.

Böse's long manifesto, read 'in rather good English', reminded Michel Cojot of 'a jumble of Ulrike Meinhof and the Palestinian revolution, of imperialism and French guilt at having provided Israel with arms and an atomic reactor – in short a leftist stew à la [Andreas] Baader, the kind that it regularly served up in certain Third and Fourth World newspapers, and even from the rostrum of the United Nations'.

When Böse asked for someone to translate the communiqué into French, the 'five or six members of the crew seated near by . . . looked at each other like pupils who have been asked for a volunteer to go to the blackboard'. They were clearly exhausted, so Michel Cojot stepped in. Handed a 'poorly typed page' and a cone-shaped megaphone to amplify his voice, he gave 'an almost faithful translation'.

As he did so, he 'took the opportunity to glance into' the terrorists' 'half-open bags' in front of him, and saw some grenades, handguns 'and a sub-machine gun loading clip – not bad for hand luggage!' He also noticed that, since landing, the terrorists had become 'less and less cautious' and that 'sometimes three of them would be in the front of the plane at once, guns in their belts with their hammers lowered, grenades in their pockets; clearly they had won the first round'.

Claude Moufflet had also noticed the terrorists' lowered guard and the fact that there were often 'only two, weapons in their pockets, installed near the front door looking after us'. He was tempted, as a result, to push both of them out of the plane and lock the door behind them. But he decided not to because he feared a violent response from the terrorists and suspected, in any case, that a sudden exclamation from one of his fellow hostages would give the game away.

Once Cojot had completed the French translation, Böse spoke again: 'I'll now tell you about our commando. It is composed of two Germans and two Palestinians. You will wonder why two Germans are part of our group. The German guerilla groups are engaged in the fight against worldwide imperialism and want to force worldwide public opinion to be interested, which they are not, in the cause of the PFLP and other revolutionary ideas. Our next objective is to obtain the release of as many of those imprisoned fighters in France, Germany, Israel and Africa at Djibouti. I excuse myself if this message seems confusing and not very clear, but English is not my maternal language, and even though I speak it often I am very tired because I haven't slept for more than seventy-two hours. I will speak to you when I have rested and you will understand better.'

After a pause he added: 'At least now you know how the mind of a crazy German revolutionary works!'

A little after the reading of the PFLP–EA's communiqué, as Böse was resting at the back of the plane, the Israeli lawyer Akiva Laxer spoke to him in German and asked why the terrorists were targeting women and children. When Böse repeated his argument about 'fighting for world solidarity' and one group of freedom fighters helping another, Laxer changed tack and asked how he had ended up at Entebbe. Böse replied that he had been involved in various terrorist activities, including the blowing up of supermarkets in Berlin and other cities, and that he thought he would end this operation 'either for many years in prison or being killed'.

1000hrs GMT, Tel Aviv, Israel

Major Muki Betser was back in his office in the bowels of the Kirya when he heard a radio report on the Voice of Israel that the hijacked plane had landed at Entebbe in Uganda where, in his words, 'President, Field Marshal and erstwhile Israeli paratrooper Idi Amin Dada (who never did jump and didn't deserve his wings)' had 'offered his services as a mediator'.

Since his and the other Israelis' 'ignominious' departure from Uganda in 1972, Betser had noticed how Amin's 'appearances on the international stage grew increasingly bizarre'. He had taken 'dozens of women from the villages of his country to serve in a harem, and fed his political opponents to crocodiles living on the banks of Lake Victoria'. Ambassadors were 'made to kneel before him if their government wanted good relations with Uganda'. And yet despite all this, noted Betser, the Organization of African Unity – set up by thirty-two signatory governments in 1963 to give African states a collective voice – had chosen Amin as its chairman for 1976.

Hearing the 'extremely sketchy' news reports from Uganda, 'mostly from the BBC relying on stringers in Kampala', Betser was highly suspicious of Amin's role. 'It was,' he thought, 'impossible to determine if he let the plane land because the pilot said he desperately needed fuel – or if Amin was aligned with the terrorists.' His own experience of Amin's 'treachery' caused him to suspect the latter.

1005hrs GMT, Entebbe International Airport, Uganda

Just after one in the afternoon, with the temperature in the Airbus a stifling 90 degrees Fahrenheit, the weary but still remarkably upbeat passengers were relieved to hear Wilfried Böse announce that they were about to leave the plane with hand luggage and be taken by buses to the Old Terminal building.

But this decision was soon rescinded and instead Bacos was told to start the engines and taxi there. Five minutes later, the plane halted on the apron directly opposite a dilapidated two-storey building that had served as Entebbe's international terminal from the airport's opening in 1929 to the construction of a newer, modern terminal in the early 1970s. A variety of aircraft had used the Old Terminal, from its first visitor, an RAF Fairey III biplane of the Cairo–Cape route, to the de Havilland Comet of the early 1950s and modern jetliners more recently. Its most famous passenger was Queen Elizabeth II, who took off from Entebbe on her way back to England after hearing that her father George VI had died and she was monarch of the United Kingdom.

Few if any of Flight 139's passengers were aware of this royal connection as they shook the stiffness from their limbs and prepared to end their excruciating twenty-six-hour incarceration in the Airbus's cramped interior. Before they did so, Böse made a final light-hearted announcement: 'Ladies and gentlemen. We thank you for having flown Air France. We hope that you were satisfied with the service and that we see you again soon on this airline.'

This released the tension and, according to Cojot, 'there was a general impression – with no basis in logic or fact – that our misadventure had come to an end'. This way of thinking was encouraged by the plane's pilot, Michel Bacos, when he told the passengers, in both French and English, that 'the nightmare is now over'. He added: 'On behalf of the crew I thank you for staying calm and for coping in exceptionally difficult conditions. I have been informed that Field Marshal Idi Amin has agreed to take charge of your security and that of the terrorists. Before long you will be allowed into the terminal to wait to hear how you will return home. Thank you.'

The applause was long and loud.

Soon afterwards, clutching their hand luggage or holding the hands of their children, the hostages were squinting in the bright sunshine as they walked down the mobile staircase to the tarmac. A handful even waved goodbye to the three terrorists stationed at the forward exit, so convinced were they that their ordeal was over.

They were quickly disabused by the sight of Ugandan soldiers, guns at the ready, lining a path to the door of the nearby terminal. It seemed 'very strange' to Gabriella Rubenstein, a twenty-nine-year-old Jerusalem psychologist who had been looking forward to a holiday in Paris with her husband Uri. 'We thought we were free,' she recalled. 'Then we watched the hijackers again greet their friends, and the real bad news followed.' No sooner had the last of the 253 passengers and crew* passed through the metal and glass double-doors into the former departure lounge of the Old Terminal – a 'huge room, dirty and dusty' with reddish-brown and white walls and a wooden parquet floor – than Böse announced through the megaphone that 'you are all still under our control'. He added: 'We have arrived in Uganda, but you are in the hands of forces of the Popular Front for the Liberation of Palestine. We are already negotiating with your governments. We hope the affair will end in the best possible way. Now, listen carefully to our instructions – then no harm will befall you.'

At a stroke, Böse had dashed the passengers' hopes and then raised them a little. The word 'negotiation' seemed to imply a peaceful solution and their eventual freedom. But would the governments of the many nationalities involved agree to the terrorists' demands? And what were those demands? Certainly none had yet been made to

---

* Of the 258 passengers and crew who left Athens, four were terrorists and one – Patricia Martell – had been allowed to disembark for medical reasons at Benghazi.

Pierre-Henry Renard, the experienced fifty-two-year-old French ambassador to Uganda, who had left for the airport soon after news of the plane's arrival had reached his private residence in Kampala. He would remain there all day and leave as night fell at 7 p.m., none the wiser. 'We still don't know what the hijackers want,' his spokesman told journalists, 'and until we do there's little that can be done.'

Meanwhile the hostages had settled down in the big hall that had formerly served as the terminal's departure lounge – a large rectangular room some forty feet deep by eighty wide, the ceiling supported by twelve concrete pillars – as best they could, some sitting on 'uncomfortable, well-worn red imitation-leather armchairs', others on the ground until more seats were brought in by Ugandan soldiers. Even then there were not enough to go round; but this did not prevent some from keeping two seats when others had none.

Families and friends tended to cluster together in small groups, as did the exhausted stewards and stewardesses, their blue uniforms now marked by a fine film of dust. The captain, the pilot and the flight engineer, meanwhile, had been kept on the plane so that it could be moved to a part of the airport where, the hostages were told, 'it wouldn't get in the way'.

About 500 yards in front of the large hall, clearly visible to the passengers through a row of large and rusty iron-framed sliding windows, was the huge expanse of Lake Victoria. A little further to the extreme right* was the control tower that served the New Terminal, itself not visible because it was located at right angles to the Old Terminal, while much closer to the left of the hall could be seen the nose cone of a Russian-made MiG fighter jet poking out of an aircraft hangar.

A cordon of armed Ugandan paratroopers stood guard twenty yards from the front of the main hall. They were also stationed on the first floor and roof of the Old Terminal, and in the old control tower, just to the right of the main hall. Their presence suggested more than a hint of collusion with the terrorists, as did the fact that the Ugandans

---

* All directions – left and right – are given from the perspective of a person looking out of the front windows of the Old Terminal on to the tarmac.

had allowed three new terrorists armed with automatic weapons to join the original four.

The most distinctive of the new arrivals was Jayel Naji al-Arjam, a thirty-nine-year-old Palestinian who was responsible for the PFLP's political activity in Latin America, and a man the hostages would soon nickname 'Groucho Marx' because of 'his cap, his moustache, and his odd gait'. To Michel Cojot he was '"the Peruvian" because he had lived in Latin America for a long time'.

The Peruvian's superior, however, was the forty-six-year-old Faiz Abdul Rahim Jaber, one of founders of the original PFLP who had stayed loyal to Haddad after his split with Habash and was now the PFLP–EA's operations' chief. A tall strongly built man from Hebron who had lived most of his adult life in Egypt, Jaber had fought in the 'Black September' war in Jordan, had participated in many missions inside Israel and held a particular hatred for Israelis since the IDF had killed at least one of his brothers in anti-terrorist actions. Wearing a moustache and a distinctive blue safari jacket, Jaber was now in overall command at Entebbe, though Böse (as the head of the hijack commando) and the Peruvian exerted some influence over him.

The last of the trio was the Iraqi-born Abdur Razaq al-Samrai (also known as 'Abu Addarda'), another founder member of the PFLP and, according to a confidential IDF report, 'a long-time participant in Wadi[e] Haddad's mechanism of terror attacks abroad', including the hijacking of a Lufthansa plane to Aden in 1972 and the attack at Lod Airport that same year.

While Jaber, the Peruvian and al-Samrai stood guard outside the entrance to the Old Terminal, the original four hijackers got some rest on camp beds in a room to the left of the main hall that had originally served as the VVIP lounge. Left largely to their own devices, the hostages were free to stretch their legs and use the two rooms housing toilets in the right-hand corners of the large hall: the ladies' at the front, next to a second entrance from the tarmac that had been blocked off, and the men's at the back, beneath a broken flight of stairs up to the first floor that had also been barricaded at the top. On the back wall of the five men's cubicles – four toilets and a shower – were circular windows, five feet off the ground, which looked through to the space between the main hall and the original arrivals' inspection hall.

The only other features of note in the large hall were an aircraft-maintenance office with glass walls (the former souvenir shop), situated in the centre of the left-side wall with its door accessed by three steps, and a small horseshoe bar at the foot of the stairs, adjacent to the opposite wall. A locked iron door in the centre of the hall's rear wall led to what had been the terminal's kitchens.

At 2.25 p.m., local press photographers arrived and were allowed to take pictures of the hostages through the windows. This prompted some of the hostages to compete for their attention, much to the disgust of one elderly American lady who exclaimed: 'Look at that! It's incredible. People are crazy. All that for a photo in a newspaper nobody will read. It's sickening.'

After they had tried to waylay the two pilots and the flight engineer as they returned from parking the plane at 2.45 p.m., the press were finally told by the terrorists to leave. Entering the hall, Bacos and the others were greeted with 'shrieks and claps' by their fellow hostages. The captain responded with a salute.

While many hostages killed time reading books and magazines, others jotted down their hopes and fears in makeshift diaries. 'A plane will arrive shortly to take us,' wrote Sara Davidson, still convinced that salvation was imminent. 'Everything is now being settled. We'll soon be flying onwards, on our family excursion . . . Illusions maybe, because a situation like this makes you want to delude yourself. Maybe the soul needs delusions, to fortify it.'

1200hrs GMT, London, UK

Foreign Secretary Tony Crosland had scarcely arrived back in Britain from the G7 conference in Puerto Rico when he received the first details of the arrival of the hijacked plane at Entebbe from James Horrocks, the British chargé d'affaires and acting high commissioner in Kampala.

According to Horrocks's cipher, the plane had been 'refused permission to land at Entebbe' – an incorrect version of events that the Ugandans had fed him – but it had ignored this instruction because it was 'short of fuel'. President Amin had arrived on the scene at 7.30 a.m. but, as the hijackers refused to negotiate through him, he had asked 'the PLO resident representative to act as intermediary'. The PLO man had since spoken to the hijackers, said Horrocks, 'from the control tower and was given their conditions for the release of the aircraft and passengers', though he had yet to reveal what they were.

Meanwhile the French ambassador, who had been at the airport since the early morning, was trying to keep abreast of developments. Having spent most of the morning at the airport with him, Horrocks had learned that an Air France plane – including a reserve crew for the hijacked aircraft – was 'en route from Paris to Nairobi where it will remain on stand by'. He was, he declared at the end of his message, 'maintaining close touch with the French Embassy in Kampala'.

Two hours later, Horrocks sent a second cable informing London that, thanks to a suggestion by President Amin, the hijackers had agreed 'to leave the aircraft and move to the old airport building with the hostages'. All the passengers were reported to be in good shape. He had heard, moreover, from the French ambassador that, contrary to initial reports, the hijackers had not yet made known their demands, and would not do so until they had received instructions from their superiors in the PFLP. The local PLO representative had said much the same thing to Horrocks, adding that the Ugandans were now dealing with the hijackers direct, and he would play 'no further role in the drama'.

Other cables read by Crosland that day included one from the British Embassy in Athens with details of the nine Commonwealth citizens who had boarded Flight 139 in Greece (three Canadians, five New Zealanders and a Cypriot); and another from the Tel Aviv Embassy stating that one more Briton, a Miss Frances Hallan, did board the plane at Ben-Gurion but got off at Athens. The latter cable also confirmed that Patricia Martell was a dual national and had been travelling on her Israeli passport, which is why 'she was not previously known to be British'.

1200hrs GMT, Jerusalem, Israel

Having spent the morning with his aides at the Ministry of Defense, Shimon Peres drove to Jerusalem for a meeting with Prime Minister Yitzhak Rabin and the coalition members of the Knesset Finance Committee. It was another hot day – with the temperature in the 80s – and most of the ministers and MKs were wearing slacks and open-neck, short-sleeve shirts. Rabin, as he tended to do when tense, was chain-smoking.

The session opened in the tall Knesset building in the Givet Ram district at 2 p.m. with Yehoshua Rabinowitz, minister of finance, arguing hard for cuts in the defense budget. Peres, who had spent the previous two years demanding and receiving an *increase* in defense spending, responded with typical pugnacity. 'It's a strange thing,' he observed with more than a hint of bitterness, 'that in Washington US senators are demanding higher allocations for military aid to Israel in the wake of the Yom Kippur War, while here in Jerusalem we're ready to vote for lower defense spending.'

Tense though the debate was, it still served as a welcome distraction from, as Peres put it, the 'relentless tension through which we had been living since the day before'. Returning to his office in Tel Aviv, Peres found 'no shaft of clarity through the pall of uncertainty and speculation that surrounded the hijacking saga'. Never before had hijackers taken a plane full of Israelis so far from the reach of the IDF. What the terrorists' intentions were was anyone's guess. Would they stay in Uganda or was it merely a staging point? Was this the usual attempt to swap hostages for imprisoned terrorists, or something more sinister? And, most importantly, was Amin helping the hijackers? If he was, Peres told his staff, it would set a very dangerous precedent. Hitherto no aircraft hijacking had enjoyed the explicit support of any president, army or state. If this hijacking now had such support, and it succeeded, no aircraft could ever be safe in African skies. So it was imperative to know what was actually happening at Entebbe. But even if the hijackers were acting alone, experience had taught Peres that, 'at the end of the day, we would have to rescue the hostages ourselves'. It was, however, far too early – if not impossible – 'to translate this principled position into an operational plan'.

Back in Jerusalem, Yitzhak Rabin was also wondering how to resolve the hostage crisis peacefully. The son of immigrants – his father was Ukrainian, his mother Russian – he had grown up a 'withdrawn, bashful child' in a Spartan home in which respect for property and public duty were the watchwords. Educated at an agricultural school, he was trained to use firearms by Yigal Allon, one of the school's first graduates who was now serving as foreign minister in Rabin's cabinet.

Destined to found a kibbutz and work the soil, Rabin saw his life and future career change in 1941 when he was invited to join the Palmach, the elite fighting force of the Haganah Jewish defence organization. He would remain a soldier – seeing action, for example, as a twenty-two-year-old brigade commander in the 1948 War of Independence – until his retirement as IDF chief of staff in 1968. Since becoming prime minister of the Labor coalition government six years later, his greatest achievement had been to work with Henry Kissinger, the Jewish US secretary of state, to bring peace to the Middle East. Military disengagement agreements with Syria and Egypt had already been agreed. Rabin took the next step, in 1975, by signing an interim agreement with President Sadat of Egypt to withdraw from part of the Sinai.

The agreement was, in Rabin's opinion, 'a first but invaluable step on the long and winding path that would lead Egypt away from war and toward peace'. His reward was much closer diplomatic relations with the United States, financial aid and a regular supply of arms (including F-16 fighter planes). Moreover the US vowed not to 'negotiate with or recognize the PLO' or 'initiate any moves in the Middle East without prior consultation with Israel'. Rabin and Kissinger then began work on further peace agreements with Egypt, Syria and Jordan. But they were interrupted by the outbreak of civil war in neighbouring Lebanon as the Christians attacked an alliance of Palestinian Arabs and left-wing Lebanese. This in turn drew in the Syrian Army in support of the Christians. It was to distract world attention 'away from events in Lebanon to the other front – the battle against Israel', a Middle East expert speculated in an Israeli newspaper on Monday 28 June, that the Palestinian terror groups had undertaken the Air France hijacking. Rabin's main concern was to liberate the hostages without making concessions. But how to achieve that in a country so far away, and one so unfriendly to Israel?

1215hrs GMT, Entebbe International Airport, Uganda

Just after 3 p.m., two hours after their arrival in the Old Terminal building, the hostages nearest the windows noticed a yellow bus pull up on the tarmac outside and smartly dressed waiters get off. They had come from the nearby four-star Lake Victoria Hotel and were carrying rectangular metal containers of rice, hot meat curry and bananas – the hostages' first proper meal since boarding Flight 139 a day earlier. Though the waiters were impeccably polite, saying 'Sir' and 'Please', some of the hostages refused the meat curry because they did not know its provenance – 'it might be from giraffes', Moshe Peretz scribbled in his diary – others out of religious scruple.

A quick census turned up twenty Orthodox Jews who rejected the non-kosher meat – including the lawyer Akiva Laxer – and the rice was served to them before it was mixed with the curry. They were also compensated with bananas. (When others realized that the 'religious observants' were being served first, they joined their ranks until, by the following morning, more than sixty were claiming Orthodox status.) Michel Cojot was shocked when 'many [of the hostages] stuffed themselves with rice and bananas'. He put the overeating down to a means of 'relieving anxiety, of alleviating fear which gnaws at the plexus. To eat is to live.' Rather unkindly, Cojot suggested to an overweight Moroccan Jewish woman that it might be a good 'opportunity to diet'. When she responded with a thin humiliated smile, he felt 'ashamed'.

A well-meaning Frenchwoman thought the solution would be for Cojot – who had become by this time, thanks to his linguistic abilities, both 'interpreter and intermediary' – to ask for apples. 'That would be enough,' she commented. 'And it's healthier.'

'But madam,' replied a flabbergasted Cojot, 'we are around the equator.'

While they were eating, Wilfried Böse came into the room with a pile of forms that he asked two stewardesses to distribute. Headed 'THE POPULAR FRONT FOR THE LIBERATION OF PALESTINE', the forms asked for a variety of personal details that included name, date of birth, profession, passport number, destination and the names of others accompanying. While Claude Moufflet was filling in his, he took a good look at Böse and observed that he was 'fairly tall, with grey-green eyes and a little scar above the arc of his left eyebrow'. His hair was short and his profile bore a 'vague resemblance' to the film star Steve McQueen, though his mouth appeared to have a 'permanent sulk'.

Shortly after lunch had been cleared away, Moufflet decided to move from the busier left front of the room to the right rear, below the broken stairs, where fewer people were gathered. There he got talking to Gilles, a tall young Frenchman with blond curly hair who soon introduced him to a smaller dark-haired work colleague called Willy. Offering Moufflet a Gitane cigarette, Gilles explained that he and Willy were coming back from a ten-day work trip to Greece where they had been filming a documentary on holiday destinations. 'We weren't supposed to be on the Airbus to Paris,' explained Gilles. 'But we had a big night out and missed our flight. In other words we tempted fate. What about you?'

'I was coming back from a business trip to Athens, Istanbul and Teheran,' said Moufflet, puffing on a second cigarette, 'and I stopped in Athens to spend the weekend with my wife who was staying with friends on the island of Mykonos. I should have taken this flight three days earlier.'

'Oh, wow!' responded Gilles. There was something in the calm and laid-back attitude of the two young men that Moufflet appreciated, and they decided to set up camp together near the wooden bar.

Soon after this encounter, the airport director and some employees arrived in the large hall with a cart full of Duty Free items such as cigarettes, soap and razor blades. They were besieged by hostages keen to buy everything they had. 'Everyone jumped on them,' remembered Emma Rosenkovitch. 'They said, "Don't worry; we'll come back every week." We said, "Every week?" Prisoners at least know how much time they serve.'

Again Cojot was amazed by the lack of community spirit. When one woman grabbed two cartons of Duty Free cigarettes, he asked her at the behest of several passengers to give them up. She refused. 'I don't smoke, you know. They are for my son.' As her son was not present, Cojot could only assume that this was 'her way of telling herself she would see him again'.

He turned to the airport director and gently chided him for not having a particular item he wanted. 'It is not easy,' said Cojot, 'to receive 257 persons unexpectedly.'

The airport director looked perplexed: 'But I expected you.'

It occurred to Cojot then that there had also been enough lunch for everyone: was such a small airport 'equipped to receive nearly 300 persons from one second to the next?' He doubted it, and the words of the airport director were for Cojot the final confirmation that Amin and his cronies had known in advance of the plane's arrival. He was in 'no doubt' that Amin 'was in agreement [with] and an accomplice' of the terrorists. Other factors were the speed and ease with which the hijackers had been joined by their three accomplices; and the loosening up of the 'military discipline' of the hijackers after the landing at Entebbe. Up to that point they had been 'extremely strict'. But once on Ugandan soil the four hijackers 'regrouped in the forward part' of the plane 'and began to arrange their material in their bags and kept only a pistol, with the safety catch on, which they slid under their belts, while previously they had kept it in their hands, even to eat'. Grenades were put in pockets and it was then, in Cojot's opinion, that 'they could have been overpowered'. They behaved this way, he thought, only because they were 'in friendly territory'.

1230hrs GMT, Entebbe, Uganda

Shortly after 3.30 p.m., Health Minister Henry Kyemba received a second call in his office from Idi Amin. He was to take the Egyptian doctor and the nurse he had put on standby to check on the hostages at the Old Terminal. Driven the two miles from Entebbe Hospital to the airport in an ambulance, they were met outside the Old Terminal, according to Kyemba, by 'officials from the Kampala office of the Palestinian Liberation Organization'. Kyemba does not name these 'officials': they could have been Haled el-Sid and other members of the local PLO, based at the former Israeli ambassador's residence on Mackinon Road; or, more likely, they were the senior PFLP–EA representatives Jaber and al-Arjam (the Peruvian).

Taken inside, Kyemba was shocked by the state of a building that was now being used as a warehouse for tea exported to England. It was an 'empty shell – dusty, with broken windows and peeling paint'. In the former departure lounge where the hostages were 'all huddled on the seats, some lying in piles of clothing, others talking in low voices', the water system was 'rusted' and toilet facilities 'virtually non-existent'. Despite having just eaten lunch, they were to Kyemba 'a miserable sight'. The hijackers, meanwhile, 'in civilian clothes and armed with pistols and grenades, were standing just inside the doorways'.

Kyemba was introduced to the 'leader of the hijackers' (Böse) and a 'woman hijacker' (Kuhlmann) whom he later misidentified – like many journalists – as Gabriele Kröcher-Tiedemann of the 2JM. He thought she was a 'strikingly good-looking woman, wearing a blue skirt and jacket with a pistol slung on her hip'. Told he was the minister of health, she said she was 'very pleased' to meet him and was about to say her name when she thought better of it. Instead she said: 'I am Miss Hijacker.'

'Well,' replied Kyemba courteously, 'I'm very pleased to meet you, Miss Hijacker.'

With the introductions over, Kuhlmann announced to the hostages in English that Kyemba, the white-gowned doctor and the uniformed nurse had come to deal with their medical complaints. At the same time a female hostage translated the announcement into Hebrew through a megaphone, while a low voice in another part of the hall, probably Cojot's, gave the same message in French.

Kyemba then told his medical staff to carry on with their work while he spoke to the hijackers. After a few minutes he left. 'I was later told by the doctor and the nurse,' he wrote, 'that the hostages were generally in good shape. They only had to distribute anti-malaria tablets and treat a few headaches.'

That was because, according to Frenchwoman Julie Aouzerate, the few medical examinations that were done by the Arab-looking doctor – some suspected he was a Palestinian – 'were hurried and superficial'. For elderly Israeli Solomon Rubin who suffered from a 'heart ailment', for example, he prescribed 'a few aspirin tablets'.

1400hrs GMT, Jerusalem, Israel

'The troubles are only beginning,' said Yitzhak Rabin with a sigh to his wife Leah.

He had returned to his official residence after the meeting of the Knesset Finance Committee, and was mulling over the likely outcome of the Air France hijacking. The historical precedents were not good. There were bound to be demands for Palestinian terrorists to be released from Israeli jails. There always were. And when they were made from countries sympathetic to the hijackers, Israel generally paid the price. It had done so after the El Al hijacking to Algeria in 1968; and again a year later when two Israelis were taken off a TWA plane and held in Damascus. More recently, after the Yom Kippur War, the Egyptians had demanded the release of 138 live and healthy terrorists and spies in return for thirty-nine Israeli corpses. Pressured by the dead soldiers' families, Golda Meir's government had done the deal. With that in mind, how could he refuse to negotiate for living Israelis?

Or as he put it to Leah: 'Can the blood of Israelis in Entebbe be spilled just because I won't allow the barter of terrorists for hostages?'

He knew the answer.

1500hrs GMT, Entebbe International Airport, Uganda

While Yitzhak Rabin agonized over their fate in Jerusalem, the hostages' spirits were raised by an unexpected visit at 6 p.m. from Uganda's president. A tall, thickly built man in a green beret and neatly pressed paratrooper's uniform (complete with Israeli 'wings'), Amin towered over the soldiers and civilians of his entourage as he entered the large hall to spontaneous applause from many of the hostages.

'Shalom,' he said, using the traditional Hebrew form of greeting. 'I think some of you know me. For those who don't, I am Field Marshal Dr Idi Amin Dada, the man responsible for you being allowed off the plane. I did it for humanitarian reasons. I support the Popular Front for the Liberation of Palestine, and I think that Israel and Zionism is wrong. I know that you are innocent, but the guilty one is your government. I haven't slept since you arrived. I haven't yet received the demands of the Popular Front, but I promise you that I am doing my best so that you can be freed as quickly as possible. Make yourselves comfortable here. I have given orders for you to have chairs and some extra mattresses. I will come back to see you soon.'

If some of the hostages – particularly the Israelis – suspected Amin of playing a double game, they tried not to show it and the end of his speech was met with more applause. One Israeli even felt the need to 'shake his hand effusively' as if he was their best hope of salvation. Cojot, for one, felt 'deeply humiliated' by the hostages' behaviour and went round the room trying to convince people that they had nothing to gain by 'lowering' themselves 'in that way'.

To revive spirits, the fifty-two-year-old Pasco Cohen told the hostages near him that they had nothing to fear. 'You are lucky to be travelling with me,' announced Cohen, partly to calm his wife Hannah and their two children Tzipi, eight, and Kobi, six. 'I'm a specialist in getting out of the most dangerous places. I was one of the few survivors of the Holocaust. I've taken part in all of Israel's wars and I've faced death many times.'

Tall, blond and blue-eyed, Cohen had indeed cheated fate. Born in the Romanian wine-producing region of Vrancea, he was just weeks from his bar mitzvah in 1940 when his father was killed by the invading Germans. He himself survived a blow from a German rifle butt and later emigrated to Israel where he worked as an administrator of the Sha'ar Menashe hospital in the north of the country. It was there he met Hannah, a Moroccan-born nurse nineteen years his junior, and together they moved to nearby Hadera with their two children. Hannah now owned a clothes shop; Pasco was manager of the local branch of health insurance and the author of two research projects on diabetes and heart disease. As a reservist he had fought many times for his country, a fact he was determined to keep from the terrorists.

1500hrs GMT, Tel Aviv, Israel

It was late afternoon when air force pilot Lieutenant-Colonel Joshua 'Shiki' Shani, unprompted by his superiors, called a meeting of his staff at Tel Nof Air Force Base to discuss the hijacking. He, like most people in Israel, had heard the radio reports of Flight 139's arrival in Uganda. But as commander of the Israeli Air Force's 131 Yellow Bird Squadron of Lockheed C-130 Hercules transport planes, he felt duty bound to carry out some 'private planning exercises' in case his superiors wanted the option of a military operation.

Born in Siberia in 1945, the son of educated Ukrainian Jews who had settled in Israel after the war, Shani had never been interested in planes as a teenager and wanted to become an electrical engineer. On his draft day for national service, sitting on the grass with other new recruits at the IDF induction base known as the Bakum, an air force major had asked if anyone present did not want to volunteer for flight school. Shani started to raise his hand, but then noticed that no one around him was doing the same. He put it down and the rest, as he said later, 'is history'.

Qualifying as a pilot in 1965, Shani started on Nord Noratlas transport planes and Fouga trainers. Six years later he was sent to Arkansas and North Carolina in the United States to learn to fly the IAF's newest acquisition, the C-130. During the Six-Day War he had flown supplies of ammunition and fuel to IDF soldiers fighting in the Sinai Peninsula. In the Yom Kippur War he went one step further by taking similar supplies in the C-130 across the Suez Canal and deep into Egypt proper.

The chief advantages of the C-130 over previous models were its greater flying range (2,175 miles), its larger load capacity and its ability to land on and take off from a relatively short runway, in darkness if necessary. With this in mind, Shani and his staff spent six hours looking at range, fuel, payload, navigation, weather problems and anything else that might affect a flight to Uganda. They concluded that the C-130 was the only IAF plane that could transport a sizeable military force the 1,900 miles from Sharm el-Sheikh in the Sinai to Entebbe.

The problem was getting back. The only C-130s with the necessary range were those with extra fuel tanks; but they could not transport the requisite number of troops and vehicles. The regular C-130s, on the other hand, would only have a brief amount of flying time after the eight-hour flight from the Sinai to Entebbe. To return to Israel, they would need to refuel. This had not been a problem when C-130s made regular supply runs to Uganda before the ejection of the Israeli military mission in 1971. They topped up their tanks at Entebbe. But if Amin was colluding with the hijackers, as many suspected, they would either have to take extra fuel in

Uganda by force or land in friendly territory nearby. The question was: where?

1530hrs GMT, Entebbe International Airport, Uganda

Aware that they might be in the Old Terminal building indefinitely, the hostages thought up ways to pass the time. They pooled books, mostly paperbacks, to set up a library (with the greatest demand for thrillers and blockbusters, and few takers for the highbrow novels by Henry James and George Eliot that the Rabinowitzes were carrying); Jacques Lemoine, the flight engineer, gave a lecture in French on the Airbus, then still a novelty in air travel; and a Frenchman nicknamed 'Teach' made ashtrays out of old fruit-juice cans for those 'who were trying to puff away their fears'.

At 8 p.m. the yellow bus returned with a dinner that consisted of beef stew, potatoes and beans, and bananas. There was also some coffee and tea, but not enough food for everyone and the bus had to make a second trip. After dinner, to raise morale, Claude Moufflet cracked open one of his bottles of ouzo and shared it with Gilles and Willy.

Michel Cojot, now the main intermediary between terrorists and hostages, was in his element. He felt like he was 'finally living out a play' he had 'rehearsed a thousand times but never performed'. Surrounded as he was by Frenchmen and Jews, under the eyes of his son, facing a death he was all but indifferent to, his chief concern was to conduct himself well. He thought a lot about his 'gentle' yet 'intense' ten-year-old second son Stéphane, back in France with his mother and younger sister, and was determined not to give him a reason to be 'ashamed of his father'.

To that end he used every opportunity to speak to Böse and the Peruvian, the most approachable terrorists, quizzing the former on his motives and using the familiar 'tu' when addressing the latter. In one of their conversations, Böse trotted out the same woolly arguments he had used in his earlier address – blaming France for sundry pro-Israeli activities – but added: 'Besides, it's useless trying anything with El Al; they have orders to shoot it out and have special bullets that won't pierce the fuselage.'

Böse wanted to be called Basil, his nom de guerre. Instead Cojot baited him with 'Klaus' and sometimes even 'Obersturmführer', and took 'sadistic delight' in engaging this post-war German child in ideological discussions. 'Doesn't it bother you,' he asked Böse, 'a leftist revolutionary from a country that made a name for itself by inventing the worst type of fascism, to torment the same victims of this fascism again?'

'No,' replied the German, 'because my goals are different.'

'And the means?'

Böse looked unsettled. 'Up to now,' he said defensively, 'you haven't suffered too much. We have been *korrect* with you.'

Cojot raised his eyebrows at this unwitting use of an adjective so beloved of the Nazis. But his response was playful: 'True, but we could all have been burned alive. And besides, you're not keeping us here to educate us.'

Another hostage who had a similar conversation with Böse at this time was Yitzhak David, deputy major of the Israeli town of Kiryat Bialik and an Auschwitz survivor. Showing the German the number tattoo on his arm, David declared: 'I was mistaken when I told my children that there is a different Germany. When I see what you and your friends are doing to women, children and the elderly, I see that nothing has changed in Germany.'

Böse paled. 'You're wrong,' he said in a trembling voice. 'I carried out terrorist acts in West Germany because the ruling establishment took Nazis and reactionaries into its service. I also know that in September 1970 the Jordanians killed more Palestinians than the Israelis did, as did the Syrians at Tel al-Zaatar [a battle fought in 1976 during the Lebanese Civil War that resulted in a massacre of Palestinians]. My friends and I are here to help the Palestinians, because they are the underdog. They are the ones suffering.'

David was unimpressed. 'Well, then,' he responded, 'when the Palestinians fulfil their promise and throw us in the sea, we'll come to you to help us hijack Arab planes.'

Slowly but surely some of the hostages – Cojot in particular – were establishing a pseudo-egalitarian relationship with Böse, exactly the type of reverse Stockholm Syndrome* that he and Kuhlmann had been warned about in the PFLP training camp in South Yemen. Kuhlmann took the advice literally and Cojot, noticing her tendency to seek the affection of children, sent his son Olivier to divert her when he wanted to be sure she 'would not meddle in a conversation'.

The only time Cojot opposed her was on this first night at Entebbe when ten mattresses had to be shared by more than 250 people. She wanted them for the children. But as most by this time were already asleep, 'curled up against their mothers', while many old people 'were having difficulty in finding a restful position on the seats or on the floor', Cojot told her the latter should be given them and eventually he got his way.

He also managed to turn off some of the lights in the large hall so that people could sleep. But the Peruvian stopped him from extinguishing them all by placing a Kalashnikov barrel in his stomach.

This was at 10.45 p.m., by which time Cojot had changed into the pyjamas, kimono and slippers that he always carried in his hand luggage. None of the other hostages had night attire because it was in their suitcases in the hold; and some of them, unaware of Cojot's idiosyncrasies, thought he must be a terrorist plant or why else would he have brought pyjamas? Others, like Moufflet, admired his stiff-upper-lip resourcefulness – like a 'British officer' – and felt it would help those who were less psychologically prepared for the situation they found themselves in.

Gradually the room settled down as people tried to ignore the swarms of mosquitoes and the dust and filth on the floor. It was 'hot as hell', Moshe Peretz recorded in his diary, and there was 'a veritable symphony of snores' with people shouting at one another to keep

* Otherwise known as capture bonding, a psychological phenomenon in which hostages develop positive feelings towards their captors, sometimes to the point of identifying with them. It was named after a 1973 bank robbery in Stockholm when several employees became emotionally attached to their captives during the six-day standoff, rejecting assistance and even defending their captors' actions after they had been freed.

quiet. It reminded him of 'summer camp at the Gadna', where Israeli teens were put through army basic training.

With most people asleep, 'an old Jewish woman, probably of Germanic origin', had what seemed to Cojot to be a 'fit of madness'. It began with her sitting bolt upright on her mattress and asking in an increasingly loud voice: 'Where am I? Where am I?'

Her voice then rose several octaves as she screamed: 'Help me! Help me!'

This woke some of the children, who began to cry. When the woman's neighbours failed to calm her, Böse intervened and led her out of the building as she 'rambled incoherently'. Instead of berating or threatening her, he put his arm round her shoulders. It was, thought Cojot, 'incredible' to see 'the heir of the Nazis speaking in a gentle voice for a good two hours to this old Jewish woman, shaking with spasms'. He was sitting with his son Olivier on a blanket taken from the plane, and together they gazed 'at the scene illuminated by moonlight, made even brighter by the reflection of nearby Lake Victoria'. Finally the woman began to sob in Böse's arms and it 'was over'.

DAY 3: TUESDAY 29 JUNE 1976

0400hrs GMT, Entebbe International Airport, Uganda

It was barely light when the yellow bus pulled up outside the Old Terminal building and waiters got out with trays of coffee, tea and rolls for the hostages' breakfast. The stewards and stewardesses helped to serve the meal, and when it had been cleared away a hostage tuned his transistor to Radio Uganda to catch the news. It was about the hijacking. 'Israel,' said the report, 'is refusing to negotiate with the terrorists, who are threatening to blow up the plane if their demands are not met.'

This was far from accurate: the Israeli government had not categorically refused to negotiate the release of the hostages, though it did issue a statement on Sunday emphasizing its unwillingness to cave in to terrorist blackmail; nor had the hijackers yet made known their demands. But the hostages could not know this and, taken at face value, the Radio Uganda broadcast was the last thing they wanted to hear. Moshe Peretz saw 'anxiety' on many faces. It may have been now that thirteen-year-old Benny Davidson murmured quietly to his mother Sarah: '*Ima*, we won't get out of here. We won't get out.'

0430hrs GMT, Sinai Desert, southern Israel

Having returned briefly to Tel Aviv the day before, Lieutenant-Colonel Yoni Netanyahu was back on exercise in the Sinai when he poured out his fears for the future in a letter to his girlfriend Bruria, now an airline stewardess who lived with him in Tel Aviv. Writing by gaslight in his tent, he explained that he was at a 'critical stage in my life, facing a profound inner crisis that has been disturbing my whole frame of reference for a long time now'. What was 'so sad and ridiculous about it' was that his only solution was to carry on. He was, he confessed, 'tired most of the time, but that's only part of the problem – I have lost the spark that is so vital for any achievement – the spark of creative joy, of self-renewal, of re-awakening'. He continued:

> I keep asking myself: Why? Why now of all times? Is it that my work doesn't absorb me, doesn't hold me? Wrong! On the contrary . . . it possesses me and I don't want it to . . . And the same haunting questions come up: Can I let myself live like this, work like this and wear myself out? And the answer always is that I must go on and finish what I've begun . . .

He admitted he was 'having a hard time as seldom before' in his life, and that 'even the alternatives outside the army' had 'lost much of their appeal'. He doubted he had the 'energy to start again from scratch' and did not want to 'burn any bridges'. Yet he knew he had to 'stop and get off now, at once or very soon'.

He closed the letter on a personal note. 'Good that I have you, my Brur, and good I have somewhere to lay my weary head. I know I'm not with you enough, and that it makes it hard for you to be alone so much, but I trust you, me, both of us to manage living our youth to the full – you, to live your youth and your life, and I my life and the last flicker of my youth. We'll cope.'

The letter reveals that the commander of the Unit, Israel's first line of defence in the war against Palestinian terrorism, was undergoing something of a personal crisis at the height of the Entebbe hijacking. He had lost faith in the government's ability to guarantee Israel's security, and feared that the hijacking would end with another capitulation. This, in turn, caused him to question his own future in the IDF. Yet it was all he had known and the alternatives – returning to Harvard to resume his studies* and possibly entering politics – were no more attractive.

---

* He had recently written to both his brother Bibi and his parents that he intended to return to Harvard the following year.

He was in an impossible position. The constant vigilance required of his job had left him mentally and physically exhausted, and close to burn-out. Yet he felt an obligation – to himself and to his country – to finish his stint as the Unit's commander. Whether he possessed the necessary reserves of strength to hold on for another year was a different matter.

0630hrs GMT, Jerusalem, Israel

Yitzhak Rabin began the day by bringing the secret weekly meeting of the Knesset's Foreign Affairs and Defense Committee – the cross-party body that oversees diplomatic relations, intelligence and homeland security – up to date on the hijacking and the decisions taken the previous day by the ministerial team. The only new information since then, he told the committee, was a brief description of the hijackers that had just arrived in a cable from Major-General Rehavam ('Gandhi') Ze'evi, the prime minister's special adviser for terrorism, who was in London when the crisis began. Containing information from Patricia Martell, the hostage released on health grounds who had been debriefed at Heathrow Airport the night before, the cable read: 'The hijackers, three men and one woman, are from the PFLP. They have pistols, hand grenades, and containers which they placed by the emergency exits of the plane.' As for demands, none had yet been made.

Shimon Peres had little to add. He had stopped off at the Ministry of Defense before leaving for Jerusalem, but there was no new information beyond a few 'colour' stories about the 'mood at the airport, visits by various dignitaries' and 'a string of bombastic but essentially meaningless declarations by the Ugandan president Idi Amin'.

With these summaries complete, the committee returned to its main business of assessing the ongoing process within the IDF of applying the lessons of the Yom Kippur War. This dragged on until the committee adjourned at midday, enabling Rabin to hold a private meeting with Menachem Begin, the leader of the Likud opposition. Almost ten years older than Rabin, a former leader of the Irgun underground movement that had violently opposed British rule, Begin was a hugely experienced political operator who, but for a spell as a minister without portfolio in the national unity government of 1967–70, had yet to taste power. But his right-wing Likud party – itself a coalition of smaller groups – had won 39 of the Knesset's 120 seats in the most recent 1973 election and Rabin was right to identify him as a rising force in politics. Having told Begin the story so far, he added: 'Mr Begin, I am of the opinion that this Entebbe business will be deadly serious and very difficult. If you have no objection, I would suggest that I keep you in the picture.'

Begin expressed his gratitude and the two parted with a handshake.

0700hrs GMT, Entebbe International Airport, Uganda

Tormented by mosquitoes, loud snoring and the discomfort of a hard floor, Hannah Cohen had slept little during her first night in the Old Terminal building. She worried constantly about the welfare of her young son and daughter sleeping beside her, and after breakfast used her Arabic to ask Khaled, the Palestinian terrorist guarding one of the doors, if they and the other children could go outside and play in the sun.

Though surprised by a request he saw as impertinent, Khaled relayed it to his superior – Jaber – and permission was given for Hannah to take Tzipi, Kobi and ten other children, including Olivier Cojot and a Dutch boy of a similar age, out on to the tarmac where they played football with an old can and other games. To give them a little more room, the cordon of unsmiling Ugandan paratroopers was moved back thirty yards.

For forty-five minutes Hannah organized games like catch and hide-and-seek. But when she encouraged the children to dance a hora – a traditional Israeli folk dance performed by a circle of people holding hands – Khaled lost his patience. 'I don't agree to you dancing,' he roared. 'All inside!'

The terrorists had, in any event, a more pressing problem to deal with as three elderly French women were becoming 'very vociferous about their detention' and insisting 'on being allowed to leave'. When the terrorists refused, one of the ladies 'urinated at the side of the hall, clearly determined to make herself as objectionable as possible until she was removed'. This prompted the Egyptian doctor to recommend their transfer to the hospital in Entebbe and, 'worried about their ability to preserve calm in such circumstances', the terrorists agreed.

They also allowed the removal to hospital of the frail French man with the suspected heart complaint. Though the doctors there could find nothing amiss, Idi Amin tried to gain credit for the man's 'miraculous' recovery by announcing to the press that he had been treated all over the world but 'only properly diagnosed and cured when he came to Uganda'.

Caring little for their real welfare, Amin ordered that all four should be returned to the Old Terminal as soon as they had been treated. Would it not be disastrous publicity for Uganda if the man died? asked his health minister Henry Kyemba. Reluctantly Amin agreed that it would and he was eventually discharged from hospital into the care of the French Embassy.

This meant that two of the original 254 hostages had been released, and more would eventually follow thanks to the efforts of Michel Cojot. 'If this lasts a few more nights,' he warned Wilfried Böse, 'one of these old people will die, and even if it is only ten minutes before the time that he or she would have died somewhere else, the whole world will consider you a murderer.' He added: 'It is in your interests and ours to rid ourselves of them. That was the logic of the SS on the Auschwitz train platform. If you don't want to resemble them you had better free the weak quickly.'

Cojot's advice was given added weight by the number of complaints to the Egyptian doctor from hostages – many of them elderly – suffering from backache. The doctor's solution was to recommend to Henry Kyemba, his boss, that additional blankets and mattresses be provided. Kyemba spoke, in turn, to Amin, and with the latter's approval the new bedding was delivered, courtesy of the Canadian Aid Agency. Even so, there were not enough mattresses to go around and some of the younger hostages had to do without.

With time on their hands, some of the hostages began speculating on the means by which the terrorists were able to smuggle their weapons aboard the Airbus. Most agreed that they must have taken advantage of the slacker baggage controls for transit passengers, a fact confirmed by a member of the crew. This prompted Captain Bacos and his co-pilot, Daniel Lom, to lament the recent announcement by Air France that all stopovers in Athens on their Tel Aviv–Paris flights would end on 1 July – the following day. It had come too late for them.

And all the while two snub-nose fighter jets of the Ugandan Air Force – identified by Daniel Lom as a Russian built MiG-17 and a MiG-21, the latter capable of supersonic speed – were paraded in front of the Old Terminal building, though they did not take off. Claude Moufflet thought this was all a bit of propaganda on Amin's part, to show the hostages 'how modern and well kitted out' his air force was. Others saw it as a form of intimidation. 'What a megalomaniac,' observed Emma Rosenkovitch. 'What was he doing with those planes and those medals, showing off?'

1045hrs GMT, Entebbe International Airport, Uganda

Several volunteers helped the members of the crew and the Ugandan waiters to serve the same lunch as the day before: rice, potatoes, beef in sauce, bananas and mineral water. After it had been eaten, most of the hostages were at a loss what to do next. Some were milling around and chatting, others playing cards or travel games they had brought with them on the plane. Claude Moufflet recognized one owned by a stewardess – a code-breaking game called 'Mastermind' – as a present his daughter had received for her birthday. He preferred chess, but made the mistake of challenging a Russian-Israeli and was easily beaten.

To pass the time, Moufflet used the single dilapidated old shower in the men's toilets, and was forced to grit his teeth as cold water cascaded from the broken pipe. Through the broken circular window-pane in front of him he could see two Ugandan soldiers – one reading a letter in a doorway opposite, and another moving along the alleyway between the departure lounge and the arrivals hall next door – and concluded that there was a double system of sentries: one fixed and one roving. It occurred to him then that if he were to chance an escape he would need a lot more information.

Leaving the shower cubicle he was met by the young Ugandan whose job it was to patrol the men's toilets and recover any written documents the hostages had left there – more proof, if any was needed, that the Ugandan authorities were colluding with the terrorists. 'You wash?' asked the young African with a smile. 'Feel good?'

Moufflet nodded, prompting the Ugandan to point and ask: 'You, cigarettes?'

Motioning with the flat of his hand for the man to wait, Moufflet went out and recovered from his hand luggage three packs of cigarettes from the carton he had bought in Athens. When he handed them over, the toilet attendant smiled broadly and put his hand on his heart.

1230hrs GMT, Jerusalem, Israel

The early-afternoon meeting of the ministerial committee was barely under way in the conference room of Rabin's office on Kaplan Street when Freuka Poran's assistant entered with a note. He handed it to Poran who passed it, in turn, to the prime minister. 'This is what we've been waiting for,' said Rabin, scanning the paper. 'The hijackers have broadcast their demands over Ugandan radio.'

Having read the note in more detail, Rabin continued: 'In return for the hostages, the hijackers want the release of terrorists – they call them freedom fighters – imprisoned in five countries: forty from us, six from West Germany, five from Kenya, one from Switzerland, and one from France. They've issued an ultimatum. Within forty-eight hours the released terrorists are to be flown to Entebbe. Those freed by us are to be transported by Air France; the other countries can decide on their own mode of transport.'

'And if not?' queried Yisrael Galili, minister without portfolio. 'What happens if they are not freed?'

Born in the Ukraine in 1911, a former Haganah chief of staff, Galili was said by a contemporary to have 'the white hair of an Einstein, the stocky build of a kibbutznik, the shrewdness of an entrepreneur, and the veiled eyes of a Svengali'. He was, moreover, Rabin's closest adviser in government and a hugely experienced political operator – and alleged lover of the former prime minister Golda Meir – who would always stay calm in a crisis.

Turning to him, Rabin replied in a portentous tone: 'If the terrorists are not freed, they threaten to begin killing the hostages as of two o'clock Thursday afternoon, 1 July. That is the day after tomorrow.'

The ministers gasped as one, but Peres was the first to speak, giving an 'impassioned address on the implications of capitulation to terrorist blackmail'.

Rabin had little time for such grandstanding, as he saw it, and quickly cut Peres short. 'Before the defense minister sermonizes any further,' he said, the contempt clear in his voice, 'I suggest we adjourn to think the matter through with all its implications. We'll meet again at five-thirty this afternoon and, hopefully, come up with some ideas.'

Once the ministers had departed, Rabin called together his personal staff – including Freuka Poran, his British-born private secretary Yehuda Avner (who had performed the same role for former premiers Levi Eshkol and Golda Meir) and Amos Eiran, director-general of the Prime Minister's Office (and in effect Rabin's chief of staff) – and vented his frustration with 'what he regarded as Peres's self-serving homilies'. He then asked if any progress had been made with attempts to encourage Idi Amin to intercede on behalf of the passengers. When he was told that, on the contrary, Amin appeared to be revelling in the media spotlight and might well be colluding with the hijackers, he exploded: 'Nothing will surprise me about what that man Amin is capable of. He runs his country like a personal fiefdom. He probably has his own fish to fry in this mess, in cahoots with the terrorists.'

Rabin's suspicions were correct. Though not part of Amin's inner circle and therefore unaware of the hijacking in advance, the Ugandan health minister Henry Kyemba soon realized that 'the whole operation was being supervised by Amin himself, working together with the Palestinians based in Kampala'. The dictator 'thought he saw', as Kyemba put it, 'a fine opportunity to humiliate the Israelis and increase his stock with the Arabs' and 'wanted all the glory'.

He crowed several times to his health minister: 'Well, Kyemba, now I've got these people where I want them' and 'I've got the Israelis fixed up this time.' He was even 'closely involved in drafting the Palestinian demands', including the forty-eight-hour deadline that was, in Kyemba's opinion, 'impossibly tight' and left 'hardly time to contact all the authorities involved, let alone get their agreement to the terms'.

Conscious of the time constraint – if not of Amin's direct involvement – Rabin told Avner to arrange another brief for the foreign media that emphasized, again, 'France's responsibility'. He then instructed Freuka Poran to ensure that the IDF chief of staff, Motta Gur, attended the next meeting of the ministerial committee at 5.30 p.m.

Poran seemed surprised. 'Why do you need the chief of staff?' he asked. 'You have something in mind for him?'

'I want to know,' replied Rabin, 'what the IDF thinks about this whole matter. I don't have the slightest doubt that Peres's pontifications about not surrendering to terrorist blackmail are for the record only, so that he'll be able to claim later that he was in favour of military action from the start. The problem is his rhetoric is so persuasive he believes it himself.'

1230hrs GMT, Entebbe International Airport, Uganda

The hostages were mostly lying around the main hall of the Old Terminal building – reading, chatting, playing games and dozing

– when a commotion was heard from the front of the building where the women and children had again been allowed to play. Seconds later they were herded back inside, followed by all the terrorists. As ever it was Wilfried Böse who spoke through the megaphone. 'I have just communicated to your governments,' he announced, 'the official demands of the PFLP. Your freedom will depend upon them being accepted.'

He then read out the demands: The release of fifty-three 'freedom fighters' in five countries, including Kōzō Okamoto and Hilarion Capucci, the Greek Catholic archbishop of Caesarea who in 1974 had been imprisoned for smuggling weapons to Palestinian terrorists in the West Bank. The list mentioned some other familiar names – notably Werner Hoppe and Jan-Carl Raspe, two leaders of the German RAF terror group (the Baader–Meinhof Gang) – but most were unknown Palestinians and meant nothing to the hostages.

All had to be flown to Uganda by noon GMT (3 p.m. local time) on Thursday 1 July, along with $5 million from the French government, or the terrorists would blow up the plane with the hostages on board. This last detail brought a collective gasp of horror from the hostages, with many now convinced that they would not leave Uganda alive. One woman was so shocked she fainted, and two of the stewardesses burst into tears. Yet while Moshe Peretz was 'almost certain' that Israel would refuse these terms, he could envisage various possible outcomes: the least probable being that the terrorists would carry out their threat to murder everyone; a more likely scenario was a compromise whereby 'a small number of detainees are released, or all the passengers, with the exception of the Israelis, are released on Thursday'.

1400hrs GMT, Tel Aviv, Israel

Lieutenant-General Motta Gur – a short, stocky forty-six-year-old in combat uniform and boots, his receding black hair hidden by a paratrooper's red beret – was about to board a military helicopter at Dov Field Airport in northern Tel Aviv for a flight to the Sinai when an aide ran up. 'Sir, the prime minister wants you to attend an emergency meeting in Jerusalem at 5.30 p.m. to discuss the Entebbe crisis. Your car is waiting.'

Gur shook his head. The hostage crisis had begun forty-eight hours earlier, and only now had Rabin seen fit to consult his chief of staff. They knew each other well from the early 1970s when Rabin had been Israeli ambassador to the United States and Gur military attaché. But as a former chief of staff Rabin had a habit of questioning Gur's operational decisions; whereas Peres, with minimal military experience, trusted him to do the right thing.

As his car sped along the highway to Jerusalem, it suddenly occurred to Gur that Rabin might ask whether the IDF had contingency plans to rescue the hostages. As things stood, the answer was no; so Gur ordered his driver to pull over at the next public telephone and told his adjutant, Lieutenant-Colonel Hagai Regev, to call the operations branch so that they could begin planning. Regev got through to Brigadier-General Avigdor Ben-Gal, the deputy chief of operations, and instructed him 'to examine military action options to rescue the hostages, and to prepare troops to carry out the operation'.

It was this telephoned order that initiated the formal start of the 'battle procedure at General Staff level', though informal planning by air force and combined operations officers like Shiki Shani had been under way since Monday afternoon. When Chief of Operations Kuti Adam was informed of Gur's order, he at once put together a 'thinking team' that included his deputy Ben-Gal and Colonel Ehud Barak, the former commander of the Unit and now assistant to the chief of military intelligence with responsibility for research and special operations.

Barak was in his Ministry of Defense office, a few floors above the Pit, when his intercom beeped. It was Adam. 'Listen, Ehud, a plane has been hijacked and the hostages are being kept somewhere in the old Entebbe terminal. All we need to do is create a surprise.'

It was obvious to Barak what Adam wanted. He knew from previous experience that the key to ending hostage situations by force was the element of surprise: with it, as few as fifteen men of the Unit could enter the terminal and kill the terrorists before they could harm the hostages. But first they would need to gather as much intelligence as they could about the situation at Entebbe: the number of terrorists, their weaponry and habits; the layout of the airport; and, just as importantly, the quality and temper of the Ugandan soldiers who were guarding the airport. Barak knew at once who to call: Muki Betser.

When Betser reached Barak's office, he found the IDF's leading counter-terrorism experts – all friends and colleagues from previous operations – sitting round a long T-shaped table: Lieutenant-Colonel Amiram Levine, a former member of the Unit who now worked for Military Intelligence; Ido Embar, an air force major with responsibility for combined operations; Major Gadi Shefi, commander of Shayetet 13, the naval equivalent of the Unit (and similar to the US Navy's SEALs); two senior officers from the staff of the Infantry and Paratroop Command, Colonel Ran Bag and Lieutenant-Colonel Amnon Biran; and Lieutenant-Colonel Chaim 'Ivan' Oren, Adam's head of special operations. Leaning back in his seat at the top of the T, Barak was chairing the meeting. 'Muki,' he said, as all eyes turned towards the late arrival, 'you know Entebbe?'

'Sure,' replied Betser. 'I know it.'

'So what do you think of Ugandan soldiers?'

Betser grinned. 'They must be good,' he said, moving towards a free chair, 'after all I trained them.'

When the laughter had died down, Barak's tone hardened. 'How good?'

'Well, they're afraid of the night. And in the best of circumstances they don't have much in the way of motivation. In this case?' Betser paused. 'I really don't see what motivation they'd have to fight us.'

This was exactly what Barak wanted to hear and he smiled.

'So,' continued Betser, 'I don't think Ugandan soldiers will be our problem. You know Solel Boneh built the terminal?'

He was referring to the huge Israeli construction firm that had completed a number of projects in Uganda before Amin turned against his former allies. Barak nodded. 'We already sent for the plans.'

And with that the preparations for a potential Entebbe rescue mission began.

1530hrs GMT, Jerusalem, Israel

Motta Gur had barely taken his place at the rectangular table in the conference room of the Prime Minister's Office, alongside the head of the Mossad and members of the ministerial committee and their aides, when Yitzhak Rabin asked him a direct question: 'Motta, does the IDF have any possible way to rescue the hostages with a military operation?'

Before Gur could respond, Shimon Peres intervened. 'There has been no consideration of the matter in the defence establishment,' he said gruffly. 'I haven't yet discussed it with the chief of staff.'

'What?' spluttered an outraged Rabin, the veins standing out on his forehead. 'Fifty-three hours after we learn of the hijacking you have not yet consulted the chief of staff?'

Rabin turned to Gur. 'Motta,' he said sternly, 'do you have a military plan, yes or no? If you do have a military plan, that will be our top preference. But remember, any operation has to provide for a way of bringing the hostages back.'

Again Peres was about to respond when Rabin insisted that Gur answer. 'When I received your message to attend this meeting,' said the chief of staff, 'I assumed it was to seek my advice on a military option. Consequently, before coming here, I ordered the chief of operations to start a preliminary examination to see whether an operation is feasible, and if so, at what cost. A major problem is our lack of reliable information on the attitude of Idi Amin. If the Ugandans cooperate with us our chances for a successful operation would be that much greater.'

'Obviously,' said Rabin, still seething that Gur had received no prompting from Peres to plan a military solution, 'but the reports we are receiving about Amin are not encouraging. The point is that, as of this moment, there is no concrete military solution, so we shall have to . . .' – he paused, as if reluctant to continue – '. . . consider negotiating with the terrorist hijackers for the release of the hostages.'

But outwardly, added Rabin, we will 'maintain our position that France was responsible and Israel would not capitulate'.

Now it was Peres's turn to seethe. His feeling was that 'a lack of authoritative information regarding the hijackers' conditions and the hostages' situation ought not . . . dictate a preference for any particular option'. Why 'rush into a decision favoring one option (free the hostages through negotiations), when its feasibility was unclear, at the expense of an alternative option (freeing the hostages by force), when there was no definite evidence to show the latter option was unfeasible?' he asked himself. But, sensing Rabin's determination to pursue this course of action, he kept his concerns to himself.

Instead Peres observed that 'there was no operational proposal, as yet, that had been thoroughly checked out', and that one would be submitted only 'after meticulous examination'. He and Gur then rose and left the room, 'presumably', commented Yehuda Avner, Rabin's aide, 'to speed back to the Ministry of Defense in Tel Aviv to see what military plan they could come up with, if at all'. This left the rest of the ministerial committee – Rabin, Allon, Yaacobi, Zadok and Galili – to engage in a 'fretful discussion about the frightening thought of attempting to rescue so many hostages, thousands of miles away in the heart of Africa, and the unthinkable alternative . . .'.

That alternative was to release forty mainly Palestinian terrorists in Israeli jails, the full list of names having just reached the Foreign Ministry in Jerusalem via a phone call from the Israeli Embassy in Paris. Hastily scribbled down on a piece of paper and delivered to the meeting of the ministerial committee by Shlomo Avineri, director-general of the Foreign Ministry, the list was 'woefully confused and full of spelling mistakes'. But most of the prisoners could still be identified and, once Avineri had read out the list, the head of the Mossad and former army general Yitzhak Hofi reviewed all he knew about the hijacking, the organization behind it, the PFLP–EA, and its ruthless leader Dr Wadie Haddad. Hofi, for one, was as unhappy as

Peres at the prospect of negotiations. But he, too, was prepared to wait on events.

The only concrete decision taken at the meeting was for Yaacobi, the minister of transport, to set up an office at Ben-Gurion Airport to liaise with the hostages' families. 'These people,' commented Peres later, 'were going through a terrible time, their desperate worry exacerbated by our frustrating ignorance.'

So desperate, in fact, that that evening the fathers of two young hostages put forward an extraordinary proposal: to offer themselves as substitutes for their sons. The man behind the offer was the former French policeman Robert Mimouni, father of young Jean-Jacques, who since his emigration to Israel in 1971 had been living in the seaside town of Natanya and working as a clerk in the French Consulate in Tel Aviv. It was because of Robert's link to the Consulate that Jean-Jacques had attended the French school in Jaffa where he became friends with the consul's son, Thierry. That friendship had, in turn, prompted Jean-Jacques' last-minute switch to Flight 139 so that he could accompany Thierry. For that reason – and, moreover, because he had encouraged Jean-Jacques to go to France in the first place – Robert felt guilty that he had placed his son in danger.

So, having first spoken to Consul Sicard, he walked into a Natanya post office and wrote out the following telegram to Idi Amin in Uganda: 'WE, THE PARENTS OF JEAN JACQUES MIMOUNI AND THIERY SICKER [sic], ARE PREPARED TO FLY TO UGANDA TO TAKE OUR CHILDREN'S PLACE AS HOSTAGES.'

They received no reply.

1610hrs GMT, Entebbe International Airport, Uganda

For much of the afternoon Michel Cojot, the pilot Bacos and some other passengers had been pestering the two most approachable terrorists – Böse and the Peruvian – to relieve the overcrowding in the large hall by giving the hostages access up the barricaded staircase to the second floor. They refused to allow that, but they did instruct Ugandan airport employees to knock a hole through the left-side wall of the large hall, behind the former tourist shop, into a smaller room – formerly a waiting hall – beyond.

Night was falling as the workmen put the finishing touches to the jagged breach in the wall: a wooden 'T' nailed across the opening to restrict rapid movement. Cojot and others were about to pass through this awkward gap when Böse, Jaber and the other terrorists entered the departure lounge. 'We're separating you,' said Böse matter-of-factly though the megaphone, 'but not because of nationality, there's no connection between that and the separation. I'll call out the names and whoever hears their names will go into the other room. Really, we're doing this so that you won't be crowded. It has nothing to do with nationality.'

The first name to be called was Emma Rosenkovitch, followed by Noam Rosenkovitch and Ella Rosenkovitch. Then more Israeli names, sparking a deep fear in many that – as in previous hijackings – Israelis were being singled out for 'special treatment'. The psychological consequences were 'disastrous', and very quickly Böse's voice was 'muffled by fearful cries, sobbing and protestations'.

Emma's more immediate concern, however, as she crawled through the low and narrow opening with her children, was for her husband Claude. His name had not been called and she feared that, as an army reservist – like most Israeli males under forty – he might be killed out of hand. She had to wait thirty long minutes before he was finally allowed through to join her.

By then more than eighty mostly Israeli names had been called. 'The feeling,' noted Moshe Peretz in his diary, 'is like an execution.' For Akiva Laxer, the shame of being forced to bend down as he passed into the other room was 'the worst feeling' of his life and he understood for the first time 'what it meant to be a hostage'. Sara Davidson also resented this deliberate humiliation of the Israelis, particularly as one of the Palestinian terrorists was standing by the gap 'armed and ready'. She noted in her diary: 'The German reads the names over a [megaphone] and everyone who hears his name goes to the exit, and grinds his teeth and crawls under the "T".' Soon Kuhlmann took her turn guarding the gap, prompting Davidson to comment: 'Tough. Wicked.'

Even those of dual nationality – like Jean-Jacques Mimouni and Dora Bloch – were sent next door: though born in Jaffa, the daughter of a famous Zionist pioneer called Yosef Feinberg, Dora had married naturalized Welshman Aarhon Bloch in Palestine in 1925 and was travelling with both her Israeli and British passports. Her son Ilan, though also of dual nationality, had brought only Israeli identity papers. They were both on Böse's list.

Not everyone living in Israel was identified. Since moving to the Middle East, Dr David Bass had become a reserve medical officer in the IDF; but because he was travelling on his US passport his Israeli links had been overlooked. The same went for a twenty-six-year-old French-born welder called Nahum Dahan who was accompanying his mother: she had an Israeli passport and was on Böse's list; as his was French he was not. Two elderly sisters were also separated because one was a naturalized Israeli and the other not, causing the former to collapse in hysterics. But there were no deliberate exceptions, and as the protests grew the terrorists made 'more and more menacing gestures'.

To try to calm the situation, the pilot Michel Bacos took the megaphone from Böse. 'It is we who have asked our guards for more space,' he said. 'All they did was grant our request, so there is no cause for alarm.' His words had little effect and Cojot was not surprised. In his view, Bacos had failed to understand 'that it was not more space but the criterion of separation that was the problem'.

Once the separation of the Israelis was complete, six Orthodox Jews were sent to join them, the men easily identifiable by their little black skull caps: two seventeen-year-old Brazilians wearing checked shirts, Raphael Shammah and Jacques Stern, who had just completed a year of studies in a Jerusalem yeshiva; the Belgian couple Gilbert and Helen Weill, the former having led many of the prayer groups; and a young American couple from New York, a twenty-eight-year-old stockbroker and his twenty-five-year-old wife. This latter couple were nearing the end of a three-week vacation in Europe and Israel when they boarded Flight 139 to Paris. Like the Weills and the two Brazilians, they did not have Israeli identity papers, and their addition to the list was probably because, as the US Embassy in Paris later put it, they 'appeared very Orthodox, ate only Kosher food and were seated with the Israelis aboard the plane and remained with them on the ground because the commandos permitted them to prepare Kosher food'. In other words they were associated with the Israelis, even if they had no direct connection beyond their deeply held religious faith.

Suddenly aware of the potential danger of his and his wife's inclusion, the stockbroker shouted: 'I'm American. I'm not Israeli. I have no connections with the Israelis. I have an American passport! I'm not going through there!'

His pleas fell on deaf ears and Emma Rosenkovitch, for one, 'felt a certain contempt' for him, though she could understand the American's predicament.

Only one person volunteered to *join* the Israelis: twenty-six-year-old Janet Almog, the American-born wife of Israeli Ezra Almog. A pretty dark-haired native of Madison, Wisconsin, Janet had fallen for Ezra – a dead ringer for tennis star Jimmy Connors – during a summer stint as a volunteer at the Ein Dor Kibbutz in Israel. They had married soon afterwards and were en route to the United States to visit her parents – Janet's first trip back for two and a half years – when the hijacking occurred. Thanks to his military training, Ezra took the shock of captivity in his stride. Janet had not coped so well and when her husband's name was called and not hers she dissolved into tears. Ezra, however, was firm. 'I want you to swear not to follow me. Stay on this side!'

Dora Bloch had tried to soothe Janet by saying her husband was right and it was best for her to remain. But the young American would not have it. 'I can't live without him,' she sobbed, 'and he told me not to follow him.'

Minutes later Bloch herself had been called through and, because of her age, she was spared the humiliation of the low entrance and instead taken outside by a terrorist and through the Israeli room's exterior entrance. There she told Ezra Almog she had changed her mind. 'You meant well,' she said, 'but you must take your wife with you. She won't be able to stand it without you.'

Ezra tried to protest. 'At least this way one of us will get out of here. There's no point in her being here with me. Perhaps they'll let her out . . .'

'No,' said Bloch, firmly. 'She must be with you.'

At last Ezra relented. He spoke to the Palestinian terrorist guarding the entrance and was delighted when Janet was allowed through. They embraced in tears.

The rectangular room the eighty or so Israelis had been moved to was much smaller than the main hall next door: still forty feet from front entrance to back wall, but barely twenty-five feet wide, its size made tinier still by a temporary side wall of cardboard boxes. It, too, was dusty and unclean, with rows of seats its only furniture. 'The terrorists warn us that [the boxes] are full of explosives,' noted Moshe Peretz in his diary, 'and if touched will go off. At first we are frightened, but in time the fear wears off and people hang their shirts over the boxes. While we are getting organized one of the hostages goes up to a terrorist and asks for a cushion for his baby. The terrorist strikes him violently with the butt of his revolver.'

Back in the departure lounge, many of the 170 or so non-Israelis were feeling just as indignant, particularly Jews like Julie Aouzerate who were reminded of Nazi practice during the Second World War. 'It was a terrible scene,' she recorded, 'that thick German accent and the *selektzia*.' It was inevitable that some of the hostages, particularly concentration-camp survivors, would be reminded of the selection process used by the Nazis: to be sent one way to live; the other to die. But, as Ilan Hartuv and others were later quick to point out, this was never a simple division of Jews and non-Jews. Many non-Israeli Jews like Julie Aouzerate, Michel Cojot and Peter and Nancy Rabinowitz remained in the original room. Appalled by the separation, Nancy had thought about joining the Israelis as a sign of Jewish solidarity and to show moral support; but Peter persuaded her to remain where she was.

Claude Moufflet and others felt so bad for the Israelis that they spontaneously picked up mattresses to take through to them. But they were stopped by the pair now guarding the entrance – Kuhlmann and Khaled – and told to pass the mattresses over the 'T', which they did. It was while he was helping to distribute the mattresses that

Akiva Laxer was struck in the back with a savage blow from the butt of Jaber's pistol, knocking him off his feet and leaving him shocked and winded. Following this unprovoked and unexplained attack by the violent and clearly anti-semitic Jaber, Laxer decided that it was dangerous for an Orthodox Jew like himself to be noticed and henceforth kept a lower profile.

A number of Israelis, meanwhile, had tried to re-enter the departure lounge with the excuse of going to the toilet. They, too, were halted and escorted individually by Kuhlmann, pistol in hand.

Moufflet now knew for certain that the separation was 'not just by hazard', but rather was 'corresponding to a very precise objective'. He felt duped, and promised himself that he would make another attempt to get access to the Israeli room the following day when the surveillance might be 'less rigorous'.

Cojot also realized the importance of 'free movement' between the two rooms and extracted an assurance from Böse that it would not be hindered. In the event, this promise was never honoured. Suspecting that it might not be, Cojot suggested to Bacos and the flight engineer Lemoine that 'two or three of the twelve members of the crew might ask to be assigned to room with the Israeli passengers' to offer moral support. Both asked for time to think about it and consult the other members of the crew. It was not until the following morning that Lemoine came back with a reply that won Cojot's respect for its candour if not its courage. 'We have wives and children,' said Lemoine, almost apologetically. 'If there is any shooting it will be in there first. We are not heroes, we prefer to remain here.'

Reminded of Cojot's suggestion, Bacos' response was blunter. 'It's not worth the trouble. We'll visit them often. It's no use complicating things.' He, other members of the crew and a few passengers did indeed pay frequent visits to, as Cojot put it, the 'people of the ghetto'. But the opportunity for the crew to make an important statement to the terrorists – that we will voluntarily share the fate of the Israelis, come what may – was lost.

Two occupants of the Israeli room were allowed back across, however, thanks to the efforts of Ilan Hartuv and Yitzhak David. They had tried to get all six non-Israeli Orthodox Jews returned by reminding Böse and the Peruvian of their earlier argument that they had nothing against Jews, only Israelis. 'We know,' came the reply, 'we didn't want to put them in your room but the German woman insisted.'

Later, Hartuv tried again on behalf of the young Brazilians. 'These fellows are just seventeen years old,' he told the Peruvian. 'They're both from Brazil and only came to Israel for a year to study in a yeshiva, a theological seminary. So maybe you'll take them back into the other room?'

'I know Portuguese,' replied the Peruvian. 'I'll go and speak to them and if the story you tell me is true I will put them back in the main room.' He honoured this promise, and before the day was out the Brazilians had been moved.

1630hrs GMT, Route 1, Central Israel

Sitting in the back of his Ministry of Defense car as it sped down the hill to Tel Aviv, Shimon Peres was still angry that Rabin could even consider negotiating with terrorists. He knew, now, that the only way to prevent this was for him and Gur to come up with a credible military option.

His thoughts were disturbed by his bodyguard in the seat next to the driver. 'Shimon,' said the man, turning in his seat, 'I was once security officer at the Israeli mission in Kampala. I think it would be possible to exploit Idi Amin. He's a great admirer of Moshe Dayan, but absolutely crazy about Zonik [Shaham] and Burka [Bar-Lev].' Peres knew he was referring to the two colonels who had headed Israel's military missions to Uganda in the 1960s and early 1970s. 'He's very sensitive,' continued his bodyguard, 'about all the Israelis who did him favours. For all his madness, he doesn't forget them. I think we should do something along those lines. Perhaps it's worth a direct talk with Idi Amin, to try and influence him.'

Peres could see the sense of this. 'Okay,' he said after a moment's reflection. 'Tomorrow, bring me Burka Bar-Lev and two or three more officers who were in Kampala, and who know Idi Amin well. At this stage we have to try everything, including Amin.'

1700hrs GMT, Jerusalem, Israel

As Peres neared the Kirya complex in Tel Aviv, a long evening of work ahead of him, Rabin was trying to unwind with a glass of whisky and a succession of cigarettes in his Jerusalem office. Realizing that Eiran, Avner and the other members of his personal staff were a little concerned by his comments at the meeting of the ministerial committee, he decided to explain himself.

'When it comes to negotiating with terrorists,' he said, 'I long ago made a decision of principle, well before I became prime minister, that if a situation were ever to arise when terrorists would be holding our people hostage on foreign soil and we were faced with an ultimatum either to free killers in our custody or let our own people be killed, I would, in the absence of a military option, give in to the terrorists. I would free killers to save our people. So I say now, if the defense minister and the chief of staff cannot come up with a credible military plan, I intend to negotiate with the terrorists. I would never be able to look a mother in the eye if her hostage soldier or child, or whoever it was, was murdered because of a refusal to negotiate, or because of a botched operation.'

1715hrs GMT, Entebbe International Airport, Uganda

'Silence!' shouted Wilfried Böse through the loud hailer, instantly stilling the raised voices that had filled the large hall of the Old Terminal building since the removal of the Israelis.

'I have good news,' he began. 'The President Idi Amin Dada has personally insisted that certain hostages will be freed as quickly as possible for humanitarian reasons. We have accepted this demand and the list of people who will be part of this will be communicated to you tomorrow morning.'

Hope rose in the breasts of many and, as Böse left the room, a vigorous debate began as to 'who will be freed, on what criteria the choice will be made, and the conditions of this freedom'. It was quickly decided, however, by the unofficial spokesmen of the hostages – Cojot, Bacos and Lemoine – that a list would be drawn up of the sick, old people, mothers and children and given to the terrorists. They knew, however, that no Israelis would be permitted to leave.

After dinner – again provided by the Lake Victoria Hotel and divided up between the two rooms – the list of sixty names was given to Böse. They included twelve-year-old Olivier Cojot but not his father Michel. When Olivier discovered this, he grabbed Böse's sleeve and pleaded in broken English: 'Put my father on the list, put my father on the list.'

Cojot intervened. 'Olivier,' he said sternly, 'one doesn't beg these people.' It was the first time he had raised his voice to his son since the start of their ordeal; but deep down he was touched by his son's unwillingness to leave him.

That night, aware that Olivier would soon be free and able to pass vital information to the French authorities, Cojot scribbled in tiny writing on a scrap of paper everything he thought might be useful: the layout of the terminal and its various entrances; the number of terrorists, their weapons and their guarding arrangements; the location of the Ugandan soldiers and their activities. When he had finished, he rolled up the piece of paper as small as it would go and put it into the turn-ups of Olivier's jeans where he assumed the terrorists would not look. He was hoping that the possession of this information might encourage the French authorities to launch a rescue mission. They still had a military base at Djibouti on the Horn of Africa that, at 1,000 miles from Entebbe, was less than half the distance an Israeli force would have to travel. As a Frenchman, albeit one conflicted by his countrymen's abandonment of Jews in the Second World War, Cojot hoped against hope that his government would do something to save the mainly Jewish hostages. Such an act might be some recompense for the behaviour of the Vichy government and the death of his father during the Second World War, not to mention the casual anti-semitism he had faced as a child, and finally give him closure. It would, he felt, be the perfect opportunity for France to act in a heroic way and pay off its long-due blood debt to its own Jewish citizens.

He knew, of course, that sending the note with Olivier was a fearful risk and that the consequences might be serious. But he reasoned that it was only information that many of the other released hostages would be able to give from memory – if not in such precise detail – and that, in any case, the terrorists were unlikely to search a child.

Others came to a similar conclusion. Convinced they were unlikely to see their families again, the Rabinowitzes wrote farewell letters and wills and asked the ten-year-old Dutch boy – also on the list of sixty names without his father – if he would smuggle them out in his shoe. He agreed.

1815hrs GMT, London, UK

With most of his day taken up by a meeting of EEC foreign ministers in Luxembourg, it was not until early evening that Tony Crosland turned his attention to Uganda and the news of the terrorists' ultimatum. 'As hijackers have claimed no animus and made no demands against us,' he cabled Horrocks in Kampala, 'we are considering, in response to a request by Mrs Russell, whether there would be any advantage in trying to get individual release for British and Old Commonwealth citizens. There is the added humanitarian consideration that Mr Good suffers from a cardiac condition.'

What Crosland was suggesting, under pressure from Tony Russell's wife Edith, was that Horrocks should use the absence of any explicit criticism of the United Kingdom in the PFLP's communiqué to secure the release of all the Britons and the 'Old Commonwealth citizens' like the Canadians and the New Zealanders. It was a course of action, however, that even Crosland had misgivings about.

'We have grave reservations about this,' he confessed, 'because of the risk of attracting to us PFLP attention and demands, the hijackers' own demands that all negotiations should be conducted through a

French-appointed negotiator, and the risk of harmful confusion in the use of more than one negotiating channel.' But it was an avenue they needed to explore, and be able to say they had explored, because of the level of press and public attention the hijacking had attracted in the UK. He concluded: 'Grateful for your urgent comments on the feasibility and usefulness of approaches solely on behalf of those for whom we have consular responsibility. You should not at this time consult the Ugandans or the French.'

Horrocks's response to this cable, sent later that evening, was to dismiss the idea out of hand. 'Although the Ugandans have ready access to the hijackers,' he said, 'I do not believe that they would be willing to exercise any influence in our favour in attempts to secure the release solely of those for whom we have consular responsibility.' Neither they nor the hijackers would, he added, 'entertain approaches from us on this subject'. As for the risks, he thought it likely that such a course of action 'would be looked upon by the other governments affected as a selfish unilateral step in a situation that requires a common stand'.

Faced with such vehement opposition to his tactic from the man on the spot, Crosland gave up all hope of playing an active role in freeing the British and Commonwealth hostages. Their lives would henceforth depend on the actions of other governments – particularly the Israelis – and, of course, on the whim of the terrorists themselves. The foreign secretary was, however, prepared to act on French requests to put pressure on the Ugandan government to improve the 'allegedly appalling conditions' of the hostages in the Old Terminal. 'If you consider it useful,' he told Horrocks, 'encourage the Ugandans to persuade the hijackers to allow [them] to bring in the necessary amenities. You should make it clear to the Ugandans that this request applies on humanitarian grounds to hostages of all nationalities.'

1900hrs GMT, Tel Aviv, Israel

Sitting with Shimon Peres round the conference table in his Ministry of Defense office were the IDF's most senior officers: Chief of

Staff Motta Gur; his deputy Kuti Adam, chief of operations; Shlomo Gazit, chief of intelligence; and Benny Peled, commander of the Israeli Air Force.

Peres opened the 9 p.m. meeting by recounting Rabin's words in Jerusalem: if the IDF could not come up with a viable scheme for rescuing the hostages at Entebbe he would have no option but to negotiate their release with the terrorists. 'So, gentlemen, what have you got to say?'

Peled spoke first. Born in Tel Aviv in 1928, the scion of a long-established pioneer family, he had joined the IAF as a mechanic and later became one of Israel's first jet pilots. He resembled a film star with his handsome fine-boned face, swept-back dark hair and pencil moustache. But his looks belied his toughness: he had twice survived the shooting down of his plane over enemy territory; he had held his nerve during the early setbacks of the Yom Kippur War; and, now that Israel was threatened by a new enemy – terrorism – he was in no doubt what the response should be. Nor had he arrived at the meeting unprepared, having earlier received assurances from Joshua Shani that Hercules planes could transport an assault force to Entebbe.

'I, for one,' said Peled, 'am strongly against giving in to terrorists under any circumstances. I would propose landing an airborne force at Entebbe Airport. Once we have eliminated the terrorists who are guarding the hostages, Idi Amin will have no alternative but to let them go. To succeed in a military operation, we must have complete control over Entebbe and the neighbourhood. It can be done by dropping a thousand paratroops.'

A thought then occurred to Peled and he turned to Peres. 'What do you want? That we conquer Entebbe or the whole country?'

Peres was intrigued: 'How many men do you need for that?'

'To conquer the whole country I need 1,000 soldiers – to conquer Entebbe maybe 200 or 300 men.' Peled went on to explain that a force of either size could be flown to Entebbe non-stop on Hercules C-130s. He had made inquiries: it could be done.

It all sounded a little far fetched to Peres, though he gave the IAF chief credit for his daring. Gur was even less convinced. Dismissing Peled's plan as 'fantastic' and one they would all do well to forget, he raised instead the possibility of a seaborne attack on Entebbe: either by troops crossing from Kenya in boats; or by marine commandos parachuting into Lake Victoria with inflatables.

The last to make a suggestion was Kuti Adam. He too was against negotiating, he said. His plan was to lure the terrorists to Israel by insisting that the exchange of prisoners and hostages take place in the Middle East. Then, once the terrorists were in reach, the Unit would launch a surprise assault to rescue the hostages. Few of those round the table thought it likely the terrorists would agree to this: yet it was, nevertheless, a tactic worth exploring.

Clearly there was much work to do and Peres closed the meeting by telling his generals to 'continue raising new ideas and checking them out – no matter how weird or crazy they sounded'.

2150hrs GMT, Entebbe International Airport, Uganda

Claude Moufflet had just fallen asleep, precariously perched on a narrow shelf behind the bar in the large hall, when he was woken by hysterical cries from the French lady separated from her sister. 'Jaco! Jaco!' she kept crying, a man Moufflet assumed was either her husband or her son.

Two stewards and a stewardess tried and failed to calm her down, and eventually resorted to wrapping her in a blanket and, with the permission of the red-shirted terrorist 'Ali', carrying her outside. So tired were most of those in the room that they didn't even wake up; those that did were quickly back to sleep, despite the hot airless atmosphere and the buzzing of mosquitoes.

Next door in the Israeli room, Sara Davidson flinched as she heard the cries. 'I've no strength left,' she wrote in her diary. 'It's hard even to write. I gaze at my children and pray that they'll emerge sound in body and spirit from this nightmare.' Like many others, Gilbert Weill felt 'broken and depressed'.

DAY 4: WEDNESDAY 30 JUNE 1976

0200hrs GMT, Tel Aviv, Israel

As the hostages slept, Ehud Barak's seven-man ad hoc operations group was working through the night at the Kirya to come up with a military solution to the hijacking. Telephones rang constantly as information flowed into Barak's office. Visitors included an engineer from the Israeli construction company Solel Boneh who arrived clutching the original plans for Entebbe Airport, and senior air force officers who had spent time in Uganda as flight trainers and pilots of the short-lived Israel–Uganda shuttle. The latter told Barak everything they could about the airport, other air bases in the country and Idi Amin's air force.

Other vital information was gleaned from an international directory of airports, notably the location of Entebbe's New Terminal in relation to its old one, and the presence of a new runway for the MiG fighters given to Amin by the Libyans.

All this enabled the planners to come up with ideas that were either rejected by the others or gradually refined. Subtly directed by Barak, and fuelled by endless cups of tea and coffee, the brainstorming went on all night. But again and again they were faced with 'holes in the intelligence', the largest of which was Amin's role in the hijacking. Was he colluding with the terrorists or genuinely trying to help? They suspected the former. They knew that Amin was due to attend an upcoming meeting of the Organization of African Unity in Mauritius, his last as chairman, and felt that the hijacking gave him just what he wanted – an international stage. His statements to the press, meanwhile, were non-committal: promising the hostages' safety on the one hand; and urging Israel to agree to the terrorists' demands on the other.

Muki Betser was not alone that 'long first night' in feeling a 'tremendous responsibility' for the safety of the hostages. Yet all were convinced that an exchange of prisoners would not only be a humiliation for Israel but 'a victory for terrorists everywhere'.

By dawn, Barak's team had moved down into the underground Pit to put flesh on the bones of four possible plans, none without disadvantages, and all dependent upon surprise. Their favourite was a combined operation for members of the Unit and the navy's Shayetet 13 to parachute into Lake Victoria with Zodiac inflatable boats, and then march the short distance from the shore to the Old Terminal at Entebbe where they would kill the terrorists and release the hostages. Only then would they hand themselves over to the Ugandans in the hope that they would arrange their repatriation. The weakness of this plan was that it assumed 'Amin wanted a rescue to relieve him of responsibility'.

The second plan – also suggested by Gur at the meeting with Peres the night before – was for an assault force to fly to Kenya and then use boats to cross Lake Victoria to the shore near Entebbe. It was dependent not only upon Amin's cooperation, but also upon that of the Kenyans who, like the rest of the OAU, had had no official diplomatic relations with Israel since the Yom Kippur War. Unofficially, however, the two countries still had close security links as proven by the recent cooperation between the Mossad and Kenyan security forces to prevent three members of Wadie Haddad's PFLP from using Russian hand-held surface-to-air missiles (SAM-7s) to shoot down an El Al jet as it landed at Nairobi International Airport, en route from Johannesburg to Tel Aviv, in January 1976. The terrorists were caught in the act, thanks to information given by Mossad agents based in Nairobi to the Kenyan internal security police, the General Service Unit (GSU), and a second pair of West German suspects – sent to Kenya to find out why the attack had failed – were captured later that week. All five were on the list of 'freedom fighters' the terrorists at Entebbe wanted released from Kenyan jails in return for the hostages. What the PFLP did not realize, however – and the Israeli government was not about to tell them – was that shortly after the arrests the Kenyan authorities had allowed the Mossad to fly the five in secret back to Israel where they later stood trial. This all augured well, of course, for an operation launched from Kenya.

The third plan – suggested by Muki Betser – was a variation on General Adam's: but instead of luring the terrorists to Israel, which all agreed was an unlikely scenario, the surprise assault would take place at Entebbe by soldiers masquerading as Palestinian prisoners. They would, moreover, be flown in an IAF Boeing painted in Air France livery, and by military pilots disguised as civilians. Once again, however, the success of the mission would require Amin's cooperation.

The final plan – and arguably the least favoured at this stage – was the so-called 'IDF Option' put forward by Colonel Ran Bag of the Infantry and Paratroop Command. Keen for his own soldiers of the Golani and Tzanchanim (Paratroop) Brigades to be involved, Bag wanted to use a force large enough to overawe the Ugandans so that the Unit's assault force could rescue the hostages. He envisaged a strike force of at least a thousand men. But unlike Air Force commander Peled's original suggestion for these troops to be dropped by parachute, Bag wanted the Hercules C-130 transport planes to land so that they could later fly the hostages to safety. The plan had the advantage of relying on neither the Ugandans nor the Kenyans. On the other hand its very size would increase the likelihood of detection as its planes flew within radar – and fighter – range of Egypt, Saudi Arabia and Sudan, three countries sworn to destroy Israel; and it would need both time and access to Entebbe's fuel tanks so that its planes could return to Israel.

That the IAF was capable of landing planes unnoticed at Entebbe, Major Ido Embar was not in any doubt. 'Believe me,' he told the others, 'I live on an air force base. I know what I'm talking about. If a plane manages to avoid radar detection up to its landing, it could land and come to a quiet halt at the end of a runway without anybody noticing.'

0500hrs GMT, Entebbe International Airport, Uganda

At 8 a.m., Ilan Hartuv was walking past the windows at the front of the Israeli room in the Old Terminal building, stretching his cramped muscles after an uncomfortable night in an armchair, when he noticed Ugandan soldiers laying rows of wires outside the building. 'They're booby-trapping us ready for demolition,' said one fearful hostage.

'No,' interjected another, 'those are electronic eavesdropping devices.'

The truth was soon revealed when a single Ugandan soldier entered the room and announced: 'The wires outside are for you.'

Nonplussed, the Israelis said nothing, waiting for an explanation.

The soldier continued: 'They are for your laundry. Anyone who wants to wash clothes may do so in the washrooms. You can hang them outside to dry.'

A collective sigh of relief went up and, minutes later, people flowed through the doorway to hang wet garments on the wires and play in the sun. The non-Israeli hostages, having received a similar message, were doing likewise. Emboldened by the relaxed atmosphere, Sara Davidson approached Wilfried Böse, on guard at the entrance to the Israeli room, and asked him: 'Perhaps we can take our bags out of the plane?'

'We wanted to bring them out,' said the German, 'but they are in special containers, and this airport doesn't have suitable equipment to unload them.'

She shook her head indignantly. 'I don't understand you! How can you hold up so many people without decent mattresses and blankets, in such terrible conditions?'

Embarrassed, Böse asked her what was needed and scribbled down a list of her requests: blankets, mattresses, soap, clean the toilets, etc. When he had finished, he said he would do his best but it was not his decision. 'I was only in command on the plane. They are the officers,' he said, pointing in the direction of Jaber and the Peruvian. 'Now they're in charge.'

·

0630hrs GMT, Tel Aviv, Israel

'I've asked you here,' said Shimon Peres, addressing the three officers seated around the conference table in his Ministry of Defense office, 'because you all served with the IDF military mission in Uganda and know Idi Amin personally. I want you to tell me everything you know about the Ugandan army, Amin's motives and methods, and to suggest any proposals for solving the hijacking crisis.'

The first to speak was Colonel Burka Bar-Lev, the tall and balding former head of the IDF's last military mission to Uganda, who had once been so close to Amin that he had known about his January 1971 coup in advance. Bar-Lev, moreover, had welcomed the new regime enthusiastically, ignoring Israeli Foreign Office advice to play an impartial role. He had used his influence to save certain 'friends' of Israel from execution and to condemn others. Yet even Bar-Lev had been unable to avert the breach with Uganda that had resulted from the Israeli government's refusal to give Amin a £10 million loan on generous terms and to supply his air force with a squadron of Phantom fighter-bombers. 'We don't manufacture Phantoms,' Prime Minister Golda Meir had told Amin during his visit to Israel in July 1971, 'we buy them from the United States, when we can. Why do you need Phantoms?' His reply: 'To use against Tanzania.'

Speaking with his trademark rapid-fire delivery, Bar-Lev told Peres that Amin obtained most of his information from talking to people. He was, as a result, 'greatly influenced by those close to him and tended to rely heavily on their judgement and their personal loyalty to him'. Bar-Lev added: 'I don't believe he will massacre the hostages, but nor do I think he will get into a firefight with the hijackers. These presumptions will remain valid as long as Amin doesn't dream something during the night. If he does, that could change everything.' Bar-Lev explained that he was referring to Amin's oft-repeated story of his mother appearing to him in a dream to warn him against ever harming the Jews.

The second of the three officers to speak was Lieutenant-Colonel Yosef Salan, the former commander of an IAF team in Uganda who had helped the country set up its own air force. He broadly agreed with Bar-Lev's assessment, but warned that if Israel tried to use force 'that could short-circuit all of Amin's fuses' and might cause him to 'go wild'. In that event there would be 'no knowing how it might end'.

While that was true, said the third officer, a major in the IAF, he also thought that the Ugandan Army would 'probably not intervene' in a battle between IDF troops and the hijackers. 'They generally prefer,' he added with a grin, 'to steer clear of other people's wars.'

'Is Amin brave?' Peres asked all three.

Their response was instant and identical: 'No, he's a coward.'

'And,' added the IAF major, 'he's also cruel. I remember once, after he had been given a rifle as a present, he immediately began spraying bullets across the courtyard of his villa, hitting innocent and unarmed people.'

Peres nodded. It had been, for him, a fascinating and revealing discussion and his silent conclusion was that Amin would be interested in 'dragging out' the drama for as long as he could, since it provided him with 'an unparalleled opportunity for getting world attention'. He 'would not, on his own initiative, kill the hostages'. He might have 'played fast and loose with the lives of his own people, but was wary of harming "white" people'. Therefore if Israel used force he 'would not intervene, even if some Ugandans were hurt or killed during the operation'. If, on the other hand, some hostages were still in his hands *after* such an operation, 'they might well be killed out of revenge'. He thus concluded that the Ugandan Army would not be a serious obstacle to any military action, and that the best way to appeal to Amin was 'not through diplomatic protocol or sweet reason', but rather 'through his ego – appealing to his pride and honour, hinting that there might be a Nobel Peace Prize in this for him, referring to his international standing, and appealing to the mystique surrounding his role as national leader'.

He determined, therefore, to set up a telephone link with Amin as soon as possible in the hope that it would provide the military planners with the detailed information they 'lacked about the hijackers and the hostages', and enable them 'to form a more accurate assessment of the situation on the ground at Entebbe'.

The officer entrusted with this task was Burka Bar-Lev, a man once described as 'Amin's personal adviser'. He was asked by Peres to call Amin and say he was speaking for people 'close to the top policymaking echelon in Israel'. Peres added: 'Burka, this entire office, all the telephones, all the secretaries, are at your disposal.'

* * *

Peres had no sooner cleared his office of Bar-Lev and the two air force officers than in trooped the senior commanders of the IDF – Gur, Adam, Peled, Gazit and one or two others – for their scheduled 10 a.m. conference. 'What have you come up with?' asked Peres.

Gur explained that his planners were still recommending a seaborne assault – either from a paradrop into Lake Victoria or by troops crossing from the Kenyan shore – and that once the terrorists were dead the commandos would withdraw. The risk, quickly identified by Peres, was that the Ugandans would then take out their frustrations on the defenceless hostages. But an even more serious obstacle was that both operations would take a minimum of thirty-six hours to prepare. With the ultimatum due to expire at 2 p.m. Israeli time the following day, there simply was not enough time.

They discussed the alternative plans – including Peled's preference for flying enough soldiers to Entebbe to take over the airport and the town – but none satisfied Peres or met with Gur's approval. An added complication was a report from Uganda that Amin had deployed an entire battalion of troops to guard the hostages. Would they put up a fight? And what about the building that was housing the hostages? Had it been booby-trapped? They simply 'did not know enough to mount a military operation – especially an operation whose success would depend, above all, on surprise'.

0830hrs GMT, Entebbe International Airport, Uganda

The distinctive whump-whump alerted the hostages to the arrival of a helicopter at 11.30 a.m. A French-made blue and white Lynx duly landed fifty yards in front of the Old Terminal building, and President Idi Amin Dada clambered out, wearing a dark-blue suit and a huge ten-gallon cream-coloured cowboy hat that was promptly blown from his head by the downdraught from the still-beating rotor blades. As his bodyguards scampered to recover his hat, Amin shook hands with Faiz Jaber, the chief terrorist, and together they got back into the helicopter for a brief conference.

Ten minutes later they re-emerged and began discussions with some of the other terrorists and a thin black man in dark glasses and a dark suit that the hostages assumed was the Somali ambassador to Uganda, the man the terrorists had nominated as their diplomatic point of contact. Their conversation over, Amin finally entered the large hall with one of his generals, his bodyguards and Jaber, Böse and the Peruvian. He was met with another burst of applause from the non-Israeli hostages – much to Michel Cojot's embarrassment and frustration.

'Good morning,' said a jovial Amin. 'I have good news for you. During the course of my negotiations with PFLP I have obtained an agreement that old people and ill people, as well as children and their mothers, will be liberated. The members of the PFLP will communicate with you a list of people in a moment. I just need to keep telling you that I don't want any of you to be killed here and I will do all I can to obtain your freedom. Your governments have still not addressed any formal response to the demands given by the FLP of Palestine, therefore it is uniquely down to me that these people will be freed. When you are freed, I ask you to say to your governments that they must stop encouraging the Zionist politics of the state of Israel.'

Amin looked round the room, pleased with the reaction so far. 'I am,' he continued, 'not only the Ugandan head of state, but also the President of all Africa and have already said to the United Nations that they must return the exiled Palestinians to their land. This is what you must repeat to your governments when you get back to your homes. The world is lucky that Yasser Arafat, the chief of the Palestinians, is a man of good sense, and also a moderate. He has publicly declared in front of all the world's nations and to the United Nations that the Palestinians are happy to live in Israel with Jews and Christians side by side. Insist that your governments make this possible.'

Again Amin paused, seemingly unaware of the contradiction between what he had just said and the ideological stance of Wadie Haddad, the mastermind behind the hijacking of Flight 139. Haddad was an extremist who sought not compromise with the Israeli state, but rather its destruction. He was, as a result, violently opposed to Arafat's tactic of seeking a two-state solution to the Palestinian problem and had, moreover, been ejected from the original PFLP and forced to set up his own splinter group because he disagreed with, as he saw it, the PLO's defeatist order not to strike at targets outside Israel.

Ignoring the perplexed look on some faces, Amin ploughed on.

'Imagine,' he said, 'that the Ugandan people are chased from their territory by an enemy people. Do you think we would accept this? No. The Ugandans would fight, even to the death, to reconquer their land. It's what the Palestinians are doing, and it's what your governments would do if it happened to you. I know that you men, women and children, young and old, are innocent and I am going to do everything I can to improve your comfort and obtain your freedom. I know that many of you have slept badly or not at all, but you should know that since you've been here I haven't slept either. I just took the time to change clothes before coming to see you today. But I am going to have some mattresses brought, and some pillows, so that you can sleep better.'

He concluded his speech by telling the hostages that those due to be freed would return home that same day on a separate Air France plane that was waiting outside the New Terminal building. He reminded them that he 'did not want anything bad to happen' to them, and that it was the responsibility of their governments to respond to the terrorists' demands. 'I will,' he said, 'come back to see you soon. Goodbye.'

As Amin was speaking, Cojot again provided a simultaneous translation into French, making corrections where he thought it was useful to do so – replacing, for example, Amin's description of himself as 'president of Africa' with 'outgoing president of the Organization of African Unity', and toning down menacing phrases like 'I don't want any of you to be killed . . .'

Their voices were occasionally made inaudible by the roar of a low-flying MiG that was surely intended, thought Cojot, 'to discourage any attempt at revolt, or perhaps to help us take down the clothes we had washed and hung up to dry'. As if that was not bad enough, the encounter was captured for posterity by press photographers and a film crew from the local television station.

The end of Amin's speech was met with a 'massive round of applause' that visibly delighted the dictator as he left with his entourage to speak to the Israelis in the adjacent room. There his reception was cooler, though a few people applauded after he greeted them with 'Shalom'. He had little to say, beyond a promise to bring more blankets and pillows, and to inform the Israelis that the terrorists had no grudge against them per se, but instead against the 'fascist Israeli government' which, if it did not agree to the terrorists' demands, was clearly unconcerned 'about the fate of its citizens'. He made no mention of the possibility that any Israelis would be released.

The man translating Amin's words into Hebrew – as he had during the president's earlier visit – was Ilan Hartuv, a former economic adviser at the Israeli Embassy in Addis Ababa who had met Amin a few years earlier during a ceremony to celebrate the construction of a big housing estate in Kampala by the Israeli firm Solel Boneh. Amin did not recognize Hartuv, and the Israeli chose not to remind him of their earlier meeting; he did, however, suggest during Amin's second visit that there was nothing he and the other Israelis could do to influence their government while they were in Entebbe, but if they were released they could 'repeat the terrorists' statements' once they were safely back in Israel.

Akiva Laxer was blunter. 'You are Field Marshal Dr Idi Amin Dada, a great leader. How can you let these terrorists harm us? Why don't you overpower them and release us?'

'Look,' replied Amin, gesturing at the wall of cardboard boxes, 'the reason I can do nothing is because you are surrounded by all these boxes of explosives.'

'But Field Marshal,' said Laxer, 'come and see. There is nothing in these boxes.'

Amin shook his head. 'I cannot do this because they have told me the boxes are full of explosives. It's too risky. They might blow up the whole building.'

Once Amin had left the room, several Israelis went to the gap between the two rooms to ask the other hostages what he had said to them. A few of the latter insisted that there was little difference between the two speeches, but one young Israeli woman was not convinced. 'You will see,' she said bitterly. 'They are going to free people from your side and they will keep all of us.'

'Surely not,' responded a non-Israeli. 'He said they would free people who were old, ill, children and their mothers. That will surely be for everybody.'

'Maybe, but on our side there is no list. You made one last night.'

The conversation might have continued but for Brigitte Kuhlmann who shooed the hostages away from both sides of the gap in the wall as Khaled returned to his post.

0900hrs GMT, Jerusalem, Israel

'Gentlemen,' said Yitzhak Rabin, addressing the first full meeting of the Israeli Cabinet since the crisis had begun on Sunday, 'I want to say that any information that leaks out today can end up costing lives. So I ask you not to behave normally regarding this issue.' In other words, speak to no one.

An hour and a half earlier he had met with Yitzhak Navon, the chairman of the Knesset Foreign Affairs and Security Committee, and with Menachem Begin and Elimelech Rimalt, the two main leaders of the opposition, to apprise them of the latest developments regarding the hijacking and to enlist their support for what he knew would be a momentous political decision if there was no alternative: to begin negotiations for the release of the hostages. Begin's response was all he could have hoped for: 'Mr Prime Minister, you can expect the full support of the opposition. The nation is united at a time like this.'

Now Rabin was looking for the support of his ministers. He told them of the latest developments – particularly the likelihood that the IDF would not come up with a workable rescue plan in time – and reminded them that the deadline for a response to the hijackers' demands was 2 p.m. the following day. Any later and the hostages would be killed.

'We know,' responded Yigal Allon, his lack of sleep obvious from the bags under his eyes and his tousled hair. 'But if we publish a statement saying we'll meet the terrorists' demands, everyone will condemn us. The French will announce they aren't planning on surrendering to pressure. West Germany is completely rejecting the possibility. In a meeting between our Washington ambassador and the assistant to the secretary of state, he mentioned that their secret approach is known to us – not to give in to demands or blackmail.'

Allon, by these comments, had made clear his belief that Israel would be diplomatically isolated if it tried to do a deal to save the hostages' lives.

Rabin was unimpressed, chiefly because he could not see an alternative to negotiation. 'At this stage,' he responded, 'I don't think a military operation is possible, because we don't have the ability to act without the consent of the countries involved. So what do we do? Attack Uganda? How would we even reach Uganda? The object is not to act militarily but to save people's lives. As of right now I can't see a way to do that. So, without befogging the issue, we are in trouble and it won't be a surprise if the hostages' families start to put pressure on us.'

After a few of the other ministers had offered their opinions, Rabin concluded: 'Gentlemen, there is still no need to decide yet, but I can see that we'll have to meet again today or tomorrow morning. My office will let you know when.'

0900hrs GMT, Tel Aviv, Israel

Once the meeting with Peres and the other IDF generals had finished, air force chief Benny Peled returned to his own headquarters building in the Kirya to continue planning a possible rescue mission. Of all the senior commanders, he was the most convinced that a military strike was feasible. 'The only danger,' he told senior members of his staff, 'is if they open fire on the planes. I think that the risks are reasonable. I don't believe that we are exaggerating. It's within normal range for a Hercules.'

'There could be a problem of discovery by radar en route,' suggested a member of his staff.

'No,' said Peled, shaking his head. 'The problem isn't radar, but rather what the enemy will do with the information he receives – if he receives it! Let's assume for a moment that we are picked up by radar in Uganda – or anywhere else on the way to Entebbe. What will they do? What will they think? The last thing that will come to mind is that these are Israeli planes on their way to rescue hostages from Entebbe. But we must make sure that the chances of being discovered en route, and particularly in the target area, are reduced to the barest possible minimum.'

0930hrs GMT, Kampala, Uganda

It was just after noon when the acting British high commissioner James Horrocks sent his response to Tony Crosland's query of the night before from the three-storey British High Commission in central Kampala. Unable to get personal access to the Old Terminal, he was forced to admit that he and his French colleagues had only 'second-hand' information about the hostages' living conditions.

He said that President Amin had assured the French ambassador that 'catering services have been organized and a Ugandan medical team was in attendance', while other sources – presumably airport workers – claimed 'that arm chairs were moved from the new airport terminal for the hostages and mattresses provided for their babies'. Although this lack of adequate sleeping arrangements 'must inevitably cause discomfort and hardship', said Horrocks, it was undoubtedly 'an improvement over their continued detention on the aircraft'.

Though not yet aware of Amin's earlier visit to the hostages, Horrocks did include in his cable the hope that, thanks to the president's intervention, some of the more vulnerable hostages – sick, elderly, mothers and children – would be released that morning. Less encouraging was Amin's refusal to allow an Air France doctor and nurse to see the hostages on the grounds that 'the Ugandans were providing all necessary medical attention'.

Horrocks's reliance on the French for his limited knowledge of events at the airport was indicative of how low Britain's stock had fallen in a country that until recently had been part of its Empire. The first British presence in what would become the city of Kampala was in 1890 when Captain Lugard established a fort on a feature known as the 'Hill of the Impala', or Akasosi k'Empala in the dialect of the local Buganda tribe. Four years later the British established a protectorate over Uganda – a loose form of imperial rule that allowed the Buganda a measure of self-government – and made Kampala its capital. Over the years the settlement mushroomed across a chain of hills, with the British building their spacious homes and government buildings on the neighbouring heights of Nakasero, Kololo and Mulago. In addition a handsome red-roofed and colonnaded State House was built in Entebbe, near the airport, for the British governor of Uganda. After independence in 1962, State House became the official residence of the Ugandan president.

With the end of imperial rule, Britain's presence in Uganda was confined to the whitewashed three-storey High Commission building on Parliamentary Avenue (formerly Obote Avenue) in the Nakasero district of central Kampala. It was from here – among the flat-roofed post-1945 modernist buildings of the administrative and diplomatic quarters – that successive British high commissioners had attempted to influence Uganda's rulers. But with increasingly little success: first President Milton Obote, in a move to the left, had angered the British by nationalizing private businesses, many of them foreign; then in 1972 his successor Idi Amin had responded to Britain's refusal to give him arms to fight the Tanzanians by expelling from Uganda the large Indian Asian community that had arrived during colonial rule. In protest, the FCO had declined to send any more substantive high commissioners to Kampala, leaving less experienced diplomats to handle trade links and the consular interests of the dwindling British community.

Horrocks was not even the official acting high commissioner: that post had been held since 1973 by James Hennessy, who was on extended leave in the summer of 1976. Small wonder that Horrocks, normally the chargé d'affaires and Hennessy's deputy, was finding it hard to get any concrete information from the airport.

0930hrs GMT, Entebbe International Airport, Uganda

'Silence!' demanded Wilfried Böse through the megaphone, and for once he got it instantly. He was standing in the centre of the Old Terminal building's main hall, flanked by his superiors Faiz Jaber and the Peruvian. All around them the hostages had stopped what they were doing, eager to hear the long-awaited announcement of who would stay and who would go.

'As we told you yesterday,' continued the German, 'we've decided to agree to the demands made by President Idi Amin, and I have here a list of people that will be freed.' The room held its breath. 'The list that we received yesterday had sixty names. We have agreed to free forty of these people.' Groans filled the air.

'However,' said Böse, raising his hand to stifle the discontent, 'for humanitarian reasons we will also free five more whose health is not good. Would you please all go to the left side of this room when I call your name, and take your hand baggage and make your way outside.'

As Böse was speaking, a yellow bus drove up to the front of the Old Terminal and out of it trooped a host of photographers and a film crew to record the moment of the hostages' release. This caused an outbreak of chatter that irked Böse. 'Silence, please!' he shouted, a plea that was echoed by many hostages.

'Yes, silence!' 'Be quiet!' 'We haven't heard anything yet!'

As the room settled down, the German continued: 'Would you please detach the tags from your hand luggage so that we can identify them. Also you must give us your cameras, tape and video recorders. We warn all of you that you are about to be searched and all disobedience will be very severely punished.'

Then he began to call out names, mentioning the very old, the sick and the mothers with children. Fathers were not included, and for some the separation was heartbreaking. One French mother of three wept as she realized her husband would not be going with them, and it took him some time to persuade her that she must go. She eventually left, holding a folded pushchair in one hand and a bag in the other, her children herded before her.

It was even harder for the children without mothers, like Olivier Cojot. When his father Michel's name was not called after his, he strode up to the Peruvian and demanded: 'Hey, hold on! What about my dad? If my dad isn't released, I'm not going.'

His father could see what was happening and quickly intervened, pushing Olivier firmly towards the line that was forming on the left side of the room. Conscious of the vital intelligence that Olivier was carrying in his turn-ups, Michel Cojot was furious that he had drawn attention to himself. But he softened for their final embrace. 'Papa,' said Olivier, 'you remember how much you missed your own father? So please don't play the cowboy.'

Though distraught, the young boy tried not to show it, keeping his head high and his expression fixed as he walked outside. The watching Claude Moufflet was astonished by Olivier's self-control and thought it must be a 'deliberate sign of affection that he wants to display for his father'. With a son about the same age, waiting for him in France, Moufflet found himself wishing that if the roles were reversed his son would display such an 'admirable attitude'.

The father of a thirteen-year-old girl – a senior officer in the Moroccan Royal Air Force – was on the list, but only because he had managed to convince the terrorists that he needed to accompany his wife who was suffering from breathing difficulties.

As the growing crowd of soon-to-be-liberated hostages sheltered from the sun under the awnings in front of the Old Terminal, some of those inside tried to pass them messages and possessions through the windows. This irritated the terrorists and caused Faiz Jaber to go outside, pistol in hand, and move the crowd further forward. When the conversations continued, Jaber ordered the windows closed.

For some of the remaining hostages, the realization that they were not to be freed was crushing. Many collapsed to their knees, hands clasped in supplication, pleading with the terrorists that they deserved to go too. Most were ignored, though at the last moment Böse signalled to two sisters that they could join the others, bringing the number of those liberated to forty-seven. Of that number, two French women – a nun and a lady in her fifties – offered to stay behind so that others could go. But their offers were rejected. 'It was soon clear,' noted Julie Aouzerate, one of the lucky ones, 'that the list was fixed and unchangeable.' It included thirty-three French nationals – among them twenty-five-year-old Annie Bracker and her two-year-old daughter Shirley – three Moroccans, two Greeks, two Americans, two Canadians, two Dutch, a Venezuelan, a Paraguayan, a Cypriot and one person defined as 'stateless'. The majority were Jews.

Once all forty-seven had been searched, counted and recounted, they were directed on to the bus and driven away, causing at least two of the women left in the departure lounge to collapse in hysterics and to require sedation. Michel Cojot, on the other hand, felt only relief that his son Olivier – whose selfless behaviour throughout the crisis had filled him with pride – was safe and that henceforth he was 'alone and free'.

1000hrs GMT, Jerusalem, Israel

Shimon Peres had missed the earlier get-together of the full Cabinet because he was consulting with the senior IDF commanders in Tel Aviv. But he was present at a brief meeting of the ministerial committee in Rabin's office at noon, having driven across to Jerusalem with General Gur.

'I called this meeting,' said Rabin, 'because a telegram has arrived from Uri Lubrani.' Everyone in the room knew that Lubrani, a former political adviser to David Ben-Gurion, had been ambassador to Uganda in the mid-1960s and was currently heading Israel's diplomatic mission in Teheran. Rabin continued: 'He and Idi Amin Dada both shared an experience where they were saved from a plane crash. Regarding this, we have a statement that will be read by Yigal.'

Allon picked up the telegram. 'Lubrani writes, "I want to offer myself as a messenger to Amin in Uganda, to try and get him to free all the hostages or trade myself in for them. I think we can try to play this card, especially with such a primitive person like Amin."'

Rabin seemed keen. 'I suggest you tell him,' he said to Allon, 'to try and get there.'

Peres was appalled. 'He is the Israeli ambassador to Iran. If, God forbid, they get their hands on him, he knows a lot of secrets.'

The defense secretary's blunt speaking seemed to bring Rabin to his senses and he decided to drop the matter. Instead he told the assembled ministers that they would meet again at nine that evening, by which time Gur would have reported on any possible rescue plan.

Only Peres stayed behind in Rabin's office for a follow-up meeting with Gur. 'What progress have you made?' Rabin asked Gur.

'We've put together a team to look into all the military options,' said the IDF chief of staff, 'and Ehud Barak is working with the air force and navy.'

'Anything workable?'

'Not yet.'

'I should say,' intervened Peres, 'that I spent this morning consulting with people who have been in Uganda. There are various suggestions, but nothing firm yet.'

Now more certain than ever that the IDF would fail to come up with a viable military option in the short time remaining, Rabin turned to a separate matter: press censorship. He explained that an article about Operation Heartburn – the foiling, inspired by the Mossad and Shin Bet (the Israeli internal security service), of a PFLP plot to shoot down an El Al plane leaving Kenya earlier that year – had just appeared in one of the daily newspapers, even though such information was thought vital to national security and was subject to a D-notice. Rabin was incensed, not least because the article laid bare the close unofficial contacts between the Israeli and Kenyan intelligence services. 'The fact,' he said, 'that we can't take a military correspondent, put him in jail and question him on how he got this information – this is a catastrophe.'

1200hrs GMT, Tel Aviv, Israel

Burka Bar-Lev was waiting nervously by the phone in one of Peres's outer offices in the Ministry of Defense when an aide informed him that Idi Amin was on the line.

Bar-Lev picked up the receiver, aware that the call was being both recorded and listened to on an extension. 'Mr President?'

'Who's speaking?' responded the familiar gruff voice.

'Colonel Bar-Lev.'

Amin's tone brightened. 'How are you, my friend?'

'How do you feel, Mr President?'

'I'm very happy to hear your voice today.'

Bar-Lev got down to business. 'I'm speaking from my home. I heard what has happened. My friend, can I ask something of you?'

'I agree, because you are my good friend.'

'I know, sir,' replied Bar-Lev. 'My friend, you have a great opportunity to go down in history as a great peacemaker. Since a lot of people abroad, in England, in the United States, and in Europe, are writing bad things about you, you have an opportunity to show them that you are a great peacemaker, and if you free those people, you will go down in history as a very great man, and that will counter those who speak against you. I thought about that this morning when I heard all these things on the radio.'

'I successfully spoke with the Popular Front of Palestine,' said Amin, keen to relay good news. 'I've just released forty-seven hostages and handed them over to the French ambassador. It's very important for you to listen to Radio Uganda at five o'clock this afternoon.'

'What about the Israeli hostages?'

'The Popular Front of Palestine are now surrounding [with explosives] the remaining hostages completely,' said Amin, his voice

135

sombre. 'They say that if the Israeli government doesn't answer their demand, they will blow up the French plane and all the hostages tomorrow at twelve noon Greenwich Mean Time. Therefore, I propose to you, my friend, to report to Rabin – General Rabin, the prime minister, I know him, he is my friend – and to General Dayan. I know he is my friend, though he isn't in the government. Your government must do everything possible to release the hostages immediately – that is the demand of the Palestinians. I am doing the best I can, I'm giving them mattresses, blankets, food, medical attention. I want you to do everything possible. I've just spoken with the Israelis now and they're very happy. What they said has been recorded on television. They asked me to pass this message to the government, immediately.'

'Mr President,' said Bar-Lev, continuing the tactic of appealing to Amin's ego, 'you are the ruler of your country. I think you have the power to liberate these people. You'll go down in history as a great man.'

Sidestepping the issue, Amin reminded Bar-Lev of their everlasting friendship and said that he was prepared 'to make peace between Israel and the Arabs', and wanted the Israeli government to know that. Rabin's best hope of saving lives, however, was for him to reply to the Palestinian demands.

'Can you do something to stop them from killing?' asked a frustrated Bar-Lev.

'I can stop them if your government accepts their demand immediately.' There was a pause before Amin continued: 'Now they're calling me. At five they will publish their final decision, so you must act quickly, otherwise they will kill all the hostages. Your government must do everything possible.'

In desperation, Bar-Lev reminded Amin of his mother's dying plea for him to help the Israelis. If he did so now he would 'go into history, and perhaps even receive the Nobel Prize'. Surely he wouldn't waste this God-given opportunity to show he was 'a great and good man'?

Amin changed the subject, asking after Bar-Lev and his wife.

'Everyone's fine. Do you want me to come to you?'

'I'll be happy to see you.'

'Can you stop them killing,' asked Bar-Lev, 'until I arrive?'

'Can you approach your government quickly, so that I will receive an answer?'

Bar-Lev conceded defeat. 'Very well, my friend. I'll call you back later.'

'Call me whenever you like,' said Amin. 'I'm waiting. I'm speaking from the airfield. I have not slept for three days. I want to save these people.'

The line went dead.

1200hrs GMT, Entebbe International Airport, Uganda

Once the 'most vulnerable' non-Israeli hostages had departed the Old Terminal building, those left behind – a total of 202 men, women and children – began to organize themselves 'for a stay' that Michel Cojot 'imagined would be long'. They were starved of news from the outside – Böse had rejected Cojot's request to have newspapers delivered – and tongues 'were wagging'. Many thought the governments concerned were unlikely to give in to terrorist blackmail and were arguing about the 'various options' open to the hijackers.

On a more practical level Tony Russell, one of the two British hostages in the non-Israeli room – and known to Cojot and the others as 'the Yachtsman' because he was 'an Englishman returning from a cruise and dressed appropriately' – devised an ingenious system of placing all the chairs in a square with both a daytime and a nighttime position. This made it possible for the hostages to move around during the day 'without bumping into' what served as their beds.

Cojot and Lemoine kept busy by drawing up an additional list of sick or elderly people who, 'through weakness, ignorance, or timidity, had not made themselves known the first time'. They included Russell's travelling companion George Good who suffered from a heart condition and had failed to notice the first list being drawn up, and an old woman 'who had simply been in the toilet at the time'.

1230hrs GMT, Jerusalem, Israel

B y mid-afternoon, having already met that day with his Cabinet, the ministerial committee and the chief of staff, Yitzhak Rabin joined Shlomo Avineri, the director-general of the Foreign Ministry, at the Knesset's Foreign Affairs and Security Committee to report on the diplomatic efforts to free the hostages.

'We have not made an official approach to the United Nations,' explained Rabin, 'because we don't want to relieve France of responsibility for the passengers of the Air France plane. But we have made a personal approach to Kurt Waldheim, the secretary-general, in the hope that he will put pressure on Amin to intervene.'

Asked about the position of the other governments involved, he admitted that the official German position not to release its Baader–Meinhof prisoners was 'troubling' and made it even harder for Israel to achieve a peaceful solution.

Returning to the nearby Ministry of Foreign Affairs, Avineri was called in to a meeting with his boss, Yigal Allon, who was wondering which member of the diplomatic community to approach. 'What about Kissinger?' asked Allon, referring to the US secretary of state. 'Do you think he might help?'

Avineri nodded, and after a brief discussion Allon dictated an urgent cable to Simcha Dinitz, the Israeli ambassador in Washington, instructing him to enlist Kissinger's support. Kissinger could help to put pressure on Amin, said Allon, by contacting President Anwar Sadat of Egypt who was known to have friendly relations with Amin and reservations about the use of terror. Allon added: 'Suggest you also ask Kissinger to activate his friends among African leaders. They will meet Amin at the end of this week at a conference of the Organization of African Unity in Mauritius.'

1300hrs GMT, Entebbe International Airport, Uganda

F aiz Jaber strode into the large hall that held the non-Israelis, picked up the loud hailer and demanded: 'Which one of you is Nahum Dahan?'

'I am,' responded the young French-born Jew who, like Jean-Jacques Mimouni, was now living in Israel.

Jaber marched over to Dahan, whose strained face betrayed his nervousness. 'You're Israeli, aren't you?' demanded Jaber in English.

Dahan shook his head. 'Je suis français.'

'Don't lie to me,' snarled Jaber. 'Your mother has an Israeli passport and we've found your Israeli identity papers. We know you live in Israel. So you must be a member of the IDF. Are you?'

'Je ne comprend pas,' persisted Dahan.

Michel Cojot was called over to translate the questions from English into French, but still Dahan answered every inquiry about his connection to the IDF in the negative. Eventually Jaber lost his patience. 'Do you speak English or not?'

'Non.'

This was too much for Jaber. 'Come with us.'

Dahan was led at gunpoint to a small adjacent room that the terrorists used as a dormitory. There he was asked again if he spoke English. His answer was the same.

'You're a damned liar!' roared Jaber, pulling Dahan from his chair and throwing him to the ground. Dahan screamed as he was kicked and punched.

After what seemed an eternity, the blows ceased and Jaber told Dahan that he would not be left in peace until he had told them everything they wanted to know. Dahan was then taken into the Israeli room and put behind a desk that the terrorists had set up near the exterior door. Given a pencil and some paper, he was instructed to write down everything he could remember about his life in Israel and the IDF. 'You won't leave this desk,' warned Jaber, 'until we're satisfied.'

1330hrs GMT, Tel Aviv, Israel

With time running out, Kuti Adam sent out urgent orders for two officers just back from the Sinai to report to his office in the Kirya. The first to arrive was Colonel Shai Tamari, the deputy chief of the Special Operations Division. Briefed on the progress made so far by Ehud Barak's team, Tamari was told to set up a separate team to 'collect together the action ideas' for a mission at Entebbe 'and organize them into a plan'. Similar instructions were given to Brigadier-General Dan Shomron, the chief of the Infantry and Paratroop Command, who, like Tamari, had just returned to Tel Aviv. Adam's intention was, in effect, to set up three separate teams in competition with each other in the hope that at least one would come up with a viable operation. Tamari, however, was given overall responsibility for coordinating the plans.

The objective of the teams, as outlined by Adam, was to 'rescue the hostages and exterminate the terrorists and anyone who disrupts the execution of the operation', such as Ugandan soldiers. The problems that needed to be overcome included: missing details about the airport, including the exact location of where the hostages were being held, their guarding arrangements and so on; the problem of refuelling the C-130 transport planes, given that only two 'were capable of flying there and back without refuelling, and this with only a small number of soldiers'; and the extent to which the Ugandans were involved in the hijacking.

But the assumption, at this stage, was 'that once the terrorists are killed the Ugandans would release the hostages'. With that in mind, the favoured option was still 'to free the hostages by killing the terrorists, and leaving them and the operation troops in Entebbe'.

Barak's team hoped to achieve this by paradropping Zodiac inflatables and soldiers from the Unit and Shayetet 13 into Lake Victoria. To prepare for this they scheduled a practice jump into the Mediterranean for Wednesday afternoon. 'We're leaving tonight,' Betser told one of his squad commanders. 'Get ready for a sortie that includes a flight, a drop and swimming freestyle among alligators.' But the Unit's drop was cancelled after some of the naval commandos' Zodiacs exploded on impact, and thereafter they concentrated on the three remaining plans: 'stealing across Lake Victoria from Kenya; pretending to be a civilian plane carrying the free international terrorists in a negotiated exchange; or as Benny Peled suggested from the start – airlifting a thousand troops to Entebbe'.

The latter option did not convince Muki Betser. 'But it's too many,' he kept saying to his fellow planners. 'If we want to keep the element of surprise on our side, we need to arrive in a more compact formation. The more elements involved in the mission, the more likely something will go wrong.' Meanwhile Betser kept his absent commanding officer, Yoni Netanyahu, constantly updated on the discussions in the Pit. 'Listen,' he told him by phone that evening, 'the chances of this going through are pretty slim.'

'Is it worth my coming?' asked Netanyahu.

'I don't think so. Believe me, what you're doing now is much more important. The Unit's represented here, and outside of us sitting here and planning, there's absolutely nothing going on. In any case, I'm keeping you posted.'

As the debate over the most effective plan continued, word reached Israel via radio reports from Uganda and Paris that the terrorists had agreed to release some of the hostages 'as a gesture of goodwill'. None of them, however, was Israeli. They had been separated from the others and were being kept in Uganda. The news was for Betser and his colleagues both a worry and an opportunity. It reminded them of Nazi methods and was proof that Israel was now 'alone'.

On the other hand, it was obvious that the freed hostages might be able to provide important intelligence and it was decided to send a trusted officer to Paris to interview them. The natural choice was Major Amiram Levine, Military Intelligence's director of operations and a man who had risen through the ranks of the Unit. He 'understood intuitively' the team's 'planning needs for a break-in at the airport' and could be trusted to know 'what to ask to get the answer' it needed.

Before catching the early-evening El Al flight to Paris, Levine changed into civilian clothes and was provided with an intelligence kit by Amnon Biran. It included a list of the 'essential information' that the team required and a set of drawings based on the Solel Boneh blueprints of Entebbe Airport. He was also given strict instructions to avoid being seen in Paris by General 'Gandhi' Ze'evi, who had been sent there from London to coordinate the diplomatic efforts to free the hostages. If Ze'evi spotted Levine at Orly Airport he 'would immediately understand that a military option was being planned' and that might affect his judgement during the negotiations and possibly alert the French. 'No matter what,' Levine was told, 'don't let Gandhi see you.'

1400hrs GMT, London, United Kingdom

Unaware that Dora Bloch and Ilan Hartuv held British passports as dual Anglo-Israeli nationals (and that the former was travelling on hers), or that British-born Isabella Poignon was a dual national, officials at the Foreign Office in London were still assuming that only two of the Air France hostages – Tony Russell and George Good – were their direct responsibility. Yet they were keeping a close eye on events in East Africa nonetheless, not least because of Britain's long colonial association with Uganda and shared security concerns with the other NATO countries involved.

The mandarin with particular responsibility for the crisis was Frank Wheeler, head of the FCO's Near East and North African Department. During Wednesday afternoon he received a memo from David Colvin, the first secretary at the UK Embassy in Paris, which contained a highly controversial theory of who was behind the hijacking.

'A contact in the Euro-Arab Parliamentary Association rang me on 29 June,' wrote Colvin, 'to say that according to his information, the hijack was the work of the PFLP, with help from the Israeli Secret Service, the Shin Beit [sic]. The operation was designed to torpedo the PLO's standing in France and to prevent what they see as a growing rapprochement between the PLO and the Americans. Their nightmare is that after the November [US presidential] elections, one will witness the imposition in the Middle East of a *Pax Americana*, which will be to the advantage of the PLO (who will gain international respectability and perhaps the right to establish a state on evacuated territories) and to the disadvantage of the Refusal Front [including the PFLP] (who will be squeezed right out in any overall peace settlement and will lose their raison d'être) and Israel (who will be forced to evacuate the occupied territory). Hence the unholy alliance of the hijacking. My contact said that the PFLP had attracted all sorts of wild elements, some of whom had been planted by the Israelis.'

It was an intriguing conspiracy theory – Israel collaborating with its arch-enemy, the PFLP, to scupper a potential PLO-sponsored peace settlement that would be to the disadvantage of both – but not one that the experienced Wheeler was prepared to take seriously.

1430hrs GMT, Tel Aviv, Israel

'We have to formulate a common line of action,' said the speaker to the tense and weeping audience in the law association's main auditorium, 'and, as necessary, pressure the responsible people to obtain the release of our dear ones.'

This first meeting of the relatives of the Israeli hostages had been organized by law professor Yosef Gross, the brother of Baruch who was being held with his wife Ruthie and six-year-old son Shay in Entebbe. It quickly became apparent that the relatives wanted only one thing: the return of their loved ones at any cost.

'We demand the release of our families,' screamed one woman, 'no matter what price asked of the government.'

'Principles don't interest me,' shouted another. 'I want my family back, safe and well.'

'If we don't use force, nothing will be done,' said a third. 'Let's go to the Prime Minister's Office in Jerusalem and demonstrate.'

'Yes, we'll present an ultimatum to Rabin. If he doesn't see us straight away, we'll start a hunger strike.'

Finally Gross intervened. 'All right, there is pain in our hearts, but we must use our heads. All these suggestions, they're exactly what the terrorists want us to do. Demonstrations will only work against us in the end.'

Ignoring the speaker the distraught relatives left the auditorium, determined to take matters into their own hands.

1500hrs GMT, Entebbe International Airport, Uganda

Faiz Jaber grabbed the six or seven pages that Nahum Dahan had pencil-written in French and got one of the hostages to translate it for him. It was, he discovered, a long and repetitive account of how Dahan had lived for many years in a kibbutz picking grapefruit. 'This is not what we want!' screamed Jaber, his chin thrust into Dahan's face. 'We want to know all about Israel. We want to know where the bases are. We want the name of your general!'

When Dahan failed to answer, Jaber had him taken to the adjacent room where he was slapped in the face, punched and had his fingers twisted back. A gun was placed against his chest, but still Dahan refused to tell the terrorists what they wanted to hear.

Eventually they gave up and took him back to the desk in the Israeli room where he was told to write another 'report' – only this time it had to be genuine. 'When you finish it is your choice,' he was told. 'But you won't sleep until you do.'

1700hrs GMT, Jerusalem, Israel

Yitzhak Rabin had called a meeting of the Newspaper Editors' Committee – a body that had been established to keep the editors of Israel's most influential newspapers up to date with the latest security issues – at the Knesset building to prepare the ground for Israel's possible capitulation to the terrorists. In particular, he wanted an assurance from the editors that they would not print stories that implied he had caved in to pressure from the hostages' families.

'There is no way out of this crisis,' he told the editors seated round the Cabinet table, 'without some kind of trauma. If there is no concession, then we must expect a massacre of Israelis. We cannot prevent it, and must not blind ourselves to the possibility.'

'Is it clear,' asked one of the editors, 'that they will put the passengers to death?'

Rabin nodded. 'We are talking about Wadie Haddad's men. I wouldn't like anyone to delude himself about the brutality of that group. They are not above any abomination.'

Having assured the editors that, despite their public pronouncements to the contrary, both Germany and France would probably back any decision Israel made, he turned to the emotive issue of the hostages' relatives.

'There is going to be,' he said, 'an assembly of all the hostage family members, demanding that the government begins negotiations. I've asked the radio and television stations not to interview them and not to publish this story. I think the extremists among them wished to protest near my house and outside the Prime Minister's Office. I know some of them have already made a direct approach to the French Embassy. They sent me a telegram, asking: "Do the dead bodies of army soldiers justify the release of terrorists, while the saving of the lives of our relatives doesn't?"* One thing is certain: it will be a disaster if the world thinks that we've been pressurized by the families to surrender to terrorists. This information cannot be published.'

The first man to respond was Shalom Rosenfeld, the editor-in-chief and co-founder of Israel's most popular Hebrew daily newspaper, *Maariv*. 'We can't,' he said, 'prevent a feature article in the newspaper

---

* The telegram was referring to the deal between Israel and Egypt after the Yom Kippur War for the release of terrorists in Israeli jails in return for the bodies of Israeli soldiers killed by Egyptian forces.

calling on the government to surrender. It's a legitimate opinion, even though I reject it.'

More sympathetic to the plight of the hostages' families was Hannah Zemer, editor-in-chief of *Davar* and the first female to assume control of a major Israeli newspaper. Born in Slovakia, a survivor from Ravensbrück concentration camp (though many of her family had perished in the Holocaust), she thought that every effort should be made to save Israeli lives. 'Even in this case,' she asked Rosenfeld, 'when the government's surrender will prevent seventy-seven Jews from being blown up in an aeroplane?'

This comment prompted Gershom Schocken, the legendary German-born editor-in-chief of *Haaretz* (a post he had held for thirty-seven years), to inquire about the ethnicity of the hostages. He clearly had in mind the example of Ma'alot a couple of years earlier when Golda Meir's government had been accused of authorizing the disastrous rescue attempt because most of the hostages were young Sephardic Jews from North Africa and not the more influential Ashkenazi from Eastern Europe.

Rabin bristled. 'As far as Israel is concerned,' he responded, 'I haven't checked the ethnicity. Anyway, it doesn't interest me. Usually people of scanty means can't afford to travel round the world. So it's the group of people who don't have much money – and it doesn't matter what their ethnicity is – who aren't there.'

Irked by the implication that most Sephardim were poor, Shocken responded: 'There are wealthy people of North African origin.' But he knew that Rabin was right: the Ashkenazi Jews were generally better off than the Sephardim, and were probably the dominant group among the hostages. Was this why, he wondered, the government was so sensitive to the political pressure that their relatives could apply?

1900hrs GMT, Glilot, Israel

Following his meeting with Adam, Brigadier-General Dan Shomron was keen to begin planning a possible rescue. But first he had to fulfil a longstanding engagement to interview newly graduated officers of the IDF Command and Staff College at Glilot, north of Tel Aviv, for posts in his command. To save time after the interviews, therefore, he summoned his planning group to meet at the college at 9 p.m. There were three men present: Shomron and Lieutenant-Colonels Ivan Oren and Amnon Biran, both of whom had attended the earlier planning meetings chaired by Ehud Barak. Neither they nor Shomron were convinced by Barak's preferred plan to 'parachute 12 fighters into Lake Victoria' from where they would 'get on to dinghies, reach the terminal, enter and kill the terrorists, and then we'd see what would happen'.

Shomron's chief objection was that there were 'two points with no answers: the one is the idea to sneak in through the swamps – indeed if someone gets spotted there's a lot of time to kill all the hostages, and then there are these twelve stuck there. The second issue is the question of evacuation. How will an evacuation be done while Idi Amin is not cooperating with us and there are Ugandan soldiers all around the terminal?' It was, he felt, 'a dud of a plan'.

It took two hours for Shomron, Oren and Biran to sketch out their own 'operational concept': they envisaged landing the IAF's two refuelling Hercules – with the ability to fly to Uganda and back – on the new runway from where an assault force would use 'innocent-looking vehicles that would fit in with the setting of the airport' to reach the Old Terminal, surprise and kill the terrorists and free the hostages. The intention was for the hostages to return to Israel on board the IAF's two tankers, though they needed to check with the IAF if it was possible to fly a Peugeot pick-up in a refuelling Hercules and return with the assault team and more than 200 hostages.

1900hrs GMT, Tel Aviv, Israel

While Shomron and his staff were working hard to come up with a viable rescue plan at Glilot, Rabin was meeting with General Gur and the ministerial committee in his Tel Aviv office, a small red-tiled building in the Kirya complex that, ironically, during the Second

World War had housed Germans suspected of espionage. It was normal for Israeli premiers to split their week between Jerusalem and Tel Aviv, holding meetings in the latter on Thursdays and Fridays. Thanks to the Entebbe crisis, and the need to be close to the Ministry of Defense, an extra Tel Aviv meeting had been scheduled for Wednesday evening.

They were gathered in the long Cabinet room, its walls empty of ornaments but for full-length portraits of the founders of Israel: Theodor Herzl and Chaim Weizmann. If Rabin felt intimidated by their gaze – as if they were judging his actions from beyond the grave – he did not show it. Instead he turned calmly to Gur, lit cigarette in hand, and asked: 'Motta, do we have a military option?'

Gur looked apologetic. 'We'll know by tomorrow at two in the afternoon. I'm sorry I don't yet have a military answer.'

'In that case, we must accept that the lack of a decision is in itself a decision. If we cannot rescue the hostages, we must assume they will be put to death when the ultimatum expires.'

The implication of this statement was obvious to all around the table. Without an alternative, they would have to consider releasing the prisoners the terrorists had named.

'I think,' said Rabin, assuming that the matter was settled, 'Gad and Amos should meet the families tonight, and try and calm them down.' The transport minister and the director-general of the Prime Minister's Office nodded in agreement.

'If there is no military option,' said one of the ministers, 'we should hear what has been done so far in the diplomatic field.'

All eyes turned to Yigal Allon, who explained that 'the French behaviour so far has been satisfactory'. He added that cables had gone out to Ambassador Dinitz in the United States to enlist the support of Henry Kissinger, and to Paris requesting pressure on African countries within France's sphere of influence. In addition Chaim Herzog, the Israeli ambassador to the United Nations, was making a personal appeal to Secretary-General Kurt Waldheim.

'What about the pope?' asked Rabin, tongue firmly in cheek.

Allon's deadly serious reply was that they were trying to get the pontiff to talk to Amin. 'After all, the Ugandan was recently received in audience in grand style – something which must have appealed to his ego. We should make good use of it.'

While on the subject of emissaries, Peres suggested sending his adviser Asher Ben-Natan, a former ambassador to France, to Paris to discuss a possible joint Israeli–French military operation. 'I do have a plan,' he insisted. 'It might work.' The advantage of cooperating with the French was that it would solve the problem of a return flight as the planes could refuel at Djibouti. Rabin, however, did not believe for a minute that President Giscard d'Estaing of France would be prepared to jeopardize French relations with black Africa to recover the hostages. There was, in any event, no guarantee that such a military operation would succeed; and for this reason, among others, France generally preferred to negotiate.

'Let us convene here tomorrow at seven forty-five,' said Rabin, ending the discussion. 'The full Cabinet will meet at eight-thirty.'

2100hrs GMT, Tel Aviv, Israel

At Rabin's suggestion, Gad Yaacobi and Amos Eiran spoke to the families of the hostages in a meeting at 11 p.m. that was 'difficult' and 'emotional'. Yaacobi explained that the government was 'sensitive' to the timetable set by the terrorists, and that its chief priority was to save the lives of the hostages. For obvious reasons he did not tell them that Rabin's mind was as good as made up and that it would soon agree to negotiations.

With the clock ticking inexorably towards the deadline of 2 p.m. on Thursday, the families were not interested in bland assurances. What they wanted to hear was that the government had abandoned every other consideration to get their relatives home safe and sound. This was not a promise that Yaacobi could give and the meeting broke up with little resolved and the families hurling insults.

Earlier, representatives of the families had met with the French ambassador to Israel, Jean Herly, and proposed that the French prime minister, Jacques Chirac, should fly to Entebbe and remain there until the hostages were released. When Herly said that that would not be possible, the families decided to take their anger and frustration out on their own government.

2105hrs GMT, Entebbe International Airport, Uganda

The arrival and distribution of more mattresses, blankets and towels meant it was past midnight before the first strip of lights in the large hall was turned off and the non-Israeli hostages went to bed. Next door in the Israeli room, on the other hand, all the lights were kept on and many had trouble dozing off. They could not stop thinking about the looming deadline and what it might bring – release or execution – and were further disturbed through the night by constant rustling sounds as people tossed and turned on the paper-covered mattresses. As they were brand new and destined for some of Uganda's tourist hotels, the hostages had been told not to remove their wrapping, and this constant crackling chorus was the result.

Still sleeping behind the bar on an old mattress, Claude Moufflet managed to get to sleep quite quickly. At 2.30 in the morning, however, he was woken by a tall, dark-haired young Frenchman he had dubbed 'the Flirt' for his persistent interest in the opposite sex. Before turning in, Moufflet had noted how the Flirt had taken his latest conquest to the semi-privacy of an L-shaped space behind three boxes at the back of the room. Now, it transpired, the new rustling mattress had made it impossible for them to make love. 'Hey,' said the thwarted lothario to a groggy Moufflet, 'do you want to swap mattresses? You understand my problem? The paper makes too much noise.'

Moufflet nodded his acquiescence and got up. 'Thanks, you're really kind,' said the Flirt, a comment echoed by his companion. Leaving them to it, Moufflet went to stretch out in their 'bedroom' where, not disturbed too much by the noise of the paper, he went rapidly back to sleep.

At 5 a.m., Moufflet was again woken – this time by someone lying down next to him. It was the companion of the Flirt who, for reasons

Moufflet did not care to speculate, had deserted her lover in the middle of the night. After a cursory 'Excuse me', she went to sleep.

2105hrs GMT, Tel Aviv, Israel

Returning to his Ministry of Defense office tired and dispirited, Shimon Peres wanted nothing more than to close his eyes and sleep. But his fear of the consequences if Rabin went ahead and negotiated with the terrorists made him determined to try every last option. One was to appeal to Amin directly, and for this he needed Burka Bar-Lev.

Urgently summoned to the Kirya, Bar-Lev was again given an office with a phone and told to call Amin. When he finally got through it was just after midnight in Uganda. Peres listened in to the call on an extension.

'I've passed on your advice to the government through a friend,' said Bar-Lev, referring to their earlier conversation. 'They said they accept your advice and will act on it, through the French government, as you proposed. Now I'm trying to find a way to visit you.'

'If you come,' replied Amin, 'you'll be at home because you're my good friend. No one will harm you.'

Bar-Lev thanked the president and asked him to 'take every possible step to make sure that nothing happens to the hostages' until he reached Uganda.

Amin's response made Bar-Lev's blood run cold. 'I am now with the leader of the Palestinian "Popular Front". He's only just arrived. He is the man who decides. The man I negotiated with previously was their number two. Now the right man has arrived. Forty minutes ago he told me that he won't change his decision, if he doesn't receive a reply by tomorrow.'

The 'leader' that Amin had mentioned could only be Wadie Haddad himself. If he was indeed in Kampala – and Bar-Lev and the listening Peres had no reason to doubt it – then it did not augur well. Haddad was known to be a ruthless enemy of Israel who would have no qualms about killing Jews if his demands were not met.

'Your Excellency,' said Bar-Lev, a little panicked, 'I'm doing everything I can to come and see you. Perhaps I can help. When I heard the news on the radio, I said: "Now my friend Idi Amin Dada has a great opportunity, a chance to do something really great. Everyone will talk about him." Please stop the bloodshed. I'll try to come and find another solution.'

Amin made it clear, once again, that events were beyond his control. 'But they've moved 145 Jews together, and they said they will surround them with high explosives, so there must be an immediate answer.'

Bar-Lev reminded Amin that he was only a 'private individual', but one who had always given him 'good advice'. He added: 'This is your country and you are the president and you have the power. If something happens, you'll be blamed; and if you save them, you'll be a holy man. What is the situation, your Excellency?'

'They refused,' said Amin, referring to the terrorists. 'They surrounded everyone and they say they can blow up all the hostages and all the Ugandan Army around them.'

How, asked Bar-Lev, could they have brought in enough explosives to do that by plane? The problem for the Israeli government was that the terrorists wanted the release of 'murderers' who had 'killed women and children'. He added: 'I don't believe that if someone tried to kill you, you would let him go. It's not easy to persuade people here to release murderers.'

Amin said he understood, but the situation was complicated by the fact that 'these people brought complete charges of TNT even on their bodies'.

Playing for time, Bar-Lev asked Amin if he could keep the terrorists 'quiet for a couple of days' to give him time to get there.

The answer was no. 'They won't wait for me. They said they will commit suicide with the hostages. They've already prepared everything to press the button, to blow up everything with themselves.'

Sensing an opportunity to obtain vital intelligence, Bar-Lev asked: 'Where are the people, in the hotel or in the plane? Where are they sleeping?'

Amin obliged. 'In the Old Terminal of Entebbe. We built a modern terminal. The old one is just a building, and that's where they're holding all the hostages. There's no plane there. They asked us to remove all the planes. All air force personnel are now out of Entebbe. They've put high explosives around everything.'

'Where is the French plane?'

'Close to me. They have some people in it with high explosives, and they're prepared to blow it up. If you can persuade your government to release those people, the ones you call criminals, it's better to save the lives of 200 people. They said they are going to kill them all. They'll start by blowing up the plane, then they'll kill everybody with high explosives. They said that if any plane comes to Uganda, they'll automatically blow up everything. They want to negotiate through France. I told them that I have some friends in Israel, like you, General Dayan, even the prime minister, that I can negotiate with them, but they said they want only the French government.'

'Remember, sir,' said Bar-Lev, a trace of desperation in his voice, 'you have a great opportunity, given to you by God.'

Amin seemed more interested in speaking for the terrorists. 'Tell your government they must put pressure on the Kenyan government to release the prisoners they caught. Otherwise something terrible will happen to Kenya. The leader of the Palestinians told me that if I can get in touch with you, I must tell you about Kenya. If not Kenya will be terribly punished.'

'Good, sir. I'll do the best I can, but I'm a private person. I saw a great opportunity for you to go down in history as a great man, a holy man. I'll try to do what you asked.'

'Tell your government,' said Amin, satisfied that Bar-Lev would do his bidding, 'I'd like to see you in a very important position.'

'Thank you very much and good night, sir.'

Peres nodded with satisfaction as he put down the extension phone. The substance of Amin's message to Bar-Lev – that there was nothing he could do to prevent the terrorists from killing the hostages if their demands were not met by noon the following day – was pretty much what he had expected to hear. The tone and content of Amin's words, on the other hand, had revealed vital intelligence that might prove crucial to any rescue mission. Peres felt certain, for example, that Wadie Haddad was not only in Kampala but actually present in the room while Amin took the call. And if that was true then it was extremely likely that the Ugandans were actively assisting the terrorists to achieve their aims. This meant, in turn, that any potential rescue mission would need enough firepower to take on the Ugandan Army and, ideally, the means to return the hostages to Israel. A simple commando mission to kill the terrorists would no longer suffice.

Amin had also confirmed where the hostages were being held – in the Old Terminal building – adding that the terrorists had surrounded them with high explosives that they would ignite if an attempt was made to rescue them. This latter threat did not convince Peres any more than it had convinced Bar-Lev. Why was Amin putting his own soldiers in jeopardy if he truly believed the explosives existed? It did not add up.

2155hrs GMT, Orly, France

It was almost midnight when the replacement Air France plane landed at Orly Airport near Paris and the forty-seven released hostages were escorted by airport officials and police to the VIP lounge where their relatives and the French foreign minister, Jean Sauvagnargues, were waiting to greet them.

Tears flowed as families were reunited with loved ones they had feared they would never see again; for some of the hostages, however, their joy was tempered by the memory of those they had left behind. Olivier Cojot raced into the arms of his mother and was so overcome with emotion that he forgot all about the note he was carrying in the turn-ups of his jeans. Julie Aouzerate – still wearing her halter-neck summer dress, headscarf and thick-rimmed glasses – hugged a pretty granddaughter. Meanwhile a smiling Sauvagnargues – a man who a couple of years earlier had caused outrage in Israel when he was photographed shaking Yasser Arafat's hand – worked the room, shaking hands, stroking the heads of children and kissing Annie Bracker's toddler.

The celebrations were interrupted by a message over the public address system. 'Ladies and gentlemen,' said an anonymous government official, 'President Valéry Giscard d'Estaing has asked me to convey his congratulations. He shares in the rejoicing at your return from captivity. The president is happy that your suffering is at an end. He hopes, with all his heart, that the other hostages will soon also be free like you.'

Sauvagnargues repeated the sentiment to a few press reporters who had broken through the police cordon. 'All our hearts are full of anxiety,' he told them. 'This is not the end of the affair.'

Meanwhile a group of unidentified men were working their way through the throng, taking notes and writing down names and addresses. They were all members of the French and Israeli security services, and their task was to single out the hostages who were likely to provide the most useful intelligence. They chose five, including Olivier Cojot and 'a veteran officer of the French army, who spent his three days at Entebbe making mental notes of all the military options, wanting revenge on the terrorists who so humiliated him and his fellow passengers'.

Olivier was interviewed by 'some Israeli people' – almost certainly Amiram Levine and agents from the Mossad – in a room at the airport. Amid all the emotion of his homecoming, he continued to forget to mention the vital document that he was carrying in his turn-ups.* But he made up for this omission by answering all the questions he was asked as accurately as he could, helped by his prodigious memory and the fact that the terrorists had given him more freedom to wander about the Old Terminal than they had the adults.

Many of the questions were very precise. Which way do the doors open? How high is the grass? Do the terrorists possess explosives? To this last vital query, Olivier said he could not be sure. They certainly had grenades, and had *claimed* they had explosives; but he had not actually seen any with his own eyes. He was not in any doubt, however, that the Ugandans were assisting the terrorists. 'Of that,' he told them, 'there's no question.'

---

* Olivier did not remember the note in his turn-ups until after it had been destroyed in the next wash.

Interviewed later in his home, the 'veteran officer' poured out another 'gold mine of details' for Amiram Levine to relay back to Barak and the other planners over a scrambled phone line. It included information about the 'separation' of the hostages into Israelis and non-Israelis – though this was generally understood as Jews and non-Jews – the layout of the terminal, the habits of the terrorists and their close relationship with Amin. 'The Ugandans definitely are working with the hijackers,' Amiram quoted the Frenchman as saying. 'They are there to prevent the hostages from escaping.' The good news, according to Amiram, was that 'the last thing the terrorists expect is for us to show up'.

One revealing interview not conducted by the Israelis was that of a British-born US citizen, Carole Anne Taylor, an 'articulate and well-educated' thirty-three-year-old graduate student in comparative literature at Harvard University, who had been released with her six-year-old son Eric. Prior to the hijacking the pair had been on holiday in Israel and Greece with Taylor's Jewish partner Sanford Freedman, another Harvard graduate student. Freedman was still in Uganda. Quizzed by US Embassy officials – most likely the CIA station chief for Paris – Taylor said the hijackers had assembled bombs on the aircraft, using 'gunpowder' packed in metal candy boxes. All the passengers had agreed that security was 'very lax' at Athens Airport. She thought the most significant event after the hijacking was the separation into two groups – Israeli and non-Israeli – on 30 June. After it there was a 'distinct change in tone and substance of the announcements made by the hijackers who spoke more harshly and abruptly to the Israeli group'.

The hijackers were made up of 'three different and distinct groups': the two Germans, 'Basil' and 'Girl Number 54', who were 'very articulate, personable, sympathetic and speak good English'; two Palestinians, 'Number 39' and 'Haifa', who were 'very young, determined, speak very broken English, and get along fairly well with the passengers, even some Israelis, by trying to be helpful'; and the three Arabs who were 'very rough in appearance, carry machine guns and grenades' (whereas the others were armed mostly with 'crude looking handguns'), and 'make no attempt to propagandize and make friends'. Yet she did not see any prospect of them falling out as all seemed determined to achieve their aims.

The living conditions of the hostages were not good, according to Taylor: the women's toilets had stopped working on the 29th; only dirty tap water was available to drink; food was inadequate; and most of the hostages were beginning to suffer from 'mild dysentery' (Taylor and her son had a touch of diarrhoea). The only hostage with medical training, as far as she was aware, was Dr David Bass, the American-born surgeon who was working in an Israeli hospital. But he seemed 'withdrawn, bitter' and was 'making no real effort to help', and other hostages resented his 'lack of assistance'. Many were 'showing signs of mental strain'.

Of the thirteen American hostages still in Uganda, most were 'young, college-educated and bearing up well except for occasional crying fits'. They had, said Taylor, established a fairly good rapport with the Germans, 'engaging in dialectic discussions on revolution and general topics'. This had, however, begun to 'break down' when the Israelis were separated from the others and Taylor's partner Freedman and another man 'nearly had serious trouble with the hijackers' when they protested.

As Taylor and her son had originally intended to spend two months in Paris with Freedman before returning to the United States, her plan was to wait there in the hope that he would soon be released. She would call her parents in England and let them know she was safe.

2200hrs GMT, Tel Aviv, Israel

As Ivan Oren finished speaking, his superior Colonel Shai Tamari leaned back in his chair. Tamari had spent the last thirty minutes of the meeting in his office in the Kirya listening to Oren sketch out the rescue mission that he had cooked up a couple of hours earlier with Shomron and Biran: a plan that hinged on the use of the IAF's two refuelling Hercules to fly a rescue force and vehicles to Entebbe and return with the hostages.

'It has possibilities,' said Tamari after a pause, 'but it needs more work. At the moment it sounds vague and half baked. You still don't know, for example, about the carrying capacity of a Karnaf tanker [refuelling Hercules] and whether it can bear the extra load that you envisage. Then there's the question of whether the Uganda troops are likely to be hostile or not. If they are, can the tankers carry enough of our troops to deal with them, and still have room to bring back the hostages? This is the sort of fine detail we have to be certain about before we can push this plan upstairs. Understand?'

Oren nodded. Though a little crestfallen, he could see the sense of Tamari's words.

'Flesh it out and bring it back to me tomorrow morning.'

'Yes, sir.'

2240hrs GMT, Washington DC, United States

At 6.40 p.m., Ambassador Simcha Dinitz picked up the phone in his office in the Israeli Embassy in Washington and asked to be put through to Henry Kissinger at the State Department.

A tall, dapper man with large black-rimmed glasses, a pencil moustache and slicked-down black hair, the forty-seven-year-old Dinitz had trained as a diplomat at Georgetown University and served as chef de cabinet to Prime Minister Golda Meir before his appointment to succeed Yitzhak Rabin as head of the Israeli Embassy in Washington – the 'most important post in Israeli diplomacy' – in 1973. Dinitz played a key role in organizing shipments of US arms to Israel during the Yom Kippur War, and had since used his 'charming effrontery, ever mitigated by his warmhearted sense of humor', to bind his country ever closer to the United States. He got on particularly well with Kissinger, the bespectacled German-born Jew and former Harvard academic who had been running US foreign policy since 1969. Kissinger was a figure of world renown – having a few years earlier brokered both an anti-Soviet Sino-American pact and a ceasefire and the withdrawal of US forces from Vietnam, the latter earning him a Nobel

Peace Prize – and Dinitz was eager to enlist his support for Israel's increasingly frantic diplomatic efforts to encourage Idi Amin to intercede on behalf of the hostages. It helped that Kissinger liked Dinitz 'enormously', finding him 'honest and honorable' and a man he could trust to 'give unvarnished accounts of Israeli domestic maneuvering' on the one hand, and to report the US government's 'views equally accurately to the Israeli cabinet'. They would have spoken sooner about Entebbe if the American had not been away from Washington on official business.

'Hello,' said Kissinger.

'Welcome back,' said Dinitz, wasting no time on an explanation of why he was calling. 'I just got a call from Israel. We have finished a meeting regarding the plane. They asked me to ask you to help on the following matters. Maybe there is a possibility for you to send an urgent message to Sadat asking him to appeal to Amin to ask that nothing happen to the passengers. Also that he won't let the hijacked Air France plane take off because we feel they will release some of the passengers and take the Israelis somewhere else.'

Kissinger did not hesitate. 'We will do it.'

Pleased, Dinitz mentioned that the Israeli government had also contacted Kurt Waldheim, secretary-general of the United Nations, and asked him to intercede. Could the United States, asked Dinitz, put similar pressure on Waldheim?

'We have done that.'

'The third thing,' said Dinitz, aware that he might be pushing his luck, 'is Rabin asked me to ask you if you know of any African country who would have contacts with Amin?'

'We have approached Mobutu on it,' responded Kissinger, referring to the flamboyant and authoritarian president of Zaire – a former Belgian colony in Central Africa previously known as the Congo – who was a close ally of the United States thanks to his anti-communist stance.

Dinitz seemed disappointed. 'You think this is the only one?'

'That is the only one we know of.'

After a moment's thought, the Israeli agreed. 'I think that is correct because the Kenyans don't . . .'

159

Kissinger finished his sentence. 'No, they are in danger from Uganda.'

'Yes. Those people they [the hijackers] want from the Kenyans,' said Dinitz, 'were those that were arrested when they were trying to shoot down the El Al plane when it was in Kenya. This is all we can think of. If you have any suggestions we would be grateful.'

Kissinger reassured him. 'We will approach the Egyptians and if Waldheim hasn't gone out we will do that too.'

'I am very grateful and sorry to bother you.'

'No, no, not at all.'

'Thank you, Mr Secretary.'

'Okay. Bye.'

Unbeknown to both Dinitz and Kissinger, the French approach to the Egyptians had already borne fruit in that Anwar Sadat's government had arranged for a special military plane to fly Hanni al-Hassan, a senior official of the PLO, down to Entebbe in the hope that he could end the hijacking peacefully. But though al-Hassan's plane was given permission to land, no sooner had it done so than it was ordered to take off again by the Ugandan authorities before al-Hassan had had a chance to speak to either the terrorists or Amin. The mission had come to nothing.

DAY 5: THURSDAY 1 JULY 1976

0330hrs GMT, Entebbe International Airport, Uganda

Claude Moufflet woke at dawn. Beside him the Flirt's former companion was still sleeping soundly, as were most of the other hostages in the main hall of the Old Terminal building. He decided to get some air and picked his way noiselessly between the bodies to where Wilfried Böse was guarding one of the large hall's two external exits (the other had been barricaded).

Sensing Moufflet's antagonism, Böse kept their conversation brief, nodding his permission for the Frenchman to go outside. It was a beautiful morning, crisp and cold, and Moufflet moved a little away from the enclosed grass area at the front of the building, enjoying his peaceful solitude. Eventually a second hostage sat down next to him: Colin Hardie, the fifty-five-year-old general manager of the *Christchurch Star* newspaper who was travelling with his wife Nula.

More comfortable covering stories than being part of them, Hardie had nevertheless coped admirably with his enforced incarceration and Moufflet appreciated his friendly demeanour and quiet stoicism. They chatted about many things: the fine weather ('beautiful and fresh'); their living conditions in the terminal ('quite rudimentary but, under the circumstances, more or less satisfactory'); their travelling companions ('an unusual lot'); and the terrorists, their objectives, and the possible outcome of their adventure (on this last point they were undecided).

As they talked, Nola Hardie came out to join them. She wanted to check if the underwear she had washed the night before was dry; and when she found that it was not, she exclaimed: 'It doesn't look good at my age to be without pants or bra under my dress.'

The men laughed.

0500hrs GMT, Tel Aviv, Israel

Yitzhak Rabin was drinking coffee in the apartment that served as his official residence in Tel Aviv when he received a call from his chief aide, Amos Eiran. 'Prime Minister, I have bad news. The families of the hostages have broken through the gates at the Kirya, pushing aside the military police, and are waiting inside your office, demanding a meeting. Would you like *me* to speak to them?'

Rabin grunted. 'That's all we need. A sign to the world that we only agreed to negotiate because of pressure put on us by the families. But, yes, could you speak to them? Don't promise them anything because, as you know, the final decision has to be made by the Cabinet. Just tell them that we're doing everything we can to bring their loved ones back to them.'

'I will, Prime Minister.'

'Good. Now do you want to take some security people with you? Emotions are obviously running high and the meeting might turn violent.'

'No, Prime Minister, that won't be necessary,' said Eiran. 'It will probably just complicate the situation further.'

Fifteen minutes later, Eiran was regretting his decision to meet the families alone. He tried to explain the government's position, but nobody was listening. Angry and afraid, they shouted him down. One man even tried to punch him. 'We don't want an explanation,' cried one. 'Just tell us that you're accepting all the terrorists' demands and will release everyone on the list. We just want our people back home, and not to arrive in boxes.'

0500hrs GMT, Entebbe International Airport, Uganda

Breakfast arrived at the Old Terminal building in a bus at 8 a.m. and was distributed by one of two service teams that had been formed of crew and passenger volunteers, with a second team assigned to lunch. Claude Moufflet was part of this first team and, assisted by his new friend Gilles, a steward and a French doctor, he took plates and cutlery next door to the Israelis. There were, he realized after a careful count, eighty-three people in the smaller hall.

It occurred to him then that he and the others left in the large hall – the former departure lounge – were refusing, probably unconsciously, to call the smaller hall the 'Israeli room'. Instead they referred to it as the 'other room', and said things like 'Are they being served?' and 'What's happening over there?' Their suspicion that the Israelis had been singled out for 'special' treatment only increased their embarrassment, as did the knowledge that the hostages themselves had provoked the separation by demanding more space.

As Moufflet and his service team were not allowed to take food through to the 'other room', three or four Israelis came through the communication door to collect it. They seemed to be in good spirits.

0545hrs GMT, Tel Aviv, Israel

With just over six hours to go to the expiry of the ultimatum in Entebbe, the ministerial committee met shortly before 8 a.m. in Rabin's office in the Kirya. Attending were the six ministers and their aides, as well as Gur, Adam and the chief of Military Intelligence, Shlomo Gazit.

Rabin spoke first. 'Gentlemen,' he said with a frown, 'I have worrying news. The terrorists have carried out a selection. They have separated the Jews from the non-Jews. The non-Jews have been released. The Jewish hostages are threatened with execution. There is now absolutely no doubt that Idi Amin is eager to ingratiate himself with the Arabs and is fully cooperating with the terrorists. The ultimatum expires in just a few hours. So, again, I ask the chief of staff – Motta, do you have a military plan?'

'We are looking at three possible options,' said Gur. 'One is to launch a seaborne attack on the airport from Lake Victoria; the second is take the assault force in on a civilian plane pretending to carry the freed terrorists; and the third is to drop parachutists over Entebbe.'

He made no mention of Shomron's IDF Option because he had not yet been briefed about it.

After a pause, Rabin asked the crucial question: 'Are any of these plans operational? Can you recommend any of them to the government?'

'No.'

'In that case, since the terrorist ultimatum is scheduled to run out at two p.m. today, I intend to propose to the full Cabinet that we negotiate with the hijackers for the release of the hostages. We will negotiate through the French. If we are unable to rescue them by force we have no moral right to abandon them. We must exchange them for terrorists held here in our jails in Israel. Our negotiations will be in earnest, not a tactical ruse to gain time. And we will keep our side of any deal we strike.'

'I object,' said Peres, horrified that such a crucial decision had already been taken.

'I'm sure you do,' muttered Rabin.

Peres continued: 'We have never agreed in the past to free prisoners who have murdered innocent civilians. If we give in to the hijackers' demands and release terrorists, everyone will understand us but no one will respect us. If, on the other hand, we conduct a military operation to free the hostages, it is possible that no one will understand us, but everyone will respect us, depending, of course,' his voice dropped to a whisper, 'on the outcome of the operation.'

'For God's sake, Shimon,' responded Rabin angrily, his jaw set, 'our problem at the moment is not more of your heroic rhetoric. If you have a better proposal, let's hear it. What do you suggest? You know as well as I do that the relatives are stalking us day and night. They are beside themselves with fear, clamouring for us to make an exchange, and for good reason. What do they say? They say that Israel freed terrorists after the Yom Kippur War in exchange for the bodies of dead soldiers, so how can we refuse to free terrorists in exchange for living people, our own people, their loved ones, when their lives are in imminent danger?'

'There is an alternative,' said Peres. 'Last night we got a lot of very useful information from the released hostages in Paris. I propose that we use this information to cooperate with France in a joint military operation.'

Rabin waved his hand dismissively. 'If anyone wants to propose an operation of this kind, let him submit to the full vote of Cabinet. It's madness. There simply isn't enough time.'

'I agree,' said Allon. 'Let's concentrate on what's possible.'

'And not,' added Rabin, looking pointedly at Peres, 'on pie-in-the-sky dreams.'

Peres stood his ground. 'If we surrender to the hijackers it will create a potentially disastrous precedent. It isn't that I lack concern for the lives and safety of the hostages. On the contrary, I am concerned for the lives and safety of the passengers in the future.'

Rabin had heard enough. 'Who is in favour of advising the Cabinet that we begin negotiations with the terrorists?' He raised his hand, as did Allon, Yaacobi, Galili and Zadok. Reluctantly, Peres followed suit.

0600hrs GMT, Entebbe International Airport, Uganda

'Wake up!' shouted Jaber, shaking the prone Nahum Dahan roughly by the shoulder.

The hostage had been forced to write the report at the desk in the Israeli room for much of the night, and allowed to sleep by Brigitte Kuhlmann only as dawn was breaking. He had, as a result, missed breakfast and would have continued to doze if Jaber had let him. Opening his eyes he could see the chief terrorist clutching a photograph of him on a burned-out Syrian tank that he had forgotten was in his hand luggage. 'I have the evidence here,' yelled Jaber, waving the photo. 'You *are* in the Israeli Army. You must be a spy.'

'I've never been in the army,' insisted Dahan in French. 'Those photos are from a tour of the Golan Heights.'

'I don't believe you. Come with us.'

Knowing that he was about to be taken back to the interrogation room, Dahan refused to get up. So Jaber and one of the other terrorists grabbed him by the wrists and dragged him there. Placed in a chair, Dahan was confronted by Jaber and Abdur al-Samrai. The former snarled: 'You work for the Israelis, don't you? You're a spy. Tell us the truth or you won't live to regret it.'

When Dahan refused to answer, Jaber lost his temper and slammed his fist hard into the young Frenchman's face, knocking him to the floor. There he was kicked and punched repeatedly by al-Samrai, as Jaber asked: 'Do you want to live or die?'

After what seemed an eternity, the blows ceased and Jaber told Dahan that he would not leave the room until he had written in English a full account of his life in Paris before he emigrated to Israel. For an hour Dahan toiled in the little room, struggling to record his biography in a language he spoke but could not write. Eventually he was allowed a break to go to the toilet and en route appealed for help to both Ilan Hartuv in the Israeli room and Michel Bacos in the one beyond. 'You must do something,' Dahan implored. 'They think I'm a spy and are going to shoot me.'

Bacos immediately consulted Lemoine, Cojot and one or two others. Cojot's response was to ask if anyone really knew his nationality.

'He has a French passport,' responded Bacos, 'but physically he is very marked.'

He was implying that Dahan was obviously Jewish in his facial characteristics and that was the reason the terrorists suspected him of being Israeli and a possible spy. But to Cojot, whose own family had suffered from such off-hand remarks, this was a hugely insensitive comment that reminded him once again of the two faces of France: light and dark. 'I was crushed by that reply,' he wrote. 'It gave sustenance once again to a racial definition of nationality, thirty years after Vichy! The hostage in question would not have caused even a novice physiognomist to hesitate. But the sole objective of the members of this ephemeral and infamous profession of the Vichy era was to identify by facial features who was Jewish, not who was French. Besides, the man, like many Sephardim, was no less Arab in "type".'

Bacos did, however, get permission from the terrorists to speak to Dahan in the little room. There he advised him to be more coopera-tive and to act less suspiciously. 'Your attitude,' said Bacos, 'is not helping.'

The French pilot then approached the Peruvian to get assurances that Dahan would not suffer serious injury. 'What would you like me to say?' replied the moustached terrorist. 'If he lies to us each time then he has something to hide.'

Meanwhile, Dahan's inability to complete the task asked of him was punished by more beatings in the small room, his screams echoing round the Old Terminal. They stopped only when Jaber put a gun to his head. Convinced he was about to be killed, Dahan prayed silently to God. 'If you plan to do something, do it quickly because I have no strength left.'

Tears poured down Dahan's face as he waited for the end. It did not come. Jaber put down his gun and left the room.

Aware that Dahan was in mortal danger, Hartuv and other members of the informal Israeli committee – including Yitzhak David and Akiva Laxer – told the Peruvian that if he wasn't returned to their room they would go on hunger strike. (Bacos had earlier made the same plea.) This time it had the desired effect – probably because the terrorists were worried that word of this would reach the press – and Dahan was released. 'Go join the others,' he was told.

Though not a religious man, Dahan put his rescue down to God and made a promise that if he returned to Israel he would regularly attend the synagogue. The beatings had left him with two cracked ribs and no appetite for food, and it was the ever-selfless Jean-Jacques Mimouni who eventually coaxed him out of this depression by bringing him bananas and pieces of pineapple.

0700hrs GMT, Tel Aviv, Israel

Once the eighteen members of the Israeli Cabinet were seated round the conference table in the Prime Minister's Office, Rabin explained the decision of the ministerial committee. 'The IDF have not been able to come up with a military option in the short time still available to us,' he said, looking grave. 'Therefore our proposal is that we negotiate with the hijackers on their terms. Our reasoning is simple: we have no right to abandon the hostages. If we're unable to rescue them by force, we must exchange them for terrorists held in our country. These negotiations are not meant as a tactical ruse to gain time. We will negotiate in earnest, and Israel will keep her side of any bargain. Any comments?'

'Yes, Prime Minister,' said Gad Yaacobi. 'Last night around 11 p.m. I met with the passengers' families. To their credit I must say their mood was very calm and responsible. Most of them claimed that due to special circumstances an Israeli military operation is impossible so the only thing they demand is to begin negotiations.' This was a far from accurate summary of the meeting he and Amos Eiran had had with the families the night before – many of whom were far from calm – but Yaacobi was trying to strengthen Rabin's point that negotiation was their only option.

Peres, however, did not agree. 'The problem isn't simply the families' claims. It should be made clear that negotiations and surrendering will simply open the door to future terror attacks.'

'Who says?' asked Rabin.

'I do.'

'Then I ask you to clarify what you mean and tell us why.'

'Until now,' said Peres, 'the Americans haven't surrendered to terrorist blackmail because the Israelis were a world-class standard. If we surrender, there won't be any country in the world that will stand up against it. It will simply lead to more and more incidents.'

Rabin could barely contain his fury. 'Let me explain to you the situation as it stands. If we don't make a decision, that in itself is a decision, including everything that comes with it, all the question marks.'

This was too much for Yigal Allon who, from the start, had felt uneasy about negotiations. 'I am,' he said, 'against accepting the terror organization's terms, and I know this is a strong statement because we truly are putting people's lives at risk. These terrorists have shown before that in certain cases where the ultimatum was not heeded, they've carried out their threat.'

As with Peres's comments, Rabin was convinced that Allon was playing politics by making sure that, if the negotiations did not work out, his opposition to them was on the record. So he cut him short. 'I wish to be clear: we don't have time for evasions. The question is: are we fundamentally willing to enter in to negotiations or not? Please don't avoid answering this question.'

'Since anyone,' said Education Minister Aaron Yadlin, 'who saves an Israeli life is actually saving the entire world, and because I'd like to preserve the lives of the innocent Israelis caught up in this situation, I support any effort to save them, including negotiations.'

Minister without Portfolio Yisrael Galili, Rabin's right-hand man, agreed. 'I suggest the government begin negotiations immediately in order to save the hostages, while showing a readiness to free detainees. We don't need to elaborate which ones.'

'I second Galili's suggestion,' said Rabin, 'and for this reason: I'm not willing to explain to the public why in recent times we've traded 130 terrorists for corpses, including eight terrorists who were guilty of hostile destructive activity, including murder. I don't wish to explain to the Israel public or anyone else why we can barter for corpses but not live people.'

Peres shook his head. 'Precedents are not the problem. The problem is what happens in the future: the future of the Israeli people and the future of Israeli aeroplanes and aviation. We should be concerned with the fate of people here, of what will happen to this country and its status regarding hijacking, terror and so on, as well as the fate of those who have been taken hostage. Up till now, all of the terror organizations, apart from Wadie Haddad's, have outlawed the hijacking of planes, and this is chiefly because of Israel's strict and persistent stance.'

'Nonsense,' responded Rabin. 'Fatah stopped hijacking as part of a broader political decision to cease their operations abroad. It had nothing to do with Israel's strict stance.'

'You think so?' asked Peres sarcastically. 'I can guarantee that if Israel had surrendered every time it was blackmailed, Fatah would have continued with *all* its terror operations at home and abroad.'

Rabin could see no profit in continuing the discussion. 'I wish to know,' he said, scanning the faces round the table, 'whether anyone is opposed to Galili's suggestion. I don't want any misunderstandings on this issue. I propose that the government authorizes the ministerial team to continue our attempts to use all means to release the hostages, including the exchange of prisoners in Israel. We'll say "prisoners", but that doesn't mean accepting the terrorists' terms. We won't specify how many we'll release and what their names are. Those in favour of this offer, raise your hands.'

One by one the eighteen ministers raised their hands, even Peres and Allon.

'It's unanimous,' said Rabin. 'Thank you.'

'Could I just add,' said Peres, 'that I would like it recorded in the minutes that I've only agreed to negotiate because I regard it as a tactical measure to gain time. I still think a military solution is possible.'

'I feel the same,' said Shlomo Hillel, the minister of police.

'So be it. You should all clearly understand that the IDF will continue to seek a military option, but this in no way detracts from the earnestness of the decision we have just taken to negotiate. Now if there's nothing else I must inform the Foreign Affairs and Security Committee about our momentous decision. Could you all wait here until I return with their response.'

Rabin then left the room and entered a neighbouring office where the members of the committee – chiefly composed of leaders of the main opposition parties – were waiting. 'Gentlemen,' said Rabin, 'the Cabinet has just made the decision to open negotiations with the terrorists to exchange killers in our hands for the hostages.'

Many of the members started speaking at once, raising objections and concerns. 'We simply have no choice,' said Rabin, interrupting. 'We have no credible military option. The terrorists' ultimatum expires in a few hours' time, at two o'clock.'

'Mr Prime Minister,' said Menachem Begin, the Likud leader, 'may I request a brief interval for consultations with my colleagues?'

Rabin glanced at his watch. 'Yes, but please be quick. Time is running out. We have yet to relay our position to the French.'

This time Begin left the room with a handful of his deputies. His voice could just be heard telling them he didn't agree with negotiating with terrorists on principle, but that 'Jewish lives were at stake' and it was imperative to rescue them 'from execution'. They would, therefore, share in the 'public responsibility' for the decision to open negotiations.

After a few minutes they returned. 'Mr Prime Minister,' said Begin, 'this is not a partisan matter for debate between the coalition and the opposition. It is a national issue of the highest order. We, the opposition, shall support any decision the government adopts to save the lives of Jews. And we shall make our decision known to the public.'

'Thank you,' said Rabin, his eyes welling with tears. He personally regretted the decision to negotiate and Begin's support had provided him with a 'certain measure of relief'. Once Likud had made its position clear, the other members of the committee fell into line, though many of them had reservations.

When he returned to the Cabinet to report, Rabin noticed that Peres seemed taken aback by the opposition's compliance. 'It seems,' he remarked sarcastically to members of his staff as he left the meeting, 'Mr Begin's display of national responsibility descended on Mr Peres like a cold shower, cooling off his demagoguery. And now I must quickly inform the French to proceed with negotiations.'

That afternoon, the *New York Post* ran the headline: 'ISRAEL SURRENDERS!'

0730hrs GMT, Entebbe International Airport, Uganda

Unaware of the momentous decision that had been taken by the Israeli Cabinet 2,200 miles away in Tel Aviv, the hostages in the Old Terminal building were uneasily counting down the hours to the deadline.

One of them, however, was thinking of how he might bring the terrorists to justice by taking surreptitious photographs of them. Having arrived in the Old Terminal with a camera and a film hidden in his briefcase, Claude Moufflet had already taken four or five snaps of the main hall and two of the original hijackers, Wilfried Böse and Ali al-Ma'ati (wearing the red shirt and known to the hostages as either 'Ali' or 'Number 39'). Now, with the assistance of Gilles, who was sitting on the bar to keep him hidden, he sneaked a picture of the other Palestinian hijacker with the moustache and the yellow shirt, Khaled al-Khalili.

Moufflet was well aware that if he was caught in the act it might cost him his life. Some hostages who saw him do it were more concerned for their own welfare and told him not to be so reckless.

By now there was a constant trickle of male Israelis passing the bar area where Moufflet was based on their way to the toilets. Several young *sabras* – native-born Israelis – stopped to chat and explained that the hijacking was not directed against France. 'It is,' said one, 'between us and the Palestinians, and very soon you will be gone and it will be easy for our country to intervene. You have to understand that we are in a constant state of war.' He was saying, in effect, that it would be simpler for Israel to launch a military strike if only Israeli hostages were still being held (and therefore at risk of dying if the rescue did not succeed). Moufflet could see the logic of this, though he was not entirely convinced that the IDF had the military capability to pull off such a long-distance operation. What was not in doubt, however, was that a significant proportion of the young Israeli hostages, particularly *sabras*, were opposed to negotiating with terrorists as a matter of principle (even if it did put their own lives at risk). The older Israelis – especially immigrants from countries like Poland, Romania, Russia and France – thought differently: many 'missed their old passports' and did not want the non-Israelis to leave because, as one told Moufflet, they saw their 'presence as protectors'. They feared the consequences of a botched rescue attempt and, in any case, did not believe it would happen.

While Moufflet mulled over this latest example of the young coping better with the stresses and strains of the hijacking than their seniors, the young Israeli he was talking to was shooed back to his room by Khaled. There was movement outside and eventually a small truck drove up in front of the Old Terminal. Out of the front stepped a Ugandan civilian who came into the large hall accompanied by Böse. The German asked Cojot to make the following announcement: 'The director of the airport has asked and obtained the Palestinians' permission to provide you with another limited service of Duty Free. You can buy cigarettes, soap, razor blades, shaving cream, toothpaste, tooth-brushes, biscuits and squash. The sale will be organized outside your room. Your purchases can be paid for in dollars, French francs, pounds sterling and deutsche marks. Can you combine your orders so that not everyone has to join the queue.'

The news was greeted with clapping, and a line of people quickly formed. With orders for fifteen others, Moufflet was behind the Yachtsman, who kept himself amused at the glacial pace of the queue by coming out with sarcastic comments like: 'Oh, c'mon, go in front of me. I've got all the time in the world to kill.'

When he eventually reached the makeshift shop Moufflet was asked by Cojot, who had been verifying the transactions, to take over his role in the hope that he could speed things up so that the Israelis could also make a few purchases before lunch. The Duty Free service, said Cojot, would finish at 12.30 p.m. and not return for at least a week, a declaration which naturally 'worried quite a few hostages'.

0730hrs GMT, Tel Aviv, Israel

While the Israeli government was hoping to end the hostage crisis peacefully, Ehud Barak and his planning team continued their work in the Pit on the assumption that a rescue mission might, at some point, be needed. Their task, however, had been considerably simplified by the arrival that morning of the vital intelligence that Amiram Levine had extracted from the freed hostages in Paris: in particular the news that Amin was collaborating with the terrorists.

It was now obvious to all the planners that most of their schemes – parachuting into Lake Victoria, ships from Kenya and 'fake identities as Palestinian terrorists aboard a plane painted to look like a civilian jet' – had 'suddenly became irrelevant'. The only plan that now counted was one that 'involved landing at the airport, freeing the hostages, and flying out'.

Dan Shomron and his staff had come up with just such a plan the night before, but it had been overtaken by events, and when Shomron repitched the improved version to Kuti Adam himself at 10 a.m. on 1 July it was deemed to be 'too limited in scope'. What a rescue force now required was the use of a 'large enough force to kill the terrorists, gain control of the airport and evacuate the hostages, with the troops returning to Israel'. That would require more airlifting power than two Hercules C-130 tankers and, moreover, meant that the planes had to be refuelled.

Coming to this conclusion, Muki Betser went to speak to Colonel Tamari. Having briefed the colonel on the new information from Paris, he suggested 'dropping everything else' and working only on a slimmed-down version of the IDF Option. Ran Bag's original suggestion had been to use 1,000 men. Barak, Betser and the other ex-Unit planners thought that was too many, and that they could do the job with a much smaller, more heavily armed force.

Nodding his assent, Tamari pressed the button on the direct intercom to Kuti Adam. 'Here's what we have,' he said, repeating the argument that the intelligence from Paris had reduced the options to an airlift rescue.

Adam was not entirely convinced. 'I want a written brief on all four options,' he said. '*All* four plans, including the failed naval one. I want a concise report on the advantages and disadvantages of each one.'

Tamari said he would have them and at once called in Barak and the rest of the planning team to draw up the briefs, 'neatly and concisely' listing all four options, 'with their pluses and minuses in meticulously drawn columns'. When he had finished he nodded, rose from his seat and 'announced he was off to see Kuti'.

A few minutes later he was back with Adam's authorization for the IDF Option. At last the planners 'could get down to details'.

0800hrs GMT, Tel Aviv, Israel

Burka Bar-Lev waited patiently for the call to be put through to Uganda. It was the third time that Shimon Peres had asked him to speak to Idi Amin from the Ministry of Defense in the hope that he could delay the executions and give the IDF more time to come up with a military option. Peres's desperate ploy was for him to tell Amin that he was ready to fly to Uganda at once with an important message from his government. But as soon as he heard the distant tone of Amin's voice, Bar-Lev knew the tactic was hopeless.

'Inform your government officially,' said Amin bluntly, 'that the People's Front of Palestine will make an announcement at 11 a.m. GMT. That's the only answer I can give you. Those are the instructions I received from the front. Okay? We had very difficult talks till now. It's best that you wait for an announcement.'

Bar-Lev asked for details, but Amin would not be drawn. So the Israeli persisted with his original tactic. 'Can you prevent them from doing anything before I arrive? I'm coming with some very interesting proposals.'

'Call me after you hear the announcement.'

Changing tack, Bar-Lev asked Amin how it was that additional terrorists – as many as twenty according to some of the released hostages – had joined the original hijackers in Entebbe.

'They were in the plane,' lied Amin. 'There weren't only six, there were about thirty from all over the world. Nobody came by another plane to Uganda. For your information, I tried to put the hostages in a bus and drive them in a different direction, but the hijackers wanted all of them to be brought to the old air terminal. It's very difficult for me, I did the best I could, but I think that your government is responsible for the fate of the Israelis and the passengers with dual nationality, and the rest of the hostages.'

Convinced that Amin was speaking under duress, and that Wadie Haddad might be listening in, Bar-Lev pleaded with him not to be 'influenced by these PFLP just because they are sitting next to you and tell you all kinds of stories'.

'I'm not influenced by the PFLP,' said Amin, his voice shrill. 'I make my own decisions, and I am doing everything I can to save the lives of Israelis and the other passengers. So what you said about wanting to come to Uganda, it isn't necessary that you should come. If you have something extremely important to tell me, listen to the announcement, phone me, and I'll tell you what to do. I want to tell you again that had I not done everything I could, all the hostages including the crew wouldn't be alive now. You must consider my position, you mustn't insult me as you did just now when you said that I am collaborating with the hijackers, who are not innocent people. But my position is extremely difficult, and you must realize it. The whole world must realize it.'

Realizing he had gone too far, Bar-Lev tried flattery, telling Amin that he was a 'great soldier' and that he alone could 'prevent a massacre and bloodshed'. He added: 'Nobody can give you instructions. The people of the PFLP have no right to do this within the territory of your country.'

'They surrounded the hostages with high explosives,' said Amin, explaining his helplessness, 'and they moved my soldiers away. The lives of the hostages are in their hands. What can I do now?'

'You can tell them that they are your guests and that they are placing your country in a difficult position. If such a thing were to happen in Israel, and it did happen, we managed to free the hostages,' said Bar-Lev, referring to the Sabena hijack in 1972. 'The front have never succeeded in doing what they want in Israel, even when they had high explosives, because we didn't permit them to. The world will never accept the claim that you and your great army couldn't overpower a small number of terrorists? How will the world believe that the PFLP can do what it likes in Uganda, and the entire Uganda Army cannot overpower them?'

'I know that you are saying that they never succeeded in your country and that I can kill the terrorists.'

'You are granting them protection. They are living in Uganda as if they were in a hotel. You are a good friend of the Palestinians and the Arabs, so they shouldn't place you in a difficult situation and harm you.' But, added Bar-Lev, 'they won't do anything if Field Marshal Dr Idi Amin asks them to do nothing and delay operations for a day until I can arrive.'

Amin denied the terrorists were living 'like guests in a hotel'. They were, he insisted, 'together with the hostages and if we take any action we are endangering the lives of the hostages'. Yet he would not deny he was their friend. 'I want peace in Palestine. It is the responsibility of your government. You must not continue with this Zionist policy and activity.'

The line went dead, causing Bar-Lev to conclude that Amin was working with the terrorists and would not intervene militarily to save the hostages. His only crumb of comfort was a suspicion that Amin's repeated references to 'high explosives' were probably a falsehood designed to discourage a rescue attempt. Not that it mattered any more. With the deadline imminent, and the government about to cave in to the terrorists' demands, such an assumption was too little, too late.

0940hrs GMT, Entebbe International Airport, Uganda

With just over two hours to go to the deadline, and the tension rising among all the hostages, the Peruvian ran into the large hall of the Old Terminal building and, without bothering to grab a megaphone, shouted out: 'I've some very important and urgent news to tell you. Before I do it's important that you make a list of all the people in this room. Hurry up. Do it quickly. This is very important and really urgent.'

The room buzzed with speculation, most of it optimistic. 'What type of news do you think this is?' asked one hostage. 'Good news or just important news? What do you think might happen?'

Before anyone could answer, Faiz Jaber began aggressively pushing those Israelis who were in the large hall towards their own room, telling Khaled who was guarding the entrance not to let them back in.

Meanwhile the interpreter Cojot had borrowed a pad of paper from Moufflet and was making his way round the room and adding each name to the list. But when he came to Bacos, Lom, Lemoine and the flight attendants, grouped near the bar, the Peruvian was adamant. 'Not the crew!' he yelled.

Close to finishing his task, Cojot was told to write each person's nationality next to his name. The Peruvian then announced to the room: 'Could you bring to the table near the door any cutlery, knives, cameras, electronic equipment, film, photos and tape recordings in your possession. You are going to be searched and if we find anything on you it will be very serious. Hurry up. It is very important and urgent. I am going to give you some good news.'

A few were hopeful that the terrorists were about to release another batch of hostages. But most discounted that possibility because they had not seen either Idi Amin or the press photographers. They thought the most likely scenario – given that Flight Engineer Lemoine had told them the hold doors were open – was that they were about to be reunited with their suitcases.

Their miscalculation was confirmed by the sudden arrival of a helicopter in front of the Old Terminal. Out of it climbed President Idi Amin, dapper in his freshly pressed combats, his four-year-old son Gamal Abdel Nasser Jwami in an identical outfit, and the president's young and very beautiful fifth wife Sarah Kyolaba, wearing an African print dress. (A former go-go dancer in the jazz band of the army's 'Suicide' Mechanized Unit – and hence known as 'Suicide Sarah' – Kyolaba had married Amin after he arranged to have her boyfriend murdered.)

Flanked by soldiers, Amin and his entourage approached the front of the terminal where a cluster of pre-warned TV cameramen and press photographers were gathering. As flash bulbs went off, a smiling Amin entered the departure lounge with his wife and son. He was welcomed, as before, with a loud burst of applause from the non-Israeli hostages who regarded him, not without reason, as a potential saviour. He spoke in English while Michel Cojot provided an almost simultaneous translation into French.

'Hello. Good morning. How are you getting on?'

Hardly pausing for a response, he continued: 'I have some good news for you. Following some difficult negotiations that I have undertaken with the representatives of the PFLP, I can tell you that I have obtained the freedom of a hundred more people for today itself, and that negotiations continue for the freeing up of others.' Spontaneous cheering broke out as the hostages realized that, with the Israelis unlikely to be included, most of those in the room would soon be on their way home.

'A plane is coming here to take those people who have been released. At the same time, the PFLP has agreed to push back till Sunday 4 July, at 11 o'clock GMT, the limit date of its ultimatum, to allow different governments to intervene or to respond to the demands that have been made. I must tell you that, for those who stay, the negotiations are continuing, and all escape would be useless and dangerous because the whole of the building is booby-trapped with explosives and you could set them off. The list of people who are to be freed will be communicated to you shortly by a representative of the PFLP. Good luck.'

Loud applause followed Amin as he left with his family and went next door to speak to the Israelis. For them he had a different, less upbeat speech. Thus far, he told them, negotiations had failed 'because of the obstinacy' of the Israeli government. Yet he was continuing these discussions through the offices of his 'good friend Colonel Bar-Lev' and had, in addition, got the PFLP to agree to extend the deadline until 11 a.m. on Sunday.

What he did not mention was that this extension had been agreed with the terrorists because it suited Amin's timetable. It gave him enough time to go to the island of Mauritius to attend the annual summit of the OAU where he was due to hand over his chairmanship to the local premier Sir Seewoosagur Ramgoolam on 2 July. His plan was to return to Uganda on Saturday 3 July in good time for the expiry of the new ultimatum the following day. He was convinced that the various governments – but particularly Rabin's Israeli administration – would have agreed to all the terrorists' demands by then and wanted to be present when that happened.

For the Israeli hostages, however, this was decidedly mixed news. Yes, it was a definite stay of execution. But, no, they would not be going home for a few more days at least, and possibly not even then. 'There is an air of depression among the Israeli group,' noted Moshe Peretz. 'People are quiet and sad; they don't talk much with one another – they've withdrawn within themselves. The children continue to play.'

1100hrs GMT, Tel Aviv, Israel

As the clock ticked towards one in the afternoon – just one hour before the terrorists' deadline and the time that Amin had told

Bar-Lev an announcement would be made on Radio Uganda – Yehuda Avner and the other members of the prime minister's personal staff were 'gnawed by a supercharged tension' that the government's offer to negotiate would not be enough to satisfy the PFLP and save the lives of the hostages.

Only Rabin himself was immune. Discussing the day's correspondence with a flustered Avner in his office, he seemed 'unnaturally composed, as if morally fortified by the principled decision he had taken'. Even when the red emergency phone on his desk began to buzz, he showed no sign of panic. 'Hello,' he answered calmly.

As Avner watched with bated breath, Rabin nodded. 'Yes I see,' he said. 'Good. Thank you. That gives us a little more time.'

Rabin had barely replaced the handset before Avner blurted out: 'Any news?'

'Yes.' Without elaborating, he pressed the intercom button to speak to his military secretary. 'Freuka, the French have just notified us that the terrorists have extended their ultimatum to 11 a.m. GMT on Sunday 4 July, to allow for negotiations to proceed. Please inform the members of the ministerial committee. I'll speak directly to the defence minister and the chief of staff. Hopefully they will come up with a military plan before then.'

1100hrs GMT, Entebbe International Airport, Uganda

Claude Moufflet was comforting some of the stewardesses who had hoped to be among those released when the Peruvian, with an amended version of Cojot's list in his hand, entered the large hall. 'I want everyone to move to that side of the room,' he said, pointing with his hand to the bar.

As the hostages began to comply, an Israeli on his way to the toilet asked Moufflet: 'What's going on? Are you going?'

'No,' he replied. 'Only some. Idi Amin Dada has just announced that a hundred people will be freed. And in your room is it all the same?'

'Yes. In our place nothing is happening. He hasn't said anything to us about that. Who is leaving?'

'We don't know yet. They're doing a list.'

As if on cue, the Peruvian started speaking again: 'I'm going to read out a hundred names. If you hear your name, take your hand luggage and stand in line on the far side of the room where you'll be searched before you're allowed to get on the bus outside.'

He began calling out names but his pronunciation was so mangled that Cojot took over. It soon became clear that apart from the crew – who were being kept for the obvious reason that they might be needed to fly the plane if the negotiations succeeded – the ones selected to stay were, on the whole, the youngest. But there were exceptions. Of the first sixty-three chosen – the maximum for the yellow bus that would take them to the New Terminal building – the majority were French, but they also included the Kiwis Colin and Nola Hardie, the Britons Tony Russell and George Good, a number of Americans, including the Harvard research student Sanford Freedman and the well-known TV producer and writer Murray Schwartz, the young Anglo-French couple Gérard and Isabella Poignon (desperate to see their eighteen-month-old daughter left in France with Gérard's mother), and four Canadians, including Louise Kourtis and Jo-Anne Rethmetakis, just twenty and eighteen years old respectively. As the young Canadians' names were called, and they looked wide-eyed with surprise at Moufflet near the bar, he responded with a 'V' for Victory. Sanford Freedman had become friendly with the Rosenkovitches, now in the Israeli room, and before leaving he passed through to them his *Complete Works of William Shakespeare* and a small box of medicines.

With the queue of departees growing ever longer, Jaber ordered them not to talk to those who were staying. Cojot concluded that the terrorists were 'very much afraid of crowd movements' and wanted to proceed as quickly as possible 'to reduce the duration of what promised to be a tense period'.

One by one this initial group was searched and then sent out to the bus, each departure from the room greeted with an explosion of flash bulbs from the press photographers. Once the bus was full it set off, and a new set of names was called.

There now seemed to be no obvious criteria for who stayed and who went. Of the two young French girls that Moufflet had shared a pair of seats with during the flight to Benghazi, only Maggy's name was called, while Agnès her friend was overlooked (because, she suspected, her surname sounded Israeli). 'There we go,' Agnès said to herself, 'it's messed up for me. If Maggy goes I won't last.' She started to cry.

Maggy was just as upset. She wanted to go; but not without Agnès. Her dilemma was 'horrific', but still she rose from her mattress in tears and joined the queue.

Then nineteen-year-old Thierry Sicard, the friend of Jean-Jacques Mimouni and son of the French consul at Tel Aviv, was named, as were the two teenage Brazilian Orthodox Jews, Raphael Shammah and Jacques Stern. By now the excitement in the room was at 'fever pitch' as it became clear to Moufflet and the others still left that 'very few of us will stay'. Yet there was little noise: people fidgeted, but the silence was 'almost absolute'.

When the names of Nancy and Peter Rabinowitz were called, the Peruvian said a 'mistake had been made' and told them to stand alone in a corner. Eventually they were returned to the group staying behind which, by this time, was chiefly composed of the crew and younger French hostages, including Moufflet's new friends Gilles and Willy; or, as Peter put it, 'the healthy, the resilient and those who would not get sick and cause problems' for the terrorists. Their hopes dashed, the Rabinowitzes were frantic. It seemed to them that there was 'no rationale behind this nightmare'. One passenger tried to reassure them by saying that *all* Americans were going; another that he had seen the list with their names 'checked and bracketed'. They could not decide if that was good news or bad. Their only consolation was that 'a couple of new-found friends seemed to be remaining too': any concern they might have felt for them was outweighed by the prospect of 'having company'.

More names were called; more friends divided. Then Moufflet was surprised to hear his own name. He quickly went behind the bar to gather his things: briefcase, camera, calculator and Dictaphone. He left behind his remaining cigarettes and a half-finished bottle of ouzo.

As he bade farewell to the group near the bar – many of whom were members of the crew – he felt ashamed. Why me? he asked himself. But they seemed genuinely happy for him, and smiled and waved when he joined the queue.

Cojot, meanwhile, was taking advantage of the haphazard nature of the selection to persuade the terrorists to release two doctors: American-born David Bass who, Cojot claimed, had a serious heart condition (it was minor); and a French doctor with a calling card that Cojot used to prove he lived in France.

All out of excuses, Cojot slumped to the ground exhausted. This prompted one of those left to approach Jaber in desperation. Falling to his knees in front of the terrorist, his hands clasped in supplication, he begged in Arabic: 'Let me go. I have done nothing to you. I don't know your histories. I have a wife and children, and I want to go home.'

'Return to your place,' responded Jaber dismissively. 'We also have wives and children. They are killed every day in the bombing of Palestinian camps.'

The one name Cojot had not called out was his own, though it had a tick next to it. The terrorists were loath to lose such a facilitator and one of them joked: 'You have been so useful that you have to stay.'

But Cojot was torn. When Lemoine asked him earlier if he was leaving, he had given a non-committal reply. He could not decide. Waiting for him back in France 'was loneliness and the agony of divorce proceedings'. Here, on the other hand, he had 'a role' and some 'small usefulness'. Nor was the threat to his life, in his opinion, very great. It seemed out of the question to him that either he or the crew 'would be among the hostages to be shot'. To stay, moreover, would be to affirm his 'solidarity' and his 'courage', and to find what he had gone to seek a year earlier in Bolivia: Franco-Jewish glory.

Then, while working as a management consultant in Peru, he had read in a newspaper that 'the Supreme Court of Bolivia had just denied the French government's three-year-old request for the extradition of Klaus Altmann, or Barbie, the former Gestapo chief who had captured and tortured' the French Resistance leader Jean Moulin and 'who had held sway in Lyons', the city from which his father 'had never returned'. Thus he came up with the idea of killing Barbie to avenge both his father and all the other French victims of the Holocaust. 'Then and only then,' he wrote, 'would I know peace. To live I had to kill.'

With the full consent of his Gentile wife, he procured recent pictures of Barbie from a photo agency in Paris, bought a five-shot revolver in Mexico, and travelled to La Paz in Bolivia where, impersonating a journalist, he spent a chilling couple of hours 'interviewing' the un-repentant Nazi. A few days later he was sitting on a bench with his gun hidden under a poncho when Barbie stopped three yards in front of him. All he needed to do was pull out the gun and shoot. But he could not. The words of the writer Elie Wiesel came back to him: 'Every murder is a suicide.'

He knew then that Barbie's killing would not be justice for his victims. 'What does a quick death mean to a purveyor of slow death?' Cojot asked himself. 'What is death to a man who has worn the uniform with skull and crossbones?' He decided it would be no punish-ment at all. Much better to leave Barbie in a permanent state of anxiety: always looking over his shoulder, hesitating before going out, mistrusting all strangers. As Cojot walked away, he told himself that he could have killed him if he had wanted to, but that he 'intention-ally decided not to do so' for 'powerful reasons'.

Staying at Entebbe would give him what he had sought and not found at La Paz: the admiration of both Jews and non-Jews, and a proper sense of belonging. It would reserve for him, as he put it, 'a stool by the Righteous'. Yet he knew, deep down, that it would serve no purpose except for himself, for his own personal glory. There was, moreover, a more compelling reason for him to go: his conviction that he could persuade the French to launch a rescue mission from Djibouti, the 'last French territory in Africa within easy reach, the distance from Paris to Madrid'.

If that was the solution to the crisis, he could provide the necessary details: 'how many terrorists, with what weapons and at which guard posts; where best to enter to minimize the risk that stray bullets would hit the hostages'. Someone who would be able to prove that, contrary to what the hostages had been told, 'the cases stored in the Israeli room did not contain explosives'. He had also observed the 'functions, positions, equipment of the Ugandan soldiers', and where those not on guard duty slept. As a reserve officer, he knew which people to talk to in France and would be able 'to prove that the terrorists and their Ugandan accomplices, with their minds at rest because of the distance, did not prevent a very formidable obstacle'.

His mind made up, he retrieved a pen he had lent to a terrorist, said goodbye to the crew and, with a nod from the Peruvian, paid a last visit to the Israelis. Spotting Ilan Hartuv, he was assailed by feelings of guilt and was tempted to stay. But Hartuv dissuaded him. 'No, you must go. You're the only one who knows all the important details. You have to go to Paris, and you'll probably be met in the airport; and if not take a taxi straight away to the Israeli Embassy and say what you know. It's of the utmost importance.' Hartuv thought, with good reason, that the Mossad would be keen to hear his story; Cojot had visions of involving French intelligence. But either way he had to leave.

Emma Rosenkovitch, who for a time after the hijacking had sat next to his son Olivier, saw Cojot's eyes glistening and asked why he was crying.

'Because,' he replied, 'it brings back memories.'

Returning to the main hall, Cojot found one of the stewardesses weeping quietly because she had to stay when others were leaving. The crew had earlier discussed their response if they were told they had the chance to go and, despite one or two gainsayers, they 'prepared the reply one might expect': in other words, they would stay until *all* the passengers had been released. But it never came to this because, according to Cojot, the terrorists did not give them the option: they were 'needed to operate the Airbus', or at least the pilots and the chief engineer were. So the crew 'remained with almost all the Israelis, as did several others, French or not, Jewish or not'.

Cojot joined the queue of those about to depart at about the same time that Moufflet was having his briefcase searched by Jaber. After reading some of the papers it contained, the chief terrorist asked: 'Are you an Iranian?'

'No, why?'

'Because in your things all these papers are concerning Iran. There's nothing except Iran. Why?'

'We have a business in Teheran and I have just been there to visit it.'

Unconvinced by this explanation, Jaber called the Peruvian over and said bluntly: 'He's Iranian.'

'Are you Iranian?' asked Jaber's deputy.

'No. I'm French.'

'What's your name?'

'Moufflet.'

Verifying the Frenchman's name on his list, he asked: 'Why does he say you're an Iranian?'

'Because he's looked in my case and he's seen some files of our business in Teheran. It's from there that I've come.'

'Okay,' he says. 'Go forward.'

The Peruvian turned to Jaber and said: 'It's okay.'

Moufflet made his way out to the bus and was joined there by Cojot and a red-eyed Gilles whose name had not been on the amended list. But earlier, while waiting in the queue, Moufflet had gestured to both Gilles and Willy – his companions of the last few days – to try and join him. Willy had obstinately remained on his mattress. But eventually Gilles had got up and presented his Athens–Paris ticket to Jaber, asking: 'How are you calling people?'

'What's your name?' demanded the Palestinian.

'Collini.'

'Are you French?'

'Yes.'

'Is this your ticket?'

'Yes.'

Jaber looked at the name on the ticket and back at Gilles. 'Go!'

The Peruvian came out of the building to count the people on the bus: there were twenty-seven, which left space for ten more. He returned to the main hall and immediately sent out five people: Dr David Bass, the Rabinowitzes and their friends. The latter four owed their place on the bus to Michel Bacos, the pilot, who assured the Peruvian that they were all Americans who had boarded in Athens and not Tel Aviv. Even then the terrorist was suspicious. 'What were they doing there?' he asked.

Nancy explained that she studied Greek literature.

'Rabinowitz?' persisted the Peruvian. 'That's not an American name; what kind of a name is that?'

Only after Peter had explained it was Polish in origin were they allowed to leave.

All this time the two young Brazilians, Stern and Shammah, as well as Maggy and Thierry Sicard, had been told to wait just outside the door. Now the Peruvian gestured for the Brazilians to leave and they boarded the bus. Maggy was in tears as she and Sicard were pushed back inside the door and an American-born woman and her Greek husband, Phyllis and Constantin Teodoropolous, were sent out. Now just one place was left and Maggy, seemingly resigned to her fate, collapsed in a chair, her face in her hands. Sicard, on the other hand, kept arguing with the Peruvian, and received a sharp push in the chest for his pains. But back he came to remonstrate and, finally realizing there was room for one more, the Peruvian grabbed him by the arms and frogmarched him out to the bus.

As the engine started, Moufflet and some of the others made signs of encouragement to the ten mostly young hostages and twelve members of the crew – not to mention the eighty-three people in the Israeli room – they were leaving behind. But, for Moufflet at least, the relief of knowing he was nearly free did not compensate for the pain he felt at abandoning the others.

1200hrs GMT, Tel Aviv, Israel

Yehuda Avner was chatting with Freuka Poran in the latter's office in the Kirya, awaiting the outcome of the prime minister's meeting with Peres and Gur, when in stormed a red-faced Rabin.

'You won't believe it,' he roared. 'Here I am, waiting for the defense minister and the chief of staff to come up with a military plan to beat the new deadline, and there they are backing the most outlandish proposal I've ever heard in my life. They want me to send Moshe Dayan – MOSHE DAYAN OF ALL PEOPLE – to Uganda to talk to Idi Amin! They have to be out of their minds, to suggest that we hand over one of our best-known public figures to that crazy tyrant so that he can hand him over to the terrorists as their prize hostage. It's outrageous!'

'But I hear,' said Poran, trying to calm him down, 'a military plan is beginning to take shape.'

Rabin was not convinced. 'I've heard that too. But I'll believe it when I see it. Motta and Peres say they might have something to show me in the morning.'

Peres's scheme to send Moshe Dayan to Entebbe had been born out of Amin's repeated comments to Bar-Lev, during their first two conversations, that the former IDF chief and defense secretary was a close friend. Peres did not imagine for a minute that Dayan would be able to secure the hostages' release; but believed rather that his presence would convince the terrorists that Israel was taking the negotiations seriously. This, in turn, would give the IDF the time it needed 'to perfect and execute a military rescue plan'. For Peres, therefore, the Dayan scheme was a means to an end.

Rabin had far less conviction that a rescue was possible – even with the extra three days' grace the terrorists had allowed – and so he scotched the scheme on the grounds that Dayan's probable incarceration would have, in his words, further strengthened 'the blackmailers' hand' and left the Israeli government 'absolutely no room for manoeuvre'.

Peres, however, was far from chastened by this rebuke as he urged Gur and his subordinates to use the extra time available to come up with a viable military plan. Their priorities, now, were first 'to procure more and better intelligence information', and second, 'to establish a safe stopover point in case a rescue operation ran into difficulties'.

1230hrs GMT, Entebbe International Airport, Uganda

As Cojot, Moufflet and the other thirty-five released hostages stepped down from the yellow bus in front of the New Terminal building they were met by Hashi Abdallah Farah and Pierre Renard, the Somali and French ambassadors to Uganda respectively. Also present was acting British High Commissioner James Horrocks.

'I'm very pleased that you've been freed,' said the Somali. 'I hope that the conditions you've been kept in weren't too painful. We are continuing negotiations with a view to obtaining the liberation of your friends. I will give you now to the care of your ambassador. I wish you good luck and I will say the only two words in French I know. *Bon voyage.*'

Renard shook his hand warmly. 'Thank you, Mr Ambassador. Thank you for your irreplaceable help in the negotiations and for all the efforts in obtaining the freedom of these people.' He then turned to the hostages and added: 'I am very pleased to see you. You are about to rejoin in the terminal those who were released before you and then you can rest. I must leave now because I must try and sort out the release of the others. An Air France plane will get here shortly to take you to Paris. Have a good journey.'

The two ambassadors departed in separate cars, while James Horrocks accompanied the former hostages into the New Terminal where they found their sixty-three comrades eating the now familiar meal of meat stew and rice. Some had already 'regained their tourist reflexes' and were complaining that the food was too cold. Others thought this basic fare had never tasted better.

Moufflet did not have the stomach to eat and thought it strange that many of the others, having eaten, were keen to buy mementoes from the souvenir shop like mounted gazelle horns, sculpted wood statues and amulets. Asked why he was not buying anything, he replied brusquely: 'I don't really need anything as a souvenir for this particular trip.'

This embarrassed the questioner who responded: 'Oh, me neither. But you understand it's just for the kids and it's not really anything.'

Horrocks, meanwhile, had been speaking to a number of the former hostages – including the Britons Tony Russell and George Good – about their ordeal. 'They seemed to be in remarkably good shape . . . given the circumstances,' he reported back to London. Moreover they confirmed earlier reports that '3 or 4 armed Palestinians had not been passengers but had joined the hijackers after the arrival of the aircraft at Entebbe' and that this, 'together with the easy relationship observed between the Ugandan authorities and the hijackers, led them to suspect Ugandan collusion'. Horrocks, however, was 'not fully convinced on this point'.

1235hrs GMT, Entebbe International Airport, Uganda

'You're moving!' announced Wilfried Böse to the Israeli hostages near the door of the small hall in the Old Terminal building.
'Where to?' asked one, hopeful that they too might be released.
'Next door. There's more room since the others left.'
Reunited in the large hall with the crew and the ten mostly young French hostages, the Israelis felt only relief that their separation was over. They found many of the non-Israelis, however, in a deep depression. One or two were still crying, including the young Frenchman Willy who – since the departure of his colleague Gilles and Claude Moufflet – was alone.

Among the new arrivals was a pretty Israeli teacher who on the plane had argued bitterly with Willy about Middle East politics. Recognizing him, she came over. 'You're here!' she said. 'Why have you not gone with the others?'

'Why would I leave,' he replied, his voice heavy with sarcasm, 'when you're still here?'

With enough mattresses and chairs for everyone, the room felt much less cramped than it had been before. But this marginal improvement was offset by the fact that many hostages had diarrhoea, probably caused by eating bad or poorly cooked meat, and some of the overworked toilets were blocked and smelling horribly. There was, in addition, a nagging fear for the older Israelis and those with children especially that, the extension of the deadline notwithstanding, the Israeli government would never agree to exchange convicted killers for their lives. And if that was so, what hope was there for them and their children?

The arrival of lunch in the little yellow bus gave the hostages the excuse to keep busy 'and think of other things'. It was the same menu – meat stew, rice and bananas – but oddly, given their reduced numbers, in smaller portions than before. Once again the crew organized the distribution of the food, assisted by several passengers.

There were now just two armed terrorists – Böse and Khaled – on guard. They seemed more relaxed than before and did not even bother to block up or guard the gap through to the Israelis' old room, now occupied by the Palestinians. Their only stricture was to ask the hostages to keep their mattresses at least two yards from the windows at the front of the room so that a walkway was left free for them to patrol. This demand was only partially complied with.

Outside, Ugandan soldiers continued to stand guard at a distance of about fifteen yards from the front of the building. Their sullen demeanour had not changed.

1400hrs GMT, Tel Aviv, Israel

Armed with Adam's authorization, Barak and his planners spent much of Thursday morning and early afternoon fleshing out the IDF Option in the war room of the Pit, the warren of underground offices that served as the nerve centre of the Israeli military. The walls were covered with old aerial photos of Entebbe Airport, up-to-date civilian flight paths for East Africa, architectural drawings of the Old Terminal, courtesy of Solel Boneh, and summaries of the intelligence sent from Paris.

Every hour, on the hour, the planners paused to listen to the latest radio news bulletins: the violent demonstrations by the distraught relatives of the hostages; the government's decision to negotiate; and lastly the terrorists' decision to extend the deadline, which they cheered because they knew it at least made a military strike possible. And yet not once did anyone in the media even raise the possibility of a rescue: they simply assumed that the distance was too great.

The planners knew better and worked hard to turn a theoretical idea into a feasible operation that both Gur and Rabin were prepared to authorize. Their chief task was to work 'on the compromise between a discreet airlift that could land unobtrusively, and the need for the firepower necessary to take the airport from the Ugandan army'.

While Ido Embar calculated fuel and cargo loads for the Hercules transports, Muki Betser concentrated on the assault force from the Unit that would travel in the first plane and tackle the terrorists: 'the landing, the ride to the terminal, the break-in, the elimination of the terrorists, freeing of the hostages and holding the building against Ugandan opposition until the arrival of troops from the second plane'. His task was made considerably easier by the intelligence from Paris which showed that the hostages were all lying down by midnight, and most were sleeping by 1 a.m. That hour gave Betser 'a cornerstone' for his timetable.

By mid-afternoon the planners had narrowed the mission down to five Hercules (four for the mission and one in reserve) – the maximum number of crews trained for a night landing in an unfamiliar airport – 'with each plane loaded far past its recommended capacity'. The break-in crews would land in the first plane, 'take out the terrorists, neutralize any interfering Ugandan troops and hold the old terminal' until the second Hercules landed seven minutes later with reinforcements, including two Soviet-made armoured personnel carriers known as BTRs that had been captured during the Yom Kippur War. These BTRs were lighter than the IDF's standard APC and 'carried plenty of firepower to protect a perimeter around the old terminal building'.

The third and fourth planes would land straight after the second one, and bring in more reinforcements, two more BTRs and medical officers and equipment that could treat up to seventy-five casualties, which was 25 per cent of the total number of hostages and soldiers. That, of course, was a worst-case scenario. They hoped the wounded would not be anything like as numerous.

Though the break-in and rescue would take just seven minutes, the planes needed at least an hour on the ground to refuel from the airport's underground tanks using mobile hand-operated pumps they would take with them. The alternative was to fly on to Nairobi and refuel there, but confirmation that that was possible had yet to be received from the Kenyans: not least because the Mossad was wary of giving them advance warning of a possible operation in case there was a security leak.

At 4 p.m. Brigadier-General Dan Shomron arrived in the Pit with authorization from Adam to take control of the planning: he was 'to determine the method of the operation, the quality of the troops and the number of the planes'. A tall, impressive man with blue eyes and a shock of thick curly black hair, Shomron had been born on Kibbutz Ashdot Yaakov in the Jordan Valley and, despite his high rank, still retained the humility and quiet confidence of a typical kibbutzim. He preferred simple cooking – eggs, meat and fresh vegetables – to haute cuisine; slacks and a shirt to a suit and tie. His combat record, moreover, was second to none: he had fought as a paratrooper in the Sinai campaign of 1956, he was the first airborne soldier to reach the Suez Canal in 1967 (a feat for which he was awarded the Medal of Distinguished Service), and in the Yom Kippur War in 1973 he commanded an armoured brigade that knocked out no fewer than sixty Egyptian tanks. A year later, at the age of just thirty-seven, he was promoted to brigadier-general and given the prestigious Infantry and Paratroops Command. As that was the formation that would supply the bulk of the soldiers needed for the Entebbe operation, it made sense for Shomron to take the plans to the next stage. His own preference, now, was to return to his deputy Ran Bag's initial suggestion of a huge airlift of at least a thousand men. It would require, he told Barak and his planners, at least ten planes.

'Dan,' responded an exasperated Betser, 'I think there's a misunderstanding here. You're making it sound as if we are going to start planning. We're almost done with planning. We don't need hundreds of soldiers. Let us brief you on the essentials of the plan, give you an idea of what we have. Then you can make up your mind.'

Amnon Biran spoke first, summarizing the intelligence available, and was followed by Ido Embar giving details of the flight and arrival ('We can land the first plane without the Ugandans noticing'), and finally by Betser explaining the assault. 'If we can reach the terminal in secret,' he said, picking up where Embar had left off, 'we can succeed.'

Shomron tilted his head, as if waiting to hear exactly *how* they would manage that. 'The break-in force from the Unit,' continued Betser, 'will land in the first plane. It's a mile from the New Terminal building to the old one. We're going to drive.'

Shomron raised an eyebrow. 'I know the Ugandan soldiers,' said Betser by way of explanation, 'I trained them. We don't need hundreds of soldiers. Instead we use a Mercedes. Every battalion commander rides around in one. A soldier spots a Mercedes, he snaps to a salute. They'll see us in the Mercedes with a couple of Land Rovers carrying soldiers, and they'll assume a general's about to drive by. They aren't going to shoot us.' Betser paused, smiling. 'You know, it's possible I'll run into one of the soldiers I trained.'

'It's lucky you trained them for only four months and not four years,' responded a wit from the back of the room.

Everyone laughed, breaking the tension. But Betser had a serious point to make. 'While we're driving to the target, we'll probably see Ugandan troops, and they'll probably see us. We can ignore them. Indeed, for the plan to work, we must ignore them, to avoid alerting the terrorists to our arrival. That's what makes a hostage situation so unique. Our first concern must be eliminating the terrorists – or they'll start harming the hostages. We're not going all that way to fight Ugandans. We're going down there to eliminate the terrorist threat to the hostages.'

After a brief pause, he continued. 'So even if a Ugandan soldier sees through our disguise, and starts shooting, we should speed on to the terminal, to the break-in. Only then should the back-up force deal with the Ugandans, while the break-in crews do their job. So, to sum up. Five minutes for us to drive across the airfield to the Old Terminal. Two minutes for the break-in. Seven minutes after we landed, the second and third planes come in carrying reinforcements. In an hour we're all on our way home,' said Betser optimistically, forgetting the extra time it would take to refuel in Uganda or elsewhere.

As Shomron nodded approvingly, a message arrived from Adam. He wanted to be briefed on the plan so that he could take it to Gur and Peres. 'Ivan,' said Shomron to Colonel Oren, 'grab the maps. Let's go.'

1400hrs GMT, Entebbe International Airport, Uganda

Maggy was undressing for a shower, and doing her best to block out the stench from the nearby toilets, when she heard happy cries and a round of applause from the large hall. Hurriedly putting her clothes back on, she ran into the room to hear one of the terrorists yelling triumphantly: 'Israel has surrendered! Israel has surrendered!'

A minute or two earlier, some of the hostages at the front of the hall had seen Pierre Renard, the French ambassador, waving frantically from behind the line of Ugandan sentries in front of the building, the nearest he was allowed to approach the hostages. 'Israel is willing to negotiate!' he shouted. 'Israel is willing to negotiate!'

As word spread, people leapt up from mattresses and armchairs to dance jigs and hug and kiss each other. Some cried, others laughed. A few even embraced the hijackers 'as if they were their good friends'. The Belgian Gilbert Weill put this down to Stockholm Syndrome.

Elated by the news, Maggy was grinning from ear to ear. It was as if, noted Moshe Peretz, they had been 'born anew'. Many of the younger Israelis, however, were fearful of the precedent that Rabin was setting. 'I'm happy that I'm about to be released,' one of them told Michel Bacos, 'but I'm certainly not happy that my government is giving in . . .' Others were horrified by the decision, with one nineteen-year-old Israeli expressing his vehement disapproval.

Talking among themselves, Maggy and Agnès began to doubt the veracity of the report. They found it curious that Idi Amin had not made the announcement in person, and doubted that Israel was prepared to release such notorious prisoners as Archbishop Capucci and Kōzō Okamoto. Yet in general the mood in the hall was festive, and to celebrate many of the Israelis suddenly removed from their hand luggage the cakes and pastries they had planned to take to France. Would the bus come for them straight away? some wondered. Or would it arrive in an hour or two? So as not to be caught out, a few started packing, anticipating the exchange of prisoners. Gilbert Weill even began making plans for when he reached France: instead of continuing on to Antwerp, he would celebrate Shabbos in Paris and give himself and his wife 'a day or two to recover'.

1405hrs GMT, Washington DC, United States

This time, on hearing the news that the Israeli government was prepared to negotiate with the terrorists, Henry Kissinger called Ambassador Simcha Dinitz from the State Department in Washington.

'I am rather astonished by their decision,' said Kissinger.

'We had no doubt,' said Dinitz, defensively, 'they were going to slaughter them. That would have created in Israel a tremendous national feeling. The pressure was up so the government decided it would negotiate the release.'

It was an argument that did not cut any ice with Kissinger. 'You are going to have Israelis picked up all over the world now.'

Dinitz seemed to agree. 'I have suggested to the Prime Minister—'

'This is,' said Kissinger interrupting, 'not an official thing.'

'I understand. We are speaking as friends. When this is over, we should take the PLO and finish it off in a very devastating way. That was my own suggestion. With the situation that exists maybe it could be done, because we cannot leave it like this. It would have been better not to surrender at all,' said Dinitz, referring to Entebbe, 'but if it was impossible . . .'

'How would you finish them off,' asked Kissinger, 'without going into Lebanon?'

Dinitz said he had only been a sergeant in the army, and would leave that to the experts. As for Entebbe, there was 'no possibility' of a military operation. He added: 'I was astonished too. We have information that Amin is participating with the kidnappers in the technical operation. Some Ugandan soldiers are joining the kidnappers in guarding the hostages.'

'That doesn't surprise me.'

'One American,' said Dinitz, referring to the released hostage Carole Anne Taylor, 'said some people joined the kidnappers in Uganda.'

After a brief interlude discussing the financing of arms shipments to Israel, they returned to the Entebbe crisis. 'I am sorry for this mess. If it was a leap year,' said Dinitz, unaware that it was, 'maybe we could reach Uganda. But not this year. He would have slaughtered them: men, women and children.'

'I wonder,' replied Kissinger, 'if that would not have been better. Then you could react.'

'Politically I'm sure you're right. But humanly and emotionally? Here we have the human element. If you look at the past, it is not like the radio reports. We have given up prisoners in the past. Algeria. It is only when we have some command over the situation that we can be useful and use force. I appreciate you calling.'

'I am worried what will happen now.'

'I just hope my suggestion will be accepted,' said Dinitz, 'because I think it should be not be allowed to go unchallenged. That is the danger, the way I see it.'

'Yes,' agreed Kissinger.

1445hrs GMT, Entebbe International Airport, Uganda

Two planes landed on the new runway at Entebbe in quick succession: a Tupolev of the Soviet airline Aeroflot; followed by an Air France Boeing 747 'Jumbo', the plane sent to bring the released hostages back to Paris by direct flight. Like the jetliner that had flown home the previous batch of hostages, the Jumbo had been on standby at Nairobi International Airport in neighbouring Kenya. It would now cross with a third plane sent by Air France to Nairobi to wait for news of a third (and hopefully final) liberation.

The Jumbo came to a halt in front of the New Terminal building, its name clearly visible on its nose: 'Château de la Roche-Guyon'. Few, if any, appreciated the irony of their rescue from German (and Palestinian) terrorists in a plane named after the famous twelfth-century French château that had served as German Field Marshal Erwin Rommel's French headquarters in the later stages of the Second

World War. They were just relieved that their departure from Ugandan soil was now a reality, and an excited chatter spread through the group.

Told that women would board first, Moufflet, Cojot and the other men waited patiently in their seats. But as the minutes ticked by, they wondered about the hold-up until a male hostage told them: 'They're searching everyone and it's me that asked them to do it. I don't have any confidence in some of our fellow travellers. You know they've freed Arabs who are going to be on this journey with us?'

Moufflet shook his head, astonished that after their shared experience such prejudices persisted. But the man he was speaking to was not the only one to doubt his fellow travellers. According to acting British High Commissioner James Horrocks, 'certain New Zealand and American hostages suspected that at least four terrorists were posing as ordinary passengers', and did not want to continue their journey with them. When he heard this, Horrocks spoke to the Air France manager 'who instituted rigorous security checks (body and baggage searches) before the released hostages embarked'.

These same American former hostages would later tell US Embassy officials in Paris that they thought two of the Arab passengers were 'working with the hijackers, at least after the event', and one in particular 'seemed to be the hijackers' spy' and 'might have helped the hijackers get their arms and explosives on board'; an American also suspected a Canadian woman of smuggling weapons 'in her heavy handbag' and passing them to the German hijackers 'when she went to the ladies' room on the weak excuse of wishing to freshen up her makeup'. No corroborative evidence was provided and the charges were almost certainly baseless.

Once the careful search of their hand baggage and persons by Ugandan customs officials was completed – just in case, thought Cojot sardonically, 'one of us had concealed a weapon with which to hijack the special return plane' – the hundred former detainees were led out one by one to the waiting Air France Jumbo. The French crew was 'really kind' and immediately offered drinks.

Among them, disguised as a steward and stewardess, was a doctor and nurse to tend to the sick. An undisguised medical team had been sent with the earlier rescue plane and, at the terrorists' insistence, forced to disembark at Nairobi. This time Air France was taking no chances.

The freed hostages were told by the plane's captain over the intercom that everything had been done to keep their families' informed of developments and that they knew the time of their arrival at Orly in the early hours of Friday morning. They would take off as soon as they had clearance from the control tower.

1500hrs GMT, Tel Aviv, Israel

While the planners continued working on a rescue mission, Shimon Peres was doing his best to convince the ministerial committee, meeting in Rabin's office for the second time that day, that negotiation was not the only option. 'We must ask ourselves,' Peres told his fellow ministers, 'whether we are willing to release all the terrorists they've asked for, without any exceptions.'

Rabin frowned. 'What does that have to do with a rescue mission?'

'It has a lot to do with it,' said the defense minister, 'because if we aren't prepared to release the ones with blood on their hands – like Okamoto – then we're going to have to explain to the hostages' families and the Israeli public why we're willing to see the hostages die for X prisoner but not for Y.'

Rabin narrowed his eyes. 'That is nonsense. If I thought we had a chance to rescue them, I would support it regardless of the price we might pay.'

'Then we both agree a military operation is preferable. But I have to confess that, as of now, there is no concrete proposal, only ideas and imagination. But we must all accept that the alternative – to release prisoners – is complete and utter surrender. If we want to negotiate, we should at least send someone to Kampala to do it face to face, and not rely on the French.'

1600hrs GMT, Tel Aviv, Israel

Shomron strode ahead, followed by Barak, Embar, Biran, Oren and Betser. Kuti Adam and Peled were waiting for them in the corridor outside the former's office in the Kirya. It was 6 p.m. 'Can you present the plan in a minute?' asked Adam.

'Sure,' said Shomron.

'Good. Motta's waiting for us with the defense minister.'

As they reached Peres's office, Betser decided it was time to call the Unit's commander Yoni Netanyahu. He had promised he would let him know when an operation was imminent; now was that time. While the others filed in to Peres's office, Betser looked for a phone to call Netanyahu in the Sinai.

'Grab your kit and get over to the airfield,' he told him when the call was finally connected.

'It's hot?' asked Netanyahu.

'It's hot.'

Betser hung up to see a beaming Shomron emerge from Peres's office. 'The plan has been approved in principle,' he told Betser, 'and I've been appointed the ground commander. Of course the full Cabinet will have to give final approval, but until then we're full steam ahead. We'll meet tonight at eight at the Paratroops House at Ramat Gan to begin work on a detailed plan. We have to organize a force and train it, and stage a full dry run, in total secrecy. Once there the troops won't leave until the operation.'

Betser immediately redialled Netanyahu to inform him of the new planning session at Ramat Gan. He then spoke to Embar and Biran, and asked them what he had missed in Peres's office. 'Dan was one hundred per cent,' said Embar. 'He presented the plan as if he planned it himself.'

'What did Peres say?'

'As soon as Dan finished, Peres asked everyone what we thought. So Dan added something. "If we can reach the terminal in secret, we can succeed." Exactly what you told him.'

'Any dissenters?'

'Only Gur. He thinks it's a charlatan plan and said he would only give his final permission if three necessary conditions were satisfied: choosing a secure flight route; gathering more intelligence about what was happening on the ground; and finding out whether the Hercules planes could land at night without runway lights. He said the plan sounded like the James Bond film *Goldfinger* and that if we did it without proper intelligence it would lead to another Bay of Pigs.'

Now that he had Peres's authorization, Shomron asked the staff of the IDF's Computer Centre for a random codename for the operation. The first name the computer came up with was 'Wave of Ash'. Declaring it 'unsuitable' for such a mission, he asked for another. This time the computer randomly suggested 'Thunderbolt' and Shomron was delighted. The name perfectly encapsulated what they were trying to do – arrive in Uganda like a thunderbolt from the blue – and was surely, thought Shomron, a good omen.

1645hrs GMT, Entebbe International Airport, Uganda

After a nerve-wracking wait on the tarmac of more than half an hour, the 100 freed hostages breathed a sigh of relief when at 7.45 p.m. the Air France Jumbo's four engines finally roared into life and the huge plane began to move. Minutes later, as the Jumbo thundered down the runway, all eyes turned guiltily to the portholes on the left through which they could see the Old Terminal that still held the Israelis, the crew and one or two others. Only as the plane's rear wheels left the tarmac were they finally able to believe that the nightmare was over.

Champagne was served, but Cojot – feeling guilty that he had abandoned the others – could not drink his glass. He felt better when a grateful female passenger commented: 'Without you my husband wouldn't be here.'

He did not consider himself a hero; just someone who had behaved decently in a difficult situation. Certainly his fellow hostages appreciated what he had done and warmly applauded him as he returned to his seat from the cockpit where he had been invited by the captain.

The Yachtsman – Briton Tony Russell – stopped him and remarked: 'One of the things that surprised me during this adventure is that you seemed prepared for it.'

Cojot smiled in response, but he knew that Russell was right. 'Actually, I *was* prepared for it,' he told himself, 'by thirty years of fantasies, reading and dreams. I had been given the opportunity to live through a version, though certainly very watered down, of my nightmare. Had I lived it well? Could I wake up at last?'

1700hrs GMT, Entebbe International Airport, Uganda

It was dark when the yellow bus returned to the Old Terminal building at 8 p.m. with dinner for the remaining 102 hostages. The menu was the same; but this time it was principally the passengers who distributed the food. The crew were curiously listless, as if suffering a delayed reaction to the terrorists' insistence that they remain in Uganda to the bitter end.

Though resigned to spending at least one more night at the airport, the hostages were still optimistic of a speedy release, and conversations and games continued in good humour. Most were settled into their new sleeping areas, with Willy joining a group of young French-speakers at the left front of the hall, near the exit, that included Jean-Jacques Mimouni. Next to them, a little further from the windows, sat a fifty-five-year-old Russian immigrant to Israel called Ida Borochovich who was travelling with her grown-up son. Opposite the Borochoviches lay Maggy and Agnès on two mattresses.

Later, finding it difficult to go to sleep, Jean-Jacques decided to tell his companions a joke. 'On his deathbed,' he said in hushed tones, 'a Jewish businessman calls for his wife, "Sarah, are you there?" She replies: "Yes, Abraham, I am here." He then calls for his son, "Jacob, are you there?" "Yes, father, I am here." Finally he calls for his daughter, "Rachael, are you there?" "Yes, my dear father, I am here." "Then who," responds the businessman, "is looking after the shop?"'

The group burst into laughter, annoying their neighbours who were trying to sleep. One went over to Michel Bacos, lying with other members of the crew near the bar, and implored him to intervene. A weary Bacos did so, telling Jean-Jacques and the others not to be so inconsiderate. He seemed to them nervous and tense, and they largely ignored his pleas.

When Willy offered round a flask of cognac, only one of the girls accepted; the others feared the reaction of the terrorists who had earlier forbidden the consumption of alcohol. But they need not have worried. Keen to celebrate the news of Israel's supposed capitulation, and to flirt a little with the girls, Khaled and Ali came over with a bottle of champagne and another of whisky. Maggy drank a little champagne; some of the boys drank whisky.

It was a bizarre scene. Seated with their backs to the door, the two armed hijackers – one holding a gun, the other with a revolver in his belt – were sharing a drink with some of the younger hostages, making small talk and laughing. Only Agnès felt uneasy and refused to join in.

The party eventually wound down and at 11.30 p.m. the terrorists turned off the first row of lights. Within half an hour the room was quiet, but for the odd snorer and the buzz of mosquitoes.

1730hrs GMT, Nairobi, Kenya

At 8.30 p.m., a secret meeting was held at the Nairobi house of Charles Njonjo, Kenya's powerful attorney-general and right-hand man to President Jomo Kenyatta, to discuss the possibility of refuelling Israeli military planes at Nairobi's Embakasi Aiport. As well as Njonjo, the participants included senior Mossad agents and three key players in Kenyan politics and security: Ben Gethi, the head of the General Service Unit; Bernard Hinga, commissioner of police; and a white former Cabinet minister with mutton-chop whiskers called Bruce McKenzie.

McKenzie was an enigmatic figure. Born in South Africa on New Year's Day 1919, the son of a farm manager, he had won the Distinguished

Service Order and the Distinguished Flying Cross with Bar flying twin-engined Wellington bombers during the Second World War, reaching the rank of lieutenant-colonel at the age of twenty-three, and commanding, for a time, an anti-shipping squadron of the Royal Australian Air Force whose motto was 'Invenimus et Delimus' ('We Find and Destroy').

After the war McKenzie settled in Kenya, then a British crown colony. Before the country gained its independence in 1963, he astutely backed the jailed opposition leader and future president Jomo Kenyatta, and was later rewarded with a post in his Cabinet as minister of agriculture. He also had interests in a number of businesses – including Cooper Motors, which held the Kenyan and Ugandan distributorships for Volkswagen Beetles and British Leyland trucks – and it was partly to protect them that he supported the toppling of Milton Obote by Idi Amin in 1971. He opposed many of Milton Obote's policies – particularly his expulsion of ethnic Kenyans and his nation-alization of foreign businesses – and assumed that a former British soldier like Amin would be a great improvement.

McKenzie was close to senior figures in both the British and Israeli foreign intelligence services. In 1966 his future wife Christina had introduced him to Zvi Zamir, then Israel's military attaché to the UK but soon to become the chief of the Mossad. Zamir became a close friend and attended their wedding. McKenzie, in return, believed passionately in Israel's cause, which he saw as that of the underdog, and during the Six-Day War he had used his contacts and influence to enable Israel to procure more military aircraft.

His links with Britain's Secret Intelligence Service, MI6, were even stronger. According to his wife Christina, he 'worked with British intelligence' and knew all the MI6 officers – or 'friends' as he called them – in Nairobi. He was not a spy as such, but rather a 'conduit for information flowing both ways'. Christina had introduced him to both Sir Maurice Oldfield, chief of MI6 (or 'C') in 1976, and David Stirling, the founder of the SAS. The investigative journalist Chapman Pincher, who lived near McKenzie in Surrey and became a close friend, often 'talked with many intelligence officials' at McKenzie's house 'who would not have wished to be seen with me in London'.

Under the circumstances it is possible that McKenzie informed either

Oldfield or his British handlers of Israel's plan to rescue the hostages. Whether this information was ever passed to the British government is doubtful. There is, for example, no hint in FCO papers that Crosland or any of his officials knew about Israeli intentions in advance.

Though McKenzie had resigned his Cabinet post in 1970, he was still 'the most influential white man in East Africa' and remained the 'chief confidant' to President Kenyatta, who 'trusted him because he knew a white man could never usurp him' and treated him 'like a son'. He now divided his time between Kenya and England – where he and Christina lived in a large mansion called Knowle Park in Cranleigh, Surrey, with their two young sons – but was in Nairobi for part of the hijacking crisis.

It was almost certainly McKenzie who, at the Mossad's request, set up the meeting at Njonjo's house. Without being too specific – for fear of forewarning the Ugandans – the Israelis told the Kenyans that the IDF was 'planning something' and 'might need your help'. They talked about the possibility of refuelling military planes at Nairobi, but did not say how many. Of course Njonjo and the others knew very well that this had to be connected to the Entebbe hijacking and said, in principle, they would be happy to help. They still owed the Mossad a favour for helping to stymie the PFLP–EA plot to shoot down an El Al plane as it landed at Nairobi Airport; they wanted to get even with Amin for, as they saw it, assisting the terrorists by smuggling their weapons into Kenya from Uganda; and, crucially, they did not want to have to admit to the hijackers – and the world – that the reason why they could not release their fellow PFLP–EA terrorists was that they had secretly handed them over to the Israelis.

They had not yet discussed the issue with an ailing President Kenyatta – in his eighties now and suffering from poor health – because they felt it was better that he did not know. That way he could claim, with complete sincerity, that he had no foreknowledge of the arrival of the Israeli planes.

After the meeting, Njonjo and McKenzie decided that once all the arrangements were in place for the Israeli planes to refuel at Nairobi Airport – with the details to be agreed between Dany Saadon, the El Al general manager in Nairobi, and the airport director – they would both leave the capital: McKenzie to return to England in time for a scheduled holiday in Norway with his wife; Njonjo to stay on a friend's farm at Nanyuki near Mount Kenya. They, too, were planning to deny any involvement. The agreed cover story for letting the Israeli planes land was that it was a last-minute humanitarian act to enable the sick and wounded to get hospital treatment.

1800hrs GMT, Ramat Gan, Israel

When Muki Betser arrived at Paratroops House, the clubhouse for off-duty airborne soldiers in Ramat Gan, to the east of Tel Aviv, he found a host of officers gathered for Dan Shomron's 8 p.m. planning session: Oren, Barak, Biran, Embar, as well as senior commanders from the signals corps, medical corps, Sayeret Golani and Sayeret Tzanchanim. Both these latter units were part of Shomron's Infantry and Paratroops Command, and had been earmarked to support the Unit's assault on the Old Terminal. Convinced that the operation would succeed, and become part of Israel's 'heritage', Shomron wanted to give both of these illustrious units, but particularly the Golani, a share in the glory.

The only key officer still absent, at this stage, was Betser's boss Yoni.

Shomron began the briefing by going over the order of battle 'from top to bottom, filling in the details of the plan'. As Hercules One taxied down the runway, he explained, ten paratroopers from Colonel Matan Vilnai's Sayeret Tzanchanim would jump from the side doors and lay electric lanterns along both sides of the runway in case the Ugandans turned off the landing lights.

Then, once Hercules One had come to a halt at the far end of the main runway, the Unit's break-in teams of thirty-six men, masquerading as Ugandan soldiers, would drive off it in a Mercedes and two Land Rovers and head down the original runway towards the Old Terminal. They would drive with headlights on and at a normal speed so as not to excite suspicion. Ehud Barak was named as the commander of this vital element of the operation. Though no longer a member of the Unit, he was hugely experienced and Shomron trusted him to get the job done. Meanwhile Shomron himself would set up his command post, consisting of a Land Rover and eight men, between the Old and New Terminal buildings.

Seven minutes later, Hercules Two would land with another sixteen men from the Unit aboard two BTR armoured personnel carriers, commanded by Yoni's former deputy, Major Shaul Mofaz. Their task would be to patrol the perimeter behind the Old Terminal and prevent any Ugandan reinforcements from interfering. The plane would also contain the balance of Vilnai's sixty-nine paratroopers whose job was to capture the New Terminal building, the nearby filling station and the new control tower.

A minute later, the third Hercules would land with two more BTRs – crewed by another sixteen men from the Unit – and thirty soldiers from Colonel Uri Saguy's Sayeret Golani. One BTR, commanded by Omer Bar-Lev, was assigned to neutralize the MiG airfield beside the Old Terminal, while the other joined Mofaz on the perimeter. The task of Saguy's men – some of whom would fly on Hercules Four – was to cover the area between the Old Terminal and the New, support the break-in teams (if they needed it) and use their Peugeot pick-up truck to ferry the hostages to the fourth Hercules.

That last Hercules would carry the lightest load so that there was room for the hostages on the return. It would contain a twelve-man surgical team and its equipment to treat any casualties, both on the ground and on the flight back; ten blue-uniformed air force techies, a portable fuel pump and another Peugeot pick-up to transport them both; and a final detachment of twenty Golani soldiers.

A second bigger medical team in a converted Boeing 707 would – if the necessary permissions were forthcoming – set up a field hospital at Nairobi in Kenya, and would be joined there by the four Hercules if the refuelling option at Entebbe took too long. All Shomron knew at this stage, however, was that discussions were taking place and that refuelling the Hercules transports at Nairobi – not least because of the diplomatic repercussions it might have for the Kenyan government – would be a last resort.

The sixth and last aircraft he mentioned was an IAF Boeing 707 that would act as Adam's and Peled's command and control head-quarters during the operation, circling the airfield at Entebbe and ferrying 'real time' information from the ground back to Rabin, Peres and Gur in the Kirya in Tel Aviv.

Shomron ended the briefing by nominating the Unit's headquarters near Tel Aviv and an adjacent base as the training locations for all the troops involved. The Unit's base not only had its own runway, but also had the tightest field security in the IDF. Once inside the bases, only the officers would be allowed out until the operation began. All non-vital phone lines would be disconnected and the remaining few closely monitored.

Shomron had barely finished speaking when a grinning Yoni Netanyahu entered the room. He had come straight from a nearby military airport, having flown up from the Sinai by light plane, and was eager to hear about the role the Unit would play in the rescue operation. As Muki Betser rose from the table to shake his hand, he thought of their shared experiences together – from the capture of the Syrian officers to the Yom Kippur War – and how much he had missed Netanyahu's calm professionalism.

1900hrs GMT, Tel Aviv, Israel

At 9 p.m., Shimon Peres picked up the phone in his office and dialled Moshe Dayan's personal number. Unperturbed by Rabin's rebuffing of his suggestion that Dayan should be sent as special envoy to Uganda, Peres was keen to hear his predecessor's opinion on the possible rescue plan.

He got through to Dayan's housekeeper who explained that her employers were out for dinner with friends from Australia. 'Do you know where?' asked Peres, stressing that it was a matter of vital national security.

The housekeeper gave him the name of a well-known restaurant on Tel Aviv's seafront. He immediately called for his military aide Arye Braun, who had also been an aide to Dayan during the latter's time as defense secretary, and together they drove the short distance across town to the restaurant. Apologizing profusely to Dayan's guests and his wife Ruth for the intrusion, Peres took Dayan to a quiet corner table where they could talk. Braun pulled out a map and Peres began to outline the rescue plan. When the defense minister dutifully listed the objections that had been raised by Rabin and Gur, and the possible obstacles, Dayan waved them aside. 'Shimon, this is a plan,' he declared, 'that I support not one hundred per cent but one hundred and fifty per cent! There has to be a military operation.'

Fortified by this unequivocal declaration of support from Israel's most famous soldier, Peres returned to the Kirya determined to win over the other members of the ministerial committee. He began by calling Transport Minister Gad Yaacobi and inviting him to a meeting at the Kirya. From the same faction of the Labour Party as Peres, Yaacobi was also a confidant of Dayan. Peres briefed him on the plan in general and on his conversation with Dayan. When he had finished, Yaacobi responded: 'Shimon, I'm with you.'

A call then came through from Rabin's office, summoning the pair to an 11 p.m. meeting of the ministerial committee.

2100hrs GMT, Tel Aviv, Israel

'We will now,' said Yitzkak Rabin, opening the 11 p.m. session of the ministerial committee in his office in the Kirya, 'discuss the arrangements of the negotiation that begins tomorrow through the good offices of the French government.'

'Surely,' responded Yigal Allon, 'the French should take the lead in this as they are directly responsible for the plane and its hijackers?'

Rabin waved his hand dismissively as if to a child, provoking a bitter exchange between the pair. When it was over, the prime minister asked Gandhi Ze'evi, the man he had appointed to conduct the negotiations via the French, to explain how he intended to do this. 'I propose to say from the start,' said Ze'evi, 'that Israel is negotiating only on its own behalf – not on the behalf of other countries that were required to release prisoners. Furthermore that we will specify the number we are prepared to release – forty – and not waver from that number. As for the list of men to be freed, Israel, and Israel alone, will compile it. The negotiations will take place in France, with France or another third party acting as a go-between. The handover of hostages for prisoners will also take place in France, at a military airfield, and not in Uganda. Failing that, a plane carrying the prisoners and another carrying the hostages would take off simultaneously from Tel Aviv and Entebbe, under mutually agreeable third-party supervision.'

Ze'evi paused before continuing. 'Our operative stages will be as follows: A. To submit our proposal to the French. B. To get their reactions, and those of Idi Amin and Wadie Haddad. C. Discuss the gap between positions, and receive lists of the passengers at Entebbe. D. To carry out the exchange.'

Rabin nodded his assent. 'Thank you, Gandhi. There is no need to go into any further detail at this stage. My feeling is that France will not provide logistical help apart from ferrying messages between the two sides.'

'They certainly won't fight Uganda,' said Allon caustically. Upset that Rabin had chosen a non-diplomat to conduct negotiations, he tried to reassert his ministry's authority over Ze'evi. But Rabin was having none of it and, as the meeting ended, Allon commented bitterly: 'If I'm getting in your way, appoint someone else to serve as acting foreign minister!'

It had been for Shimon Peres a 'particularly tense' session. With the military plan still taking shape, he did not want to mention it to Rabin until it had Gur's full support. He was, however, pleased with the outcome of the meeting. There would, he knew, be 'much diplomatic activity to span the two and a half days until the hijackers' latest ultimatum ran out – and to create a convenient cover beneath which' the IDF could continue its 'preparations for a military rescue'.

2200hrs GMT, Near Tel Aviv, Israel

It was past midnight when Yoni Netanyahu and Muki Betser settled down at a long Formica-topped table in Yoni's office, situated at one end of a low hut, its walls covered with maps, photos and weapons donated by previous commanding officers.

Briefed on the plan by Betser as they drove to the Unit's base, Netanyahu now set to work fine-tuning the various roles his men would play and the equipment they would use. He chose Betser to be his deputy for the operation and to command the four break-in teams, three of three men and one of six. Mindful of the mistakes made at Ma'alot, Betser said he wanted to lead the first break-in team. 'C'mon, Muki,' responded Netanyahu, 'you know it's against doctrine.'

'I do,' said Betser, fully aware that senior ranks were never first through the door. 'But I don't want a repeat of Ma'alot where I should have gone up the ladder first. I want to make sure the job's done properly. I insist upon it.'

Yoni sighed. 'You're impossible,' he said, conceding defeat.

Betser then assigned the break-in teams to specific jobs: Captain Giora Zussman's team of six would go through the two doors into the Israeli hall and the adjacent VVIP area where the terrorists slept; the team under Yiftach Reicher, Yoni's new deputy, was tasked with entering the first door into the customs hall, climbing the stairs to the second floor and neutralizing the Ugandan soldiers who were sleeping there; while Betser himself would lead two break-in teams through the doors that led from the tarmac into the main hall.

Just fifteen men were assigned to these four break-in crews, leaving a further nineteen outside to hold off with rocket-propelled grenades (RPGs) and heavy machine-guns any Ugandans who tried to intervene. Yoni would direct operations from the front of the Old Terminal, assisted by Tamir Pardo, his communications officer, Dr David Hassin and a reserve company commander Alik Ron.

While Netanyahu drew up the order of battle – selecting his most experienced soldiers, many of whom had just been given pre-discharge leave, for the most difficult tasks – Betser supervised the building of a model of the Old Terminal from blueprints provided by Solel Boneh. Using two-by-four timber for a frame, his men put up burlap and canvas sheets to mimic the exterior and interior walls and doorways of the terminal building. As soon as the model was ready, and sited alongside the Unit's runway, just like the real thing at Entebbe, they began practising the break-ins.

Eventually Ehud Barak arrived at the base, having just attended a meeting at the Kirya, and there was obvious tension between him and Netanyahu as they went over the entire plan, Barak making various suggestions. Netanyahu resented the fact that he had been superseded as leader of the assault troops – telling Betser earlier, 'I don't see any alternative to my being in command' – and he made little attempt to hide his disgruntlement.

Barak understood this and would have felt the same himself if their roles had been reversed. But he was not going to stand aside. He may also have felt his appointment was for the best: the tension between Netanyahu and some of his men was well known to Barak and other ex-members of the Unit, and there were even rumours that Shlomo Gazit, the general with overall responsibility for the Unit, was about to replace Netanyahu a few months early with Amiram Levine.

Once they had finished going over the plan, Barak gave Netanyahu a lift home – they lived in the same Tel Aviv apartment building, one floor apart – so that they could both snatch a couple of hours' sleep.

Meanwhile the support troops from the Golani and Tzanchanim Sayerets were arriving at an adjacent base to begin rehearsing their own roles in the operation. Among them was a promising twenty-one-year-old junior officer in the Golani called Noam Tamir. Having recently passed out first of a class of officer-cadets, Tamir was training with his squad when word arrived of an impending operation. They speculated on the destination, but Tamir did not make the connection with the Entebbe hijacking until he had attended the initial briefing at the Unit's base. He felt both relief and pride that he had been selected, but no fear.

Feeling just as upbeat was Colonel Dr Ephraim Sneh, the chief medical officer for the Infantry and Paratroops Command and the man chosen to head the field medical team earmarked for Entebbe. Sneh's Polish-born father Moshe, also a doctor, had been one of the leading figures in the Haganah before entering the Knesset where he was a member of various left-wing parties. Sneh himself had begun his training as a doctor in 1964, at the age of twenty, after completing an initial two years' military service with the Nahal infantry battalion. The IDF had released him six months early on condition that, having qualified as a doctor, he agreed to serve two more years as a medical officer.

He eventually joined the Tzanchanim (paratroopers), initially as a battalion doctor and then with the brigade. After a spell out of the army, training as a surgeon, he returned to the Tzanchanim at the start of the Yom Kippur War and commanded the paratroopers' medical unit during the costly and brutal Battle of the Chinese Farm in the Sinai. The experience of treating a huge number of para-troopers and armoured soldiers in combat conditions, almost constantly under fire, had convinced Sneh that he could cope with anything. He was, therefore, quite unfazed by the orders he received late on Thursday 2 July that he needed to put together a medical plan for the Entebbe operation and command the teams on the ground.

He decided to take with him a surgical team of eleven: a chief surgeon (Lieutenant-Colonel Eran Dolev, a future surgeon-general of the IDF), an anaesthetist, a gynaecologist and an orthopaedic surgeon; a liaison officer whose sole task was to keep the hostages calm during the flight back; and six male medics. A further six doctors would be embedded with the various combat troops.

One of Sneh's surgical team was a thirty-six-year-old South African-born gynaecologist and obstetrician called Jossy Faktor. When Faktor got the evening call to report for duty he was with his wife Barbara celebrating some friends' tenth wedding anniversary in the town of Ra'anana, north of Tel Aviv. The two couples were close, having grown up together in South Africa through the Habonim – a socialist-Zionist cultural youth movement – and were literally clinking champagne glasses when Faktor had to leave. Faktor's job the following day was to obtain large supplies of blood plasma without arousing suspicions, particularly among the media, that a rescue operation was about to be launched. He managed this by spreading a story that 'a crisis was developing on the northern border with Lebanon and we would need medical teams and blood'. It worked.

Sneh himself, on hearing that many of the hostages were suffering from stomach complaints, was preoccupied with the problem of 'a hundred shitting people and no toilets' on the Hercules. So he arranged – via a 'very smart' logistics officer called Rami Dotan* – to take along two aluminium milk cans that the hostages could use *in extremis*. Dotan sourced them from a local moshavim.

Neither on Thursday evening nor later did Sneh have doubts. Instead he had 'total confidence that the operation would be accomplished and we'd come home'. Why? Because he knew all the senior men involved – Shomron, Vilnai, Barak and Netanyahu – and regarded them as the IDF's 'A-team'. Such a team, he felt certain, was 'invincible': there was 'none better than these guys to tackle unexpected problems, to overcome and prevail'.

Others were not so certain. Twenty-one-year-old First Sergeant Amir Ofer was enjoying the customary pre-discharge leave given to soldiers who were about to finish their military service, having spent the previous two and a half years in the Unit, when he received a phone call from Yoni Netanyahu's secretary. He was to report to the base in the morning. 'Are we going far?' he asked, knowing it had to be an operation.

'Very far,' she replied.

He realized at once it had to be Entebbe and that the Unit would spearhead any assault. His mind flashed back to earlier rescue attempts that had not gone well: Ma'alot and, a year later, the storming of the Savoy Hotel in Tel Aviv that had cost seven Fatah terrorists, eight civilian hostages and three soldiers – one of them, Itamar Ben-David, from Ofer's own squad – their lives. How much harder, then, would be an operation so far from Israel and in a country where the army appeared to be cooperating with the hijackers?

Tormented by such doubts, Ofer lay awake until he finally convinced

---

* Dotan later became the IAF's procurement chief with the rank of brigadier-general. Convicted in 1989 of embezzling $10 million from US military aid packages, he was reduced to the rank of private and spent thirteen years in prison.

Soldiers of the elite Sayeret Matkal ('the Unit') in a dry river bed in the Negev Desert in 1960. Ehud Barak, a future commander of the Unit and prime minister of Israel, is sitting on the left in a cap.

Soldiers of the Unit practise a house entry in 1971. Bibi Netanyahu, brother of Yoni and a future prime minister of Israel, is on the right.

The bloody aftermath of the Lod Airport Massacre when three pro-Palestinian members of the Japanese Red Army shot and killed twenty-six travelers, most of them Christian pilgrims from Puerto Rico, in 1972. Two of the attackers were also killed; the third, Kozo Okamoto, was wounded and captured.

Shocked hostages are evacuated from a hijacked Sabena Airways Boeing 707 after soldiers of the Unit had successfully stormed the plane at Lod Airport in 1972. The Unit's commander Ehud Barak (left) is dressed in white overalls and holding a pistol. One of the two dead Black September terrorists is at his feet.

Brigitte Kuhlmann, co-founder of the German left-wing terrorist group Revolutionary Cells (RC) and one of the four Air France hijackers. Some Israeli hostages thought her a brutal 'Nazi'; her boyfriend and fellow RC terrorist Gerd Schnepel insists she was 'a friendly, caring person with social commitment'.

A police mugshot of Wilfried 'Boni' Böse, the former sociology student who helped form the RC and led the Air France hijackers.

Japanese Red Army terrorist Kozo Okamoto listens through headphones as he is sentenced to life imprisonment for his part in the Lod Airport Massacre.

Relatives of Israeli passengers on Air France Flight 139 arrive at the Tel Aviv office of Israeli Prime Minister Yithak Rabin on Thursday 1 July 1976 to demand that the government releases 40 'freedom fighters', including Okamoto, in exchange for the hostages' lives.

Israeli Prime Minister Yitzhak Rabin, seated between IDF Chief of Staff Motta Gur (left) and Defense Secretary Shimon Peres.

US Secretary of State Henry Kissinger (right) and Israeli Ambassador Simcha Dinitz in Washington in 1975.

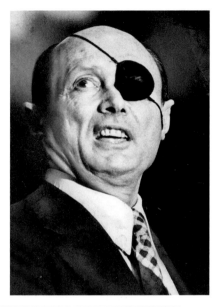

Moshe Dayan, former IDF chief of staff and Israeli defense minister. Peres wanted to send Dayan out to Entebbe to negotiate with the hijackers. Rabin vetoed the plan because his capture would have 'strengthened the blackmailers' hand' and left the government 'no room for manoeuvre'.

West German Chancellor Helmut Schmidt holds an emergency session with members of his cabinet and opposition leaders on Thursday 1 July 1976 to discuss the hijackers' demands for the release of six imprisoned terrorists.

French hostage Michel Cojot in Switzerland with his daughter Yael. After his release by the terrorists on Thursday 1 July 1976, Cojot gave Israeli intelligence vital information that saved many lives.

President Idi Amin of Uganda (in dark suit and broad-brimmed hat) visits the hostages in the Old Terminal building at Entebbe in the morning of Wednesday 30 June 1976. Michel Cojot (right) is holding the megaphone; Cojot's 12-year-old son Olivier is second from the left.

Idi Amin comforts a Ugandan soldier wounded during the Entebbe Raid in Kampala's New Mulago Hospital on Sunday 4 July 1976.

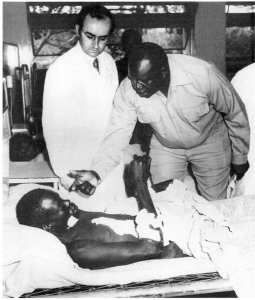

Israeli hostage Dora Bloch, pictured with her granddaughter a year before the hijacking. Mrs Bloch was in New Mulago Hospital when the raid took place and was later murdered on Amin's orders.

Henry Kyemba, Ugandan minister of health, shortly after he fled to London in 1977. Kyemba kept Dora Bloch in hospital after her treatment because he thought it would be more comfortable than the Old Terminal. His good intention cost Bloch her life.

South African born Bruce McKenzie with Kenyan President Jomo Kenyatta around the time of the hijacking. A former minister of agriculture and the 'most influential white man in East Africa', McKenzie helped to broker the secret deal that allowed Israeli planes to refuel at Nairobi.

Charles Njonjo, the attorney general of Kenya. It was at Njonjo's Nairobi house that the secret deal with the Israelis was agreed.

Julie Aouzerate (second left), an Algerian-born French Jew, is met by her granddaughter at Orly Airport after the arrival of the first batch of 47 released hostages in the evening of Wednesday 30 June 1976.

Some of the 100 hostages released in the second batch enjoy refreshments at Orly Airport after their arrival from Entebbe in the early hours of Friday 2 July 1976.

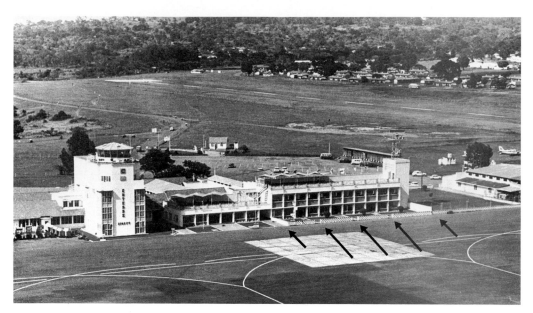

The photograph of the front of the Old Terminal building that the IDF used to plan Operation Thunderbolt. The arrows mark the doorways through which the Unit's break-in teams would enter: (from L to R) the customs hall, large hall (the former departure lounge where the hostages were being held), small (Israeli) hall and VIP hall (not built when photo was taken). The control tower is to the left.

One of the photos taken of Entebbe Airport by a Mossad agent in a small plane on Friday 2 July 1976. The Air France Airbus is parked at the end of the old runway (top). In the centre are two rows of MiG fighter jets. The Old Terminal building is out of picture to the right. This vital intelligence reached the assault teams shortly before their departure from Lod Air Force Base on 3 July.

The charred remains of MiG fighter jets destroyed by the Unit at Entebbe Airport, thus fulfilling the Israeli side of the secret deal with the Kenyans.

The black Mercedes used by the Unit to fool Ugandan soldiers that it contained one of their senior officers. Here it is being reversed out of Hercules One on its return to Tel Nof Air Force Base, south of Tel Aviv, on Sunday 4 July 1976. Major Muki Betser is standing on the right in Ugandan uniform.

Lieutenant-Colonel Yoni Netanyahu, commander of the assault force at Entebbe, who was shot and killed by a Ugandan sniper.

Motta Gur, IDF chief of staff, briefs the media on Operation Thunderbolt at a press conference in Tel Aviv. Beside him is a map of Entebbe Airport.

Hercules Four, with its distinctive high tail, lands at Ben-Gurion Airport
with the released hostages on the morning of Sunday 4 July 1976.

Some of the hundreds of relatives and well-wishers at Ben-Gurion Airport
to welcome the return of the hostages from Entebbe.

Israeli Foreign Minister Yigal Allon (back to camera) welcomes the hostages as they disembark from Hercules Four at Ben-Gurion Airport. Michel Bacos, the chief pilot of the hijacked Air France Airbus, is on the left.

A female hostage is hugged by an emotional relative.

Israeli lawyer Akiva Laxer talks with a neighbour at his Tel Aviv home after his return from Entebbe. The table is piled high with gifts from friends and well wishers.

Relatives weep as the body of Ida Borochovich, one of three civilians killed during the raid, is buried with military honours in Bat Yam, south of Tel Aviv, on 5 July 1976.

Members of the Israeli Knesset – including Shimon Peres and Yitzhak Rabin (centre right) – stand in silent tribute to the casualties of the Entebbe Raid.

Brigitte Kuhlmann's grave at a military cemetery in Jinja, Uganda. The Muslim headstone gives Kuhlmann's nationality, nom de guerre 'Halime' and date of death '3-7-76'.

The abandoned and derelict Air France Airbus at Entebbe Airport in 1994.

In 2009, Israeli Prime Minister Bibi Netanyahu climbs out of one of the Hercules C-130s used in the Entebbe Raid. Netanyahu's political career has been boosted by his late brother's status as a national hero.

himself that a criminal like Amin would surely be open to bribes. If Amin agreed to look the other way, Ofer reasoned, the rescue would not be nearly so dangerous. Only now could he sleep.

2230hrs GMT, Tel Aviv, Israel

Before turning in for the night, Shimon Peres invited Motta Gur to his home in the hope of persuading the IDF chief, who still had serious reservations, that the proposed military option was both necessary and viable. Gur arrived after midnight. 'Motta,' said Peres, 'I don't intend to suggest a plan against the judgement of the chief of staff, but I want you to understand that, in my opinion, the future of this country and the nation is in the balance. This is the time for boldness. You can have nothing without sacrifices. And I'm not deluding myself – there are likely to be some along the way. Failure will mean that I have to draw some personal conclusions. But if we give in to terrorists, not even the faintest memory of us will remain.'

The most Gur would concede, after a long discussion, was for the planners to set up a model of Entebbe based on the data then available (an undertaking that was already under way at the Unit's base). It was a step forward, but the plan was still a long way from becoming reality. Peres noted in his diary for 1 July: 'I spoke to Motta with all my powers of persuasion . . . Today was the hardest of my life.'

DAY 6: FRIDAY 2 JULY 1976

0010hrs GMT, Orly Airport, France

A spontaneous cheer broke out among the hundred former hostages as the Air France Jumbo touched down on French soil at 2.10 a.m. Their nightmare was finally over.

Twenty minutes earlier, as the descent began, they had been advised over the intercom to be careful what they said and to whom: to their families and friends they were 'to appear as reassuring as possible'; to the authorities they were to 'tell everything they could remember in the minutest detail'; and to the press they were to say nothing that might 'make the Palestinians or Ugandans angry' and that might lead to 'a deterioration of conditions' for the hostages still at Entebbe, or 'put their lives in danger'.

Once on the ground they were told that their families and a high-level delegation were waiting to greet them in the airport's VIP suite. What they were not expecting, at two in the morning, was to have to run the gauntlet of the world's press as they left the plane. Amid popping flashbulbs and shouted questions, they were ushered by a line of police into the temporary refuge of the VIP suite where most of the forty-nine French nationals enjoyed a tearful reunion with their families: Claude Moufflet, for example, was met by his wife, his parents, his brother and his sister-in-law. (Later that day he posted the 'urgent' letter that had been entrusted to him at Athens the previous Sunday.) British-born Isabella Poignon and her French husband Gérard left at once for their home in Versailles where Gérard's mother was caring for their eighteen-month-old daughter Emma. On hearing of Isabella's release, her mother Dr Kathleen Murray said from her home in Middlesex:

'I'm so relieved that I can't stop smiling – it has been ghastly these last four days.'

Waiting to greet Michel Cojot, much to his surprise, was his 'future ex-wife' and they 'embraced almost as warmly as a real couple'. They were still locked together when a soberly dressed official from the Ministry of the Interior tapped Cojot on the shoulder and asked if he could speak to him urgently and in private. Cojot was delighted. 'France needs me,' he told himself, before arranging to meet the official at his home a couple of hours later.

The official never appeared. Instead Cojot was closely questioned at work that Friday by Amiram Levine and agents from the Mossad who had been pointed in his direction by other former hostages. He told the Israelis everything he knew about the layout of the Old Terminal and the number, habits and descriptions of the terrorists; and, as before, the information was quickly phoned back to Israel. A lot of what he said was simply confirmation of what the Israelis already knew from the testimony of other hostages; yet, at the same time, it was more up to date and more precise. There would most likely be, he explained, at least four terrorists guarding the hostages at any time, day or night, while the others slept in the VVIP room at the end of the building. Exactly how many in which room he could not say: he had left before the remaining hostages had been reunited in the big hall and, as far as he was aware, they were still in separate rooms.

For the non-French nationals, there was no tearful reunion at Orly. Instead they were met by consular officials and given details of hotel accommodation and onward flights. Most of the Americans were put up at the Hôtel Concorde La Fayette, near the Porte Maillot in Paris's 17th Arrondissement, though Sanford Freedman chose to join his lover Carole Anne Taylor and her son at the Hôtel Le Littré in the city centre. Not all were impressed by their welcome. After all they had been through, the Rabinowitzes were expecting the waiting US diplomats to be sympathetic and helpful. They were anything but. 'We were expecting a hero's welcome,' remembered Peter. 'But instead their attitude was, "You've made me get up at two o'clock in the morning, so don't expect any of my time tomorrow." They were essentially hostile to us.'

It went from bad to worse when one US diplomat told the Rabinowitzes that, since their old passports had been confiscated by the terrorists, they would have to buy new ones at 'full price, but good for only three months'.

Peter then asked: 'Have you contacted our families?'

'No, that's *your* responsibility.'

'Could we charge the cost of the calls to the Embassy?' queried Nancy.

'Do that and we'll break your arm.'

After 'five days at gunpoint' this was hardly, as the Rabinowitzes put it later, a 'diplomatic joke'.

Later that day, after they had got some rest, a selection of the Americans were debriefed in their hotels by US officials – probably from the CIA – and the composite report was distributed to, among others, the US Embassy in Tel Aviv.

They claimed that, as far as they were aware, the only Americans still in Entebbe were the young stockbroker and his wife, both from New York. They did not know why they had been kept back, though one of them suggested that 'their flaunting of their Jewishness might have alienated some of the Arabs in the commandos'. One or two thought their retention might simply have been 'an oversight'. As for Janet Almog, not one of them had been 'aware of her presence'. She was probably held back, they thought, because she was 'seated with the Israelis' and had 'Israeli documentation'. The dual nationals, they noted, had 'made no attempts to destroy or discard the evidence of their national citizenship'.

They explained that the four hijackers were 'two Germans and two rather inexperienced young Arabs'. The German male was the 'obvious leader', though the woman was 'often the most virulent'. They were, thought some of the Americans, 'sincere revolutionaries who were not working merely for the PFLP . . . but also to free their colleagues imprisoned in Germany whom they appeared to know personally'.

Once they had reached Entebbe the hijackers were joined by 'four PLO' who assumed 'principal command', though some Americans thought 'Basil' continued to be the 'General Manager' of the group and 'was able to make a major input into the decisions as to who should be released'. The four 'Arab leaders', on the other hand, were 'more authoritative' and 'much tougher' than the original hijackers. They were 'clearly' anti-semitic – unlike the Germans, who insisted they were only anti-Zionist – and 'took a certain sadistic pleasure in forcing the old Jewish passengers to plead to be among those sent to France'. Two of the group were tall (one weighing over 200 pounds) with black moustaches. Another was short and heavy-set, with a 'comical face', as though he was wearing the stereotyped big nose/hornrimmed glasses mask, and 'appeared to be the most influential'. He was thought to have connections with Peru, and spoke Spanish as well as French and English.

As for Idi Amin, all the Americans found him 'repellent and duplicitous in his treatment of the prisoners'. They were convinced that he knew Uganda was the plane's destination 'before it landed' and that he had probably been 'aware of the plot before the hijacking'. He had let the terrorists bring in 'more lethal weapons' and the Ugandan troops were 'clearly there as a back-up force'. It would have been easy for the Ugandans, had they so wished, to disarm or kill the terrorists. But they had chosen not to. Amin, moreover, had made clear his support for the terrorists' aims. He had told the hostages that 'if their governments wished to see them alive, they must cooperate in meeting the just demands of the hijackers'.

The most controversial aspect of the composite report, however, was the section that dealt with American suspicions that three of the released hostages – two Arab men and a Canadian woman – had collaborated with the terrorists. The female, said the report, had 'left [Orly] airport quickly (with an American) without checking in' with Canadian Embassy officials and had 'not been staying at the hotel where reservations had been made' for her. These were, the authors of the report hastened to add, 'merely the impressions of some of the passengers, speculation induced by their surprise that even the lax security at the Athens Airport had permitted the introduction of substantial arms'.

Asked about the intentions of the hijackers, the Americans said they did not think they intended a 'general killing of the Israelis or the young French passengers and crew', but that they might start by shooting one or two Israelis first 'to emphasize the seriousness of their demands'. Overall the terrorists' optimism was justified 'since they held all the cards and eventually even Israel would be forced to yield'.

Amin had warned the hostages that if an assault was launched from outside, or if there was an uprising from within, the terrorists would blow up the building. The Americans did not believe this, and thought the boxes allegedly filled with dynamite were 'really designed just to block off a door'. In any event, 'the chances of rescue or escape are nil'. The Israelis knew this, and while their distress had increased as two planeloads of passengers had left, they had 'remained stoic'. Whether this would continue the Americans could not say. A few more days might 'cause some of the old and infirm to break'.

0200hrs GMT, Tel Aviv, Israel

Yoni Netanyahu waved good night to Ehud Barak and climbed the stairs to his apartment. Inside he was surprised to find Bruria asleep; she had been scheduled to work on a night flight that had clearly been cancelled.

Letting his clothes fall in a heap, he got into bed without showering. He was exhausted, but also intensely excited. This was the moment he had been waiting for all his life: to lead – albeit with Ehud Barak looking over his shoulder – Israel's finest soldiers against its most implacable foe. If their mission was successful, and he had no doubt on that score, it would do much to erase the growing tension between himself and some of his men. They would finally understand that his methods were the right ones, and that his leadership in battle was second to none. Then, and only then, would he be happy to relinquish command of the Unit to another man, convinced that he had done his bit.

Yoni quickly fell asleep. But by 5.30 a.m. he was awake again. Watched by a bleary-eyed Bruria, he rose from the bed, dressed and left for the base without saying a word.

Only later did Bruria find on the kitchen table the four-page letter that Yoni had written to her in the Sinai but never posted. It moved

Bruria to tears, particularly the closing passage: 'I know I'm not with you enough . . . but I trust you, me, both of us to manage living our youth to the full – you, to live your youth and your life, and I my life and the last flicker of my youth. We'll cope.'

0230hrs GMT, Entebbe International Airport, Uganda

It was still dark outside as Maggy rose from her mattress in the Old Terminal building and went to take the shower she had postponed a day earlier. Returning after her wash she discovered Jean-Jacques Mimouni reading a favourite journal of hers called *Science et Vie*. So she sat down next to him and together they discussed an article on sub-Saharan Africa that mentioned Uganda.

All around them people were beginning to stir, though dawn was still some way off. Excited by the prospect of their imminent release, few had slept well. 'Everybody's possessions are packed,' noted Moshe Peretz in his diary, 'and we await notification [of] when we move off.'

0400hrs GMT, Tel Aviv, Israel

At 6 a.m., Shimon Peres woke from a fitful sleep with severe tooth-ache. He had felt it coming on all week, but had tried to ignore it because he did not have time to go to the dentist. Now, with no option, he called Dr Langer and fixed an appointment for later in the morning. He then headed in to his office at the Kirya where a very welcome piece of news awaited him: Kenya had agreed to let the rescue planes 'land on its soil in the event of difficulties during the flight'.

Peres was delighted that one of the major obstacles to the operation – how to get the planes safely back to Israel – had been overcome. He hurried across to Motta Gur's office to deliver the news in person, and saw with satisfaction the glint in the chief of staff's eyes. They both agreed that a solution to the refuelling problem made it possible to launch the operation on Saturday night. This was 'much to be preferred, since the ultimatum would not have elapsed by then and negotiations would still be in progress'. As for the danger that the Kenyans might leak news of the plan, neither was worried. They knew that the Kenyans' policy 'was to continue denying that they held any of the terrorists demanded by the hijackers' – which technically was true, though they could not admit why – and that 'their interest was in a successful operation by Israel'.

With Gur slowly warming to the idea of the Hercules rescue mission – and as the plan was 'rapidly becoming operational' – Peres felt it was the right time to inform Yitzhak Rabin of its existence. So he called the Prime Minister's Office and told Rabin that 'at this moment, speaking personally rather than officially, I am convinced that we have a real military option available'.

Having repeated his view that releasing prisoners 'would gravely demoralize the public at home and seriously weaken Israel's standing and prestige abroad', he described the plan in broad terms.

Rabin seemed unimpressed. 'If it fails,' he said, 'the blow to the IDF and to Israel itself will be very great. Moreover it seems to me that the plan is flawed at its outset. What if the first plane is identified and attacked before the rest of the force has time to land and deploy? They won't stand a chance. Anyway, I'm bound by the Cabinet's decision.'

Peres knew that this last comment was not strictly true: technically the prime minister did need the support of his Cabinet before authorizing such a risky military operation; but in reality it was hard to believe that any minister would withhold his approval if the prime minister, defense minister and chief of staff were all supportive of a military strike. His toughest hurdle, Peres knew, was getting both Rabin and Gur on board. 'You should know, prime minister,' responded Peres, 'that Benny Peled is confident that the first plane can land without arousing suspicions.'

Rabin grunted, as if that was typical of Peled.

Realizing that Rabin still needed some convincing – and that the person most likely to do that was the chief of staff – Peres said he would bring Gur to the Prime Minister's Office at 10.30 a.m. As he put down the phone, his aching tooth reminded him of his dental appointment. He left at once for Dr Langer's surgery. Naturally there was no mention of an upcoming military operation until the dentist, during a pause in his treatment, asked an open-mouthed Peres if he knew why his soldier son had had his weekend leave cancelled. The defense minister shook his head.

0400hrs GMT, Entebbe International Airport, Uganda

The hostages were surprised and delighted to see President Idi Amin enter the Old Terminal hall at seven in the morning. He was wearing a civilian suit and his cowboy hat, and was accompanied, once again, by his fifth wife Sarah 'in a beautiful green dress' and his young son Gamal Abdel Nasser Jwami. On his last two visits he had announced the release of hostages, and few doubted that was the reason for his return.

'Good morning,' said Amin in English, his expression stern. 'I can confirm that yesterday your government agreed to negotiate with the PFLP, and that was the reason that more hostages were released. But since then Israel has not accepted the PFLP's demands and this puts you in grave danger. This building is surrounded by TNT and will be blown up if the demands are not met.'

This was not what the English-speaking hostages expected to hear, and many murmured their dissent. Amin raised his hand for silence. 'This morning I leave for the conference of the Organization of African Unity, of which I am president, in Mauritius. While I am there I will keep in touch with the various negotiators and will continue to do everything I can to secure your final release. To assist with that process I ask that you write a letter to your government, urging it to accept the PFLP's demands, and that you have it ready for the one o'clock broadcast on Radio Uganda. I will come and see you on my return on Saturday. Goodbye.'

As Amin turned to leave, many of the hostages applauded, though not all had understood his words. The non-English-speaking Israelis had to wait for Ilan Hartuv to translate his words into Hebrew, while the French hostages in a similar predicament went to the pilot Michel Bacos for enlightenment. Once all had been updated, a huge depression fell over the group. They had been led to believe the night before that Israel had agreed to release the forty prisoners. Now they realized that this was not the case and that the negotiations were ongoing. The danger for them now was that the two sides would fail to reach an agreement.

With this in mind, some of the hostages argued vehemently that they should follow Amin's suggestion and write a letter to the Israeli government; others disagreed. The split, noted Moshe Peretz, was between 'most of the family men, and the crew members, except for the captain', who were in favour; and the younger Israeli hostages, who were against.

For Ilan Hartuv, the Israelis' unofficial spokesman, the decision whether or not to write the letter was an agonizing one. He and his fellow committee members – Yitzhak David, Uzi Davidson, Baruch Gross and Akiva Laxer – argued about it back and forth, and eventually decided to write a watered-down version that American-born Janet Almog translated into English. But for a long time they delayed giving it to the terrorists, in order both to miss the one o'clock broadcast and to show, as David put it, 'that our spirit is not broken'. It was Bacos who eventually persuaded them to hand it over. 'Look,' he told Hartuv, 'you have to give them the letter. They are very agitated and I don't know what they'll do.'

So together they went outside and gave the letter to Böse and the Peruvian. Addressed to the government of Israel, it read: 'We, all the Israelis hijacked near Athens and flown to Entebbe airport, personally thank H[is] E[xecellency] Field Marshal Idi Amin, President of the Republic of Uganda, for his personal concerns for our safety and comfort and for his many visits to our group. The President informed us of his unflinching efforts to obtain our release. We, therefore, ask the Government to react positively to the effort to obtain the safe release and return of all our persons held here.'

Having read the letter, the Peruvian shook his head: 'It's not what we asked you to do.'

'Look,' replied Hartuv. 'Our government knows Israelis and how they think. They know we would never ask them to release prisoners unless we had a gun to our foreheads. It's the best we can do.'

The Peruvian shrugged and took the letter. It was not broadcast to the world, via Radio Kampala, until 5 p.m. the following day.

0600hrs GMT, Central Israel

Sergeant Amir Ofer climbed out of the car with his pack, thanked the driver for the lift and approached the gates of the Unit's base. He could see all the usual signs of an impending operation: tight security at the entrance and lots of activity beyond. But what hardened his suspicions that Entebbe was the target was the mock-up of the Old Terminal near the perimeter fence.

Inside the base he received the final confirmation from his team commander, Lieutenant Amon Peled, who had arrived the night before. 'There's going to be an operation to free the hostages at Entebbe,' Peled told him. 'The Unit will spearhead it, and our team will be the tip of the spearhead.'

Most of the Unit's soldiers would have been both honoured and excited to hear that they had been selected for such a vital job. Not Ofer. He felt his chest constrict and a shiver of fear go through him. He knew only too well how dangerous it was to be among the first to enter a room full of hostages, and felt cursed that such a job had come up so close to his discharge. But he kept his thoughts to himself and merely nodded.

Leaving Peled, he went to recover his ammo vest that he had given to a young recruit in anticipation of his discharge, and then to the quartermaster's hut to replenish his supplies. Other soldiers were swarming round the counter, and when it came to Ofer's turn he asked for all the usual equipment. But as he was holding a helicopter landing light it suddenly dawned on him that no helicopter could rescue him from Entebbe, which was practically at 'the end of the earth'. He handed the light back and carried the rest of his kit to a nearby barracks to prepare his ammo vest before the briefings and drills began.

Yoni Netanyahu, meanwhile, was giving the 'warning orders' for the operation to the Unit's officers, including one or two like Peled who had missed the late-night briefing. The only major change from the plan agreed with Betser was that Netanyahu would now command one of the break-in teams. On hearing this, Betser and others tried to convince their commander to remain outside and let his subordinates storm the terminal. But Netanyahu was insistent: and the reason was that Ehud Barak, who had been given overall command of the assault, intended to position his command post in front of the Old Terminal. Knowing this, Netanyahu felt that if he did not take part in the assault he would be, in effect, redundant.

0630hrs GMT, Entebbe International Airport, Uganda

Once breakfast had been cleared away, Brigitte Kuhlmann entered the large hall and announced in English: 'Could everyone take their mattresses and their belongings and move to the back wall of the room so that the Ugandan staff can sweep and polish. Do it now!'

Hebrew and French translations followed, but not quickly or accurately enough for everyone to understand, and as people dithered Kuhlmann lost her temper. 'I asked you to go over there!' she shouted, waving her pistol at the back wall, 'now move!'

Hostages bumped into each other, and stumbled over their possessions, as they hastened to obey. Once most of the room had been cleared, three airport workers entered with brooms and proceeded to sweep the floor, while another pushed a large polishing machine. Some optimists saw the clear-up as a sign that they would soon be leaving; but most were resigned to staying a few days longer.

At 10 a.m. Wilfried Böse took Bacos and Lemoine, the pilot and flight engineer, out to the Airbus that was still standing on the apron in front of the Old Terminal. Once in the plane they were told to start the engines and taxi it closer to the building – for what purpose

Böse did not explain. Having done this, Bacos and Lemoine were given permission to collect from the cabins any discarded books and magazines to distribute to the hostages who, five days in to their their Uganda stay, were running out of things to read. Jean-Jacques Mimouni was delighted to recover his copy of *Atlas* magazine, and turned to a report on the Poitou-Charentes region of France with a particularly beautiful photo of two peasants in front of a table filled with wine, country bread and Camembert cheese. When any of the non-kosher-eating Jews saw the picture, they were literally salivating.

Outside, the yellow bus was making regular trips to and from the plane, prompting Agnès to speculate that it was being cleaned for their departure. Certainly the terrorists in general, and the Palestinians in particular, seemed remarkably relaxed, as if the negotiations were nearing a satisfactory conclusion.

A stiff breeze was coming off the lake and providing some relief for the hostages sweltering in the large hall. It was also causing the Airbus's engines to whine as the blades were spun round. 'Why are the engines still on?' Jaber asked Captain Bacos.

The Frenchman raised his eyebrows. 'They're not on. It's the wind.'

0800hrs GMT, Tel Aviv, Israel

Once his tooth had been fixed, Shimon Peres went to speak to Justice Minister Chaim Zadok. He reckoned that two members of the six-man ministerial committee – Yigal Allon and Gad Yaacobi – were likely to support his call for a military strike, and that one more would give him an outright majority. He tried to convince Zadok by saying that Zionism and Israeli sovereignty would be forfeit if the hostages were not rescued.

Zadok shook his head. 'The question is not about that. It's whether there is a plan for a military rescue – one with a high probability of success.'

'There is such a plan,' replied Peres.

Having explained in more detail, Peres left Zadok knowing he had 'a firm ally'.

He next called a meeting in his office of Gur, Adam, Peled, Gazit and their senior aides, and Yitzhak Hofi, chief of the Mossad, to discuss the rescue. 'What should our troops do,' Gur asked Peres, 'if they encounter resistance from Ugandan forces at Entebbe Airport?'

'Shoot to kill,' was the instant response.

Gur nodded in satisfaction. 'That will make the detailed planning of the operation much easier.'

Next they discussed the news that Amin had left for the meeting of the OAU in Mauritius and would not be back in Uganda until Saturday evening at the earliest, and possibly Sunday. 'In that case,' suggested one of those present, 'we should appoint one of our soldiers as a stand-in. We just need to find one of suitable height and girth, dress him up as Amin and black his face. The Unit is already planning to take a limousine so that the Ugandans think it contains a senior officer. Why not put our Amin "double" in it?'

'Because,' said another, 'if he returns from Mauritius *before* our planes arrive the Ugandans are bound to smell a rat.'

Gur then summarized the flight plan and the various stages of the ground operation. 'The planes will take off from Sharm el-Sheikh, the closest point, late on Saturday afternoon. They'll fly straight down the middle of the Red Sea, only turning right when they reach Ethiopia, which does not have radar that can track high-flying aircraft. Finally they'll approach Entebbe from over Lake Victoria, the route used by most commercial airlines coming in to land. The rescue will take a maximum of fourteen minutes: two for the lead Hercules to taxi to a halt; two more for the troops and vehicles to disembark, shortly after which the other planes would start to land; five minutes to reach the terminal building; and another five to complete the rescue.'

'It sounds possible,' said Peres. 'Do you still have any concerns, Motta?'

'I have a couple. First we need to examine what the level of risk to the hostages is. We still don't know exactly where all the hostages are being held – whether they've been reunited in the big hall or split between the two rooms – and where the terrorists are stationed. We need more intelligence about this. I also need to know that the Hercules crews can land on an unfamiliar airstrip in darkness. I've asked Benny to arrange a demonstration for me tonight,' said Gur, nodding towards Peled. 'I'll be in the cockpit and if I don't come back you'll know the answer.'

'What about the air defences at Entebbe?' asked Peres. 'You were worried about them before?'

'We don't think there are any,' said Hofi, 'but we'll know for sure when one of my men has taken photos of the airport from a light plane. He's on his way to Nairobi where he'll hire a light aircraft for the job. We should have the pictures by tomorrow morning.'

'Good. Well, if that's everything, I think it's time for Motta to present the plan in detail to the prime minister.'

Peres took with him to this vital meeting Gur, Hofi and their aides. Greeting them in the conference room of the Prime Minister's Office were Rabin and Freuka Poran. Rabin spoke first, bringing them up to date on General Ze'evi's ongoing efforts in Paris to conduct negotiations with the hijackers. Then Gur outlined the rescue plan, with Rabin 'interjecting questions about conditions on the ground'.

It was, said Rabin, the first operational plan that he 'could consider as reasonably feasible'. But there were still, he felt, two unanswered questions: 'How was the assault force to reach its objective by surprise? And how would it take over the area held by the terrorists and the Ugandan troops before they had time to kill the hostages?'

Initially, he had worried about Amin's warning that the Old Terminal was rigged with explosives. But various reports from the released hijackers – including the latest from the Americans and Cojot – had caused him to doubt that was the case. Perhaps the clincher was the conviction that Amin would never have quartered some of his troops on the first floor of the Old Terminal, above the two halls where the hostages were being held, if the building really had been mined with explosives.

After an hour, the meeting was broadened to include Zadok and the other members of the ministerial committee. As Gur expounded his proposal anew, he kept stressing the 'supreme importance of maintaining total secrecy'. When he had finished, Yigal Allon asked: 'So it's a flight without aerial defence?'

'Yes,' responded Rabin, 'without. The problem, as you rightly point out, is interception en route.'

'The plan does have an advantage,' interjected Peres, 'and that's the element of surprise. They won't know we're coming.'

'That's as may be, but it's still the riskiest operation we've known,' said Rabin, adding that the final decision would rest with the full Cabinet, and that all ministers would be told to stay in Tel Aviv pending a meeting of the secret ministerial defense committee on Saturday. That way the Orthodox ministers, who did not drive on the Sabbath, would remain within walking distance of the government offices in Tel Aviv.

'There are,' concluded Rabin, 'more than eighty Israelis trapped in that terminal. Yet the intelligence we possess is far from adequate. I am in favour of all the preparations going ahead, but I propose we still see this thing as subsidiary to ongoing negotiations.' He paused, deep in thought, before continuing: 'If only I could get them to release the women and children. That would change everything.'

0850hrs GMT, Ewhurst, Surrey, UK

Chapman Pincher, the debonair *Daily Express* investigative journalist and security expert, was writing in the study of his Surrey farmhouse when the telephone rang. It was a Mossad contact based in Paris. 'Would you be interested,' said the agent, 'in an exclusive on what the released hostages told us about their experiences at Entebbe?'

'Certainly. Tell me more.'

The agent did, concentrating chiefly on the hostages' conviction that Amin was working hand in glove with the terrorists. He particularly stressed their claims that Amin had let other terrorists join the original hijackers, had given the terrorists extra weapons, including sub-machine guns, and had told Ugandan troops to help guard the hostages so that the hijackers could sleep. 'I suggest,' added the contact, 'that you give it maximum publicity.'

'I will,' promised Pincher, and no sooner had he put down the phone than he began to write the article for publication in Saturday's *Daily Express*.

After a while he stopped. Something was not right. He had detected from the tone of his informant that it was vital this information was published as quickly as possible: but why? He mulled it over for a while, and eventually decided it was part of a typical Israeli PSYOPS exercise – the dissemination of selected information to influence public opinion – against the hijack and all associated with it. He was, in any event, 'completely confident about the accuracy of the statements' because, having known the contact for many years, he had never yet been given false information.

He continued writing.

0900hrs GMT, near Paris, France

'I actually noticed two of the hijackers when we were in the departure lounge at Athens,' said George Good to the junior British diplomat who was driving him and his friend Tony Russell (the Yachtsman) to the airport for their flight back to London. 'They were the German girl and the taller of the two Palestinians. He had long fair hair and looked a bit like Mick Jagger. The reason I remember him is because of his wild look.'

'What do you mean by that?' asked the diplomat.

'Well, he had wild staring eyes as if he was high on drugs. He didn't look right. Which makes me think that the most effective form of security at airports would be for trained observers simply to study the looks and deportment of passengers waiting to board international flights.'

'Did the hijackers have explosives?'

'I think so,' said Russell. 'They certainly attached what looked to me to be sticks of gelignite to the doors of the aeroplane at Benghazi.'

'What was the low point of the week?'

'It was when we were separated into two groups: Israelis and the rest. You could have cut the tension with a knife, and to reassure us one of the terrorists said there would be freedom of movement between the two rooms. That never happened. Access between the two rooms was blocked except for those Israelis who wanted to use the toilet.'

'Any moments of light relief?' inquired the diplomat.

George Good smiled. 'A few. Like the time Idi Amin's Stetson was blown from his head by the downdraught from his own helicopter. But that same downdraught also blew clothes that the hostages had hung out to dry on to the roof of the building.'

They pulled up in front of Departures. 'It's been quite an adventure for you hasn't it?' said the diplomat.

'Yes,' replied Russell. 'But our families wouldn't agree. My wife Edith has been through hell, and it's not over for the relatives of the hostages still in Uganda.'

'It wasn't so bad for me,' interjected Good. 'I'm a widower and my children are grown up. I've had a good life so I wasn't too worried.'

Once back at the British Embassy – the beautiful eighteenth-century Hôtel de Charost on the Rue du Faubourg Saint-Honoré, the former home of Napoleon Bonaparte's sister Pauline – the diplomat sent a report of this conversation to the Foreign Office in London. The only really useful information about explosives was almost certainly shared with the Israelis.

0905hrs GMT, Central Israel

Just after 11 a.m., the excited chatter died away as Ehud Barak, Yoni Netanyahu and intelligence officer Captain Avi Livneh entered the packed briefing room at the Unit's base. The temperature was in the high 80s and, despite ceiling fans and open windows, most of the waiting soldiers were perspiring freely. Barak and Netanyahu took their seats in the front row, next to Muki Betser, while Livneh climbed the steps to the dais where a diagram of the airport and a schematic drawing of the various halls in and entrances to the Old Terminal had been set up on a stand.

Livneh began by summarizing the available intelligence: '102 mostly Israeli hostages are being held in the Old Terminal at Entebbe Airport, either in the large hall, here,' he said, tapping the schematic diagram with a stick, 'or the smaller hall next door. Possibly both, but we suspect the Israelis have been put back with the others in the large hall. Seven to ten terrorists – the reports vary – armed with pistols and sub-machine guns, are taking turns to guard the hostages, patrolling from time to time inside the halls. The terrorists say they've booby-trapped the buildings with explosives, but we've just received intelligence from some of the released hostages in Paris that the explosives are fake.'

Livneh went on to say there were reports of sixty to a hundred armed Ugandan paratroopers guarding the terminal and working hand in hand with the terrorists. They were typically deployed thirty yards from the building, and spaced ten yards apart, but at nighttime most were barracked on the first floor of the building. At least once the Ugandans had been seen on the roof of the building.

Livneh finished his briefing by explaining the layout of this part of the airport: the adjacent control tower that dominated the surrounding area; the military base 200 yards to the east that contained one or two battalions of infantry and a squadron of MiG fighters; and a road that connected the north of the airport to the town of Entebbe, itself the location of Amin's presidential palace and another garrison of troops.

As Livneh left the dais, Barak took his place. He had scarcely begun his briefing on the assault of the Old Terminal when a young duty officer entered the room. 'I'm sorry, colonel,' said the officer, 'but I've just been speaking to General Adam. He wants you to report immediately to his office in the Kirya.'

'What, now? Didn't you tell him I was in a briefing?'

'I did, sir, but he was very insistent. He wants you to hand over to Colonel Netanyahu and leave at once for Tel Aviv.'

Barak sighed and turned to Netanyahu. 'Yoni, you'll have to take over. I'll be back when I've sorted this out.'

Netanyahu nodded, trying to hide his delight. Something told him Barak would not be returning.

Half an hour later, Barak walked into Kuti Adam's office in the Kirya. 'I'm sorry, Ehud,' said Adam ruefully, 'but there's been a change of plan. We're taking you out of the assault phase of the operation and putting Yoni in charge. Please call to let him know.'

Barak was stunned. 'Why?'

'We have another job for you that's just as important. In two hours we want you on a flight to Nairobi. Your task when you get there is twofold: firstly, to guarantee that it will be possible for the planes to refuel in Kenya on their way back; and secondly to make contingency plans in case the operation fails, because it can fail.'

Back at the Unit's base, Yoni was wrapping up the briefing. 'Some of the assault teams,' he said, 'will be given bullhorns [megaphones] so they can give clear instructions to the hostages – particularly to tell them in the first moments to lie down and stay still. The hostages won't necessarily respond as they might in a similar situation in Israel, where they'd expect the army to rescue them. At Entebbe they'll be taken completely by surprise and their behaviour will be unpredictable. The bullhorns will help with this, and also after the shooting when some might panic and try to flee the building. Any questions?'

One soldier raised his hand. 'Sir, you said the APCs would not move to support us until they were all on the ground. Wouldn't it make sense for the first pair to move towards the Old Terminal as soon as they're disembarked? That way we'll have more firepower sooner.'

'Good point. We'll look into it. Anything else?'

'Sir, what if we can't take off from Entebbe, for whatever reason? What do we do then?'

Yoni smiled. 'Don't worry. We'll have a huge amount of firepower, and if all else fails, we'll use our vehicles and commandeer any others we manage to find, and cut our way through to Kenya overland. We'll be taking maps that show the possible routes to the Kenyan border.'

'Yes,' quipped another soldier, 'and we'll be the only ones with enough vehicles to get that far. The paratroopers and Golani will have to stay behind, as usual.'

As the laughing subsided, Netanyahu asked: 'Is that it?'

A stern-faced veteran raised his hand. 'Sir, it seems to me that we're breaking all the rules of combat with this operation. There might be as many as ten armed terrorists in the large hall when we arrive. That's more than the six soldiers assigned to the hall's two entrances. We'll be outnumbered, as well as exposed and vulnerable. And because of the hostages we can't throw grenades or use bursts of fire. It doesn't make sense.'

'Maybe not,' said Netanyahu, 'but we have no option. The first Hercules can only take so many vehicles and fighters. We'll have to read and react to the battle as it unfolds. And don't forget: we have the element of surprise and Shaul [Mofaz]'s APCs will be with us in no time. If everyone does his job, we won't have a problem. It can be done.'

1000hrs GMT, Entebbe International Airport

The usual lunch was delivered to the Old Terminal building at 1 p.m. – meat in sauce, rice, potatoes, a little bit of bread and half a banana – and was enlivened a little by the donation of olives and harissa from two of the hostages. Jean-Jacques Mimouni was prominent among the team of servers, making sure, as Moshe Peretz put it, 'that no one is left without his portion, and that no one is deprived'. Exuding good spirits, the young French-Israeli had also been handing out tea and coffee, while demanding 'nothing for himself'.

Dora Bloch, one of the grateful recipients, had no sooner eaten a mouthful of her meal than she began to cough uncontrollably.

'What is it, mother?' asked her son, Ilan Hartuv.

She pointed to her throat, as if something was stuck there. Hartuv sighed. Once before her doctor had removed a piece of meat that was lodged in a cavity in her throat. Now it had happened again. He thumped her on the back to no effect. Next he called over an Israeli doctor named Hirsch who tried and failed to remove it with his finger.

Finally Yitzhak David's wife Hadassa, a trained nurse, took Mrs Bloch to the toilet and tried to make her throw up. Nothing worked.

So Hartuv asked the nearest terrorist, Brigitte Kuhlmann, to fetch Dr Ayad, the Egyptian medic provided by Idi Amin. Ayad asked what was wrong and between coughs Mrs Bloch, who had grown up in Egypt, was able to explain in Arabic. Worried that she might choke in her sleep, Ayad persuaded the terrorists that she needed hospital treatment.

'I want to go with her,' said her son.

'No, absolutely not!' shouted Kuhlmann. 'What an idiot you are to think we'll let you both leave. She will go and you will stay here.'

So Dora Bloch, accompanied by Ayad and the Ugandan nurse, was taken by ambulance to the 1,800-bed New Mulago Hospital in northern Kampala, the largest and best equipped in the country. Though sorry that her son could not accompany her, Mrs Bloch was relieved to escape from the Old Terminal where the living conditions were increasingly smelly, uncomfortable and dangerous.

Health Minister Henry Kyemba was out of town and did not learn of her admittance to Mulago until the evening, by which time the piece of meat had been 'easily removed by one of the surgeons in a minor operation'. Kyemba told the hospital director to let Mrs Bloch rest, and he would return to Kampala to visit her the following morning.

1015hrs GMT, Central Israel

Yoni Netanyahu was waiting with members of his staff outside Dan Shomron's office, sited on a base a couple of miles from the Unit's, when he was called to the phone. He returned soon afterwards, a big smile on his face. 'Ehud's gone,' he announced. 'He's cleared out. I'm in command of the assault.'

Moments later a relieved and excited Netanyahu was summoned into Shomron's office to present his refined plan. It was approved without amendment. One of the last-minute changes that Netanyahu had made to the plan concerned his own role. With Barak out of the picture, he would direct affairs and not take part in the actual assault. That job would be left, as originally agreed, to Betser. Netanyahu and the command group, meanwhile, would station themselves outside the central entrance to the Old Terminal. From there, Netanyahu would be able to control the movement of all his troops, as well as enter the large hall if necessary.

By the time Netanyahu returned to his own base, the stretch Mercedes – such a vital component of the assault plan – had arrived. But apart from having three rows of seats, it was far from ideal. Muki Betser had stipulated a black Mercedes in good condition, similar to the type used by the military in Uganda. This one was old, white and falling apart. 'It needs a lot of work,' was the verdict of forty-two-year-old Master Sergeant Danny Dagan, an expert mechanic who would drive one of the APCs.

'Whatever it needs,' Betser told him. 'But just make sure it works for the ride from the plane to the terminal. Put in a second ignition, just in case. And paint it black.'

Dagan began work on the car, but the extensive repairs – which included realigning the alternator, replacing the tyres, patching up the fuel tank, making a dummy number plate and fixing a little Ugandan flag to the bonnet – took up the rest of the day and most of the night. It did not help that the work was repeatedly interrupted as the car was taken away for various practice runs. All in all, it was hardly the ideal preparation for a major operation and was an example of the constant penny-pinching that all armies – even special forces – are faced with.

Meanwhile the men selected for the mission were drilled incessantly. 'When the Ugandan soldiers see the Mercedes,' Betser told them, 'they are going to assume it's an officer's. They won't try to stop a senior officer. As far as they are concerned, we will look just like a Ugandan brigadier and his escort. They are not going to shoot at us – at least not until we start shooting. And even if they aren't sure about our identity, the dilemma will make them hesitate long enough for us to reach the terminal. But, if for any reason they do start shooting, let the back-up crews handle it. We concentrate on the break-in, eliminating the terrorists, and then defending the hostages until the time comes to get them on the plane.'

1200hrs GMT, Tel Aviv, Israel

At 2 p.m., the eighteen members of the full Cabinet filed into Yitzhak Rabin's conference room in the Kirya. The purpose of the meeting was not to inform them about a potential military plan – it was too soon for that – but rather to discuss the ongoing negotiations and to make sure the ministers stayed the night in Tel Aviv.

Rabin began by mentioning his conversation with opposition leader Menachem Begin of a day earlier. 'Begin,' he said, 'advised the government not to get entangled in the pre-negotiation proviso that we won't commit to the number of prisoners or their names. He was worried that we might be forced into another humiliating climbdown. My response was that I agreed with his proposal. We should all be aware that from the moment they separated the hostages into Israeli and non-Israeli, releasing the latter, it became Israel's problem. No one will stand with us now. The decision will be ours, and ours alone. Frankly, the rest of the world couldn't give a damn. At best, they'll be sympathetic – or not. We have, as a result, no one to turn to except ourselves, and the decision isn't going to be made by anyone but the Israeli government.'

Pausing, Rabin looked round the table, waiting for a comment. When none came, he continued: 'We're conducting negotiations regarding the release of the prisoners, but I've told our negotiators not to start arguing about numbers. Nor have we told them to exclude terrorists with blood on their hands. I wouldn't want to see this whole thing fail.'

When it was Peres's turn to speak, he gave the first hint that a military option was being considered. 'Starting tomorrow,' he told the room, 'we only have half a day left, and I recommend that all ministers be prepared to stay here for a while. Tomorrow is going to be a dramatic day.'

1300hrs GMT, London, UK

With the news that the two released hostages, Tony Russell and George Good, had arrived safely back in Britain that morning on a flight from Paris, officials at the Foreign Office in King Charles Street withdrew their gaze from Uganda. As far as they knew, no more British passport holders were being held in Entebbe. It was, henceforth, an Israeli problem.

As the Foreign Secretary Tony Crosland was busy for most of the day in Cabinet committees and at the House of Commons, junior ministers and senior officials took on the responsibility of tying up the loose ends. It was, therefore, Peter Rosling, head of the East African Department, who instructed the acting high commissioner at Kampala, James Horrocks, to thank 'Amin on behalf of HMG for his success securing the release of the British subjects from the hands of the hijackers'. He should add, said Rosling, 'that HMG very much hope that [Amin's] efforts to secure the speedy and safe release of the remaining hostages and the aircraft will be equally successful'.

On a more practical level, David Goodall of the West European Department informed senior colleagues that if Helmut Schmidt's West German government chose to assist the Israelis by releasing some of its six prisoners – three of whom, all Baader–Meinhof terrorists, were being held in West Berlin – it made sense for Britain, as the current chair of the three-power Allied Kommandatura set up to govern the western half of the city in 1945, to agree in principle to provide air transport if necessary. The precedent for this was just a year earlier, during a similar hostage crisis at the Embassy of the Federal Republic of Germany (FRG) in Stockholm, when Britain had offered a Royal Air Force plane in West Berlin. 'In the event,' wrote Goodall, 'the Federal Government decided not to accede to the terrorists' demands, and the aircraft was not needed.' This time, however, it might be different.

Officially, the spokesman of the FRG government was still insisting that all the countries concerned 'should reach a common position'. Yet German press reports on 2 July were predicting that the Emergency Unit – a committee of senior ministers and opposition politicians set up a few days earlier to handle the crisis – was about to release the six German terrorists. Certainly the prisoners themselves believed that to be the case, and two in West Berlin 'were said to have packed their bags and cleaned out their cells'.

In truth, Schmidt and his colleagues in the Emergency Unit were following the Israeli lead. On 1 July, Yigal Allon had assured the German foreign minister Hans-Dietrich Genscher that the Israelis would bring the Entebbe crisis to an end 'on their own responsibility'. From this the Germans drew the conclusion that they should not take any hasty decision to release the hostages, 'but should rather leave the Israelis the maximum freedom of manoeuvre'.

1300hrs GMT, Central Israel

To coordinate the movement of the assault team with the plane taking it to Entebbe, Yoni Netanyahu and his senior officers held a meeting at their base at 3 p.m. with the crew of the Hercules: Lieutenant-Colonel Joshua Shani, his co-pilot and his chief navigator.

It was an uncomfortable hour for Shani. Their conversation was frequently interrupted by phone calls for Netanyahu who, between times, was absentmindedly taking apart and reassembling a silenced revolver. Every now and again the barrel pointed in Shani's direction, causing the airman to shift in his seat.

But eventually the main points were agreed: the plane would land and taxi almost to the end of the new runway where there was an access strip on the right to the old diagonal runway. The assault troops would disembark here and use their vehicles to drive up the old runway to another access strip, this time on the left, that led to the front of the Old Terminal. It was to this second access strip that the fourth Hercules would taxi after the assault, to reduce the distance the hostages would have to walk or be driven to get them aboard.

Nothing was left to chance: they discussed which side of the Hercules they would drive by as they headed for the Old Terminal building; even the difference in height between the propellers and the top of

241

the vehicles, in case they decided to save time by driving under the wings. Yoni also asked about the runway lights and what would happen if they were off when they arrived. 'Don't worry,' said Shani, sounding more confident than he felt, 'we have a radar that enables us to land in complete darkness. It's not a problem.'

It was the first time that Shani's co-pilot had worked with the Unit and he was hugely impressed with their professionalism and attention to detail. They seemed to him 'amazing' and from 'another world'. He left the meeting convinced that the assault team could pull off its part of the operation. The question now in his mind was whether he and Shani could accomplish theirs. They would soon find out because, at 6 p.m., they were scheduled to fly Gur and Peled to Sharm el-Sheikh in the Sinai and demonstrate a landing in total darkness.

1300hrs GMT, Entebbe International Airport, Uganda

The hostages passed the afternoon with the usual activities: chatting, playing cards, reading and sleeping. Some handwashed their clothes and went outside to hang them on the improvised lines. They wore, in the meantime, borrowed shirts and towels around their waists.

People talked about their lives, jobs and families. A few discussed sport, chiefly the cycling Tour de France which had begun on 24 June with the Dutchman Joop Zoetemelk as favourite; the last anyone had heard, first-time rider Freddy Maertens of Belgium was wearing the leader's Yellow Jersey. (Zoetemelk eventually finished second, behind the Belgian Lucien van Impe, with Maertens winning the Points classification Green Jersey.)

The subject of preference for the young French group, however, was sex. 'I told you when we arrived,' said the tall brown-haired man known as the Flirt, 'that the youngest would stay the longest and have quite a party. Was I right?'

'You tell us,' said one of the group. 'You seem to have been the busiest among us.'

The Flirt laughed. 'I've done my best. During the flight I got talking to a cute young woman with a kid who told me her husband was the jealous type and she'd only got married out of desperation. We slept together the first night in Uganda, but never got beyond kissing because she was always busy with her kid. Then the evening before her departure, on a whim, and I'm not sure why, she dropped me and hooked up with a steward.'

'Poor you!' heckled a girl. 'Who did you target next?'

'*I* didn't target anyone. Marianne', he said, nodding towards a pretty dark-haired French girl, 'approached me and we started chatting. That night we slept together behind the bar. We kissed and I felt her breasts, and a bit more than that. She fondled me in turn. But we stopped there.'

'Really?'

'Yes, really. Anyway, the following morning – that's Wednesday – Marianne introduced me to another girl and, to cut a long story short, I slept with her that night in a "room" made by the first girl I was with. She relaxed without any problem. But as the paper on the mattress was making too much noise, we woke up Claude and asked if he would swap places. He agreed and we were finally getting down to business when . . .'

'When what?'

'. . . I lost the urge,' said the Flirt, his face reddening.

Everyone in the group laughed. 'Do you mean,' said one, 'you couldn't get it up?'

'That's exactly what I mean. And I think I know why: they're putting something in our food to make us less likely to rebel.'

'Like what?'

'Bromide, probably. I've heard they use it in prisons to make inmates easier to handle. But it was also given to troops in the First World War to curb their sexual urges.'

'He might be right,' said one of the girls. 'I got together with someone and the same thing happened.'

The group started laughing so hard that an older Israeli woman came up and said: 'Please, my lovelies, you must not make so much noise. You're going to antagonize the Palestinians.'

But, far from being irritated, the terrorists joined in the laughter, as did the Ugandan sentries outside. None of them had a clue what the joke was about.

1400hrs GMT, Entebbe International Airport, Uganda

The hostages closest to the windows could see the Peruvian – easily distinguishable by his green cap and moustache – moving the Ugandan soldiers to a distance of at least fifty yards from the front of the building. Then he entered the main hall, a smile betraying his good humour, and picked up the megaphone. 'Good news,' he announced. 'You can go outside and get some exercise. Older people and children go first. Then the rest.'

Most people complied with the Peruvian's instructions, and an initial group of about fifty young and old went out to walk and play on the tarmac, with Wilfried Böse standing on a line they were forbidden to cross. After about half an hour, and unbidden by the terrorists, this first group started to come back in and were soon replaced by the remaining hostages. The sporty ones began to do stretching exercises, little sprints and star jumps, and often strayed further from the building than they should have. But the terrorists seemed unconcerned and let them get on with it. They were chatting among themselves, visibly relaxed, and their laid-back mood was transmitted to the hostages. This time, however, there was no fraternization between prisoners and keepers.

1700hrs GMT, Israeli airspace above the Sinai

A tiny bead of sweat trickled down the side of Joshua Shani's face as he squinted through the Hercules C-130's windshield, trying to locate the runway of Ofira Air Force Base near Sharm el-Sheikh that had been chosen for the practice run because, like its counterpart at Entebbe, the final approach was over water. He was in the lead pilot's left seat of the plane's spacious cockpit. To his right sat his co-pilot, Avi Einstein, and behind him were squashed his navigator, Chief of Staff Motta Gur and IAF chief Benny Peled.

Shani and his crew had flown down to Ofira a couple of hours earlier to familiarize themselves with the airfield. Now they were back in total darkness to prove to Gur that they could land at night without lights. Shani felt the weight of the world on his shoulders: he knew that, if he failed to convince Gur, the operation could not go ahead and Israel would face humiliation. He looked down at the Adverse Weather Aerial Delivery System (AWADS) radar screen on the large instrument panel in front of him. It was showing a faint line that was in roughly the right place. But was it the airstrip? He would soon find out.

He slowly decreased altitude until he was just a couple of hundred feet from the ground, at which point he turned on his landing lights. Directly beneath him was the thin taxiway that ran parallel to the runway; the radar had locked on to the chain-link fence that ran along the taxiway. Realizing his error, he banked steeply to the left, straightened out over the runway and let the wheels almost touch down before quickly gaining altitude.

If Gur noticed something was wrong, he said nothing beyond: 'Do it again.'

On his second attempt, Shani aligned the plane closer to the main runway, though not dead centre. Gur seemed satisfied. 'I knew you could do it all along,' he said with a grin, slapping the two pilots on their backs. 'Let's get back to Tel Aviv.'

After landing at the Unit's base, ready for the full dress rehearsal of the operation at 10 p.m., Shani voiced his concerns to Peled. He was worried that with no moonlight it would be even darker when he tried to land at Entebbe. Therefore, he said, even if the radar could find the runway he intended to use the plane's landing lights. But if the radar did not work, he would 'get on the radio' and tell the Entebbe control tower that he was 'East African Airways Flight 70 with a general electrical failure'. He would then ask them to turn on the runway lights. There wasn't an air traffic controller in the world 'who wouldn't flip the switch if he heard that', said Shani. No one would be 'crazy enough to take the risk of causing a plane with 200 passengers on board to crash'. By the time he realized what was happening, 'the operation will be over'.

Peled gave his blessing. 'It's a good idea and you should use it if you have to. But keep it to yourself.'

1700hrs GMT, Nairobi, Kenya

Soon after arriving in Kenya on the scheduled El Al flight from Tel Aviv, Ehud Barak and his intelligence colleagues – including, according to some accounts, the legendary Mossad officer Mike Harari who had led the Wrath of God operation – were driven to Attorney-General Charles Njonjo's house in Nairobi. The subject of discussion was the same as it had been a day earlier – Kenya's cooperation in the event of an Israeli rescue mission – as were most of the personalities on the Kenyan side: Njonjo, Ben Gethi and Bernard Hinga. Only Bruce McKenzie was absent from the original negotiating team, having flown back to Britain that morning so as to distance himself from any involvement. He was, however, being kept informed of developments by telephone.

The exact terms of the highly controversial deal that was struck between the Kenyans and Israelis at this second meeting have been kept secret for almost four decades – and with good reason. But recently Charles Njonjo, the lead negotiator on the Kenyan side, confirmed who was present and what they spoke about. The conversation began with Njonjo asking the Israelis: 'How can we help?'

'First and foremost,' said the chief Israeli negotiator (probably Barak), 'we need the option to refuel all our planes at Nairobi Airport tomorrow night if we can't get supplies elsewhere. Secondly we want to put a Boeing 707 with medical facilities, but with El Al livery, on the ground at Nairobi before the operation so that we can set up a field hospital, including an emergency room and an operating theatre. The casualties could be heavy, and we need to be able to treat them as quickly as possible. And lastly, if anything goes wrong and the planes can't take off from Entebbe, we want your help to arrange an overland evacuation of troops and hostages from Uganda.'

Njonjo glanced at Gethi and Hinga who both nodded. 'I think we can help you,' said Njonjo. 'We'll cordon off a section of the airport for the 707 and the other planes. I'll inform the airport director that you're coming under the guise of El Al. When you know the planes are coming, make sure the El Al representative is in the control tower so there are no misunderstandings. The fewer people who know about this the better.'

As for the overland option, they would warn the border guards at Malaba that an Israeli military force might want to cross from Uganda and that they were to let it through. 'We're happy to assist you,' continued Njonjo, 'but you must realize that we can never admit publicly that this meeting took place. It would not make us popular with the others members of the OAU who, as you know, have a strong anti-Israel bias. When we're asked if we knew about your plans in advance, we'll deny any knowledge. We'll simply say that you asked permission to refuel at Nairobi at the last minute, and that we agreed out of humanitarian considerations. The fewer people that know about this the better, which is why I haven't even consulted my Cabinet colleagues.'

'What about President Kenyatta?' asked the Israeli.

'No, we haven't spoken about this yet. He's not well and should not be bothered. That way he can say with complete honesty that he made no deal.'

'I see,' responded the Israeli. 'Well, thank you, Mr Njonjo, you're doing us a great service. Is there anything we can do for you?'

Njonjo paused, the faint trace of a smile on his lips. 'There is one thing you can do for us. If Amin gets wind of what we've done, he might try a revenge attack. But it will have much less chance of success if you've already destroyed his air force.'

'You mean his MiGs?'

'Yes.'

'I think we can manage that.'

'And if, of course, Amin happens to be at the airport and is killed during the operation, that would be a bonus.'

'For us too,' said the Israeli.

The two sides shook hands on a deal that, had it been made public, would have badly damaged Kenya's credibility in the eyes of its fellow OAU members: not only was Kenya plotting with a country that had been blacklisted by the OAU but the chief target of the plot, President Idi Amin of Uganda, was the serving president of the OAU (albeit one who was coming to the end of his year in office).

Yet the benefits of the deal for both sides were significant. The Israelis now had landing facilities close to Entebbe that would enable them to treat their casualties and refuel their planes for the journey back to Tel Aviv, not to mention a fall-back plan if the planes could not take off. Without this assistance, Operation Thunderbolt would almost certainly not have been authorized. For the Kenyans the agreement promised sweet revenge for Amin's recent hostility – particularly his support for a terrorist act on Kenyan soil – in the form of an Israeli attack on his international airport and the destruction of his air force which would tip the local military balance in Kenya's favour. Amin's assassination would be the icing on the cake.

1730hrs GMT, Tel Aviv, Israel

'Shabbat Shalom,' said a smiling Shimon Peres, holding the door open for his American dinner guest. 'Welcome to my home.'

Spending the evening with a man he had never met before, even one who was tipped to become the next US president's national security advisor, was not an activity Peres would have chosen at such a time. He wanted to keep an eye on the preparations for Operation Thunderbolt, particularly the dress rehearsal. But the dinner invitation had been issued some weeks earlier, at the behest of the Foreign Ministry, and to cancel at the last minute might have aroused suspicions.

'Thank you, Mr Secretary,' said the guest, Professor Zbigniew Brzezinski, 'I'm delighted to be here.'

Peres led Brzezinski through to the lounge where his wife Sonia and the other guests were waiting, drinks in hand, to be introduced. They included two of Israel's senior soldiers – Kuti Adam and Shlomo Gazit – who, like Peres, had their minds on other things. Gur, too, was originally on the guest list with his wife Rita; but Rita's father had died that day and Gur was needed elsewhere. In his absence, Adam and Gazit played their parts to the letter, chatting amiably and never allowing a nerve in their faces to betray the tension they must have felt.

Another guest was Gershom Schocken, editor-in-chief of the leading liberal newspaper *Haaretz*. As he knew nothing of the plan, it was only in retrospect that he could appreciate 'the great performances of his fellow diners'.

The most uncomfortable moment for Peres came when Brzezinski asked him why Israel was *not* sending a military rescue operation to Entebbe. Unwilling to lie, yet unable to tell the truth, he lamely trotted out the potential obstacles: distance; lack of reliable intelligence; the presence of 'hostile' Ugandan troops. With Brzezinski seemingly unimpressed, Peres turned to Schocken, a well-known 'dove' in foreign and security affairs, in the hope that he would support his argument. But Schocken held his tongue.

Only later, after Brzezinski had left, did the editor speak his mind. 'I didn't say anything earlier because I didn't want to embarrass you in front of your American guest,' he told Peres. 'But you should know that I'm completely against the government's decision to do a deal with the hijackers and would wholeheartedly support a rescue attempt.'

This time, Peres was silent.

1830hrs GMT, Cranleigh, Surrey, UK

Chapman Pincher and his third wife Billee often dined with Bruce and Christina McKenzie at the latter's imposing Regency manor house Knowle Park, just a couple of miles away from their own Tudor farmhouse in the village of Ewhurst. What made this evening different was that Pincher was desperate for the ladies to retire so that he could discuss with Bruce, just back from Nairobi, the story he had written about Ugandan collusion with the hijackers. Pincher was aware of his friend's close contacts with both the Kenyan government and the Mossad, and knew that if anyone could verify the validity of the story, he could.

Yet he found McKenzie in a 'very mysterious mood', unwilling to say much about the situation at Entebbe beyond the fact that he hoped the *Daily Express* would make the 'fullest use' of the information Pincher had been given which he 'knew to be true'. The only other thing McKenzie let slip was that he had 'hardly been off the telephone' since his return. To whom, he would not say.

1830hrs GMT, Entebbe International Airport, Uganda

As the evening wore on, the terrorists guarding the large hall became increasingly tetchy and tense, nervously fingering their trigger guards and shouting at any hostage who did not at once do their bidding. The contrast with their earlier good humour was stark.

Suddenly a car pulled up outside and Faiz Jaber got out. Stern-faced, he came into the room and ordered an immediate head count of the hostages. Two terrorists did separate counts, to avoid error, and came up with different totals: 103 and 104. So they both recounted – only this time with the hostages lined up one behind the other – and agreed on 104, of whom ten were under the age of ten, seventy-eight were of Israeli or part-Israeli nationality, two were Americans (the stockbroker and his wife, though most people in the room assumed they were Israeli-Americans), two were Belgians (the Weills), one Swedish (the stewardess Ann-Carina Franking) and the rest French (including eleven members of the crew).

As soon as the count had been completed to his satisfaction, Jaber left the room and the hostages settled down for the night. Jean-Jacques Mimouni, Willy and Isa – a twenty-two-year-old French interior designer who had spent the last three years travelling in Afghanistan – pushed their mattresses right up against the windows at the front of the room. This annoyed the terrorists, who had earlier insisted the hostages leave a walkway in front of the windows of at least three yards, and they were forced to move them back a little.

Once everyone was lying down, Jean-Jacques' group began to speculate on the terrorists' change of mood, concluding that the negotiations with the Israeli government must have hit an impasse. Their nervousness was exacerbated by a rumour that soon spread round the room that, for reasons unknown, the terrorists were on a high state of alert. They were soon given evidence of this when Khaled, who was guarding the door, refused to allow any of the lights to be turned off. The only dark part of the room was above Willy, Jean-Jacques and Isa, where a row of neon lights was not working.

As the hostages prepared for bed, Gilbert Weill and some of the Orthodox Jews were determined to observe the onset of Shabbat, the Hebrew term for the Jewish holy day – in Yiddish it is Shabbos – that traditionally begins just before sunset on Friday and ends on Saturday night. They would normally have lit candles; but, as none was available, Weill took the advice of a woman who had been at Auschwitz and lit two matches instead. Ruthie Gross simply walked up to the window and 'chose two stars in the sky', and they became her candles. As she contemplated their predicament she burst into tears and prayed that she, her husband Baruch and son Shay 'would get another chance to light candles back home'.

Then drying her eyes she rejoined Weill and the other Orthodox Jews who were chanting the zemiros – the blessing – and sharing bananas and a bottle of cola as their festive meal. They followed this by quietly singing religious songs, at which point a nervous Michel Bacos tried to intervene. 'Please stop!' implored the French pilot. 'You've seen how tetchy the terrorists are tonight. If you sing you'll make them angry and who knows what they'll do to us.'

They continued singing despite his protest, and Weill felt it was 'the nicest Shabbos of my life'.

2000hrs GMT, Central Israel

'There's just one problem that I can see,' said Motta Gur. 'What are you going to do about the control tower? A single soldier up there with an automatic rifle will be able to dominate the ground in front of the Old Terminal.'

Gur and other senior officers – including Adam, Peled and Shomron – had just listened to Yoni Netanyahu's final briefing at the Unit's base before the full dress rehearsal. It was the last opportunity to fine-tune the plan of assault.

'I'm aware of that, sir,' replied Netanyahu. 'But we simply don't have enough men on the first Hercules to be able to assault the control tower as well as the main building. The hostages are the priority. We're taking a calculated risk, but if all goes well we'll be in the building before the terrorists and Ugandans know what's happening. If necessary, the covering force in the Land Rovers can tackle the tower; and if they don't silence it the APCs will.'

With the briefing over, the officers were driven the short distance to the adjacent base where the dress rehearsal was due to take place. While Netanyahu and Shomron joined the assault troops on the first Hercules, Gur and the other senior officers climbed into a Jeep so that they could watch the exercise as it unfolded.

The first Hercules trundled down the runway as if it had just landed, disgorging the paratroopers with their lights. But as it came to a halt and the rear ramp was lowered, the Mercedes refused to start. It could not be jump-started because it was an automatic, so its driver Amitzur Kafri shouted to the occupants of the Land Rover behind to give it a shunt to shake up the starter motor. He knew that the success of the practice run, and therefore the operation itself, was hanging in the balance. Fortunately the blow worked: the engine roared into life, and Kafri drove the car off the plane and headed towards the mock-up of the terminal, followed by the two Jeeps.

Once the rehearsal was over, and the Unit's assault troops had gathered round the vehicles again, Gur said to Netanyahu: 'The one thing I didn't like was the overcrowding on the Jeeps. You're drawing attention to yourselves and it looks chaotic. They'll get in each other's way. You need to take a couple of men off each vehicle.'

'Sir,' said Netanyahu, 'if I do that we won't have enough firepower to secure the Old Terminal. We've worked this way before without any problems.'

'Yoni, I'm not asking, I'll telling you. Lose the men.'

'What if I take one off each, sir? That way we're both happy.'

Gur looked from Netanyahu to the Jeeps and back again. 'Okay, one it is,' he said, before turning to his adjutant. 'Yegev, assemble the senior officers and unit commanders in the field tent. The debrief will begin in five minutes.'

Once all the officers were together in the tent, sitting on wooden benches at the folding tables that had served as a mess for the paratroopers and Golani soldiers, Gur asked them one by one to give their opinion on the mission's chance of success. Dan Shomron spoke first. 'It will succeed,' he said, 'if the first plane lands without detection. But it all depends on that first plane.'

Others agreed, including the Tzanchanim commander Matan Vilnai whose job was to secure the New Terminal building, the runways and the fuel tanks. Though he did not say it, he felt the rehearsal had been 'very bad'. But that did not worry him, because in his experience 'you need to have a bad rehearsal' for the actual operation to go well. He, too, was not in any doubt that the mission could, and would, succeed.

The final officer to speak was Netanyahu. He had had little sleep for the last few days and looked exhausted. But his tone was upbeat.

'I think, sir, after the rehearsals and training we've done, that it's going to work. There are a few points that need touching up a little, but nothing we can't handle. Yes, I think the risks are acceptable. If the hostages are where we think they are, we can do it.'

Gur stood up, and paused before he spoke. The decision he was about to make was the hardest of his life. He had been sceptical about a rescue mission from the start. Entebbe was too far away; the intelligence picture was incomplete; and the probable hostility of the Ugandans made the element of surprise doubly hard to achieve. But the events of the last forty-eight hours had changed his mind. He now felt confident that the pilots could land the planes unnoticed, and that once on the ground the hand-picked troops he had just watched perform – the best the IDF had to offer – would do the rest. The problem of refuelling had also been solved.

Yet he knew that it was still a hugely risky operation with potentially disastrous consequences: either the death of most or all of the hostages before the soldiers could reach them; or the loss of the cream of Israel's special forces if they were unable to withdraw by air. Either scenario would be a military and political catastrophe from which Israel would find it hard to recover. But Gur – heavily influenced by the optimistic Peres – managed to banish such gloomy thoughts from his mind. 'From what I've seen tonight,' he told the assembled officers, 'and from what I've heard, I also think you can do it and I'm going to recommend to the defense minister that the operation be approved.'

Many of the officers present breathed a sigh of relief, aware that a major obstacle to the mission had just been removed. But there were still more hurdles to be cleared, as Gur stressed. 'It's now up to the prime minister and the Cabinet,' he continued. 'In the meantime the planes and vehicles will be moved to Lod to be ready for the flight to Sharm el-Sheikh tomorrow. Thank you and well done.'

2230hrs GMT, Central Israel

It was after midnight when Netanyahu, Betser and their men returned to base. The two officers retired to Yoni's office to discuss the rehearsal and to tie up any loose ends. All the while Betser was thinking, but not saying out loud, that in the light of his experience at Ma'alot the number of dead hostages was likely to be as high as ten, and perhaps even twenty. Once their discussion was over, Netanyahu called in the squad commanders for another briefing. They were, he said, to make certain that all the terrorists were dead before they tried to move the hostages.

The men, meanwhile, were checking their equipment, fitting sighting lights to their assault rifles, and studying the intelligence material in their mission files, particularly the layout of the Old Terminal and the runways and roads near to it.

Like most of his colleagues, Amir Ofer filled his ammunition vest with as many bullets and grenades as it could hold, and fastened a second magazine to the one in his Kalashnikov, thus reducing the time it would take to load the new clip. He also practised the best way to carry the megaphone for warning the hostages and the kit for breaking open locked doors. One man per team was to carry this extra kit and Ofer had drawn the short straw.

Too nervous and excited to sleep, he sat up for hours studying the photos and diagrams of the Old Terminal. His job was to follow his commander Lieutenant Amnon Peled through the right-hand entrance into the large hall where the hostages were being held. But if anything happened to Peled he could not afford to go through the wrong door. He voiced the concerns of many when he told a soldier in his room: 'It will either be the IDF's most successful operation of all time, or its biggest failure.'

Ofer's pessimism had been enhanced by what he saw as a hopelessly unrealistic dry run. 'In a real rehearsal,' he noted, 'you should take a flight of eight hours to see how you function and storm a "real" building. We just hung some fabric to imitate the . . . terminal. We didn't even shoot. God knows why Motta Gur was happy with the dry run and approved the mission.'

Similar doubts were being expressed by a small group of the Unit's junior officers – most of whom had never warmed to Netanyahu's style of command – in a room near the flagstaff. They had been working on the rescue plan – one of the most audacious ever conceived by the IDF – for just eighteen hours when it was approved by the chief of staff. It seemed to them the height of madness. Typically they would prepare for weeks, sometimes even months, for an operation of this magnitude. At the very least they would expect to practise on a real building, not on a few pieces of burlap and masking tape. One spoke for all when he declared: 'The top brass are leading each other on. The troops aren't ready. It wasn't a proper dry run. The intelligence isn't convincing. We can't even be sure the hostages are where they say they are. It's all a load of baloney. The Unit is fooling itself and the army, Shomron is fooling his superiors, and on up.'

'I agree,' said another, 'and the only way to stop this, before it ends in disaster, is for us to go over Yoni's head, even over Gur's head, to one of the ministers so that the Cabinet knows what the situation really is.'

But for the others in the room this was a step too far – tantamount to mutiny – and the meeting ended without a decision. Sullen and resentful, they would wait on events. Their mood, however, and the serious reservations they had about the mission, held the potential for disaster.

2300hrs GMT, Tel Aviv, Israel

Peres picked up his home phone at 1 a.m. 'Hello.'

'Shimon, it's Motta,' said Chief of Staff Gur. 'There's no point in my coming over so late. I just wanted to tell you that the rehearsal went well and I think the plan will work. To reach Uganda at the optimum time – which is 11 p.m. here – the planes will need to leave by 3.30 in the afternoon. So I just need your authorization to fly the planes down to their jumping-off point at Sharm el-Sheikh before the Cabinet meets.'

'You have it,' said Peres. 'Thank you. We'll meet at my office at nine. Good night.'

'Good night.'

Peres closed his eyes in gratitude. With Gur now fully supportive, Rabin would find it almost impossible not to approve the military option. He would tell him in the morning.

DAY 7: SATURDAY 3 JULY 1976

0200hrs GMT, near Tel Aviv, Israel

Bruria was washing clothes when Yoni Netanyahu finally returned home at four in the morning. He was covered in grime and looked exhausted. 'I bet you haven't eaten,' she said. 'I've made your favourite lemon meringue pie. Why don't you have a piece?'

He went to the fridge and took half a mouthful with a spoon. 'Delicious. I'm going to have a shower and then bed. Will you be long?'

'No.'

Ten minutes later, she went into the bathroom and found Yoni still under the shower, his head propped against the wall, his eyes closed. She helped him to wash and got him into bed. Within seconds he was asleep.

0330hrs GMT, Entebbe International Airport, Uganda

Maggy woke in the Old Terminal building with nausea and severe stomach cramps. 'I feel terrible,' she moaned, curling herself into a ball.

'Me too,' said Agnès. 'It must have been something we ate.'

All around them people were groaning in pain or making rapid visits to the toilet. Too ill to move was Isa, the young French interior designer. 'Oh my stomach hurts!' she complained to Willy, one of the few not affected.

'Could it be your period?' he asked helpfully.

'I don't think so.'

Also stricken with cramps and nausea was the Israelis' unofficial spokesman, Ilan Hartuv. But as he hastened to the toilet he was stopped by Faiz Jaber. 'I saw you talking to President Amin,' said the terrorist chief in Arabic. 'What are you plotting against us?'

Hartuv could understand Arabic but not speak it very well. 'I wasn't talking to him,' he replied in English. 'I was translating his words into Hebrew.'

'Why do you move about so much?' Jaber persisted.

'I just want to go to the bathroom.'

'You're lying, you're lying!' snarled Jaber, using his rifle butt to push Hartuv out of the large hall to the spot where he was on guard duty.

'Stand there,' said Jaber, pointing to a muddy puddle that had formed from the overnight rain. 'And don't move.'

After a short time, Hartuv complained that he was cold and his thin cloth slippers were soaked. Jaber responded by chambering a round into his weapon, the sound terrifying the Israeli. He stood rooted to the spot, awaiting his execution. But then the Peruvian intervened. 'What's the problem?' he asked Jaber.

After Jaber had responded in expletive-laden Arabic, the Peruvian told Hartuv to go back inside. 'He's in charge,' he told the Israeli. 'You must be very careful what you say and do around him.'

In the large hall the majority of the hostages were sick and the symptoms – stomach pains, nausea and diarrhoea – made the Egyptian doctor suspect they had eaten contaminated meat. This inference was given added weight by the fact that none of the Orthodox Jews, all of whom had refused to eat the non-kosher meat, was ill. The doctor offered antibiotics as an antidote, and one by one the stricken hostages rose from their mattresses to get an injection or some tablets.

A few refused, including Isa who was given permission by the terrorists to go outside and get some air. There, while chatting with other sick hostages, she was challenged by the pilot Michel Bacos. 'Surely,' he said, 'if you were genuinely sick you would not be talking like this. You'd be lying down.'

Disdaining to respond, she brushed past him and returned to her mattress, ignoring all who came to comfort her. These commiserators were mostly young French hostages who had not fallen ill, including Cécile, Marianne, Willy and Jean-Jacques Mimouni. As ever, Jean-Jacques was selflessly making tea for anyone who wanted it.

Worried by this outbreak of sickness and the unsanitary conditions in the bathrooms, the terrorists arranged for the Ugandans to bring in a tanker of fresh water and a pump to clear the blocked toilets. As they were doing this, Willy saw an eighth terrorist – another Palestinian – arrive in the main hall. He was of medium height, fairly muscular with a moustache and dark hair, and wearing green trousers and a green tee-shirt with a yellow border on its sleeves and neck. Most of the hostages had not seen him before and he has never been identified. It is just possible that he was Wadie Haddad, the leader of the PFLP–EA and mastermind of the hijacking, a man that Gerd Schnepel of the Revolutionary Cells later insisted was in Uganda that day.

0500hrs GMT, Tel Aviv, Israel

Amos Eiran arrived early at Yitzhak Rabin's apartment with, as requested, a draft briefing for a government decision on a military operation. He found Rabin chain-smoking, a full ashtray at his elbow.

'Amos,' he said, cigarette in hand, 'I've been thinking about the plan all night and I'm about to give it my approval. The pilots have shown they can land in the dark and that the element of surprise is possible. I'm also satisfied that the airport is not rigged with explosives. I think it's worth the risk. Besides, the hijackers have rejected the list of terrorists we've said we'll release on the grounds that they aren't the ones they've asked for. We're at an impasse unless we cave in completely and free men with Israeli blood on their hands. And that's something I'm not prepared to do while there's an alternative.'

Once they had finished correcting the briefing draft, Eiran left to get the document typed up. Accompanying him to the lift, Rabin asked: 'By the way, can you prepare a resignation letter for me in case the mission fails.'

Eiran raised his eyebrows. 'What is your definition of failure?'

Rabin shrugged. 'If twenty-five are killed, I will regard the operation as having failed and assume personal responsibility. Fewer than that and it's a success.'

'What are the chances of that?'

'I would say not greater than fifty–fifty. Many things can go wrong.'

0600hrs GMT, Teheran, Iran

Israeli Ambassador Uri Lubrani was having his weekly meeting with Abbas Ali Khalatbari,* Iran's urbane French-educated foreign minister, when the door opened and a secretary entered. She walked over to Khalatbari and whispered in his ear. As she spoke, the foreign minister's eyes widened and swivelled towards his guest.

'Uri,' said Khalatbari in English, 'your secretary is asking to speak to you urgently. You can use the phone next door.'

Lubrani rose to his feet. 'I apologize,' he said. 'I won't be long.'

Angry that his meeting had been interrupted, Lubrani was about to tear his secretary off a strip when she pre-empted him. 'Please don't be cross,' she implored. 'I've just been called by the Prime Minister's Office in Tel Aviv. You must return to Israel as soon as possible. The plane is on the tarmac. Please ask your wife to prepare some clothes. They'll be waiting for you at the airport.'

Lubrani was perplexed. 'What's this about?'

'They didn't say. But they want you back in Israel as soon as possible.'

---

* Khalatbari was Iranian foreign minister from 1971 to 1978. Found guilty of treason and corruption in the wake of the Islamic Revolution, he was executed by firing squad on 11 April 1979.

As Lubrani put the phone down, it suddenly dawned on him. 'It must be to do with Entebbe,' he said to himself. 'They've taken up my offer.'

Having made his apologies to Khalatbari, he left the building.

0700hrs GMT, Ewhurst, Surrey, UK

Retrieving the recently delivered copy of the *Daily Express* from the hall floor of his Surrey farmhouse, Chapman Pincher noted with satisfaction that his Entebbe story was the front-page splash. 'AMIN'S DEADLY HIJACK GAME' read the banner headline, above a brief 450-word article that accused the Ugandan president – a 'fanatical Moslem' who was 'bitterly opposed to Israel' – of assisting the terrorists. Citing freed hostages as its source, the article claimed that Amin had given the terrorists extra weapons, including sub-machine guns; allowed at least two more terrorists to join the original four hijackers; and provided Ugandan troops to help guard the hostages so that the terrorists could sleep. He had, as a result, made it impossible for the Israelis to use the standard tactic of prolonging negotiations to exhaust the hijackers and break their resolve.

Amin's priorities, said Pincher in the article, were twofold: to save the lives of the hostages; and to secure the release of as many Palestinian prisoners in Israel as possible, which in turn would bring him prestige in black Africa and in several Arab countries. He had been, moreover, a recent target for assassination and was 'relying on the airport crisis to keep his troops occupied'.

As Pincher finished reading his article, the phone rang. It was his Mossad contact in Paris. 'I've just seen what you wrote and wanted to thank you. It's exactly what we were hoping for.'

Pincher's suspicions were immediately rekindled. It was usually him expressing his gratitude to a source, not the other way round. There was, he felt, more to the story than met the eye. It had been deliberately placed for a reason: but what? All the press reports coming out of Uganda were claiming that Amin was playing the role of honest broker, and had helped to secure the release of the non-Israeli hostages. Why, then, were the Israelis keen to accuse him of complicity? It was not likely to help the negotiations with the terrorists. It did not make sense and his source had given him 'no clues' to the real reason.

0700hrs GMT, Tel Aviv, Israel

Bruria woke as Yoni was putting on his olive-green combat fatigues. 'I'm late for work,' he complained. 'People are already waiting for me. If I don't come back tonight you'll know there's something on.'

Bruria frowned. 'A few minutes more won't make any difference. You need to eat and we need to talk,' she said, thinking about the letter he had left her the day before.

When there was no reply, she asked: 'It's Entebbe, isn't it?'

'Okay,' he said, after a pause, 'you're right.'

'Is Ehud doing it?'

'No. This is my operation. But you're not to worry because I doubt the government will have the courage to approve it.'

She sat him at the table and put the lemon pie in front of him. He ate half of it in silence. 'Why aren't you saying anything?' she asked.

'I'm thinking of my soldiers.'

'Yoni, you must learn to be a little more open with me, with everybody.'

He changed the subject. 'Tell me where you'll be today. I don't want you to leave home.'

She was about to ask him about the letter when he stood up and kissed her. 'I've got to run.'

When he had gone, she suddenly remembered their German Shepherd. She rushed out of the flat and down the stairs, shouting: 'Yoni! You forgot to say goodbye to Mor!'

But he was already driving away.

0730hrs GMT, Tel Aviv, Israel

Shimon Peres had called a final meeting at 9.30 a.m. in his Kirya office for the generals and senior officers involved in the planning and control of the operation, including Motta Gur, Kuti Adam and Benny Peled. It was a fiercely hot day, with the temperature heading for the 90s, and the single whirring fan on the sideboard was merely circulating hot air. 'Motta,' said Peres, mopping his brow with a handkerchief, 'can you go over the plan once again, but slowly, stage by stage.'

'Of course,' said Gur, standing with a pointer in front of a diagram of the airport. 'Five Hercules – one in reserve – will fly down to the Sinai with the troops and the vehicles at 1130 hours. Then, if we get the go-ahead from the Cabinet, four Hercules will take off from the Sinai at around 1530 hours and be over Entebbe at 2300 hours. The first plane will come to a halt at the end of the runway and disgorge two Land Rovers and the "presidential" Mercedes, all with soldiers aboard, guns at the ready. These vehicles will head immediately for the Old Terminal building where, as we know from the released passengers, the Israeli hostages are being held. They will then neutralize the hijackers and take over the building. Five to seven minutes later, the other three planes will land in close succession, protected on the ground by a detail from the fighting force aboard the first plane. They will unload armoured cars which could be used, if necessary, to fight the Ugandan troops. They will also bring the medical team and a unit whose job it is to take care of the hostages and help them to emplane. At this point one plane will draw up near the Old Terminal building, board the hostages and take off. The other three planes will taxi to the New Terminal building and board the troops and vehicles there, before taking off. Any emergency medical treatment can be performed aboard the planes.'

'How long will it all take?' asked Peres.

'Well,' said Gur, 'the whole ground operation during the dress rehearsal last night took fifty-five minutes. If all goes well, therefore, we should be in and out in under an hour. But if a firefight develops with the Ugandan forces, or if we suffer a lot of casualties, it could take much longer. In any event, the operation on the ground should end before 2 a.m. our time at the latest. I should add that the latest intelligence from Entebbe, received via the released hostages, is very encouraging: the Air France plane seems to be empty and there is no reason to believe that the terrorists have mined or booby-trapped the approaches to the Old Terminal building.'

Peres thanked Gur and closed the meeting. He realized that the timetable was beginning to look very tight. The planes were due to leave Lod Air Force Base for Sharm el-Sheikh at 1.20 p.m., and be in the air again, bound for Entebbe, no later than 3.30 p.m. They could be recalled, of course, but the earlier the Cabinet made its decision the better. He therefore called Prime Minister Rabin and asked if he could bring forward the noon meeting of the ministerial task force by an hour. Rabin's compromise was 11.20 a.m.

0800hrs GMT, Kampala, Uganda

Health Minister Henry Kyemba climbed the stairs to the sixth floor of the Mulago Hospital and was directed by a doctor to a private room in Ward 6B, reserved for VIPs. A policeman was guarding the door. Inside he found a frail white-haired old woman in bed, still wearing the light-grey dress she had been admitted in. Her handbag and cane were propped in a corner.

'Hello,' said Kyemba, 'how are you? I hope you will soon be well.'

'I'm all right,' replied Dora Bloch, 'but I'm worried about my son Ilan.'

Realizing that she was referring to a son still at the airport, Kyemba tried to reassure her. 'Don't worry. Everything will be all right.'

'I hope so.' She looked towards the door. 'Could you say something to the guard. He keeps looking through the window and it's frightening me.'

Kyemba went outside and told the guard to stay on his bench and not keep checking on Mrs Bloch. 'After all,' he added, 'she's very old and can't walk very well.'

After she had thanked him for speaking to the guard, he left the room, much moved by the old lady's 'gentleness' and 'helplessness'. She reminded him of his mother who was about the same age and had recently been hospitalized. Though Mrs Bloch had made a good recovery and could have gone back to the airport, he was anxious to look after her and so arranged with the doctor for her to stay another night in the hospital 'rather than face the discomfort of the airport hall'.

0800hrs GMT, Central Israel

Once word had spread through the Unit's base that the mission to Entebbe was still on, a group of junior officers approached their team commander Captain Giora Zussman. They were the same officers who had expressed reservations the night before, and now they wanted Zussman to speak to Yoni. 'You've got to tell him,' said one, 'that the details haven't been properly worked out.'

After Zussman had passed on the message, Netanyahu called all the officers involved to a meeting in the office of his deputy, Yiftach Reicher. Their first complaint was that the covering team had been ordered not to open fire at Ugandans in the control tower or on the Old Terminal's roof unless bullets came from there, by which time it might be too late.

Yoni's patient response was that the firefight was unlikely to last longer than a minute, and that during that time he would be at the front of the building, 'deciding if a team is stuck and another needs to be called in', or even to go in himself. But if he had a team behind him 'pouring heavy fire in the direction of the tower or the upper floors', it would result in 'so much havoc and noise' that he 'might lose control at the critical moment' and not be able to communicate with the different teams. He reminded them that they were undertaking 'a rescue mission, not a conventional assault', and that their priority was 'to secure the rooms' where the hostages were. For that reason he did not want any covering fire until the terrorists were dead.

Seemingly convinced by Yoni's argument, the officers raised other issues. They asked questions like: What happens if one team is knocked out? Who would replace it? Yoni's response was: 'We'll do it this way or that.' After an hour, recalled Zussman, the officers departed 'feeling completely different, feeling that a lot of things . . . that hadn't been clear were settled now. It was an excellent meeting.'

0920hrs, Tel Aviv, Israel

For thirty minutes, using maps, diagrams and notes, General Gur gave Rabin and the other five members of the ministerial task force a detailed briefing of Operation Thunderbolt in the Prime Minister's Office in the Kirya. Most of them already knew of the plan's existence, thanks to Peres, but this was the first time they had been led through it step by step. 'After attending last night's exercise,' Gur concluded, 'I can recommend that the Cabinet approve the plan.'

Peres, his voice cracking with emotion, spoke next. 'Prime Minister,' he said, 'the prospects for a successful rescue operation are better now than they have ever been. The chief of staff is now totally in favour, as are, I've been led to believe, the foreign, transport and justice ministers. My position is well known to everyone in the room. That just leaves you and Yisrael to make up your minds.'

Despite his earlier words to Amos Eiran, Rabin still had reservations. 'We have to accept,' he said, after a lengthy pause, 'that there is still a real possibility the operation will not succeed. And if it doesn't, that failure will badly damage the IDF's prestige and its ability to act as a deterrent force. We can't forget that we're relying on yesterday's intelligence, and that things on the ground might have changed in the last twenty-four hours. We must remember that there's an alternative.'

Was this hesitation typical of Rabin's inability to make up his mind, particularly as he got closer to the point of no return? Or was he deliberately tweaking Peres's tail for lobbying behind his back? It is hard to know, but it caused the defense secretary to lose his temper.

'It is Israel,' he said sharply, 'that has lectured the world against giving in to terrorism. If *we* give in now our prestige will suffer greatly. Should we ignore the fact that the hijackers have conducted a "selection", separating the Jews from the others aboard the plane? If the operation succeeds, the mood of the entire country will suddenly and dramatically improve. It's true that the operation will put our finest soldiers at risk. But we have always been ready to risk lives to save a larger number of lives by using our own forces, and without recourse to outside assistance.'

Rabin rubbed his forehead. The raw emotion of Peres's words had finally convinced him: the operation had to be authorized. 'When do the planes have to go?' he asked Gur.

'They must leave central Israel for the Sinai shortly after 1300 hours,' responded the chief of staff, 'and be in the air again by 1530 hours.'

For Peres, it was the first indication that the prime minister was 'coming round'. He slowly exhaled. Barring a mutiny in the full Cabinet, the operation was on.

1000hrs GMT, Entebbe International Airport, Uganda

For the sick and exhausted hostages, the morning hours seemed to crawl by as they lay on their mattresses in the large hall. Few had the strength to talk or play cards, and tempers were short. Pilot Michel Bacos seemed particularly out of sorts as he wandered the room, urging people to obey the terrorists' orders to leave a three-yard zone in front of the windows and not to discuss politics. The more generous of the hostages 'put his bad mood down to tiredness' and an attack of arthritis.

By the time the yellow bus brought lunch, people were beginning to get back on their feet, though few had much of an appetite. This did not, however, stop them complaining. 'Madame,' said one to an Israeli female teacher who was giving out food, 'that's three times you've served the same people.'

As soon as lunch was over, Jean-Jacques Mimouni restarted his drinks service. He had been given fresh supplies by the Ugandans, and was now able to offer coffee and tea with sugar. He also told jokes, and his cheery presence was for many hostages a rare ray of sunshine on a depressing day.

1100hrs GMT, Tel Aviv, Israel

'What I'm about to say is top secret,' said Rabin, staring down the long conference table in his Kirya office at Motta Gur and the seventeen Cabinet ministers. 'We have a military option.'

Some of the ministers sat there open mouthed; others gasped. Having been told to stay in Tel Aviv on the Sabbath for this vital meeting, they had been expecting an update on the negotiations; perhaps even the news that a deal had been done and the hostages would soon be coming home. But not this.

'It has been thoroughly examined and recommended by the chief of staff,' continued Rabin in his usual flat emotionless tone. 'As long as we had no military option I was in favour of conducting serious negotiations with the hijackers. But now the situation has changed.'

A minister intervened. 'Can you give us an idea of anticipated casualties?' he asked anxiously.

Rabin looked him in the eye. 'The rescue operation will entail casualties both among the hostages and their rescuers. I don't know how many. But even if we have fifteen or twenty dead – and we can all see what a price that would be – I am in favour of the operation.'

'And are you positive,' asked another minister, 'there is no other way out, besides negotiating with the terrorists?'

'Yes, I am. If we have a military option, we have to take it, even if the price is heavy, rather than give in to terrorists.' Rabin paused to gauge the mood of his colleagues. Their pinched faces and frowns said it all.

'I have said all along,' he said, his voice cracking with uncharacteristic emotion, 'that in the absence of a military plan we have to negotiate in earnest. Now that we have a military plan we have to implement it, even at a heavy cost.'

Shimon Peres spoke next. 'I wholeheartedly agree with the prime minister. The heart-wrenching question is whether we risk the lives of innocent unarmed civilians, and save the future of this country, or not. If we surrender, terrorism will gain strength and more copycat outrages will follow. In the eyes of the world, Israel's prestige will collapse as will her capability to defend herself. Countries around the world might understand why we did it, yet mock us just the same.'

It was now Motta Gur's turn to take the ministers step by step through the operational details. He described the 'stealth, caution and subterfuge that lay at the heart of the plan, all designed to catch the terrorists and the Ugandans off guard'. He concluded: 'Gentlemen, having attended the rehearsal of Operation Thunderbolt last night I can recommend it to the Cabinet. The risk is, as I see it, very calculated and can be taken. There is a possibility of casualties, just like in any other operation we've ever done to rescue civilians, but overall I think the circumstances are reasonable and a military operation can be done.'

This prompted Industry and Trade Minister Chaim Bar-Lev, a former IDF chief of staff (and father of Omer Bar-Lev), to ask what would happen if the planes could not refuel. 'They won't be able to return home,' replied Gur.

'What about weather issues over there?' said Bar-Lev.

'It's risky.'

'What if,' asked Yosef Burg, the German-born minister of internal affairs and founder of the National Religious Party, 'we found out they moved the hostages' location overnight?'

This time Rabin responded. 'The mission,' he said bluntly, 'will be a complete and utter failure.'

Having observed that they were entering into uncharted territory, in the sense that the IDF had never previously launched a military operation outside the Middle East, Peres asked that he and Gur be excused from the rest of the meeting. They wanted to wish the soldiers the best of luck before they took off from the nearby Lod Air Force Base for the Sinai.

Once Peres and Gur had departed, Rabin assured the ministers that the planes did not need to leave the Sinai for Uganda until 3.30 p.m. and could fly for five hours and still have enough fuel to return to Israeli territory. There was, as a result, still plenty of time for them to cancel the mission if that was their decision.

1140hrs GMT, Lod, Israel

Shimon Peres and Motta Gur reached Lod Air Force Base, adjacent to Ben-Gurion International Airport, as the last of Operation Thunderbolt's 190 soldiers, twenty non-combatants and ten vehicles were being loaded aboard the four Hercules C-130s at 1.40 p.m. They made straight for Hercules One, the lead plane, where a knot of senior officers was standing on the tarmac. With the sun beating down mercilessly, and the mercury topping 100 degrees, many of the soldiers were wearing sunglasses.

The pair got out of their car and approached the officers, all of whom were in 'full webbing and obviously in high spirits'. When they spotted Peres, their first question was: Would the Cabinet approve the mission? Peres replied that they were deciding at that very moment, and that he hoped with all his heart they would do the right thing. 'Don't worry, Shimon,' said Dan Shomron, 'everything will work perfectly.'

Next to shake the defense minister's hand was Yoni Netanyahu. The plan, he assured Peres, was 'one hundred per cent'.

Having embraced Peres and Gur, Shomron and the others climbed 'into the bellies of the vast planes, smiling as if they were off on a holiday jaunt'.

The pilots of the four Hercules C-130s started their engines. In the hold of Hercules One, the lead plane, were crammed Dan Shomron's five-man command group, Yoni Netanyahu's assault force of thirty-four and Matan Vilnai's fifty-two paratroopers, a total of ninety-one men and three vehicles. Every square inch of floor was occupied, and the men were relieved when the rear ramp began to rise, hopeful that the temperature at altitude would be cooler.

Suddenly the ramp was stopped and lowered again. Muki Betser could see through the gap a Jeep racing across the tarmac towards the plane. It screeched to a halt and an intelligence officer got out and ran to the rear door, waving an envelope. 'It's for Brigadier Shomron,' he said.

The flight engineer took the envelope and threaded his way past the mass of humans and vehicles to the flight deck where Dan Shomron was sitting with the pilots, Joshua Shani and Avi Einstein. Soon afterwards, Yoni Netanyahu and Muki Betser were summoned to join Shomron. The envelope, they were told, was from the Mossad. It contained 'photographs, shot from a light plane over Entebbe' the day before. The pictures were 'snapshots, raw data with no legends or explanations about the buildings in view'. But they were much more up to date than the ones in the mission files and included images of the New Terminal building and the fuel tanks; the military airport with eleven MiG fighters on the tarmac and the hijacked Air France Airbus clearly visible in the background at the end of the diagonal runway; and the complex of buildings that made up the Old Terminal. This latter photo seemed to confirm that only a thin cordon of Ugandan soldiers was guarding the Old Terminal. Earlier verbal confirmation of this intelligence had encouraged Gur to authorize the operation.

At 1.55 p.m., the heavily laden Hercules One lumbered into the clear blue sky above Lod, followed at five-minute intervals by the other three C-130s and a fifth in reserve. At first they flew in different directions, to confuse onlookers, and turned south only when they were well away from the area. But the need to elude Jordanian radar and Soviet surveillance ships off the coast meant that they never got much above a few hundred feet. As they were flying at such low altitude over the Negev and Sinai deserts, the upcurrents of hot air caused severe turbulence – so severe that almost all the soldiers were soon vomiting into sick-bags. Amir Ofer threw up so many times he did not think he could carry on. Another veteran of Hercules flights thought it was the 'worst of them all by far', and remembered his head being 'pounded' against the roof of the Land Rover because the plane was 'rocking so badly'.

After an hour of this torment, the planes finally landed at Ofira Air Force Base in the southern Sinai. While the C-130s' fuel tanks were being topped up, the groggy soldiers got off and congregated in underground hangars, one for the paratroopers and the Golani, a second for the men of the Unit. Food and drink was available, but only a few took advantage. The worst affected by the flight were still lying by the planes. They included Captain Alik Ron, a reservist who had been assigned to Netanyahu's command team, and a young soldier who was part of Muki Betser's break-in crew, and therefore a vital component of the plan. Ron recovered, but the young soldier did not and was replaced by Amos Goren, a fighter from Omer Bar-Lev's BTR (leaving the total complement of Unit fighters one short). Nervous but proud, Goren was handed the soldier's megaphone and backpack, and told by Netanyahu that he would be properly briefed on his role during the flight.

There was still no decision from the Cabinet that the operation could go ahead.

1300hrs GMT, Tel Aviv, Israel

Yitzhak Rabin looked at his watch as yet another minister rose to have his say. It was 3 p.m. The Cabinet had already been meeting for two hours and still the discussion continued.

'You have put us,' said the speaker to Rabin, 'under unacceptable pressure by allowing the planes to take off before we've made our decision.'

'No,' replied the exasperated prime minister, 'this is not the first time that forces drawn up for an operation were subsequently called back when the Cabinet did not approve its execution. The ultimatum runs out tomorrow, as you know, and since such a mission cannot be launched by daylight this is the last opportunity. But now you must excuse me for a moment. I asked Yitzhak Navon and the leaders of the opposition, Begin and Rimalt, to meet me at three so that I could tell them about the military option.'

Rabin left the room and found the three members of the Foreign

Affairs and Security Committee in an adjacent office. He quickly briefed them on the plan and the Cabinet's deliberations. Begin responded for all three: 'Mr Prime Minister, yesterday when you had no military plan, I said that since the issue was a matter of saving Jewish lives we of the opposition would lend the government our fullest support. Today, now that you have a military rescue plan, I say the same thing. And may the Almighty bring home all our people safe and sound.'

'Thank you,' said Rabin, embracing each of them. He then returned to the Cabinet meeting where he declared: 'We're going to execute a complex mission with expected casualties. Nonetheless I recommend the government approve it, though not with a light heart. Gentlemen, who is in favour of the decision that I shall now read? "The Government resolves to approve implementation of a rescue operation of the hostages held in Entebbe by the Israeli Defense Forces, according to the plan submitted by the Defense Minister and the Chief of Staff."'

Seventeen hands – including Rabin's – rose around the table. It was unanimous: the mission would go ahead.

The tension drained from Rabin's body and he felt calm for the first time in a week, convinced the decision they had come to was the right one. He returned to his office and sat alone, lost in his thoughts, until Freuka Poran came in. 'I've just received the signal. Our forces are on their way.'

'So be it,' said Rabin, rising to pour himself a glass of whisky. 'There is nothing more I can do.'

1341hrs GMT, Sinai, Israel

Pilot Joshua Shani steadily increased the power as Hercules One headed down the runway of the Ofira Air Force Base and into the wind. So overloaded was the plane – carrying a payload of 14.8 tons when its safe maximum was two tons lighter – that it felt like it was taxiing rather than accelerating. The 100-degree desert heat reduced still further the power of the four engines and as Shani neared the end of the tarmac he was just two knots over the stall speed. He took off anyway and, like some prehistoric bird, the great metal beast lumbered slowly into the air.

For some minutes Shani continued flying Hercules One north in the wrong direction until he had picked up enough speed to turn the plane. Even then he struggled to keep control of the juddering C-130 as he brought it slowly round and headed for international air space above the Red Sea. Following close behind were the remaining three overloaded Hercules, their pilots finding it equally hard to manoeuvre. Forced to fly at barely 100 feet above the water to avoid Egyptian and Saudi Arabian radar, and observing strict radio silence, Shani had no means of knowing if the other planes were still behind him. So every now and again the pilots of the other C-130s would fly alongside him to show that all was well.

As during the first leg, the belly of Hercules One was crammed with soldiers: the paratroopers in the space between the three vehicles and the side of the plane; the Unit's men in and on the Land Rovers and the Mercedes. Standing in the tiny gap between the Mercedes and rear cargo gate, Yoni Netanyahu and Muki Betser briefed Amos Goren about his role in the mission. To help the young soldier, Yoni sketched a plan of the Old Terminal on the back of a sick-bag using crosses and arrows to mark the point at which the vehicles would stop and where the various break-in crews, including Goren's, would enter the building.

The briefing was interrupted by the message from the cockpit they had all been waiting for: the government had authorized the operation. Netanyahu merely nodded in satisfaction and continued explaining Goren's job to him as though they were 'going to do an exercise'. When the briefing was over, Goren folded the sick-bag and put it in the pocket of his tigerstripe combat fatigues, part of a consignment of Ugandan paratrooper uniforms that the men of the Unit had changed into during the stop at Ofira.

The two officers got into the front seat of the Mercedes and chatted about what the other had missed during the week they spent apart. Netanyahu talked about the operation in the Sinai, while Betser went through the days and nights he had spent in the Pit, 'planning the rescue'. But eventually 'exhaustion from a sleepless week of non-stop preparation took over', and Betser nodded off.

Netanyahu pulled from a pouch his dog-eared copy of Alistair MacLean's *The Way to Dusty Death*, a bestselling thriller about motor racing. He loved edge-of-the-seat stories and had been teased by his family for watching *The Great Escape* film three times in quick succession. He also liked the popular American TV series *Mission: Impossible* about an elite covert-operations unit, and would watch it while puffing on his pipe and making critical comments like 'That would never work!'

After reading a few pages, Netanyahu turned to the dozing Betser: 'We could do with a few of MacLean's "real men" tonight, eh?'

All around men were sleeping. But a few could not, including Amir Ofer, who kept going over in his head what he was supposed to do and how he was going to do it. Though not quite quaking in his boots, he was 'very tense'. So too was Sergeant Surin Hershko of the Tzanchanim Sayeret, but for a different reason. Like Ofir, Hershko was twenty-one years old and about to be discharged when he was nominated for the mission; yet he trusted his officers to get him back safely. He was sitting beside the Mercedes and could see Netanyahu, a man he knew and admired from the latter's command of a tank battalion, reading in the front seat. The reason Hershko could not doze off was because he was too cramped. The only way to straighten his legs was to put them under the Mercedes. But that was not an option when turbulence bounced the car to within inches of his limbs.

1400hrs GMT, Tel Aviv, Israel

At 4 p.m., Yitzhak Rabin called for his driver to take him home. There was nothing more that he could do, and he wanted to get some rest before he returned to the Kirya to listen to reports from Entebbe on a loudspeaker link-up in Shimon Peres's office. The first plane was not due to touch down until 11 p.m. Israeli time, which gave him plenty of time to have a nap.

'Well,' he told his aides as he rose from his chair, 'if there's going to be a tragedy, God forbid, I know I will be the target for criticism. Me, and nobody else!'

He had reached the door when he was called back: Gandhi was on the line from Paris. He hesitated. General Ze'evi was the last man he wanted to talk to. 'What am I going to tell him?' he asked his assistants in a whisper. 'I can't tell him the truth . . .'

No, replied one, but you should still take the call.

Rabin picked up the phone. 'What's going on, Yitzhak?' asked a plainly exasperated Ze'evi. 'After all, tomorrow is Sunday. The ultimatum expires at midday and, so far, I don't know what is being done about it.'

'Gandhi,' responded Rabin in a slow clear voice, 'you ask me what to do? Right now you are the man who has to give the answers. Go back to the French one more time, and ask them what's happening in Uganda. Ask them whether they have any answers to our proposals in principle. I don't have enough to convene the ministerial team, or anything to discuss.'

Rabin then repeated his previous instruction: there would be no exchange in Entebbe under the auspices of Idi Amin, who could not be trusted. 'I personally would be happy with Paris or even Cairo,' said Rabin, adding: 'I want you to understand that it isn't the number of terrorists to be released that counts, but rather the list of names. Capucci isn't the main thing for me. I'm far more concerned about releasing someone who has committed murder . . .'

Realizing he was putting Ze'evi in an impossible situation, Rabin hinted that a resolution was imminent. 'You know what? I'll contact you again later. Perhaps I'll have something to tell you.'

Replacing the receiver, he murmured: 'Gandhi will kill me . . .'

Back home Rabin could not sleep. 'Every detail, every phase' of the operation was 'etched' in his brain. He kept going over and over the sequence of events. Convinced in his own mind that the plan would work, he finally fell asleep.

1530hrs GMT, International airspace over the Red Sea

With the restraining straps not enough to prevent turbulence bouncing the Mercedes up and down, Yoni Netanyahu got out and made his way to the flight deck of Hercules One. It was packed with people: the two pilots, navigator and reserve pilot; but also the senior officers on board, Dan Shomron, Ivan Oren and Matan Vilnai, all sitting on small wicker stools.

Told by Shani that all was well, and that they were now heading on a southerly course that would take them into Eritrean, Ethiopian and finally Kenyan airspace before they reached Lake Victoria, Netanyahu agreed with Shomron that they would land come what may. He then went over a number of points with Shomron – including the exact time the latter would arrive at the Old Terminal in his command Jeep, which was being brought by Hercules Two – and remarked to Oren: 'If he's there I'll kill him.'

Oren looked mystified. 'Who are you talking about?'

'Idi Amin.'

'You can't do something like that,' said Oren, frowning. 'It hasn't even been discussed. You'd have to ask for approval.'

'I don't intend to ask. If Idi Amin is there, I'm going to kill him.'

Soon afterwards, Netanyahu queried if there was anywhere he could rest and was told by Shomron to use one of the two narrow bunks at the rear of the flight deck. 'You sleep on the way there,' said the operation's commander, 'and I'll do the same on the way back.'

Asking the navigator to wake him up when they were thirty minutes from Entebbe, Netanyahu climbed into the bunk, placed a blue inflatable pillow under his head and promptly fell asleep.

1630hrs GMT, Lod, Israel

Uri Lubrani was forced back in his seat as the IDF's Boeing 707 medical plane – disguised as an El Al civil airliner – accelerated up the runway and took off from Lod Air Force Base for Kenya where it was scheduled to land at 10.20 p.m. Israeli time, about forty minutes before Hercules One touched down at Entebbe.

As part of the deal agreed with the Kenyans the night before, the

707 would fly direct to Nairobi to give its medical personnel enough time to set up, in a secure corner of the airport, a field hospital to treat the many casualties that were expected from Entebbe. In that same location the five planes directly involved in the rescue – the four Hercules and the command and control 707 – would be refuelled, thus enabling the whole force to return to Israel.

Lubrani's task – as explained to him shortly after his return from Iran a few hours earlier by Prime Minister Rabin himself – was twofold: firstly, to act as a high-level representative of the Israeli government who could smooth any difficulties that might arise in Kenya *before* the arrival of the strike force from Entebbe; and secondly to be on hand to intercede personally with Amin if the rescue failed or the planes, for whatever reason, were unable to leave Uganda.

As the Boeing continued to climb to its optimum cruising altitude, Lubrani's mind went back to that chilling experience in 1968 when he and Amin, Israeli ambassador and Ugandan chief of staff respectively, had been returning from a military exercise to Kampala in a Piaggio light plane when its single engine began to splutter. Realizing they would not make it to Entebbe Airport, more than an hour's flying time away, Lubrani persuaded Amin to order the Ugandan pilot to turn back to the airstrip they had left twenty minutes earlier. With Amin praying in Arabic they made it with seconds to spare, the plane skimming the tops of trees as it glided towards the dirt runway and crash-landed. Incredibly both Amin and Lubrani were unhurt, prompting the superstitious Ugandan to declare their deliverance a miracle and to make Lubrani his 'blood brother'.

It was because of this 'close bond' that Lubrani had made his original offer to fly out to Uganda. While that offer had not been accepted, it had got Rabin thinking that Lubrani, with his close knowledge of East African politics, might be useful in other ways. Hence his speedy recall from Iran and his presence on a plane that, but for him and the crew, was reserved for doctors and nurses.

Lubrani had been quick to accept Rabin's offer. But now that he was on his way, one thought was uppermost in his mind: If the rescue fails, what can I say to Amin that will make any difference?

1655hrs GMT, Tel Aviv, Israel

Shimon Peres was sitting at his desk in the Kirya, lost in thought, when his military aide entered the room. 'Shimon,' said Colonel Ilan Tehilla, 'we have just had confirmation that the Boeing 707 command and control plane, with Generals Peled and Adam on board, has taken off from Ofira Air Force Base.'

Peres nodded his acknowledgement. All six planes were in the air: the slower-moving Hercules C-130s had been the first to leave Ofira at 3.40 p.m.; followed by the Boeing 707 medical plane from Lod just under three hours later; and now the command and control plane had departed from Ofira. This last plane's vital task was to close within sixty miles of the C-130s and circle Entebbe Airport while they were on the ground, directing events and providing a communications link between the operation and Peres's office where the action would unfold in real time.

Since the departure of the C-130s from Ofira, Peres had been monitoring the operation's waveband on a loudspeaker in his office. The planes had orders 'to maintain complete radio silence unless any problems arose', and no news thus far had been interpreted as good news. Peres listened for a few minutes longer and, when he heard nothing, decided to honour his previous acceptance of an invitation to the bar mitzvah party for the thirteen-year-old grandson of Dr Herzl Rosenblum, a noted Revisionist and editor-in-chief of the mass-circulation newspaper *Yediot Aharonot*. Peres did so because he was anxious to 'keep up the façade of discretion that was working so well to protect the secrecy of the operation'.

At the party he saw 'all the big names of Israeli journalism', and 'not one of them had any inkling of what was afoot'. One or two even remarked on how well Peres was looking; others said he looked tired.

He interpreted both comments as an attempt to elicit hints of what he was 'doing, if anything, in connection with the hijack saga'. He stonewalled them; and when some asked him directly about the hostages, he replied that they 'would be back home very soon, perhaps within twenty-four hours'. This had the desired effect of heightening 'speculation as to the state of the behind-the-scenes negotiations between Israel and hijackers'.

At 10 p.m., his aim achieved, Peres left the party and returned to his office with his aides and Transport Minister Gad Yaacobi. He wanted to be back well before the scheduled landing time of the C-130s at Entebbe an hour later.

1700hrs GMT, Tel Aviv, Israel

The Israeli government's success in keeping both its own people and foreign diplomats completely in the dark about its operation to rescue the hostages was proven by a cable sent from the German Embassy in Tel Aviv to the Auswärtiges Amt (the Federal Foreign Office) in Bonn during the evening of 3 July.

The message noted that the 'Israel crisis committee' had met at noon 'for some hours, without making any new decisions', and that a further meeting of the whole Cabinet was scheduled for the following day. This was wrong on two counts: the 'crisis committee' had come to a decision – to launch Operation Thunderbolt – and one that had already been authorized by a lengthy follow-up meeting of the full Cabinet. Clearly the disinformation put out by the Israeli Foreign Ministry was having the desired effect.

The message went on to state that while there had not yet been an official response from the terrorists to the latest Israeli terms, the Somali intermediary had hinted that 'the ultimatum might be extended if there is a reasonable chance of getting a result at the end' of the negotiations. The Embassy, meanwhile, had left the Israelis in no doubt that the German government 'would release prisoners if the Israeli government were to ask them to do so'.

The conclusion of the German Embassy was that the Israeli government wanted to 'win some time' and was showing no sign of being 'willing to release' its own prisoners. It would eventually be forced to do so, however, 'if there are no alternatives'.

Meanwhile back in Bonn, according to a well-informed senior diplomat at the British Embassy, Schmidt's Cabinet had already approved a hardline draft statement that was to be released before the expiry of the second ultimatum the following morning. It described those held in the FRG as 'criminals', and said 'no link could possibly be established between their release and that of the hostages'. The diplomat added: 'One wonders what might have been the effect had such a communiqué been issued on the evening of 3 July. In the event, the decision was taken to hold back the communiqué overnight.'

1700hrs GMT, Entebbe International Airport, Uganda

Hardly had the hostages begun to put out the chairs and mattresses so that people could get ready for bed than shouts and running feet outside heralded the arrival of President Idi Amin. Wearing the smart grey-blue uniform of a Ugandan field marshal, he entered the main hall of the Old Terminal building with Faiz Jaber, the Peruvian and a small entourage.

'Shalom!' said Amin.

The response from many hostages was hearty applause, though some of the younger ones like Willy and Isa refused to join in and remained lying on the mattresses, looking daggers at Amin and his people.

The president continued in English: 'I've just got back from Mauritius where I presided over a meeting of the Organization of African Unity. During my absence I stayed in contact with the negotiators, and I continue to do everything I can to save you. I was disappointed by the attitude of the Israeli government who do not reply quickly enough, and if there is a problem it will be their fault. However, the negotiations are moving forward despite this. We are going to continue into the night and I think you will all be gone by Sunday night. Sleep well.'

After this brief speech, Amin turned on his heel and exited the building, leaving behind consternation among the many hostages who could not understand English. When it was translated for them, most looked relieved. The upbeat mood was seemingly confirmed a short while later when the yellow bus arrived with a welcome change of menu: chicken instead of boiled meat. It seemed to be a good omen.

1833hrs GMT, Hamilton, Bermuda

British Foreign Secretary Tony Crosland was on board the Royal Yacht *Britannia* in Bermuda when he heard about the latest domestic repercussions of the hijacking crisis. He was accompanying the Queen on her week-long royal visit to the United States for the celebrations marking the 200th anniversary of the country's Declaration of Independence on 4 July 1776 – a largely ceremonial duty he was not looking forward to – and had just flown in to Hamilton, where the yacht was moored, on a VC-10 with the royal couple and his American-born wife Susan.

The news, in the form of a Foreign Office cable 'laboriously decoded' by one of the *Britannia*'s naval officers, was that Eric Moonman, Labour MP for Basildon and president of the Zionist Federation for Great Britain and Ireland, had written a letter urging the Foreign Office to raise the allegations contained in Chapman Pincher's article in that day's *Daily Express* at the United Nations.

In Crosland's absence his deputy Ted Rowlands, the minister of state in charge of African Affairs, had told Moonman that 'cool heads' were required and that it 'would not be right' for the British government to intervene in a matter in which it was 'not primarily involved'. It was important, added Rowlands, not to 'cross wires' with the other governments more directly involved like the French.

Crosland agreed with this response, and repeated the information to the British ambassador in Paris in a cable timed at 1833 hours GMT. 'Please take an early opportunity,' he wrote, 'to inform the French of the above, making it clear that we are not – repeat – not initiating or suggesting action.'

1900hrs GMT, Entebbe, Uganda

At 10 p.m. – having just finished dinner at State House with guests that included Wadie Haddad, the leader of the PFLP–EA – Idi Amin phoned the home of his health minister Henry Kyemba.

Recognizing Kyemba's voice, Amin said: 'It's the president. I got back from Mauritius this evening and spoke to the hostages. They don't look well. What medical treatment are they receiving?'

'I arranged for a doctor and nurse to be available at all times, Mr President, as you requested. A few *are* sick but that's because the sanitation in such an old building is not adequate.'

Amin grunted.

'Only one hostage has been admitted to Mulago,' continued Kyemba. 'A Mrs Bloch, an old Israeli lady, who was brought in yesterday with a piece of meat caught in her throat. That was dealt with and she is almost fit again.'

As he finished speaking, Kyemba felt a flutter of fear in his belly. He had deliberately lied to Amin to spare the old lady another night of discomfort in the Old Terminal. If Amin discovered the truth – that she was already well enough to be discharged – it would not go well for him. But the president suspected nothing.

'Good,' he replied. 'Make sure she is returned to the airport before the expiry of the deadline tomorrow at 2 p.m.'

'I will see to it.'

2000hrs GMT, Entebbe International Airport, Uganda

For the hostages it had been a curious evening. After dinner there had been much toing and froing of Mercedes limousines in front of the Old Terminal building, one of which had delivered Faiz Jaber from an unknown appointment. He and the other Palestinians seemed to have 'a very satisfied air' as if something was being prepared. They then spent a few minutes discussing something on the tarmac with a group of official Ugandans, before coming back into the building with smiles on their faces. No explanation, however, was given to the hostages.

At 11 p.m., something even odder occurred. Jean-Jacques, Isa and Willy were lying on mattresses in their usual position close to the exterior door, while next to them Agnès and Maggy were sorting out their bedding. They were approached by a white-haired Israeli man of about forty, dressed in shorts and white shirt, who asked them: 'What are you doing? Why are you getting ready for bed when we will be leaving later?'

Staring first at the man and then at each other, they wondered if he was joking or mentally ill. He gave no hint. 'Tonight we're going to be freed,' he repeated. 'They will come to get us.'

Willy asked the man what he meant, but he could not – or would not – explain. After he had walked away, they speculated among themselves. Had he misinterpreted Idi Amin's words to conclude they would be free tonight? Had the Israelis received a secret message from their government 'to hold themselves in readiness for this night'? Or had the Israelis simply assumed that their government would not wait until the last minute to conduct an exchange of prisoners? Agreeing that this last scenario was the most likely explanation, they thought no more about it and got ready for bed.

By now most of the hostages were lying down. Among the exceptions was a group of four – including Akiva Laxer and Ilan Hartuv – playing bridge on a fold-up table at the left rear of the room, just beyond the glass-fronted aircraft-maintenance office. This was possible because, for the second night in a row, the terrorists had decided not to turn off any of the lights. The only dimly lit area of the large hall was where Jean-Jacques and the others were camped, thanks to the faulty row of neon lights.

Meanwhile the four terrorists on guard – Jaber, Böse, Kuhlmann and the Peruvian – were keeping cool by 'sitting just outside the main door, talking with some Ugandans'. The remaining three were resting in the former VVIP room next to the Israeli hall.

2025hrs GMT, Nairobi, Kenya

The first of Operation Thunderbolt's six planes to touch down on African soil was the Boeing 707 medical plane with Ambassador Uri Lubrani on board. Under the guise of a scheduled El Al flight, it landed at Nairobi's Embakasi Airport at 11.25 p.m. local time and was at once directed to Bay 4, a cordoned-off area for aircraft requiring security precautions. There its medical teams quickly set up under canvas both an emergency room and an operating theatre in preparation for the arrival of casualties from Entebbe that were expected at around two in the morning.

Lubrani, meanwhile, had been taken to meetings with senior officers of the Kenyan GSU to coordinate the arrival of the planes from Entebbe. As only a very small number of Kenyan security officials – among them Ben Gethi, the head of the GSU – knew about the decision to let the planes land, it was agreed that Dany Saadon, the local El Al manager, would inform the Nairobi control tower only at the last minute. Even the airport director was kept in the dark, though his boss the transport minister had been informed.

Most of the senior members of the government – including President Jomo Kenyatta, Vice-President Daniel Arap-Moi and Foreign Minister Dr Munyua Waiyaki – did not yet know what was planned. But now that the first plane had landed, Charles Njonjo decided to call the president at his country home. He told him that the Israelis were about to try and rescue their hostages at Entebbe and wanted to refuel their planes at Nairobi. He also said they hoped to be able to treat any casualties on Kenyan soil. He, Ben Gethi, Bernard Hinga and Bruce McKenzie were all of the opinion that they should be allowed to do this.

There was silence for a moment as Kenyatta digested what Njonjo had told him. Then he replied: 'Njonjo, I have not heard what you just said. If something goes wrong I shall deny knowing anything about it. I'm not saying that they shouldn't land. What I'm saying is that officially I shall deny any knowledge of this and if it goes wrong you and the others will burn your fingers alone.'

Before Njonjo had a chance to respond, the line went dead.

2030hrs GMT, Kenyan airspace

Yoni Netanyahu felt a hand press his shoulder. 'Wake up,' shouted the navigator, above the drone of Hercules One's four engines. 'We're nearing Lake Victoria. Time to get ready.'

Netanyahu turned in the narrow bunk at the back of the flight deck and blinked the sleep from his eyes. 'How long?' he asked.

'Thirty minutes.'

Netanyahu swung his legs off the bunk and stood up. All along the length of the hold, men were preparing for battle by pulling on their shirts, checking their weapons and buckling on their webbing. As he moved down the aircraft, walking on the vehicles where the press of soldiers was too great, he shook hands with all his men, murmuring words of encouragement and last-minute reminders of the contingencies they had practised: 'If there is a cordon of Ugandan troops round the terminal, the Mercedes keeps going whatever happens and the Land Rover teams mop up. If the lights are out in and around the terminal, the Land Rovers swing their headlights to illuminate the hall through its plate-glass windows and the assault groups use the light-projectors on their guns. If the terminal doors are locked, each team has the charges to blow them open. If one team is knocked out, the reserves fill in. If any force fails to carry out its objectives, radio me for immediate reinforcement.'

His last word of advice to them all was: 'Remember. We are going to be the best soldiers at that airport tonight, and there's nobody there who can beat us. And above all – speed, speed.'

Suddenly the plane rocked from side to side as it was hit by a fierce electrical storm. Through the small portal windows 'the sky flashed with streaks of lightning' and the 'thunder clapped louder than the Hercules engines' rumble'. Most of the soldiers felt nervous. But for Muki Betser the storm held no fears: it reminded him of the red skies of Jinja and, moreover, was oddly appropriate given the name of the mission: Operation Thunderbolt.

Noticing that one of the Tzanchanim officers was having trouble buckling his web-belt because his fingers were trembling, Betser tried to reassure him. 'Relax,' he said, 'we're still twenty minutes away.'

Once the storm was behind them, Netanyahu moved up to the crowded flight deck to watch the final approach. The sky ahead was clear and already, in the distance, they could see the runway's landing lights. They all breathed a sigh of relief, knowing they were not expected.

A voice came over the radio: 'Everything all right?'

It was Benny Peled, speaking from the command and control 707 which had caught up with them and was circling overhead.

'A-okay,' replied Shani. 'No problems.'

To the right of the runway they could all see the New Terminal building with its lights blazing, and further to the east, less distinct but also lit up, the Old Terminal. 'So far, so good,' said Netanyahu. As he turned to rejoin his men, Shomron put a hand on his shoulder. 'Now just remember,' said the older man, 'you're the Unit commander and not the first man in the storming party.'

Netanyahu grinned. 'It'll be okay.'

He then made his way back to the Mercedes and pulled on his own heavy web harness that, like most of the Unit's officers, he had had custom-made: eight drab brown magazine and grenade pouches sewn on to a wide foam-rubber backing for comfort; field dressing, knife, rope; and silenced Beretta .22 pistol tucked into his combat blouse.

His preparations complete, Netanyahu opened the front right passenger door of the Mercedes and climbed in beside the driver Amitzur Kafri. On the next row of seats were sitting Betser, directly behind Kafri, and three more fighters, including Giora Zussman by the right rear door. Squashed into the last row of seats, designed for just two people, were three more soldiers.

The rest of the break-in crews, including Amir Ofer, were crammed aboard the first open-topped Land Rover directly behind the Mercedes. In the equally overloaded second Land Rover was the covering force whose first job was to prevent any Ugandan fire from the control tower. Both Land Rovers were mounted with a single belt-fed MAG 7.62mm general-purpose machine gun. Most of the Unit's soldiers were armed with Kalashnikov AK-47s, though a few had Galil ARMs, an Israeli-made assault rifle modelled on the AK-47 but with a folding stock and firing a smaller 5.56 round. All the paratroopers on board were issued with Galils.

With a soft hiss of hydraulics, the massive rear ramp ahead of the Mercedes was partly lowered in the air to save time once the plane had landed. Through the open gap, Netanyahu and the others could see the huge black expanse of Lake Victoria. 'Start the engine,' said Netanyahu.

Kafri turned the key and the repaired starter motor did its job: the Mercedes engine roared into life. He then turned on the car's head-lights. The drivers of the two Land Rovers did the same.

Up ahead in the cockpit, Joshua Shani was holding his breath as he guided the heavily overladen plane towards the still-lit runway. He kept saying to himself, 'Don't screw this up! Don't screw this up!', fully aware that one mistake would wreck the entire operation and cost many lives.

He had judged the approach beautifully and the plane touched down with just a minor jolt and a faint screech of rubber from tyres not fully inflated to deaden the sound. Muki Betser exhaled in relief.

With the runway lights racing past the back of the plane, one of Netanyahu's soldiers glanced at his watch. It was 11.01 p.m. Israeli time – just after midnight in Uganda.

2045hrs GMT, Tel Aviv, Israel

Yitzhak Rabin and his aides arrived at Shimon Peres's office in the Kirya with just fifteen minutes to spare. They found the defense minister and his staff, Motta Gur, Gad Yaacobi and Yitzhak Hofi, the Mossad chief, sitting silently round the large conference table, many of them smoking to relieve the tension. The only sound was static from the loudspeaker on Peres's desk.

At 11.03 the first momentous news came crackling through the receiver: the lead plane had landed safely.

Keenly aware that the operation was now entering its most dangerous phase, Israel's political, military and intelligence leadership held its collective breath for what seemed like an age. In reality barely a minute elapsed before they heard a loud staccato sound that the military men – Rabin, Gur and Hofi – at once identified as gunfire. They gave each other querying looks. Were Yoni's men already at the Old Terminal? Or had they run into trouble en route? The latter scenario, they knew, might spell disaster – not just for the hostages and soldiers in Uganda, but for every man in the room. Their reputations, and more importantly Israel's future security, were balancing on a knife-edge.

2100hrs GMT, Cranleigh, Surrey, UK

For the second night in a row, Chapman and Billee Pincher dined with their friends the McKenzies at Knowle Park in Cranleigh. It had been a strange evening as Bruce was 'more mysterious than ever and somewhat exhausted after another day of hectic international telephone calls'. When Chapman asked his host if he 'thought it possible that the Israelis might somehow attempt a rescue' of the hostages at Entebbe, he pointedly refused to reply.

It was only when the Pinchers were driving the short distance home to their farmhouse in the nearby village of Ewhurst that Billee, who had visited Entebbe with her husband and Bruce a few years earlier, suddenly piped up: 'I know what the Israelis are going to do. They will stage a surprise attack by plane, blow up the MiGs to cause a diversion and then free the hostages.'

Chapman laughed. 'It's a nice idea,' he said, 'but it won't happen. Entebbe is too far from Israel. The only way such a venture could work is if it was launched from Nairobi. But even with Kenya's close links to Israel, and Bruce's undoubted influence over Kenyatta and some of his senior aides, that scenario is simply unthinkable.'

2101hrs GMT, Entebbe International Airport, Uganda

Reducing power and braking hard, Joshua Shani was able to slow the huge bulk of Hercules One almost to walking pace by the time it had reached the runway's mid-point. This enabled ten of Colonel Vilnai's men to jump at intervals from the plane's side door and place, on either side of the tarmac, two battery-operated lanterns so that the follow-up planes could land even if the permanent lights were turned off. At the same time the flight crew released the blocks and lashes securing the three vehicles.

Shani continued taxiing the plane past the New Terminal building with its lights still blazing and down the access strip that led at right angles from the main runway to the diagonal runway. He halted the plane halfway down the access strip, enabling the flight engineer to drop the rear ramp the remaining couple of feet to the tarmac. No sooner had the ramp clanged to the ground than Netanyahu tapped Kafri on the shoulder and shouted 'Go!'

Kafri drove the Mercedes down the ramp and was forced by the narrowness of the access strip to turn sharp right under the wing, only just missing the outer engine's still turning propeller. He was closely followed by the two Land Rovers.

Sitting behind Kafri with his window rolled down, Muki Betser thought of his last time in Africa as he drank in the cool freshness of the African night. He felt 'calm, almost serene, looking out in the darkness' as Kafri 'drove slowly but steadily, like any convoy of VIPs in the Ugandan army', not so fast as to attract attention, not so slow as to cause suspicion.

In the back of the first Land Rover, Amir Ofer had a strong sense of loneliness and foreboding as they moved towards the faint glow of the Old Terminal. He felt they were 'approaching quietly, silently, to

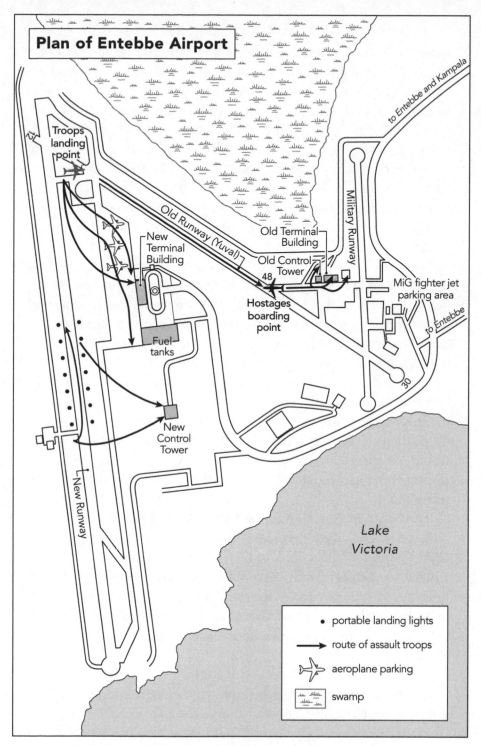

Based on a map in the Confidential IDF Report of
Operation Thunderbolt.

some sort of inevitable explosion, to a terrible clash that was about to begin'. He asked himself: How many of us will come through this?

Turning right on to the diagonal runway, Kafri drove at a steady 40 miles per hour with full headlights as 'the distant halo of the Old Terminal's lights sharpened into detail'. Betser could see the 'canopied entrances' to the building and began the countdown in his mind to the moment when the vehicles would stop and he and his men would rush into action. He broke radio silence to utter the codeword for his break-in teams to chamber a round and set their weapons 'to single shot mode for selective shooting'. All three vehicles were filled with the ratcheting sound of assault rifles being primed.

Then, just as they turned left on to the approach road that led to the Old Terminal, the occupants of the Mercedes could see in its headlights two armed Ugandan sentries who were 100 yards in advance of the control tower. The one on the left quickly vanished into the darkness; but his comrade on the right lifted and aimed his rifle at the Mercedes and called out 'Advance!'

Betser assumed from his time in Uganda that it was a routine challenge and that the soldier was unlikely to fire. That was why they were in the Mercedes. They could drive right by him. 'Eighty, seventy, sixty,' he said under his breath, counting down to the moment when they would leave the car. He was concentrating on the first canopied entrance that he would use to enter the large hall and tackle the terrorists.

'Amitzur,' said Yoni. 'Cut to the right and we'll finish him off.'

Betser was horrified. 'Leave him, Yoni,' he said quietly but emphatically. 'It's just his drill.'

After the briefest pause, Netanyahu repeated his order to change direction. He was convinced that the sentry was suspicious and about to open fire. They had to take him out before he did. As Kafri swerved towards the soldier, Netanyahu and Zussman drew and cocked their silenced Berettas.

'Giora, let's take care of him,' said Yoni.

The memory of Ma'alot flashed through Betser's mind. He felt they were making a fatal mistake before they had even reached the terminal. 'Yoni, no!' he urged. 'Don't shoot!' But his warning was ignored.

Netanyahu and Zussman pointed their pistols out of the window and aimed at the sentry, who was wide eyed with astonishment. At a range of ten yards they opened fire from the moving car, the silencers turning the crack of their shots into a 'bare whisper'. It was a difficult aim, but at least one of the bullets hit its mark and the sentry tottered and fell. Netanyahu and the others could breathe again.

Kafri began to accelerate when suddenly the silence was shattered by a long burst of automatic fire. Betser jerked his head round to see the Ugandan sentry, who must have got back on his feet with his gun, crumple in a hail of Kalashnikov bullets fired from one of the Land Rovers. This prompted yet more unsilenced firing from all three vehicles at both the downed sentry and his fleeing comrade, who was eventually cut down by bullets from a mounted machine gun.

The sound of the unsilenced gunshots had put the whole operation in jeopardy. The element of surprise had been well and truly lost and Betser, for one, expected the terminal building to vanish at any moment 'in a fireball of explosions as the terrorists followed through with their threats to blow up the hostages'.

'Drive!' shouted Netanyahu at Kafri, who had braked at the first sound of unsilenced fire. 'Fast!'

Kafri stamped on the accelerator but had only covered a short distance when bullets spat out of the darkness. Aware that they were easy targets packed into the vehicles, Yoni and Betser both yelled, 'Stop!'

The car screeched to a halt, as did the Land Rovers behind. They had stopped short of the control tower and at least fifty yards from the edge of the Old Terminal, rather than the five they had planned for. Flinging his door open and shouting at the others to follow him, Betser began running towards the Old Terminal, careful to veer left to avoid the pool of light in front of the building. He could hear the thumping of boots behind him and knew that his break-in teams were close behind.

From the darkness to his right came a burst of fire. Flicking his AK-47 to automatic, he fired back as he ran, his bullets hitting his assailant and causing him to fall. On reaching the corner of the Old Terminal he paused 'while the rattle and crack of rifle and sub-machine gun fire shook the air, kicking up bits of asphalt at our feet'. Behind him the rest of the assault teams were 'bunched up, instead of heading to the assigned entrances'. It was a 'complete contradiction of the battle plan', caused no doubt by the loss of the surprise and the threat of incoming fire.

Netanyahu shouted at Betser to move forward, passing him as he did so. He then moved a little to the right to let Betser, Yiftach Reicher and the rest of the assault teams go beyond him. As Betser ran on, staying close to the front of the building, he could see an armed man come out of the second canopied entrance to the large hall and take up a position behind the low concrete wall. Betser fired a couple of shots at the man before his magazine emptied. They missed and the man ran back inside.

Betser paused briefly to reload, flipping the empty magazine round and replacing it with a full one, before continuing on to the first can-opied entrance. Finding it blocked off and no way through, he ran on to the second entrance, followed by Amos Goren. But in the lead now was Amir Ofer, part of the squad assigned to the second entrance. Ofer's job was to watch the back of his officer, Amnon Peled. But on leaving the Land Rover his legs had momentarily gone to jelly and he lost sight of Peled. Terrified that he would not arrive in time to do his job, Ofer ran as hard as he could to the second entrance, ignoring the cover of the building and overtaking both Betser and Peled in the process.

Yoni Netanyahu was almost opposite the first entrance, and not far from the point where he planned to set up his command post, when he stopped and turned to his left. He may have wondered why Muki Betser's squad had run past the blocked entrance; or he might have been checking on the progress of Yiftach Reicher and Giora Zussman, the leaders of the other assault teams. But by pausing in open ground, when most of his men were hugging the front of the building, he was vulnerable to Ugandan snipers.

Shots rang out from the control tower – the vantage point barely eighty yards away that Motta Gur had warned about – and Netanyahu was struck in the chest and lower right arm. Sighing, he collapsed to the ground. 'Yoni's been hit,' shouted Tamir Pardo, his communica-tions officer, who was following close behind him.

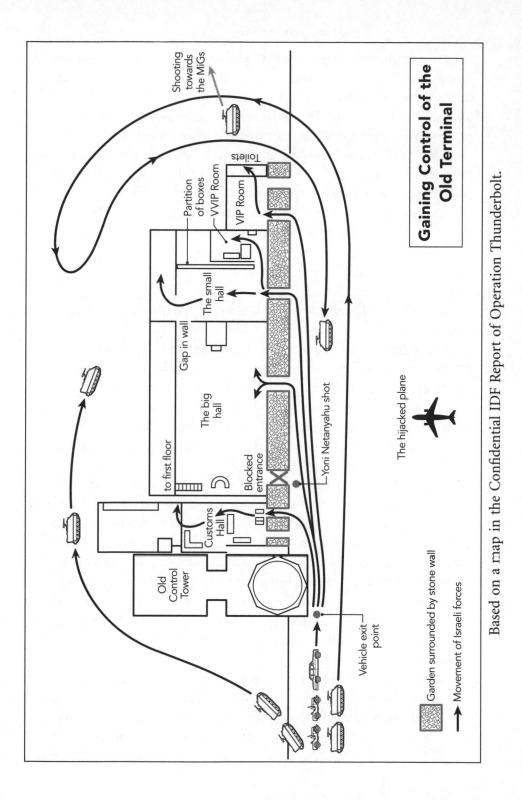

Based on a map in the Confidential IDF Report of Operation Thunderbolt.

Ofer was within twenty yards of the second entrance when he heard Pardo's yell. He continued running, keenly aware of his task 'to reach the door' as quickly as possible because the terrorists 'could blow up the building in a matter of seconds'. He had reached the canopied path and was approaching the door when its lower glass panel exploded outwards in a hail of bullets that seemed to pass on either side of Ofer, missing him by inches. Spotting a terrorist shooting from a prone position beyond the door, Ofer fired back through the shattered panel from a distance of five yards. The terrorist's head dropped. He pushed the door open and shot the body again to make sure.

2104hrs GMT, Entebbe International Airport, Uganda

Akiva Laxer was sitting with Ilan Hartuv and two others at a card table to the left rear of the large hall, just finishing off a round of bridge, when he heard a burst of gunfire from outside. Two possibilities flashed through Laxer's mind: either the terrorists had decided to kill them, or the Ugandans had decided to attack the terrorists. Hoping it was the latter, he advised his shocked companions to join the rest of the hostages on the ground.

Among those woken by the noise of gunfire were Willy and Cécile, lying with the French group near to the door. Willy stayed stretched out on his mattress, trying to work out what was happening. Hearing more shots, he concluded that either the Ugandans were firing on an escapee or the negotiations had reached an impasse and the terrorists were killing hostages. Others feared they were about to be executed, including Emma and Claude Rosenkovitch who were lying with their children Noam and Ella behind the glass-fronted aircraft-maintenance office. They at once rolled on top of their offspring, hoping to act as human shields.

Also now awake, Maggy and Agnès saw tracer bullets flashing across the front of the building from right to left. They could hear terrorists and Ugandans shouting orders outside – but to whom and what about they did not know. Then suddenly the four terrorists on guard tumbled back through the door, led by Wilfried Böse who was holding a sub-machine gun in one hand and a grenade in the other.

Looking from the back of the room, Ilan Hartuv could see Böse pointing his weapon at the hostages on the floor, many of whom were sobbing, and was convinced he was about to open fire. So too was Michel Bacos who, a day or two earlier, had been told by Böse: 'If any army from any country comes to save you, you can rest assured that we will hear them first, and before they get to you we will kill every last one of you.'

Now Bacos felt certain Böse would carry out his threat. The German certainly had the opportunity, as did the other terrorists. But, instead of pulling the trigger, Böse jerked his head towards the back of the room and told the hostages near him to 'retreat' and take cover. He and Kuhlmann were prepared to die for their beliefs, but not to murder women and children in cold blood.

Having shooed away the hostages, Böse turned to face the door, tugging the pin from his grenade as he did so.

Assuming Böse was about to throw the grenade in among the hostages, the chief steward got to his knees and begged him not to. But the German had already made up his mind and, after glancing again at the hostages, he hurled the grenade through one of the open windows, the flash from the explosion lighting up the darkness outside. This prompted Maggy to flee towards the back of the room, her back tensed in anticipation of a bullet that never came. Agnès followed her, the two of them throwing themselves stomach down on the floor behind the office. Next to head for the same corner were Willy and Cécile, both fearing that the terrorists were about to kill them. They piled on top of the large number of people who were already there, including the Rosenkovitches and their children.

Looking around her, Maggy could see a 'young kibbutz guy' she had got to know, 'face down on the floor, under the chairs'. She noticed the Belgians Gilbert and Helen Weill praying for deliverance; others were 'white with fear'. Of Jean-Jacques Mimouni, Isa and Brigitte there was no sign.

Böse, meanwhile, had fallen to the floor and had his AK-47 trained on the door ahead of him. Crouching slightly to the right of the door were two more terrorists, Faiz Jaber and Brigitte Kuhlmann, while a fourth, the Peruvian, had retreated into the room and was hiding behind a pillar towards the right rear of the hall.

Suddenly Böse opened fire through the door at an approaching figure who shot back at him. The noise of automatic gunfire was deafening and more than one hostage screamed in terror. Then Böse's head twitched as a bullet hit it.

Amir Ofer burst into the hall, fired more shots into Böse to make certain he was dead, then moved slightly to his right to scan for more terrorists. His heart was pounding as he looked on the scene of chaos before him. Distracted by hostages screaming and fleeing in all directions, Ofer failed to see two terrorists – Jaber and Kuhlmann – kneeling below the window to his left rear. As they turned their weapons on Ofer, Amnon Peled, who should have led the assault, burst through the doorway, spotted the danger and shot them both. Running over to them, he kicked away their AK-47s in case they were still alive, prompting Ofer to shout out in Hebrew, 'Amnon, don't advance!' He knew that more terrorists were unaccounted for and was worried Peled would obstruct his field of fire.

By now Muki Betser and Amos Goren had also come through the doorway. Betser immediately shot Jaber and Kuhlmann 'to make sure they were out of action'. For a second there was silence. Then more shooting could be heard outside and one of the hostages began screaming. At this point Betser was standing just ahead of the doorway, Peled to his left and Ofer and Goren on his extreme right, 'totally focused on the fully lit hall, searching for more terrorists'.

Scores of hostages were strewn 'all over the floor on mattresses', some frozen with fear, others screaming and shouting. Many 'covered their heads with blankets as if to protect themselves from the bullets'.

Then a small object arced across the hall, from the soldiers' left to right, before bouncing to the ground and igniting with a flash. It gave off large quantities of smoke and set fire to a number of blankets under which hostages were huddling. It was an incendiary grenade and had been thrown by the Peruvian, who was still hiding behind a pillar.

Perhaps hoping that the grenade would distract the soldiers, the

Peruvian emerged from the pillar and brought his AK-47 up to the firing position. Betser and Goren saw him and opened fire simultaneously, their bullets striking the Peruvian's weapon, head and chest. He fell to the floor.

2106hrs GMT, Entebbe International Airport, Uganda

Only a minute had elapsed since the soldiers had fired live rounds at the Ugandan sentries, and barely three minutes from the time the vehicles had rolled off Hercules One. In that short time Yoni Netanyahu had been wounded and Muki Betser and his men had killed all four armed terrorists who posed an immediate threat to the hostages in the large hall; which just left the trio who had been sleeping in the VVIP room unaccounted for. As more of the Unit's fighters poured in through the door, Betser continued to scan the room for danger.

Suddenly to his right front a figure leapt up from a pile of smoking blankets and mattresses that had been set on fire by the Peruvian's incendiary grenade. It was the only part of the hall in shadow, thanks to the broken lights, and the smoke made it harder still to identify the figure. In a split second Betser took in the man's youth, olive skin, moustache and curly hair and assumed he was an Arab terrorist. He opened fire, as did at least one of the others, their bullets striking the figure in the body as he tried to turn and run.

It was Jean-Jacques Mimouni, the handsome young French-Israeli who all week had kept the hostages' spirits up with his stories, jokes and a constant drinks service. When the shooting started and some of those around him fled to the back of the room, he and Isa stayed on their mattresses under some blankets. But after the Peruvian's grenade had caused those blankets to catch fire, they were forced to get up – a desperate manoeuvre that, for Jean-Jacques, was fatal.

Though he did not fire himself, Ofer felt that this mistaken killing was entirely justifiable, if very sad. 'It's important to understand,' he later admitted to Jean-Jacques' nephew, 'that according to our drill anyone who stood up, or was even suspected of being a terrorist, even if there was a one per cent chance of that, would have been shot.'

Moments after Jean-Jacques' shooting, a half-dressed Isa also jumped up and fled towards the back corner, jumping over Jean-Jacques' corpse on the way. But as she was clearly an unarmed and nearly naked European woman the soldiers did not fire.

Maggy could still hear the odd burst of fire in the room, and see bullets hitting the wall behind her, but most of the shooting now seemed to be coming from the direction of the Israeli hall and the floor above.

It was only now that Amir Ofer remembered the megaphone he was carrying. Raising it to his lips, he meant to shout out in Hebrew and English: 'Lie down, we're the IDF. Don't get up.' But so stressed was he that the words came out only half formed. His second attempt was clearer.

Ofer's words did not, however, prevent a small figure from climbing to its feet in the far corner of the room, near the stairs. Peled and Goren pointed their weapons and were squeezing their triggers when they realized it was a young girl. They jerked their weapons up just in time, and the bullets hit the wall above her.

A young Greek man who worked for the French holiday company Club Med had a similar escape after getting to his feet in the centre of the hall. As a number of Kalashnikovs swivelled towards him, a voice cried out in Hebrew, 'He's one of ours!' The soldiers lowered their weapons.

Only now that the firing had stopped did the majority of Israeli hostages realize that the soldiers in the room were IDF. 'They are here!' cried Emma Rosenkovitch to her husband Claude. Most of the French were uncertain as to their identity until an Israeli explained in their language: 'They're ours. These are our Israeli soldiers.'

Instructed in Hebrew and English to stay lying down, to remain calm, and assured that the situation was under control, the shocked hostages remained where they were. Seeing a hostage with his arm in the air, Muki Betser went over to talk to him. 'Are there any terrorists among you?' he asked.

'You got them all in here. Apart from that one,' said Akiva Laxer in Hebrew, pointing at Jean-Jacques' bloodied corpse. 'He was one of us. A hostage. But there are more terrorists in a small room to the side.'

'Don't worry,' said Betser, 'we'll take care of them. Are all the hostages here?'

Laxer nodded. 'Yes, apart from one. An old woman called Dora Bloch who was taken to the hospital in Kampala.'

Betser frowned. 'We won't be able to take her back with us.'

2106hrs GMT, Entebbe International Airport, Uganda

While Muki Betser and his men were securing the large hall, the other two assault teams also entered the Old Terminal building. Using flashlights, Reicher and two men led the charge into the unlit customs hall where they found and killed three Ugandan soldiers before locating, in the adjacent reception hall, the stairs to the first floor. As he climbed the staircase, Reicher shot two more Ugandan soldiers at close range, their bodies tumbling past him. In the hallway at the top he discovered that the door to the platform that overlooked the large hall was barred by a locked metal grille. Leaving one man to guard it and the top of the stairs, he continued with the other to the large room at the end of the corridor that had been a restaurant and was now a dormitory for Ugandan soldiers guarding the Old Terminal. It was full of blankets and sleeping bags – Reicher estimated more than sixty – but no people. Hearing shots, the bulk of the soldiers had jumped from a window to the open area behind the terminal.

Having briefly checked that no one was on the terminal roof, Reicher used his radio to call Lieutenant Arnon Epstein, leading his second team, and ask him where he was. Epstein should have followed Reicher through the customs hall and posted his men at the stairs. But, failing to find the staircase in the darkness, he and his men had instead entered a side room where they found and killed several Ugandan soldiers. They were back at the front of the terminal – helping to suppress the Ugandan fire from the control tower that continued intermittently throughout the operation – when Reicher came down to meet them. Together they re-searched the customs and reception halls as far as the door at the end, shooting two more Ugandan soldiers in the process. Reicher's teams killed at least twelve of Idi Amin's men. Not one was taken prisoner.

With his team strung out behind him, Giora Zussman made a solo entry into the small hall that had held the Israeli hostages. He could see several empty mattresses with sheets, a number of suitcases and a table piled with passports; but no hostages or terrorists. Just in case, he sprayed the hall and the gap in the wall of boxes with bullets from his Kalashnikov until his clip was empty. As he ducked back out of the hall to reload, the two missing members of his team moved past him and into the hall, firing as they went. Reaching a room at the far end that had been used as a kitchen, they found and killed two Ugandan soldiers.

By now Zussman's team had been joined by Shlomo Reisman, one of Amnon Peled's men who had missed the entrance to the large hall, and Tamir Pardo, the communications officer who had been left with nothing to do after Yoni was hit and the command post ceased to function. With Pardo following close behind, Zussman and Reisman moved cautiously through the gap in the wall of boxes and down a corridor that led to the former VVIP lounge, throwing mini-grenades and firing as they went. In the first room they came to – the one that had earlier been used for Nahum Dahan's interrogation – they saw emerging from the smoke two men with their hands out from their sides. Reisman called out in a mixture of English, Hebrew and Arabic: 'Stop! Who are you?'

They ignored him and continued walking past Zussman.

'They're terrorists!' Zussman shouted to Reisman as he jumped out of his line of fire. 'Shoot them!'

Reisman hesitated and, unable to fire himself for fear of hitting his men, Zussman repeated the order.

'No,' replied Reisman, still under the impression he was near the large hall, 'they're hostages!'

But as the duo went past him, Reisman spotted a grenade on one of their belts. 'Stop!' he yelled, and when they ignored him he shot them both.

One of them must have been holding a grenade in his hand because as he fell the detonator gave off a blue flash. 'Grenade!' shouted Reisman as he pulled Pardo into a small alcove. Zussman also dived for cover.

The explosion shook the small room and left a pall of smoke. When it had cleared, Reisman confirmed that both terrorists were dead. His lip was bleeding from a minor shrapnel wound; other than that the Israelis were unharmed. As they worked their way back down the corridor to the large hall they found the body of a third terrorist. It was unclear how he had been killed.

By now Zussman's second team had got through a window into the final part of the Old Terminal – the former VIP lounge – and found it empty. Their initial attempt to gain entry had been foiled by a barricaded door. When they tried to throw grenades through a window, one rebounded from the frame and wounded an Israeli in the leg.

It was not until the entire Old Terminal building had been secured that the stricken Yoni Netanyahu was dragged behind the relative cover of a low wall and treated by Dr David Hassin, the medical officer. This was in accordance with Yoni's own order that the wounded were to be left where they fell while the battle was in progress. Hassin could tell by the paleness of his face and other indicators that Netanyahu had already suffered significant blood loss. There was little blood on Yoni's clothing and he feared the haemorrhaging was internal. At first, having cut off Netanyahu's ammunition belt and shirt with a knife, the doctor could only find an exit wound close to the spine on his lower back. But on closer examination he located a small slit below the collarbone on the right side of Netanyahu's chest. That confirmed that the bullet, fired from above, had passed obliquely down through Netanyahu's torso, tearing organs and most likely arteries as it went. He put dressings on the wounds, but knew that Netanyahu was unlikely to survive.

2107hrs GMT, Entebbe International Airport, Uganda

Muki Betser had just finished his conversation with Akiva Laxer when his hand-held radio squawked into life: 'Muki! Muki!'

'Muki here.'

'Giora here. Mission accomplished. Three terrorists down. No casualties on our side.'

Betser breathed a sigh of relief. The threat from the rooms beyond the large hall – where the terrorists were known to have set up their dormitory – had been neutralized. Unaware that Netanyahu had been shot, Betser tried to reach him on the radio. 'Yoni!' he called.

No response. He tried again. 'Yoni? Muki here. Mission accomplished.'

A long silence, finally ended by a squawk. 'Muki, it's Tamir here,' said Yoni's communications officer, just returned from helping to clear the VVIP room. 'Yoni's down.'

Ordering the soldiers in the room to collect the terrorists' weapons and treat any wounded hostages – the most serious of whom was Holocaust survivor Pasco Cohen who had been shot in the pelvis as he tried to shield his children from the hail of bullets that killed the Peruvian – Betser went outside to check on Netanyahu. He found him lying on his back on the tarmac, his shirt torn open, with David Hassin 'kneeling by his side . . . trying to treat him'. The scene reminded him of another doctor's desperate attempt to save the life of an officer shot during the failed operation to destroy the PLO camp at Karameh in 1968. He had failed, and Betser suspected that Hassin would too.

Looking around, Betser could see Shaul Mofaz's BTR parked near to the Airbus in front of the terminal, his machine gun pointing at the control tower which, for the moment, had fallen silent. All the Israeli soldiers were surprised to see the Airbus so close to the terminal. According to the Mossad photos taken a day earlier, it should have been parked at the end of the diagonal runway. But, unbeknown to them, the terrorists had earlier that day instructed Michel Bacos to move the plane in anticipation of a press conference to celebrate Israel's capitulation.

Betser used his radio to call Dan Shomron. 'Dan. Muki here. Yoni's wounded. I'm taking command.'

'Okay.'

By now all four planes had landed: the last two with the assistance of the paratroopers' lanterns after the Ugandans in the new control tower had realized a raid was in progress and turned off the runway lights. The first three Hercules were parked on the apron close to the New Terminal building that Matan Vilnai's paratroopers had secured as Netanyahu's men were storming the Old Terminal. They had found it well lit but mostly deserted apart from a few Ugandan civilians who were quickly rounded up. But as Sergeant Surin Hershko climbed the external stairs at the corner of the building, his Galil assault rifle slung from his neck, he came across a Ugandan policeman and a woman coming the other way. The policeman raised a pistol and, before Hershko could release his safety, fired two shots. The second hit Hershko in the neck, severing his spinal cord. He collapsed to the ground, conscious but unable to move his hands or legs. His assailant escaped.

2107hrs GMT, Entebbe International Airport, Uganda

No sooner had Hercules Two landed – at around seven minutes past midnight local time – than Shaul Mofaz drove his two BTRs towards the Old Terminal and patrolled as far as the eastern end of the building, where he found no opposition. Leaving Omer Bar-Lev's BTR to guard that flank, he returned to the main entrance and parked near the Airbus in case he was needed. It was here that Betser spotted him. Meanwhile the remaining two BTRs had deplaned from Hercules Three and were stationed to the north of the Old Terminal to intercept any Ugandan reinforcements coming from the direction of Entebbe town. During their patrol they shot and killed seven Ugandan soldiers and made contact with some of Yiftach Reicher's men at the back of the reception hall.

Hercules Four touched down at 12.08 a.m. local time. Its pilot was Amnon Halivni, a hugely experienced reserve officer and former head of the Yellow Bird Squadron who had been part of Israel's military delegation to Uganda in the early 1970s. Because of his familiarity with Africa's air routes, weather patterns and airports – particularly Entebbe – Halivni felt he should have been chosen to fly Hercules

One. But Benny Peled had faith in Joshua Shani and Halivni was instead assigned to the plane that would carry the hostages to safety.

Once on the ground, Halivni taxied Hercules Four past the other three C-130s that were parked near the New Terminal building. The agreed pick-up point for the hostages and any casualties was the junction of the diagonal runway and the approach road to the Old Terminal (a point marked on the maps as 'Yuval 48'). But at first Halivni stopped the plane well short of the turn because he saw one of the Golani soldiers waving a torch. The medics were in the process of setting up their equipment beside the runway when Alik Ron arrived on foot from the Old Terminal with a request from Muki Betser for the plane to move to the agreed embarkation point. The medics duly repacked their equipment and the plane was taxied to 'Yuval 48', and turned round so that its tail was 'pointing in the direction of the terminal and the nose towards the runway'.

By then both Peugeot pick-up trucks on Hercules Four had left on their respective missions: one to ferry Ephraim Sneh and the Golani soldiers – including Noam Tamir – to the Old Terminal; the other to take the air force technicians with their pump to the fuel tanks. As they approached the Old Terminal building, Sneh and Tamir could see tracer bullets being fired from the control tower to the ground, and machine-gun bullets and rocket-propelled grenades (RPGs) going in the opposite direction. This caused the driver to halt, and only continue when the firing had stopped.

As Sneh reached the Old Terminal, Betser and Hassin were loading Netanyahu's stretcher onto the back of a Land Rover for evacuation to Hercules Four. A few hostages, spilling out from the large hall, tried to get on as well; but they were told to wait. 'They should take very good care of Yoni,' said Hassin to Sneh, 'because he's in a bad way.'

En route to the plane, the driver of the Land Rover heard Netanyahu mumble something, but could not make out his words. By the time he was unloaded at the back of the Hercules, his heart had stopped. A resuscitation team – two doctors and a senior medic – administered CPR and gave him blood through a central venous line. But it was too late. He died beside the plane.

Back at the Old Terminal building, a soldier had told the hostages

– some of whom were walking around blank-faced and in a state of shock – to leave their possessions, put on their shoes and get ready to depart for the plane. Most ignored him and wasted valuable time scrabbling for their bags. As Willy collected his from behind the bar – twisting his knee in the process – he saw the pilot Michel Bacos, 'very pale', changing from his sports shirt into his captain's uniform, presumably because he wanted to look the part when he returned home; and all the time Bacos was shouting to the other hostages, 'Don't forget your shoes!'

Outside Betser had corralled the first batch of hostages into a tight group, protected by a wall of soldiers. As he began to lead them down the access strip to where the Hercules was waiting on the edge of the diagonal runway, another heavy burst of fire came from the control tower, the bullets ricocheting off the tarmac and causing the soldiers and panicked hostages to scurry back to the cover of the building. 'Shaul,' shouted Betser into his radio. 'Take out the control tower please.'

Mofaz opened up with everything he had, as did one of the Land Rovers, their machine-gun bullets and RPGs tearing chunks out of the balcony from where the Ugandan soldier was firing. After another false start, Betser ordered a second burst of sustained fire that lasted for nearly a minute. Only then did he allow the hostages to leave the building.

The departure was more stampede than orderly procession as the terrified hostages, many weighed down by children and possessions, fled the building. Some were told to get on the two Land Rovers waiting outside, but many preferred to run, fearing that the shooting would start again. The latter included the Rosenkovitches: Emma holding young Noam's hand; Claude carrying his daughter Ella and using Sanford Freedman's bulky copy of the *Complete Shakespeare* to try to protect her from stray shots. From far behind them they could hear gunshots and explosions. But Emma did not care. She was just relieved to be out in the open again, free of her captors, and heading for safety.

Having grabbed her things, Agnès was about to leave the large hall when she saw an elderly Israeli man – probably Yitzhak David, who had been shot in the arm – sitting on a chair, covered in blood. He seemed to be waiting for something. She was about to go up to him and say, 'Come on, you must get up and run!' But at the last minute her courage failed her. Worried that he might be dead already, she ran past him. So too did Maggy, passing Jean-Jacques' bullet-riddled body as she did so. It was obvious that he was dead, but she could not bring herself to believe that.

Willy was loath to leave the terminal without his sandals. By the time he had located them under some blankets, the fire was out, but the room was still full of smoke and reeking of cordite. He went outside, jumped over a wall and was directed by soldiers to a Land Rover parked thirty yards away. It was already packed with people, but he got in and soon found himself lying half on his back, his cheek pressed against the side panel. Near him was a wounded man who sobbed in pain every time someone pressed against him. Agnès was also in the truck, complaining that she could not breathe. She was holding a plastic bag with a big wooden spoon that she had bought as a present for her sister. Realizing that it was digging in to people, she threw the bag out of the vehicle, forgetting that it also contained another hostage's belongings. Despite the crush, and the driver's warnings that the truck was overloaded and some people might fall off, hostages continued to clamber in.

At last the Land Rover moved off on the short drive to the Hercules. It was pitch black but the hostages could hear the plane's engines and feel the wind from its propeller wash before they saw it. When the vehicle stopped, there was an unedifying scramble to get off it and into the plane. To haul herself up, Maggy grabbed a machine-gun barrel that was still hot from the firefight and burned her hand. Willy lost a sandal and had to scrabble around to find it. Eventually they all got off – including the wounded man who was put on a stretcher – and were herded up the plane's rear ramp by the Golani soldiers who were fanned out on either side to prevent hostages from disappearing into the long grass.

One of the last hostages to leave the terminal was a beautiful young stewardess wearing only a pair of red panties and matching camisole top. Lightly wounded in the thigh by a tiny piece of shrapnel, she refused to walk and became hysterical when the soldiers threatened to leave her. So Amir Ofer hauled her on to his shoulder and carried her outside. When a bullet narrowly missed his head, he shifted the stewardess's body on to his exposed right side 'so that, if they shot again, she'd take the bullet'. He was determined not to die 'because of her stupid stubbornness' and, as luck would have it, they both made it unscathed to one of the Land Rovers that was ferrying the hostages.

Inside Hercules Four the hostages were welcomed by Israeli medics wearing a red Star of David on a white armband, and told to move as far forward as possible because more were arriving all the time. They sat where they could: on the floor, on boxes and on bags of medicine. Only now did they start to look at each other to see who was there, who was hurt – or worse. In tears, Maggy embraced Willy. So too did Agnès. Not far from them were sitting Marianne, Cécile and Isa, the latter still struggling to come to terms with Jean-Jacques' brutal killing.

The crew was sitting nearby in various states of undress: Bacos had his uniform on, but Lemoine was wearing a dressing gown and pyjama bottoms that only came to his knees. One of the stewardesses had lost her glasses and had covered a little yellow petticoat with her uniform jacket; another, the fiancée of a famous Israeli footballer, was wearing just a towel until the medics made her some knickers out of crêpe paper, almost like a nappy.

One grim-faced hostage, however, was in two minds about leaving Uganda. 'My mother was taken to Kampala Hospital yesterday after a piece of meat got stuck in her throat,' explained Ilan Hartuv to Dr Dolev, the head of the surgical team. 'Maybe I should stay to make sure she's safe.'

Dolev shook his head. 'If you stay they'll kill you for sure. But an elderly woman like your mother has a good chance of being left alive.'

By now the Land Rovers had returned from the Old Terminal with the remaining wounded – civilian and military – who were carried up to the front of the cargo hold and laid out on the floor so that they could be treated. Nearby was the body of Yoni Netanyahu, his face covered with an aluminium blanket.

Willy counted six injured people and two dead. Two were from the

Unit: Netanyahu and the young soldier wounded by an Israeli grenade. The rest were hostages, including fifty-five-year-old Ida Borochovich – who had been shot in the heart and killed as she fled with her son to the back of the room – Pasco Cohen and Yitzhak David. Of Jean-Jacques Mimouni there was no sign. But shortly after Maggy had explained to Willy that she had seen Jean-Jacques badly hurt, another stretcher arrived. Though the face was obscured, they at once recognized the sweater on the blood-soaked corpse as belonging to their friend. All the girls started weeping.

On the flight deck the pilot, Amnon Halivni, was anxious to leave. He knew how vulnerable the unprotected Hercules was to gunfire, and how a single well-aimed RPG round would cause carnage in its hold. The longer they remained on the ground, the more likely a Ugandan counter-attack became. 'How many hostages are on board?' he asked the loadmaster.

'We've got everyone.'

'That's not good enough. I need the exact number in writing.'

Moments later the pilot was handed a slip of paper which stated that ninety-three live hostages and the dead bodies of two more were on board. Halivni shook his head. He knew that there should have been 105 hostages in the terminal. Where were the others? He asked the loadmaster to count again and list, in writing, the names of the dead. Back came a second note with a total of 102 alive and dead: still fewer than it should have been. On the back were written the names of the dead: 'Ida Borokovich', 'Jean-Jacques Mimouni' and 'Lt. Col. Yoni'. When Halivni again queried the number with the loadmaster, he was told that no two counters could agree, but that the hostages themselves were convinced that everyone, apart from Dora Bloch, was on the plane. Halivni reported the problem to Amnon Biran – call sign 'Butterfly' – who was manning the radio in Shomron's Tactical Headquarters Land Rover.

Biran, in turn, told Kuti Adam who was circling in the command and control Boeing 707 – call sign 'Two Hundred' – above the airfield. 'Look,' Adam responded, 'the numbers are not making sense to me. I want you to check. Have you searched all the places and verified that you have removed all the people? Over.'

'Uh, the search of the building has been done,' said Biran. 'That is all I can tell you at this stage. Over.'

'Roger. Okay.'

A minute or two later, Adam asked for an update. 'Butterfly, Two Hundred here. Over.'

'Butterfly here,' said Biran. 'Roger. Over.'

'Well, what's going on? You're not saying anything.'

'We are continuing to organize for the evacuation. When I have more specific information other than general words I will inform you. Over.'

'Okay. When the first takes off, tell me as well.'

'Of course. Of course.'

'Roger. Over and out.'

But Adam was not silent for long. 'Don't forget,' he reminded Biran, 'that I also asked you about the French crew.'

Biran replied: 'At this stage I don't have specific details yes or no.'

'Okay. I just don't want you to forget it.'

'There is no one left in the hall. If they were taken out of there beforehand . . .' he said, a pause completing the sentence. 'The hijacked plane is standing right in front of the terminal, with stairs beside it, so maybe it was preparing to take off or something like that. Over.'

'Fine. Okay.'

Adam's next request a minute or two later was for 'more reports on the people'.

A clearly harassed Biran responded: 'At this moment, I don't have any, it's being checked. When I have, I will report back. Over.'

'Roger. Okay. Other than that, is there more gunfire?'

'If there is, it is only from our side. Isolated gunfire towards additional places. Over.'

'Fine. And regarding injuries, do you know anything yet? Over.'

'There are a number of injured. At this moment we don't know precise numbers. Over.'

'Roger. Okay.'

Biran reported to Adam moments later: 'What is happening now in this area, in the area of the army hangars of their air force, is that black smoke is rising, and there are fires. In the area of the Old

Terminal it is quiet. There are more of our security forces there. We're near the plane that is evacuating the wounded, and there are lights on at the New Terminal. Over.'

'Is Dan near you?' asked Adam, referring to Shomron.

'He's currently supervising the loading of the vehicle on to the plane; he's at a little distance from me.'

'Okay. Tell me, has the plane with the wounded left yet?' asked Adam as if he had not heard Biran's two previous comments.

'Not yet,' said Biran, biting his tongue. 'They're currently transferring the last vehicle to it; then it will take off.'

'Okay.'

It was shortly after this conversation that Biran asked the pilot of Hercules Four to check in person on the Airbus's crew. Leaving the flight deck for the first time since landing, Halivni found the hold packed with people but eerily silent. Directly ahead, doctors and medics were working on the wounded who had been arranged in two triple tiers on either side of the fuselage, their stretchers fastened to the fuselage by straps. As Halivni passed the man on the top left tier – the young soldier from the Unit who had been injured in the arm and leg – he put a hand on his shoulder to comfort him.

Beyond the stretchers were the unwounded hostages, most sitting and staring straight ahead with glassy eyes. Interspersed among them were some of the Golani, the medical team and the aircrew. At the very back, closest to the ramp, was the grey Peugeot 404 pick-up that had transported Sneh and the Golani. It was full of sleeping soldiers.

Identifying Michel Bacos by his white shirt and pilot's epaulettes, Halivni beckoned him forward. 'You're the Air France pilot?' he asked in halting French.

'Yes.'

'Is your whole crew here?'

'Yes. But what about my passengers?'

'They're all here, except for Dora Bloch. We have to take off right away.'

Pausing briefly to talk to Uzi Davidson whom he knew from the IAF reserves, Halivni returned to the flight deck and assured Biran that the Airbus's crew was on board. He added that he could see tracer fire from the direction of the Old Terminal and was worried that the vulnerable Hercules might be attacked. He wanted to take off as soon as possible. Having spoken to Shomron, Biran told a relieved Halivni that he could leave. His destination, said Biran, was Nairobi International Airport. The air force technicians had finally managed to connect their portable fuel pump to one of the ducts; but as it would take far too long to fill all four planes, the decision had been taken to head for Kenya.

While Halivni did his final checks, Biran was asked by Adam for another update. 'At this stage,' he said, 'we've finished loading the plane that is evacuating the wounded. The first plane is still standing in place, but it will soon start taxiing for takeoff.'

'Good.'

'Look, it's closing its doors.'

'Good.'

Once its rear ramp was up, Hercules Four began to move on to and up the diagonal runway, back the way it had come. It had been parked at the start of the access road for just twenty-six minutes.

Watching the plane depart, Muki Betser was reminded of the last time he and the other Israelis had departed from Entebbe four years earlier. Then nobody had offered a helping hand as they 'climbed heavy-hearted on to the plane to Nairobi', feeling 'like refugees, helpless and defeated'. This time the hostages were neither helpless nor alone. They were 'freed citizens of Israel' and Betser felt a surge of pride that he and his men had 'fulfilled' their roles 'as their protectors'.

Reaching the end of the main runway, Halivni opened the throttles and the Hercules – with its cargo of 101 hostages, including two dead and a number of wounded – accelerated past the New Terminal and rose slowly into the air above Lake Victoria. Still stunned by their sudden and violent rescue, and fearful that the plane might be pursued and shot down by Ugandan fighters, the surviving hostages were in no mood to cheer. Instead they clung to each other as Halivni banked the Hercules steeply to the left and set a course for Nairobi's Embakasi Airport.

It was 12.52 p.m. local time. The rescue had taken just fifty-one minutes.

2125hrs GMT, Ugandan airspace

Kuti Adam knew that Operation Thunderbolt's first priority was to rescue the hostages. But once word had reached him in the command and control plane that the evacuation was under way, he gave the soldiers on the ground permission to destroy the eleven MiG fighters of the Ugandan Air Force that had been identified in the Mossad aerial pictures. It was, of course, the reciprocal part of the deal that had been struck with the Kenyans to allow the Israeli planes to refuel at Nairobi; but Adam had been reluctant to order such an action until he knew the hostages were safe.

When the message reached Shomron it was waved aside. The ground commander had his hands full with the hostages and intended to deal with the MiGs when the evacuation was complete.

Meanwhile Omer Bar-Lev, who had been assigned the task of destroying the MiGs, was sitting in his BTR at the far end of the Old Terminal. He could see eleven planes – four MiG-17s and seven MiG-21s – in his searchlight and was waiting for permission to open fire. When none came, he tried to get in touch with Shaul Mofaz, but the radio link was poor. So he eventually made a unilateral decision. The noise was deafening as his men opened up with both machine guns and RPGs. All eleven planes were destroyed: some perforated by bullets; others bursting into flame as their fuel tanks ignited. It was the black smoke from these explosions that Biran was referring to when he spoke to Adam about 'fires' in the 'area of the army hangars'.

Not long after this, Hercules Four took off and Shomron asked Muki Betser to carry out one last search of the Old Terminal building for stragglers before withdrawing his force to the New Terminal, where the three remaining C-130 planes were parked on the concourse. Finding no one, Betser ordered his men aboard the

Mercedes and two Land Rovers, and they set off down the diagonal runway. Shaul Mofaz's four BTRs followed soon afterwards, leap-frogging each other in pairs and dropping demolition charges 'to create a smoke screen' for any Ugandan soldiers 'who might decide to be heroes'.

The two rearguard BTRs – commanded by Mofaz and Bar-Lev – were halfway down the diagonal runway when Mofaz received a call from Shomron to return and check the Air France plane. Adam was worried that some of the hostages might have been left behind, and wanted to be certain they were not on the plane. Shomron told Mofaz to take a look, but not to enter the plane in case it was booby-trapped.

The two BTRs drove back through the smoke screen and, as they neared the Old Terminal, saw the headlights of two vehicles approaching down a side road from the direction of Entebbe. Mofaz ordered the BTRs to stop and turn off their lights. This prompted one of the vehicles to do the same, but they kept advancing. When they reached a bend in the road, Mofaz ordered his men to open fire at a distance of 200 yards. The lights on the first vehicle went out – either hit by bullets or turned off to provide a cloak of cover – and the occupants dispersed.

The BTRs moved on towards the plane and, as they neared it, were shot at by the brave Ugandan soldier (or soldiers) in the control tower whom the previous firefights had failed to subdue. They fired back, prompting the Ugandan to take cover. Reaching the plane, Omer Bar-Lev dismounted from his BTR and climbed the mobile stairs that led up to the rear door. It was open but he did not enter. Instead he called out and used his flashlight to look inside. There was no sign of life and no response. 'The plane looks dark and we didn't hear anything from it,' Shomron told Adam after getting a report from Mofaz. 'Everything is currently quiet. A few Ugandan soldiers remain, here and there a bullet. But overall, quiet.'

His task completed, Mofaz ordered the BTRs to head for the New Terminal. By the time they arrived, only Hercules Two – earmarked to carry them and Shomron's Jeep – was still at the parking concourse. Hercules One had taken off with the Unit's assault team and vehicles at 1.12 a.m. local time, a good twenty minutes earlier; Hercules Three, with the other two BTRs on board, was waiting on the main runway. While the last two BTRs were driven aboard, Shomron made his final report to Adam. 'We've begun to load the fourth plane. See you later.'

Biran then dismantled the radio's huge antenna and the Jeep was driven up the ramp. With everyone on board, Hercules Two began to taxi towards the main runway and, in the pitch-blackness, almost ran straight into the ditch that ran along the access strip. A yard or two further and at least part of the rescue force would have been stranded. But the pilot realized his error just in time and corrected his line. Joining Hercules Two at the top of the main runway, the two planes took off one after the other.

It was 1.40 a.m. local time. The rescue force had been on the ground for just one hour and thirty-nine minutes.

2145hrs GMT, Kampala, Uganda

Henry Kyemba was woken at 12.45 a.m. by the ringtone from his bedside phone. Answering it, he was surprised and not a little irritated to discover that the caller was one of Idi Amin's mistresses. What she had to tell him, however, soon dissipated his anger.

Amin had just called her from State House with the astonishing news that 'there was fighting at the airport and that the situation was out of control'. According to the president, the airport had been 'captured' but he did not know by whom. He was, as a result, 'taking care of himself, and advised her to do the same'. To that end he was sending a car for her and suggested she go 'into hiding'. Which is why she was calling Kyemba. She could not think of anywhere to go and wanted the health minister's 'advice and help'.

Kyemba told her there was little that he – or anyone else – could do to help and quickly ended the conversation. But he was not in any doubt about the identity of the attackers. 'It's the Israelis,' he told his wife Teresa. 'It must be. They've come to take the hostages.'

Then, after making a couple of calls to let family members know what was happening, he and his wife went back to sleep.

It was only later that Kyemba learned of the panic the Israeli assault had caused among the country's political and military leaders: that Amin himself had assumed it was 'some sort of mutiny backed by a foreign power' – either Kenya or Tanzania – and could not discover the truth because 'as soon as the fighting started' his senior officers, many of whom had been carousing at the Lake Victoria Hotel near State House, simply 'vanished'. When the first bursts of gunfire ripped through the night, the officers had fled from the hotel's bar and swimming pool to their own homes where they went into hiding, 'telling their families that if anyone phoned . . . they were not available'. They too had assumed that the troops had mutinied and 'until it was clear who was fighting whom, no officers wanted to risk becoming involved with the wrong side'.

Amin took refuge in a 'driver's quarters near State House', trying without success to contact his military chiefs to find out what was happening. Only after the Israelis had departed did he discover the truth: it was not a mutiny but a foreign incursion.

The military response, therefore, was too little, too late. Kyemba and his wife were woken again at around 3 a.m. by the 'rumbling of tanks and trucks' on their way to the airport. But even then two of the armoured personnel carriers 'broke down' en route, according to acting British High Commissioner James Horrocks, and had to be 'towed back to Kampala'.

It was around three in the morning that Horrocks himself set off for the airport with two colleagues from the West German Embassy. He had received a call about a fire at the Old Terminal building and, after failing to contact the airport by telephone, had decided to go there in person in a consular capacity 'out of concern for the hostages'. But Horrocks and the two West Germans were stopped by Ugandan troops near the Lake Victoria Hotel, two miles from the airport, and told they could not go any further. Instead they were taken to the nearby officers' mess of the Ugandan Air Force and detained for a number of hours. Only at 10.30 a.m. were they finally given permission to return to Kampala by General Mustafa Adrisi, the Ugandan minister of defense, and Colonel Isaac Malyamungu, a former Jinja gatekeeper who had risen swiftly through the army ranks to become one of Amin's leading henchmen. Idi Amin would later suspect that Horrocks's nighttime drive to the airport meant he had 'prior knowledge of the Israeli invasion', a charge the British diplomat vehemently – and truthfully – denied.

Henry Kyemba, meanwhile, had been woken again at six by a call from a senior officer who had finally returned to the airport. He had found twenty-seven dead bodies, including seven terrorists, and another ten seriously wounded, and wanted the health minister to send ambulances to ferry the casualties to Mulago Hospital. 'It was the Israelis,' said the officer, confirming Kyemba's suspicions. 'All the hostages are gone.'

Kyemba made the necessary calls before heading to the hospital to supervise the admissions. There he discovered 'army trucks and ambulances passing in and out, delivering the injured, while relatives crowded around, wailing'. The dead – including the terrorists – had been taken to the mortuary for identification. The seriously injured were in emergency wards, while those with minor wounds were treated and discharged. Later a number of civilians were admitted after they had been beaten up for laughing at Amin's humiliated troops.

2210hrs GMT, Frankfurt, Germany

Gerd Schnepel was listening to the radio in the Frankfurt apartment of Magdalena Kopp, another Revolutionary Cells terrorist and the girlfriend of Johannes Weinrich, when the programme was interrupted by a newsflash from Entebbe in Uganda. A gun battle had broken out at the airport, said the reporter, and in the distance could be heard the muffled if distinctive sound of automatic fire. Schnepel and Kopp were stunned.

They debated what it might mean. Had the Ugandans turned on their comrades or was it a rescue attempt by the IDF? The latter was the last thing any of them were expecting. But either way the shooting was bad news and they feared the worst.

2240hrs GMT, Tel Aviv, Israel

The ministers, security chiefs and aides gathered in Shimon Peres's office in the Kirya had mostly listened in silence to the intermittent reports coming through the radio receiver as the drama unfolded in real time.

At first, having heard gunfire, they endured an agonizing wait until the static was interrupted by Dan Shomron's cool, calm voice: 'Everything is all right. Will report later.'

More shooting could be heard – or was it the plane's engines? Time seemed to stand still. Then a single codeword was uttered – 'Shefel' – meaning that all four planes had landed safely at Entebbe.

Another wait for news, but this time shorter, until Shomron spoke again: 'Everything is going well. You will soon receive a full report.'

The room seemed to relax. People dared to look at each other and nod. The troops were on the ground and, despite the firing, Shomron did not seem unduly concerned.

The next codeword was 'Falastin' – denoting the start of the attack on the terminal. This was it: the moment of truth. Most of those present stared hard at the receiver, willing it to give them good news. At last, after an agonizing wait of twelve minutes, it came in the form of the codeword: 'Jefferson'.

It meant the evacuation of the hostages was under way: the terrorists were dead and the attack had been successful. Were there casualties? Almost certainly, but how many they could not tell. They felt like throwing their arms around each other and dancing for joy. But it was too early for that: the terrorists had been killed but there was still the small matter of the Ugandan Army.

'Move everything to Galila,' said a voice over the radio. They deduced from this that the hostages were being moved to one of the planes. Everything so far had gone perfectly.

Then the first setback: a call for medical assistance for 'Mateh Skedim', the Unit. There were 'two Ekaterina' – two casualties. 'Who were they?' Peres and the others wondered. They would have to wait to find out.

Finally, at around 12.40 a.m. local time, they heard the single word they had been waiting for: 'Carmel'. It meant that all four planes had taken off, and the hostages and soldiers were safe. The operation had succeeded.

For a moment the occupants of Peres's office looked at each other in stunned silence, scarcely able to believe what had just happened. Then a week of bottled-up tension exploded in hugs and shouts of triumph: 'We did it!'

Peres's heart 'leapt with joy' as champagne was opened and a toast drunk to the success of the mission. Then the group dispersed: Rabin to his office and the others to Motta Gur's suite of rooms in the Kirya where 'all the members of the General Staff' had been told to assemble. Not all of them knew about the operation in advance, and 'their shouts of enthusiasm mingled with the jubilation and relief of those who had known and had shared the anxiety and anticipation'.

Before heading over to Gur's office to join in the celebrations, Peres called for Burka Bar-Lev and asked him to telephone Idi Amin at the presidential palace in Entebbe to discover whether the Ugandan dictator 'had learned yet of the nocturnal visit to his country' and to gauge his reaction.

When Amin's voice came on the line it was 1 a.m. Israeli time, and just twenty minutes after the last Hercules had departed from Entebbe. 'Sir,' said Bar-Lev in his most matter-of-fact tone, 'I want to thank you for your cooperation. Thank you very much, sir.'

Amin seemed nonplussed. 'You know I did not succeed.'

'Thank you very much for your cooperation,' repeated the Israeli, before feigning surprise. 'What? The cooperation didn't succeed? Why?'

Amin asked what the Israelis had done, and Bar-Lev replied that they had done exactly what he, Amin, had wanted.

'Wh— Wh— What happened?' stuttered Amin, perhaps realizing for the first time that the fighting was not a mutiny by his own troops but an Israeli raid.

'I don't know.'

'Can't you tell me?'

'No,' said Bar-Lev, lying. 'I don't know. I have been requested by a friend with good connections in the government to thank you for the cooperation. I don't know what was meant by it, but I think you do know.'

Amin continued to insist he knew nothing and Bar-Lev, his task accomplished, said he would call back.

At Gur's office, meanwhile, the chief of staff's driver had procured more bottles of champagne and the drink continued to flow. Gur 'made a little speech in which he said that apart from Netanyahu' – who, as far as they knew, was injured but still alive – and 'another paratrooper' (Hershko), the force had apparently suffered 'no casualties' (no mention was made of the soldier wounded by the grenade). All the hostages, he added, had been 'rescued unharmed' – this of course was not true – 'save for one woman, Mrs Dora Bloch' who had been taken to hospital in Entebbe. The hijackers, 'who were Arabs and Germans', had been 'shot dead'. It was, said Gur, 'certainly one of the most successful' operations the IDF had ever undertaken. He added that he could not conclude even this preliminary assessment of the mission 'without singling out the one man whose determination made it happen – the minister of defense'.

All eyes turned to Peres, as Gur elaborated: 'I don't know if it's possible to apportion credit among those responsible for the decision to undertake this operation, but if it is, the biggest share of the credit goes to the defense minister.'

To those listening, this accolade was fully justified. Peres was the one minister who, from the very start, had warned of the consequences of caving in to the terrorists' demands. It was largely thanks to his determination that the quite understandable objections of both Rabin and Gur to a military operation had eventually been overcome. Yet Peres – unlike the other two – had no operational military experience and his support for some of the earlier options put forward by the planners is an indication that he was prepared to support almost *any* military strike against the terrorists – regardless of the risk. It was for him both a matter of principle and an opportunity to label his political rival Rabin as a leader who was 'weak on terrorism'.

For Rabin and Gur, on the other hand – particularly the former – there was an absolute conviction that a failed military operation would do more harm to Israel's standing in the world than even a negotiated settlement and the release of imprisoned terrorists. It was for this reason that both withheld their support for a strike until they were convinced that the proposed plan had a reasonable chance of success. To both of them, and to the people chiefly responsible for planning and carrying out the operation – Ehud Barak, Iddo Embar, Muki Betser, Dan Shomron, Yoni Netanyahu, Benny Peled, Kuti Adam and the others – must also go a sizeable share of the laurels of victory.

At 1.15 a.m. Peres telephoned Rabin to inform him of Bar-Lev's conversation with Idi Amin. The prime minister burst out laughing on hearing of Amin's hapless response, and invited Peres over to his office. When the defense minister arrived he found in situ the various opposition leaders who had supported the mission, including Begin, Rimalt and Navon. Even the abstemious Begin, who preferred tea, was drinking whisky.

While Peres was there, Rabin phoned a number of senior politicians – including President Ephraim Katzir, Speaker of the Knesset Yisrael Yeshayahu, and former Prime Minister Golda Meir – to give them the good news. Peres took the opportunity to call his wife Sonia, who was 'thunderstruck' but delighted.

Meanwhile Amos Eiran had been asked by Rabin to make two important telephone calls: the first to Professor Yosef Gross, the chairman of the Relatives' Committee, who cried when he heard the hostages had been rescued; and the second to the White House to let the United States president Gerald Ford know about the successful operation. With Washington six hours behind Tel Aviv, it was around eight in the evening when one of Ford's aides came to the phone. Having listened to what Eiran had to say, the aide responded: 'Tell Mr Rabin I can't think of a better way to celebrate the Bicentennial.'

Finally they drafted a 'laconic statement' to be issued by the army spokesman. It read: 'IDF forces have tonight rescued the hostages and aircrew from Entebbe Airport.' The plan was to withhold the statement until the planes had reached the safety of Israeli airspace. But this was brought forward to 3 a.m. – when it was broadcast on the IDF's radio station Galei Zahal – after the Agence France-Presse had reported, on the strength of Ugandan sources, 'an Israeli attack on Entebbe'.

At around the same time Peres lay down on the couch in his office and closed his eyes. But he could not sleep. He kept 'thinking of the hostages', and 'what they must be feeling now, in the belly of the Hercules'. Sensing a presence in the room, he turned round to see a distraught-looking Motta Gur. 'Shimon,' whispered the chief of staff, 'Yoni's gone. The bullet went through his heart. He was shot from the control tower.'

Peres turned away and, 'for the first time that week', gave vent to his 'feelings' by weeping. His joy at the operation's success would forever be 'tinged with sadness because of Yoni's death'.

2255hrs GMT, Kenyan airspace

For much of Hercules Four's short flight to Nairobi, the medics worked hard to stabilize the more seriously injured by fixing up blood and serum drips. When a woman who had been shot in the buttock was undressed, however, the sight and smell of blood was too much for young Maggy, who preferred to move to the back of the plane and settle in next to the Peugeot pick-up.

Sitting next to her was an Israeli youth called Frank,* fat with frizzy hair, who two days earlier had been one of the most vociferous opponents of Israeli negotiation. 'I was one of the last to leave the terminal,' he told her with a self-satisfied smirk, 'because I was helping to evacuate the wounded and the dead. When that was over I borrowed a gun from an Israeli soldier I know and used it to finish off the German woman by firing a round into her ear.'

He seemed genuinely pleased with what he had done and proudly showed Maggy his bloodstained hands, exclaiming: 'Look!'

Ignoring Maggy's grimace, Frank added that he had taken a bullet

---

* Not his real name but a pseudonym given to him by Claude Moufflet in his book *Otages à Kampala*.

from the chest of a dead woman – Ida Borochovich – and wanted to enlist with the Unit that had carried out the raid. But the commandos had said no because he was too young. He then showed her the souvenir he had brought with him: Böse's megaphone.

By now the hostages could see that two of the dead, wrapped in aluminium blankets, were stacked on a single stretcher at the front of the plane: a woman – Borochovich – on the bottom; and an Israeli soldier dressed in green – Netanyahu – above her. The body of Jean-Jacques Mimouni, meanwhile, was still at the back of the plane.

Sitting close to Netanyahu's corpse, a female hostage felt a lump under her bottom. Reaching down, she picked up something round and metallic. 'What's this?' she asked Ephraim Sneh, who was tending to the wounded nearby.

Sneh recognized it immediately as one of the small and very unstable mini fragmentation grenades that the Unit carried for special operations. It must have fallen off Yoni's webbing and rolled to the floor. He took it carefully from her and stored it in a locker. Had its pin come loose, the explosion would have caused carnage in the tightly packed cargo hold and might even have brought the plane down.

2258hrs GMT, Nairobi International Airport, Kenya

Informed by the pilot of the Boeing 707 medical plane that the rescue aircraft were on their way, Dany Saadon climbed the stairs of the control tower and opened the door. As the local El Al manager, Saadon was well known to the senior air traffic controller who, looking up from his radar screen, asked the Israeli how he could help.

'I just wanted to let you know', said Saadon, 'that there are a few El Al flights coming in that you won't be expecting. But I have authorization from both the minister of transport and the airport director for them to land. They are to taxi to Bay 4 where I'll arrange for them to be refuelled. They won't stay long.'

Knowing that Saadon had good relations with both the minister and the head of the airport, the air controller took him at his word.

But when he identified no fewer than five blips approaching Nairobi from the direction of Entebbe – two within a few minutes' flying time – he frowned and asked: 'Are you certain that you have permission for this?'

'Yes, I'm certain,' replied Saadon. 'But if you're unsure you can call the airport director for confirmation.'

Hesitating for just a moment, the air controller replied: 'No, I won't call him. It's too late. I'll do that in the morning.'

Minutes later – having announced itself as El Al Flight 167 from Tel Aviv – the command and control Boeing 707 landed at Nairobi, followed immediately by Hercules Four. It was 2.12 a.m. local time.

Once Hercules Four had come to a halt in Bay 4 – the quarantined area guarded by armed Kenyan GSU men – its ramp was lowered and the Peugeot 404 driven off to make it easier to unload the wounded. Told to remain on board, the hostages moved to one side as the six stretchers were carried off. The two most seriously wounded – Pasco Cohen and Yitzhak David – were taken by ambulance to Kenyatta National Hospital on the western edge of Nairobi, a distance of eleven miles. Pasco's wife Hannah had wanted to accompany him but was told by a doctor: 'That's not possible. In any case, your husband will fly home on a Boeing and be there before you.'

Both men were rushed into theatre for emergency operations: David came through his, but not Cohen – the self-confessed survival 'specialist' – who finally ran out of luck and died of a coagulation disorder, the fourth Israeli fatality of the raid.

The other casualties were treated in the field hospital before being put on the Boeing 707 medical plane. Most of the remaining hostages, however, were told they would leave Nairobi on Hercules Four, an announcement that hugely disappointed Willy, who imagined an Air France plane, or a French army plane at the very least, would be waiting in Kenya to take them home. The exceptions were two mothers – Emma Rosenkovitch and Yael Brotsky – who accepted Kuti Adam's offer to travel with their children on the command and control 707 because it would be 'more comfortable'. Their husbands stayed on the C-130.

Soon after Ephraim Sneh had got off Hercules Four to stretch his legs, he felt a tap on his shoulder. It was Ehud Barak, wearing a blue suit and tie; Sneh had last seen him in uniform in Israel. 'I understand,' said Barak, 'that Yoni was killed.'

'Unfortunately yes,' replied Sneh.

Wanting to see for himself, Barak got on the plane and pulled back the blanket covering Netanyahu's corpse. Staring up at him was a 'white face, pale, strikingly handsome – Yoni's face'.

Shortly after Hercules One had landed at Nairobi at 2.32 a.m. local time – allowing Joshua Shani to turn off the engines for the first time since leaving the Sinai – Barak went onboard to tell Muki Betser and his men that their commander was dead. Their chatter died in an instant. Betser tried to raise spirits. 'We did our duty,' he told them. 'We succeeded. Successfully. This is the painful price we sometimes have to pay in this kind of war. But we continue.'

Like Barak, Matan Vilnai wanted to see Yoni's body. As he passed the hostages he was struck by how depressed they seemed, 'completely stunned, shadows of men'. The downbeat mood prompted in him a 'totally illogical' feeling that 'if Yoni was dead, then the whole thing wasn't worth it'.

When the final two planes – Hercules Two and Three – landed at Nairobi at around 3 a.m. local time, they were given just over two hours to refuel, pack up and leave. The rushed timetable was the result of an ill-tempered conversation about forty minutes earlier between Ben Gethi, the head of the GSU, and President Kenyatta, who was out of Nairobi for the weekend. With Uri Lubrani standing beside him, Gethi had called Kenyatta to let him know that Israeli military planes were on Kenyan soil. After wincing at Kenyatta's expletive-laden response, Gethi turned to Lubrani and said: 'The president wants you out of Kenya in three hours. Can you do it?'

'Yes, we can do it,' replied Lubrani. 'Tell him yes.'

DAY 8: SUNDAY 4 JULY 1976

0004hrs GMT, Nairobi International Airport, Kenya

Just four minutes after the arrival of the last two planes from Entebbe, Hercules Four accelerated down the main runway and took to the sky on the last leg of the hostages' week-long odyssey. A nightmare journey that had for most of them begun in Israel, before taking in Greece, Libya and Uganda, was about to end where it had started.

Not that the hostages yet knew of their final destination: that had been deliberately kept from them in case the twenty or so French nationals objected. Instead the Golani soldiers on board tried to raise spirits by passing round their water bottles and offering sweets. They also gave the hostages makeshift ear-defenders to drown out the noise of the engines and help them sleep. Most found the ear-defenders heavy and uncomfortable, but kept them on. A few lucky ones, like Maggy and Agnès, used cotton wool instead.

Since the wounded had been removed, there was now more room for those left and the soldiers helped by fixing up some hammocks. Isa, Cécile and Marianne were now sitting rather than standing, and others had settled in 'where they can': Willy was by a port window, perched on a box of medicines; Maggy was in the car with the soldiers; and Agnès was sitting further forward with a young Frenchman called Julian who was nursing a twisted ankle. Suddenly, Agnès' nerves gave out and she burst into tears. 'Don't cry,' said Julian, stroking her arm. 'You'll make all the others cry.'

'I'm thinking,' she replied between sobs, 'of Jean-Jacques.'

'Please don't cry. They don't all know he's dead.'

Maggy, too, was haunted by flashbacks of the injured man in the chair and of Jean-Jacques' bullet-riddled body. As hard as she tried, she could not dispel them from her mind.

Ignoring the instruction not to smoke, some hostages accepted cigarettes from the soldiers and improvised ashtrays from the boxes that had held their ear-defenders. They were then encouraged to lie down and sleep, because it was going to be a long flight. Before she did so, Agnès asked one of the soldiers who could speak French: 'Where are we going?'

'You'll soon see.'

'Come on,' she persisted. 'Tell me, where are we going?'

'To a beautiful country.'

She concluded from this that they were bound for Israel. Looking around her, Agnès could see a variety of costumes: Isa was wearing an oversized tee-shirt that she had borrowed from Jean-Jacques and a skirt made from an Air France blanket; Willy had lent his jumper to the stewardess who had left the Old Terminal dressed only in a camisole top and small pair of knickers. Many were wearing just their underwear, and the makeshift clothes were more to protect people from the cold than to preserve their modesty.

Before long, all conversation had ceased: there was too much noise and everyone – soldiers and hostages alike – was exhausted. Most people fell asleep, some stretched out next to the dead bodies.

By now all six of Operation Thunderbolt's planes were in the air: Hercules One was airborne by 3.13 a.m. local time, followed by the command and control 707 at 3.40 a.m.; Hercules Two and Three took off at 4.07 a.m. and 4.15 a.m. respectively; and the last to leave Nairobi – with Surin Hershko and the other seriously wounded on board – was the Boeing 707 medical plane at 5.18 a.m.

Uri Lubrani's promise to President Kenyatta at around 2.20 a.m. that the Israeli planes would be gone in three hours had been kept almost to the minute.

0400hrs GMT, Tel Aviv, Israel

On hearing the incredible news from Entebbe, Uri Dan raced into the city centre office of the popular daily *Maariv* newspaper where he worked as chief correspondent. Like every other Israeli journalist, he was hoping for a scoop; but, unlike them, his method was to go straight to the horse's mouth by calling the office of the Ugandan president and asking to speak to Idi Amin himself.

It was a long shot, he knew, and one he did not expect to succeed. But it did. After a lengthy delay, and much consultation at the other end of the line, Amin came to the phone. 'I am,' he told Dan, seemingly on the verge of tears, 'holding in my arms my soldiers who died from the bullets of your people. In return for the good I did, you caused me harm.'

He was speaking, he said, from the airport where they were 'counting the victims' of last night's action. It was all so unnecessary. 'I was planning to seek the release of the Israelis and came back earlier from Mauritius for that purpose, and all that's left now is for me to count the dead.' His soldiers could easily have shot all the Hercules down, he added, but they chose not to.

'Why,' asked Dan, 'were your soldiers there? Isn't it true that they, as well as the Palestinians, were holding the hostages?'

Amin denied this. 'My soldiers were 200 yards from the building,' he said, not entirely truthfully, 'and the Palestinians were inside. As your people will confirm when they return to Israel.'

And so the conversation went on, with Amin continuing to insist that he had been working to resolve the crisis. 'I treated them very well. We did everything for them. We gave them food, we gave them toilet articles, and we protected them, in order to exchange them. And what do I have left now? Instead of thanking me, you kill my people.'

Why, asked Dan, were your soldiers killed if they were not cooperating with the Palestinians?

'My soldiers were there to guard the Israelis,' insisted Amin. 'I saved their lives. Tell them when they get to Israel that I wish them happy lives. I even said that to Colonel Bar-Lev when I spoke to him by phone. If my soldiers had shot at the planes they would have killed your soldiers. But we did not want to fight. We can fight – but we did not want to.'

After yet more of Amin's protestations of innocence, Dan asked if he planned to declare a state of emergency. 'Don't you fear that after an operation like this, a blow like this, you may lose your position?'

'No . . . no,' stuttered Amin, '. . . my soldiers are with me and they help me and there are no problems at all.'

'Will you declare a state of emergency?' Dan persisted.

'Yes.'

0530hrs GMT, International airspace over the Red Sea

While most of his men slept, Muki Betser sat up front in the cockpit of Hercules One with Joshua Shani and his crew. Usually after an operation he and Yoni Netanyahu would talk together 'about what had just happened' and what they planned to do next. But Netanyahu was dead and the 'natural loneliness of the commander' had 'never sat so heavily' on Betser's shoulders.

As the plane thundered homewards, Betser kept trying to understand what Yoni 'was thinking when he decided to take out the Ugandan'. He must have thought, Betser concluded, that the sentry was a threat, and that he and Giora Zussman, with their silenced guns, could 'quietly eliminate' him. Yet, as far as Betser was concerned, it was contrary to the plan: which was to allow nothing to distract them from their central aim of getting to the Old Terminal as quickly as possible.

And yet Betser, as he mulled over the events of the night, was able to take comfort from the fact that 'despite everything – the wounded Ugandan, the bunched-up run to the building from fifty metres away, the blocked entrance' – the Unit was still able to react fast enough to 'surprise the terrorists before they could harm the hostages'. Or so Betser thought as he flew back to Israel. What he did not realize, however, was that the Unit's premature burst of firing had given the terrorists the opportunity to start killing people – but for some reason they had chosen not to.

Deep in thought, Betser was brought back to reality when Shani tuned his radio to the Voice of Israel and a newsreader announced that Israeli government sources had confirmed international media stories that Israeli troops had rescued the hostages from Entebbe. Betser was furious. They were, he knew, still facing 'three hours of flight within reach of enemy aircraft from Egypt and Saudi Arabia'. Yet someone in Israel 'couldn't wait to make the announcement' and was 'endangering' their lives by doing so.

0600hrs GMT, Frankfurt, West Germany

A few hours after hearing the radio report of fighting at Entebbe Airport, Gerd Schnepel and Magdalena Kopp received the news they had been dreading: Israeli commandos had mounted a successful rescue mission, rescuing the bulk of the hostages and killing seven terrorists in the process. Their comrades Kuhlmann and Böse were among the dead.

Schnepel and other RC members were 'furious' about the killing of their comrades and immediately plotted revenge. 'We wanted to do a very brutal response,' Schnepel recalled. 'We were checking out aeroplanes and things like that, to just blow them up in flight. That was our first idea. But luckily we didn't go through with it.'

0630hrs GMT, International airspace over the Red Sea

Forty-five minutes ahead of Betser's plane, Hercules Four was flying so low that Willy was able to see through his porthole the spray from the waves sweeping across the Red Sea. The sight of the low sun glinting on the water was beautiful. But Willy could not appreciate it: he was desperate for the seemingly interminable flight to end.

Suddenly land came into view and, as the plane gained altitude, Halivni's voice came over the intercom. 'Ladies and gentlemen,' he said in Hebrew, 'we are now flying above Sharm el-Sheikh.'

They had reached Israeli territory: they were safe. This was the moment when all the hostages – but particularly the Israelis – knew that their long and traumatic ordeal was finally over. They let out a great cheer and embraced those near to them. Some were in tears. It was now that Eran Dolev, the head of the surgical team, revealed his dry sense of humour. 'I have to tell you,' he said over the intercom, 'that last night Israel introduced VAT for the first time at eight per cent. If you don't like it, you're free to return to Entebbe.' No one laughed.

0700hrs GMT, Kampala, Uganda

Having overseen the admission to Mulago Hospital of the wounded from Entebbe, Health Minister Henry Kyemba went home for a couple of hours. But he returned to Mulago at 10 a.m. to check on Dora Bloch, the Israeli hostage that he had deliberately kept in hospital because he thought it would be more comfortable for her than the Spartan conditions in the Old Terminal.

Now, however, he realized his mistake. Because she was in Kampala during the raid, Dora Bloch had not been rescued with the other hostages. The presence of injured Ugandan soldiers in nearby wards, moreover, meant the risk of her being killed in revenge by Idi Amin's humiliated troops was very real. Kyemba had considered moving her to a different hospital with Amin's approval so that it could be done 'under proper guard'. But he decided against this because it would 'only have drawn attention to her' and might have encouraged Amin to 'order her execution on the spot'. Kyemba's reason for visiting Mrs Bloch, therefore, was simply to say 'hello' and warn the staff 'not to talk to her about the events of the previous night, in case she became unduly frightened'.

During their very brief conversation, it was clear to Kyemba that Mrs Bloch knew nothing of the raid. Her only request was to be allowed to wash the grey dress she had been wearing for the last couple of days. Kyemba made this possible by procuring a three-quarter-length white hospital gown – one of the few available – for her to wear while her dress was drying. He then departed for his official residence, hoping against hope that by leaving her where she was, and keeping quiet about her, 'the problem would solve itself'.

0740hrs GMT, Rehovot, Israel

Waiting beside the runway of Tel Nof Air Force Base near Rehovot, twelve miles south of Tel Aviv, Israel's political and military leaders craned their heads upwards for the first sight of the plane carrying the rescued hostages. It was a beautiful summer's day and many of the VIPs – who by this time included Generals Kuti Adam and Benny Peled, their faster Boeing 707 having landed two hours earlier – were shielding their eyes from the glare of the sun.

At the centre of the group was Prime Minister Yitzhak Rabin, wearing a white short-sleeved shirt and sunglasses, his hands placed expectantly on his hips. On his left stood Shimon Peres, in a blue shirt and cream slacks; and next to Peres was Motta Gur, dressed in olive-green combat fatigues, consulting his watch.

Eventually someone spotted a tiny speck approaching from the south. As it got closer, the distinctive high-tailed shape of a Hercules C-130 became visible. It eventually landed and came to a halt close to the VIPs who, meanwhile, had surged on to the tarmac. Once the rear ramp was lowered, the hostages emerged blinking into the sunlight. They were greeted with shouts and applause, and one or two of them – including Michel Bacos, the Airbus's pilot – spoke briefly to Rabin and Peres. The rest were directed by air force personnel towards a couple of waiting buses that would take them to a nearby hangar where refreshments had been prepared. Though their families and the press were waiting to greet them at Ben-Gurion, the hostages had been brought first to Tel Nof so that they could be debriefed and the soldiers and equipment taken off Hercules Four.

The IDF had arranged for a film crew to capture for posterity the hostages' arrival at Tel Nof: from the moment the plane landed to the departure of the buses. In the secret film – released in 2010 – many of the hostages are waving or giving the thumbs-up to the camera; others look dishevelled and disorientated. On one bus they can be seen celebrating their arrival by sipping from a distinctive bell-shaped bottle of chocolate-orange-flavoured Sabra liqueur.

In the hangar the hostages found a huge table, about sixty feet long, piled high with fruit, cakes, toast, coffee and drinks. Agnès devoured a bunch of grapes, crying and laughing as she did so. Willy ate two pieces of toast and ten peaches. Then Yitzhak Rabin and Shimon Peres arrived to speak to some of them. Approaching Agnès and Maggy, the defense minister asked in halting French: 'Are you happy that the Israelis have freed you? Did the attack last a long time?'

'No, no,' replied Agnès. 'It was very quick.'

'Did it all pass by okay?'

Thinking of Jean-Jacques and the other dead and injured, they both hesitated before Maggy replied: 'Not for all of us.'

A short while later, Peres spoke to all the French former hostages in Hebrew while someone translated for them. 'We are very happy to have got you here,' he said, 'and freed you after all the difficulties that stood in our way. Once you get back to France, you will be able to tell everything that you would like to about your experience. But we ask you now – and it's the only thank-you that we expect – to keep total silence about what happened from the moment the Israeli soldiers arrived. Please consider this a military secret and that you do not have the right to speak about it.'

To Willy this request seemed superfluous. He approved, however, of the special mention that Peres then made of the crew of the Airbus who were applauded by everyone in the room.

The one awkward moment came when Emma Rosenkovitch, who had returned earlier with her two children in the Boeing 707, spoke to Rabin and Peres. 'Thank you for what you did,' she said. 'I hope you have as much success with the peace process.'

Angered by this jibe, Rabin frowned and stalked away. Peres was more conciliatory. 'Don't worry,' he said, clapping Emma on the shoulder, 'we will do it.'

Not long after this, the hostages reboarded the buses and were taken back to Hercules Four – which, in the meantime, had been 'emptied, washed and swept' – for the short fifteen-minute flight to Ben-Gurion. While waiting to re-embark, they saw another C-130 land and were told that it, too, had participated in the operation. It was Hercules One. The time was 10.29 a.m.

As the hostages took off a few minutes later for Ben-Gurion, the VIPs were welcoming back the soldiers on Hercules One. Rabin and Peres shook hands with each of the soldiers as they disembarked from the side door. When Betser appeared, Peres asked him: 'How was Yoni killed?'

'He went first, he fell first,' said Betser.

Rabin reserved his warmest welcome for Joshua Shani, the pilot, who was enveloped in a bearhug that seemed to last an age. 'Thank you,' said the prime minister.

Finally the black Mercedes was backed out of the Hercules by Amitzur Kafri and driven away. It was packed with soldiers of the Unit keen to get back to their base as quickly as possible. Betser and the others had to wait for helicopters. While they did so, the last two Hercules landed and Rabin and Peres gave short speeches to most of the soldiers who had taken part in the operation, thanking them for their efforts. Rabin spoke 'like an army commander'; Peres talked of the soldiers' 'contribution to the fight against international terror'.

A few hours later, once all the Unit's soldiers had returned to base, a debriefing was held by Yoni's replacement, Amiram Levine. Normally this would have involved only those who took part. But Levine decided to break with precedent by inviting everyone on the base. First the officers, then the team commanders and finally the individual soldiers reported on what they had seen and done. The soldier who had fired the live burst from the Land Rover explained that when he saw 'the Ugandan get back up on his feet, and aim at us', he 'feared for our safety'.

That night there was for the Unit no victory celebration. Even a single casualty was proof that the Unit's performance 'did not match' its plan. Betser knew that to 'maintain its abilities' the Unit needed to learn from its mistakes. It was for that reason that he and the other participants talked long into the night 'about what happened, each of us from our own point of view, trying to understand what went wrong on the night of our most famous initiative'.

0901hrs GMT, Lod, Israel

During the fifteen-minute flight to Ben-Gurion International Airport, the hostages were offered a fresh set of clothes by Hercules Four's aircrew so that they could look their best when they met their families and the press. Still wearing her Air France blanket, Isa accepted a whole outfit: pale-green cotton jumper and skirt, and black sandals.

Nothing, however, could prepare the hostages for the fervour of the welcome that awaited them at Ben-Gurion. As Hercules Four's rear ramp was lowered to the ground, those nearest could see a huge crowd threatening to surge through the police cordon towards them. The sound it was making was deafening: shouts of joy, applause, songs and even blasts of welcome from a *shofar*.*

The first hostages to leave the belly of the plane were assailed by well-wishers and members of the press, the latter taking photos and asking questions. They struggled towards buses that would take them to their families. Agnès had almost reached one when she noticed a girl running from the crowd, crying and screaming, 'Judith! Judith!'

The girl was the sister of a young married Israeli hostage who had received a slight graze from a bullet. When she reached Judith, she threw her arms around her neck, and was soon joined by other family members, all equally delighted. It was too much for Judith who promptly fainted.

Willy held Isa's hand so they would not be separated, and they eventually got into one of the buses which took them and the other hostages to a large building – half hotel, half military barracks – where the other families were waiting. 'Men and women began shrieking with joy,' read Terence Smith's report in the *New York Times*, 'as the rumpled and weary-looking hostages disembarked from buses . . .

---

* A ceremonial ram's-horn trumpet associated with holy festivals.

Flinging their arms about each other, whole families stood locked in swaying, weeping embraces. There were old women in babushkas, young girls in slacks, men with a week's growth of beard. There was near-chaos when several political leaders arrived on the scene. Mr Rabin and Mr Peres were mobbed by a happy crowd and Menachem Begin, the leader of the opposition, was lifted on shoulders and carried about to rhythmic cheers of "Begin! Begin! Begin!"'

The Israelis were submerged by hordes of emotional relatives, leaving the others – the twenty or so French, two Belgians, two Americans and the lone Swedish stewardess – feeling more than a little 'left out' of the celebrations.

Willy and Isa grabbed a Coke from the drinks table before asking a female soldier: 'What are we going to do now? Where will we go?''

She took them to a little side room where people from the French Consulate were arranging provisional passports. The consul was there, but when Willy and Isa were introduced he responded: 'I haven't seen anyone else. I will see you in a minute.'

Neither took kindly to being snubbed and formed the impression, as did Agnès and Maggy, that while the crew were expected the other French hostages were not. All of them opted to return home imme-diately on the next Air France flight and not to stay on in Israel for a short all-expenses-paid holiday. In the meantime, after speaking to journalists and doing a brief interview for Israeli TV, the non-Israelis were driven to the Plaza Hotel on the beachfront in Tel Aviv where a large and vociferous crowd was waiting to greet them. In their rooms they found bottles of champagne and baskets of fruit. But journalists continued to harass them, and eventually Willy responded to one who asked his profession: 'I'm making missiles for Israel.'

At 3.30 p.m. they were taken back to the airport for the direct flight to Paris in an Air France Boeing 707. Many fell asleep immediately and woke up only as the plane began its descent. Waiting for them in the VIP room at Orly were their families and some of the released hostages. Agnès was met by her dad; Willy by his wife and Gilles, who also embraced Maggy. The ordeal, for them, was finally over.

For four Israeli families, however, there would be no celebration and no closure. Woken by her father at 4 a.m. with the news that the hostages had been freed and they must head for Ben-Gurion Airport, Martine Mimouni-Arnold was convinced that she would soon see her brother Jean-Jacques. But shortly after Hercules Four had landed, she and her parents were waiting in the building set aside for the hostages' families when an ominous message came over the public address system: 'Would the Mimouni and Borochovich families please come to the Officers' Club.'

Robert Mimouni was perplexed. 'Why are they calling us?' he asked.

Martine had no answer. Her chief fear at this point was that Jean-Jacques had been injured. With Martine hobbling on crutches, they eventually found the Officers' Club and were taken into a side room where an officer inexplicably told them: 'I'm very sorry, but your son had an asthma attack and died.'

Unable to take in the awful news, Robert turned to Martine and said: 'That's impossible. Nobody dies from an asthma attack. It's impossible.'

As Jean-Jacques' mother Rachel fainted, his father started screaming that the officer was lying and he wanted to see his son. Eventually they took Robert and Martine to a nearby room where Jean-Jacques' corpse was lying beneath a sheet. The intention was to let Robert see only his son's face. But he pulled away from the soldiers holding him and tore off the sheet. There, plain for his father and sister to see, was the cause of his death: seven livid bullet wounds from his throat to his lower abdomen.

Enraged as much by the unnecessary deception as by the fact of his only son's death, Robert screamed at the officer: 'You lied to me!'

He smashed a chair to the ground and when two officers tried to intervene he attacked them. Losing patience, the doctor warned him to calm down or he would be given a sedative. This prompted Martine to shout: 'Leave him alone! He has just lost his son. Let him scream! Let him cry! Get away from him!'

But when Robert continued to shout, they held him down and injected him. Only now, as the sedative took effect, did he stop screaming. He was finally led away by Jean-Jacques' aunt and uncle who had arrived from their nearby home in Moshav Ramot Meir. As he left, Robert lamented: 'Look at all the people here! They are all singing and dancing, and my son is dead!'

Robert would never discover the truth of his son's death – that he was accidentally killed by Israeli bullets – though he made many attempts to find out. By leaving for the airport so early that day, he narrowly missed two IDF officers who had been sent to his house to inform the family of Jean-Jacques' death. They might at least have told him that his son died in the firefight between the terrorists and the IDF. Instead he was told at the airport that the cause of death was an asthma attack – possibly on the orders of senior government officials who did not want any gloss taken off the successful operation – and it would not be until 2006 that Jean-Jacques' nephew Jonathan Khayat, just two months old in July 1976, heard the truth first-hand from Muki Betser. In 2012, to honour the memory of his uncle and the other Israelis who died at Entebbe, Khayat narrated and appeared in a moving documentary called *Live or Die in Entebbe*. In it, ex-Sergeant Amir Ofer tells him: 'I know this is painful to hear, but had I seen him I would also have shot him. It was the right thing to do. You have no choice in some situations. It wasn't me, but I don't blame the people who did it. They did not make a mistake, they did the right thing, the thing we planned to do.'

Khayat's only regret was that his grandfather was never given such a frank admission before his death in 1996. 'I think,' says Khayat on the documentary, 'it would have definitely helped him to heal . . . He felt they were put aside.'

Because the other two hostage fatalities – Pasco Cohen and Ida Borochovich – were travelling with family members, there was never the same mystery as to how they had died. For a time Hannah Cohen clung to the conviction that her husband would survive his injuries. Told that he would be back in Israel before her, she checked all the hospitals. There was no sign of him. Eventually she was informed by the IDF that he was in hospital in Nairobi and would be back 'in a few days'. So she returned to her home in Hadera with Tzipi and Kobi, only to receive a knock on the door at four in the afternoon. Standing outside were soldiers with bad news. Pasco had lost too much blood and died on the operating table.

The first member of the Netanyahu family to hear of Yoni's death was his younger brother Iddo, himself a member of the Unit's reserves.

First Iddo received a mysterious telephone call at his Jerusalem home in the early hours of 4 July from an officer in the Unit who asked him to stay indoors and once 'all this is over, you can go back to your usual routine'. Iddo was then asked for the number of his other brother Bibi, who was studying in the United States. He gave it, and realized a rescue had taken place only when he heard it announced later on the radio.

He next got a call from Bibi who was 'overjoyed at the news of the raid' and wanted to know if Iddo had heard from Yoni. The answer was no, and the reason became clear when officers came round to Iddo's home to inform him in person that Yoni was the only Israeli soldier to die at Entebbe.

During his lifetime, thanks to the secret nature of his work, Yoni was 'virtually unknown' to the Israeli public. But within twenty-four hours of the rescue his name would become a household name throughout the country.

At the first post-operation Cabinet meeting, held shortly after the return to Israel of the command and control Boeing 707, Kuti Adam told the ministers that the commander of the Unit, Yoni Netanyahu, had been shot and killed by a Ugandan soldier as he 'ran to the terminal'.

Yitzhak Rabin's chief concern was that Yoni's father Benzion, 'the father of Revisionist Zionism' and a professor of Jewish history at Cornell University, should find out about his son's death 'from us and not from the press'.

Shimon Peres added: 'I want the government members to know that today we lost one of the greatest soldiers the Jewish people have ever had. Yoni and his brother served in the same unit. They both risked their lives many times. He was one of the most wonderful people this country's ever had.'

1445hrs GMT, Jerusalem, Israel

Just a few hours after the return of the hostages to Israel, Yitzhak Rabin addressed a special session of the Knesset in Jerusalem. 'Mr Speaker,' he declared, 'Members of the Knesset, in a bold, resourceful and sophisticated effort, the Israel Defense Forces have succeeded in carrying out the decision of the Government of Israel to save and liberate from captivity the passengers of the Air France plane, who were hijacked by Palestinian terrorists and kept prisoner in Uganda, with their lives in danger.'

Explaining that four Israelis – three civilians and one officer – fell in the fight (a suitably neutral description that deliberately avoided identifying the killers), he described the rescue as one of the IDF's 'most exemplary victories from both the human and moral and the military-operational points of view, a remarkable manifestation of Jewish fraternity and Jewish valour'.

He then explained how the decision to launch the operation had been taken by his government 'on its sole responsibility', and without consulting any other government in advance. It did so because it had become 'clearer and clearer that the attack against the Israeli and Jewish passengers was the principal objective' of the terrorists. All indications showed, moreover, that the Ugandans were collaborating with the terrorists.

He had, he added, only praise for the opposition politicians in their support of the government throughout the crisis: first for the decision to negotiate a release of terrorists in exchange for the hostages' lives; and then for launching the rescue operation once a viable plan had been put forward by the IDF.

Characterizing the rescue as 'Israel's contribution to humanity's struggle against terrorism as an international manifestation', he predicted that it would long be 'a subject for research, for song and for legend'. He concluded by expressing his 'special thanks and appreciation' for the 'IDF, the Chief of Staff, the General Staff, the Arms of the Forces, and those who personally participated in the operation – for risking their lives in the fulfilment of their duty as Jews and human beings, and for being an example and a source of pride to us all'.

Not a natural orator, the ex-soldier Rabin had given a heartfelt and compelling account of why his government had authorized the raid of another country's territory, killing a number of its soldiers and destroying much of its air force. It was left, therefore, to that silver-tongued demagogue Menachem Begin, leader of the Likud party, to sum up the significance of the rescue to Israel and its people. Responding to Rabin's statement, he began: 'Not since the Six-Day War has our nation known such a profound sense of unity. We shared a common anxiety and a sense of fraternal love for our people, emanating from the resolve to rescue our brothers and our sisters in peril. Perhaps it was because of this unity that we found within ourselves the capacity to mount such a momentous operation – a rescue mission unprecedented in gallantry and daring.'

Having paid tribute to those who had lost their lives, including 'a most valiant commander who charged at the head of his troops', he described the soldiers and airmen who carried out the mission as 'Maccabees . . . risen anew'. But his greatest praise he reserved for Yitzhak Rabin. Turning towards the prime minister, he declared:

> You and I belong to different political factions. Our outlooks differ . . . But not today. On this day . . . Mr Prime Minister, I salute you. I salute you for what you have done. I salute, too, the Minister of Defense, as indeed I do all the members of the Cabinet, and everyone involved in the most difficult decisions a nation's leaders can possibly make. But you, Mr Prime Minister, you who are the leader of a team – and I have some knowledge of being a leader of a team – I say that while all your colleagues have a share in the decision-making responsibility, upon your shoulders rests an extra morsel of responsibility. And who can measure the weight of that extra morsel?

Begin then made the inevitable – if inaccurate – analogy between the German-sanctioned *selektzia* at Entebbe and the more infamous actions of Dr Mengele at Auschwitz when a finger to the right had condemned Jewish men, women and children to death. Then there had been 'no one to save them'; now there was. 'Now,' he said, his voice rising for emphasis, 'we declare for all to hear: Never again! Our generation has taken a solemn oath consecrated in the blood of our slain mothers, our butchered fathers, our asphyxiated babes, and our fallen brave – never again will the blood of the Jew be shed with impunity. Never again will Jewish honour be easy prey.'

The world should know, he added, that if 'anyone anywhere' is 'persecuted, or humiliated, or threatened, or abducted, or is in any way endangered simply because he or she is a Jew', then Israel would marshal all its strength 'to come to their aid and bring them to the safe haven of our homeland'. This was 'the message of Entebbe'.

The thunderous applause went on for some minutes as politicians of all hues registered their approval. For this one day, at least, Israel's Jews were united.

1530hrs GMT, Kampala, Uganda

British diplomat Peter Chandley was at home with his wife, still digesting the incredible news from Entebbe, when he received a call from his boss James Horrocks, the acting high commissioner. Horrocks had just heard from the French Embassy that one of the hostages, a seventy-three-year-old Israeli-British dual national called Dora Bloch, had been admitted to Mulago Hospital two days earlier and was 'still there'. Aware that Mrs Bloch's life was in mortal danger, Horrocks asked Chandley to get over to Mulago as quickly as possible to arrange her release from hospital and speedy departure from Uganda, preferably via Air France.

At around the same time, but many thousands of miles away in the Caribbean, British Foreign Secretary Tony Crosland was still recovering from sea sickness on board the royal yacht *Britannia* when he received a cable from his deputy Ted Rowlands informing him that, according to the Israeli Embassy in London, a hostage with dual British and Israeli nationality called Dora Bloch 'hadn't got away from Entebbe' and was in a Kampala hospital. He immediately cabled Horrocks in Kampala with instructions 'to get Mrs Bloch on the first available flight out of Uganda'. But Horrocks had already acted.

Accompanied by his wife to make the visit seem as innocent as possible, Chandley arrived at Mulago Hospital at 6.30 p.m. and was waved through the main gate. Up on the sixth floor they found the door to Mrs Bloch's room locked and a nurse inside. When they gestured through the glass panel for her to open the door, she said she needed the authority of either the doctor in charge or the matron. When the matron arrived, she said that one of the two plainclothes men guarding the room would have to give permission. Chandley showed his diplomatic identity card to the men and asked what they were doing.

They refused to say, though one eventually claimed, none too convincingly, that he was a nurse. While being questioned, the two men showed not 'the slightest change of expression' and Mrs Chandley thought they were 'frightening'.

Eventually, after much discussion, the Chandleys were allowed into the room to speak to Dora Bloch. This was the result of a phone call from the hospital to Henry Kyemba, the minister of health who had visited Mrs Bloch earlier that day. Kyemba knew that Amin would not have approved of a British diplomat 'talking' to Mrs Bloch; but he gave his permission for a 'quick visit' because he thought it 'would provide some kind of reassurance to both parties'.

The Chandleys spoke to Dora Bloch 'in the presence of the nurse, the matron and the two plainclothes men', who insisted on listening in. Still unaware that the raid had taken place, the old lady confirmed to Peter Chandley that she 'was a British subject, though all her documents were lost'. She told him that she had been 'on her way to America to attend her son's wedding and another son was accompanying her as far as Paris'. His name was Ilan Hartuv and she wanted Chandley to give him the message 'Mother is all right'. The diplomat said he would.

When Chandley asked how she was feeling, Dora said she was 'fit and able to leave', but did not like the food and had hardly eaten since her admittance on Friday. Turning to the two plainclothes guards, Chandley suggested that he and his wife should be allowed to take Mrs Bloch home with them until her departure from the country could be arranged. But the 'nurse' shook his head. He was arranging transport to take her to the Imperial Hotel in Kampala and 'that was that'. Eventually admitting defeat, Chandley said he would go home to prepare some food for Mrs Bloch and return within the hour. This the men agreed to, as did the guard on the main gate when they drove out. Before they departed, the

Chandleys gave Mrs Bloch 'some toilet articles' they thought she might need.

It was now 8.30 p.m. When the Chandleys returned to Mulago with food at 9.15 p.m. they were stopped at the main gate by a new guard. No cars with 'CD' – Corps Diplomatique – number plates were being admitted, he told them. Even when they returned with a police escort they were refused entry. Eventually, having handed the food to a nurse who promised to give it to Mrs Bloch, they drove away. They later discovered from a senior British medic who worked at the hospital that the food had indeed been delivered, 'but it was too late as Mrs Bloch had been taken away'. The nurses, added the medic, 'were in tears'.

It would take many days before Chandley and Horrocks discovered what had happened next. According to Henry Kyemba, Idi Amin was still 'smarting with humiliation' at the brutal ease with which the Israelis had rescued the hostages when he discovered that, contrary to his orders, Mrs Bloch had not been returned to the Old Terminal and remained in the hospital in Kampala. He at once sent four men to exact revenge on the defenceless old lady. Two of them – Major Farouk Minawa, the head of the State Research Centre (Amin's secret police), and Captain Nasur Ondoga, chief of protocol to the president – marched up to her ward where they ordered hospital staff to stand aside and the guards to open the door. They then hauled the terrified Mrs Bloch out of bed and 'frogmarched her' down the flights of stairs, 'leaving behind her cane, handbag, shoes and dress'. She 'screamed continuously'.

By now the commotion had alerted staff, patients and visitors who watched in horror as the two men dragged Mrs Bloch, 'still screaming, through the casualty department and out of the main hospital door'. Put into the back of one of two waiting cars, Mrs Bloch was then driven away at high speed. And through all this, though they must have known she was going to her execution, the spectators did nothing. 'Interference,' noted Kyemba, 'could mean death. And after all, this was not the first public kidnapping in Uganda. It had become an everyday occurrence.'

Minutes later Kyemba received two separate calls from the hospital, telling him what had happened. He in turn called Amin, who did not seem unduly concerned. 'Is that so? Okay. I'll see.'

Kyemba had no doubt that Amin 'already knew what had happened'. No one would have dared do such a thing 'except on Amin's orders'. His initial hope was that Amin 'might try to use Mrs Bloch – the only remaining hostage – as a pawn to enforce the Palestinians' demands'. But when he reflected on the fact that she had been 'seized in public by Amin's own thugs', he realized there 'was no doubt that she was going to be executed'.

He soon received confirmation from Amin himself. The call from the president was chiefly to discuss the care of those wounded in the raid and the burial of the dead – including the terrorists – that was scheduled for the following day. Amin added: 'Oh, by the way, that woman in hospital – don't worry about her – she has been killed.'

Though shocked, Kyemba had by this time learned to keep his reactions to Amin's excesses as neutral as possible. 'Oh dear,' he muttered.

Having put down the phone, he vented his anger to his wife Teresa and a visitor. 'This is outrageous!' he told them. 'That poor lady, to take revenge on her like that. This is terrible.'

But there was nothing he could do. The hostage crisis had claimed its fifth and last Israeli victim.

AFTERMATH

Monday 5 July 1976, Israel

The day after the return of the hostages, not all of Israel's Jews were celebrating. Instead the distraught families of Jean-Jacques Mimouni and Ida Borochovich – two of the three hostages killed during the rescue – were laying their loved ones to rest in private funerals in Netanya and Bat Yam respectively. Both were buried with military honours, their graves covered in wreaths from, among others, the Israeli government, the IDF and Air France.

'This is a harsh land,' declared Borochovich's weeping husband, a Russian immigrant who had finally achieved his lifetime's ambition to bring his family to Israel seven years earlier. 'It was a magnificent, courageous operation,' added Brigadier Mordechai Piron, the chief military chaplain. 'But it is the fate of this nation that every joy and delight be mixed with pain and mourning.'

Elsewhere in Israel, border troops were on high alert as they watched for revenge attacks by Palestinian guerillas. But the main priority of Yitzhak Rabin's government on 5 July – the day after the return of the hostages – was minimizing the diplomatic fall-out of its military action by impressing on foreign governments that it had had no option. The British ambassador to Israel, for example, was told by Yigal Allon that the 'Government of Israel had no alternative means to secure the safety of its citizens, particularly in view of the fact that the Ugandan authorities collaborated with the hijackers and practically formed part of the extortionist action against Israel'. Yigal added: 'An Israeli surrender . . . would have served as an added blow to international security and an encouragement to uninhibited blackmail.' In other words, Israel had acted in self-defence.

In private Roy Hattersley, then a minister of state at the Foreign Office, told the Israeli ambassador to the United Kingdom that his 'personal congratulations' were 'strongly felt and warmly meant'. But the official response of the British government – mindful of the safety of its 500 or so citizens living in Uganda – was to avoid any explicit praise of Israel. Prime Minister Jim Callaghan's actual statement to the House of Commons on 5 July made clear his 'satisfaction at the successful outcome of a daring and skilful operation which frustrated a senseless act of terrorism'. He added: 'We very much regret the loss of life at Entebbe.'

This anodyne public statement infuriated many Britons who wrote to their MPs and the Foreign Office to complain. They wanted Jim Callaghan to send a personal message of congratulation to the Israeli prime minister. But senior officials at the FCO advised against this. 'We see no particular need,' wrote one to Callaghan's private secretary on 5 July, 'for the Prime Minister to send a message to Mr Rabin. President Ford, President Giscard [d'Estaing of France] and Chancellor Schmidt have sent messages. However all three had more obvious motives for doing so than exist in the case of the UK. We have nothing to gain from sending one, and need to bear in mind both the doubtful legality of the Israeli raid on Entebbe and the strong feelings it has aroused in Africa as well as the Middle East.'

The official was right: other Western countries, more directly involved in the crisis, had good reason for thanking Israel. In West Germany both Chancellor Schmidt and Dr Kohl, the leader of the opposition, sent telegrams of congratulation to Rabin, while Foreign Minister Genscher phoned his counterpart Allon 'to express his relief and satisfaction'. Senior officers in the West German Bundeswehr told a British diplomat that they 'could not decide which to admire more: the technical brilliance of the operation or the clear political directive behind it'. But the main relief for Schmidt's federal government lay in the fact that it had been spared the dilemma of whether or not to release the terrorists held in West Germany. As a diplomat at the British Embassy in Bonn put it:

Release of the prisoners held in the FRG would have been a very difficult step for the Federal Government. They include some of the most important remnants of the Baader–Meinhof gang and of the 2 June Movement . . . [and] the Government would inevitably have been exposed to criticism and unpopularity. But had they received a direct request from the Israeli Government to release the prisoners, it is hard to see how they could have refused – they simply could not have afforded to be accused of causing, even indirectly, the deaths of innocent hostages who moreover were Jews.

France and Switzerland were also broadly supportive of Israel's action, while Sweden followed Britain's lead by welcoming the rescue of the hostages.

The US president Gerald Ford sent a message to Rabin expressing his country's 'great satisfaction that a senseless act of terrorism has been thwarted'. Behind the scenes at the US State Department, however, there was some disquiet that Israel had clearly broken the terms of its agreement not to use American-supplied military equipment like the Hercules C-130 outside its own country. This prompted Henry Kissinger to phone Simcha Dinitz, the Israeli ambassador to the US, on 5 July and threaten to freeze all new military shipments. But Dinitz talked him round and, towards the end of their chat, Kissinger agreed to the ambassador's request to protect Kenya from Ugandan retaliation. His exact words were: 'We will not let Kenya get [screwed] for this.' As for pulling off the raid, Kissinger had nothing but praise for the Israelis. 'It was,' he told Dinitz, 'a terrific thing to do.'

True to his word, Kissinger arranged for the US Seventh Fleet – including the aircraft carrier USS *Ranger* – to sail towards East Africa, a naval frigate to dock at Mombasa in Kenya, and a US naval patrol aircraft to fly to Nairobi's Embakasi Airport. All these moves were designed to discourage a Ugandan attack on Kenya that had seemed imminent after Idi Amin had sent letters to both the Organization of African Unity and the Security Council of the United Nations, accusing Kenya of allowing Israeli planes to land in Nairobi both before and after the operation, and warning that 'Uganda reserves her right to retaliate in whatever way she can to redress the aggression against her.'

The response of Sir Seewoosagur Ramgoolam, president of the OAU, to Amin's letter was to send a telegram of his own to Piero Vinci, president of the UN Security Council, condemning Israel's 'unprecedented aggression' as 'a danger not only to Uganda and Africa but to international peace and security'. He and the OAU heads of state therefore requested the immediate summoning of the Security Council 'to consider this wanton act of aggression against a member state of the UN'.

Because only a few people in the Kenyan government knew about the secret deal with Israel, the official reaction to Amin's accusations was confused. In Mauritius for the meeting of the OAU, and therefore unacquainted with the facts, Vice-President Daniel Arap Moi insisted that Kenya 'has not been used as a base for aggression against Uganda' and unreservedly condemned 'this naked Israeli aggression against one of our OAU Member States'. But the cat had already been let out of the bag by a special edition of the Kenyan *Sunday Nation* newspaper which confirmed that the Israelis had passed through Nairobi, accused Amin of collusion with the hijackers and praised the Israeli action.

'It remains to be seen,' a well-informed British diplomat in Nairobi reported to the FCO on 5 July, 'whether the Kenyans will elaborate on Moi's disingenuous view or whether they will eventually concede some involvement on humanitarian grounds. They are in a dilemma since there will be strong misgivings about Kenya's public and close identification with Israel in a military attack on her neighbour. At present the Government appear to be still at sixes and sevens over their public stance.' Later that day, he added:

> The Kenyans continue to remain silent about the extent of their role in the Israeli operation. They have not attempted to deny that the aircraft passed through Nairobi on their way back from Uganda . . . Preliminary contacts here suggest the Kenyans will elaborate on the theme that [they] received minimal warning and acted purely on a humanitarian basis . . .
>
> On balance it is our view that a very small number of senior Kenyans were informed perhaps two days in advance in general terms of the Israeli plans. The information was not spread within the

government and whatever support the Kenyans arranged was probably authorized and laid on at a very late stage. The silence of the Kenyan government reflects considerable indecision among ministers as to what should be said and suggests again that there was no advance knowledge or discussion outside a very limited circle.

The diplomat's assessment was entirely correct, as was his suspicion that Kenyatta had been told in advance of the operation (yet 'only in such a way that he could not realize its full implications'). Fortunately for Kenya, it had the full military backing of the United States, and Amin knew, under the circumstances, that it would be foolhardy to attempt an invasion. So instead of making new threats against Kenya, he stressed that the 'people of Uganda and Kenya are brothers' and that he forgave Kenya 'for its mistake'.

Most of the opprobrium for the raid, however, was directed not at Kenya but at Israel. As well as the OAU, the chief accusers were mostly Arab and communist countries. It was, said Egypt, nothing less than 'government terrorism' and particularly regrettable because it came 'at a time when negotiations would have led to saving the hostages'. The Soviet Union described it as 'the latest act of piracy by the Israeli military', while Austrian Kurt Waldheim, the UN secretary-general (who had served with the Wehrmacht during the Second World War), condemned the raid as 'a serious violation of the national sovereignty of a United Nations member state'. The meeting of the Security Council to consider this 'violation' was set for 9 July.

Monday 5 July 1976, Kampala, Uganda

As well as avoiding war with Kenya, Idi Amin's chief concern on the day after the raid was to cover up the murder of Dora Bloch. To that end he told his health minister Henry Kyemba that if 'any inquiries were made about the sick hostage' he was to say 'she had been returned to the airport one hour before the Israeli commandos had arrived, and that the commandos had taken her with them'. To back up this lie, Kyemba was instructed to 'fix the records' at the hospital so that it appeared as if Mrs Bloch had indeed been discharged.

Kyemba did as he was asked, and also collected Bloch's belongings and hid them. 'I felt sickened by my actions,' he wrote later. 'But I justified it by reflecting that everyone involved knew the truth of what had happened.'

Amin also tried to muddy the waters by accusing James Horrocks, the acting British high commissioner, of knowing about the raid in advance – an accusation the diplomat categorically denied. But Horrocks was not taken in. Both from Peter Chandley's account of his visit to Mulago Hospital on 4 July and from further reports received from the staff at the hospital, he knew that Mrs Bloch 'had been dragged screaming from her hospital room to the lift and that her few items of luggage were left at the hospital'. Yet the same staff had also stressed their belief that it was 'unlikely that as the sole remaining Israeli hostage left in Uganda she was being taken away to be killed to assuage the wrath of the Ugandan Army over their own losses'.

When the FCO learned of Amin's denials, it instructed Horrocks to deliver a strongly worded note to the Ugandan Ministry of Foreign Affairs, demanding 'access to Mrs Bloch with a view to facilitating her early departure from Uganda to the destination of her choice'. It produced no immediate response.

Tuesday 6 July 1976, Jerusalem, Israel

A day after the burials of Jean-Jacques Mimouni and Ida Borochovich, Yoni Netanyahu was interred at Mount Herzl, Jerusalem's military cemetery, in a service attended by his family and thousands of mourners. Many of his former comrades from the Unit wept as his simple wooden coffin, adorned with dozens of wreaths, was lowered into the ground. Also in attendance were Israel's senior military and political figures, including Yitzhak Rabin and Shimon Peres, who delivered the graveside eulogy.

'There are times,' said the defense minister, 'when the fate of an entire people rests upon a handful of fighters and volunteers. They must secure the uprightness of our world in one short hour. This young man was among those who commanded an operation that was flawless. But to our deep sorrow, it entailed a sacrifice of incomparable pain: that of the first among the storming party, the first to fall. And by virtue of the few, the many were saved, and by virtue of the one who fell, a stature bent under the heavy weight rose again to its full height . . .'

Almost overnight Yoni Netanyahu had become an Israeli national hero. 'Yoni's passing,' wrote his biographer Max Hastings, 'unleashed one of those immense catharses that shake Israel from time to time.' Schools and newborn children were called after him. 'Operation Thunderbolt' was renamed 'Operation Yonatan'. The Jonathan Institute was created to serve his memory.

In the United States, too, Netanyahu's name lives on. His obituary in the *Harvard Crimson* was read into the Congressional Record. A part of the Bronx–Pelham Parkway in New York City was redesignated 'Lieutenant-Colonel Yonatan Netanyahu Lane'. 'The American people,' wrote Hastings, 'like the Israelis, seemed to find in Yoni a symbol to erase the Vietnam image of the warrior as a man of My Lai,* mindless bombardier of society, and to replace it instead with the older, more brilliant version of the hero in arms as the saviour of innocents.'

Yoni's hero status is a source of great pride for the Netanyahu family. Moreover it has aided – and is still aiding – his middle brother Bibi's political career. Bibi was studying at MIT in the United States at the time of the raid and probably thinking of a career as a management consultant. But his brother's death in battle, and instant fame, opened up possibilities. After a brief spell as a diplomat, including the post of Israeli ambassador to the United Nations, he joined the right-wing

---

* An infamous incident in 1968 when a company of US troops ran amok in two Vietnam hamlets, killing more than 300 men, women and children, and raping and mutilating many of the victims. Their officer William Calley was found guilty of murder and sentenced to life in prison with hard labour. He served three years under house arrest before being freed by a presidential pardon.

Likud party and – at the time of writing – is serving his third term as Israel's prime minister, only the second man after David Ben-Gurion to achieve such a feat.

Tuesday 6 July 1976, Paris, France

Two days after the rescue of the hostages, Michel Cojot gave a written account of his experience at Entebbe to a young French official who was collecting testimonies 'for the sole benefit of the archives'. Cojot also, as spokesman for the hostages, wrote a letter to the Air France management 'praising the crew's behaviour' and omitting any inconvenient details such as the fact that, contrary to all the reports in the press, the crew were never given the option to remain behind with the other passengers. He wrote later:

> In the elation of the liberation, I threw my reservations to the wind. There should be no false notes in the general rejoicing. So I wrote a fine letter . . . suggesting unity of behaviour among the crew, which had numbered twelve very different people. Without writing anything false, thanks to the marvellous instrument that is the French language, I succeeded in bending the truth. I, too, wanted things to be as I would have wished them.
>
> But official France, annoyed that Israel had succeeded in her stead, and without even consulting her, maintained a pinched silence. She offered neither congratulations nor thanks. The secretary-general of the Elysée [Presidential Palace], one of the first in France to be informed, did present his felicitations on the telephone 'in a personal capacity'; the prefecture of police was unusually nice to those who needed new documents; Air France was unusually generous in compensating the hostages for lost baggage; but silence, a great milky silence, prevailed. I wanted to cry out, but I no longer had a loudspeaker.

Cojot was particularly unhappy that the French government chose to obscure the fact of its own inaction by making heroes out of the crew. 'France is the State,' wrote Cojot, 'and what could be closer to the State than the uniformed servants of its own nationalized airline? The captain was hastily made a chevalier of the Legion of Honour . . . The rest of the crew were awarded the Cross of Merit.' He added:

> The press, books, films – including the Israeli film ['Operation Jonathan', starring Sybil Danning and Klaus Kinski] – joined in the chorus: the crew was composed solely of lion-hearted heroes who had protected their terrified passengers . . . There were other French hostages who had remained with the Israelis until the end, but only the crew was worthy of praise because collectively they symbolized France . . . Certain details were expanded while others disappeared. Roles were glossed over. Thus the truth was gradually retouched . . . Was I jealous of these cut-rate decorations fallen from the sky? . . . Sincerely, I do not think so. None of the hostages had voluntarily risked life or even an hour's freedom; none deserved a Cross. But I had a tremendous feeling of injustice, of exclusion. Again I was rejected by France.

Only in Israel was Cojot's contribution truly appreciated. Chief of Staff Motta Gur later told Ilan Hartuv, one of the rescued hostages, that had it not been for the information that Cojot gave to Amiram Levine after he returned to Paris on 2 July, 'many more hostages and soldiers would have died'. Yigal Allon, the foreign minister, told Hartuv the 'same thing'.

Michel Cojot, his son Olivier and Ilan Hartuv were among a group of sixty-seven hostages who later sued Air France in an Israeli court for security failures in Athens prior to the hijacking. On 4 July 1981, exactly five years after the rescue, the airline agreed to an out-of-court settlement of almost $2 million in compensation, giving each hostage $21,000 and a similar amount for the relatives of each fatality. Hartuv's written deposition contained the odd criticism of crew members, such as one or two injudicious remarks they had made. He was convinced that Air France settled because it did not want discussions of this type in open court. 'It's a moral victory,' declared Hartuv's brother Daniel Bloch. 'I didn't care so much about the compensation. I cared about the principle, the lack of security on Air France.'

Thursday 8 July 1976, Kampala, Uganda

Flown back out to Uganda at Prime Minister Jim Callaghan's request to investigate the disappearance of Dora Bloch, acting High Commissioner James Hennessy went straight to the Ministry of Foreign Affairs building in Kampala but was told that both the minister and the permanent secretary were in a Cabinet meeting. He later called on his French and West German colleagues, Renard and Ellerkman. Renard said that Amin had accused him of collaborating with the Israelis and that 'the Palestinians would get him or his family sooner or later'. Despite this, Renard did not think that Amin was in league with the terrorists and believed that the 'Israeli intervention was unjustifiable and unnecessary'.

West German Ambassador Ellerkman, who like Hennessy had been on home leave when the raid occurred, did not go quite so far, but still took the view 'that Amin was capable of and had intended a happy ending to this hijack affair'.

Hennessy reported to London: 'All the reports I have had so far suggest that [Mrs Bloch] is dead and has already been buried. My French colleague supports this view. While it is unlikely that we shall get any firm evidence it seems that she was shot in an act of revenge on the day of the Israeli commando raid, when so many Ugandan soldiers died. At this stage we have no firm evidence to suggest that the murder was directed by the government.'

Friday 9 July 1976, New York City, United States

Uganda's foreign minister Juma Oris Abdallah opened the Security Council debate at UN headquarters in New York City by thanking the members of the OAU for requesting such a meeting to consider 'the aggression of Zionist Israel'. During his long, rambling speech, Juma went through the sequence of events in exhaustive if inaccurate detail. He denied any collaboration with the hijackers and accused Israel of 'naked aggression'. His demand was for the Council 'unreservedly to condemn in the strongest possible terms Israel's barbaric, unprovoked and unwarranted aggression against the sovereign Republic of Uganda'; and for his country to be given 'full compensation from Israel for the damage to life and property caused during its invasion'.

In his spirited and extremely detailed response Chaim Herzog, Israel's ambassador to the UN, said he was standing before the Council 'as an accuser of all those evil forces which in their inherent cowardice and abject craven attitude see blameless wayfarers and innocent women and children – yes, even babes in arms – as legitimate targets for their evil intentions'. He also took aim at 'all those in authority throughout the world who for reasons of cynical expediency have collaborated with terrorists' (a clear dig at Idi Amin); and even at the United Nations itself 'which has been unable, because of the machinations of the Arab representatives, and their supporters, to coordinate effective measures in order to combat the evil of world terrorism'.

Israel's action at Entebbe to release its hostages, on the other hand, 'had given rise to a worldwide wave of support and approval, such as has rarely been seen from every continent, including Africa; from every walk of life; from countries hostile, as well as friendly, to Israel'. He added: 'The ordinary man and woman in the street have risen behind us and proclaimed "enough" to this spectre of terror . . .'

Herzog's one false note was to claim that, during the rescue, 'three of the hostages were killed by the terrorists before the terrorists were gunned down by Israeli troops', and that 'a senior Israeli officer was killed, shot in the back'. But overall his speech was compelling, particularly the detailed section that dealt with Uganda's alleged complicity. He even mentioned Dora Bloch's disappearance, suggesting that it 'and the by now all-too-familiar picture of the terrifying happenings in Amin's Uganda provide ample justification in themselves for the premonition which prompted' the Israeli government to act.

Insisting that the rescue was justified in both international and moral law, Herzog concluded 'with a simple message to the Council':

> We are proud of what we have done, because we have demonstrated to the world that in a small country, in Israel's circumstances, with which the members of this Council are by now all too familiar, the dignity of man, human life and human freedom constitute the highest values. We are proud not only because we have saved the lives of over 100 innocent people – men, women and children – but because of the significance of our act for the cause of human freedom.

In his reply to Herzog, the Ugandan foreign minister maintained the ludicrous and easily rebutted falsehood that Mrs Bloch had been returned to the airport with the other hostages on 3 July, and that therefore it was Israel's responsibility to say what had happened to her.

The argument continued back and forth, with claim and counter-claim, for four days: supporting the draft resolution condemning Israel were, among others, Mauritania, Libya, China, Guyana, Tanzania, Cuba and the Soviet Union; broadly supportive of Israel – or at least not prepared to condemn it – were France, the United States, Sweden, West Germany and the United Kingdom. As it was by now clear that at least three of the five permanent members of the Security Council – France, the United Kingdom and the United States – would use their veto to block the draft resolution, it was never put to the vote.

Fearful of jeopardizing the safety of British nationals in Uganda in general, and Dora Bloch in particular, the FCO had instructed its ambassador to the UN to tread a middle ground by suggesting a separate draft resolution that condemned aircraft hijacks, deplored the loss of life at Entebbe and reaffirmed 'the need to respect the sovereignty and territorial integrity of all States'. Because many anti-Israeli countries refused to vote, the resolution did not garner the requisite majority to be adopted.

Tuesday 13 July 1976, London, UK

Arriving back at Heathrow from what had been a draining royal tour of the United States – and minus his wife Susan, who had been hospitalized in Maryland with a broken jaw, the result of a fall – Foreign Secretary Tony Crosland was given the grim news that Dora Bloch's body had been found. The British High Commission in Kampala had eyewitness statements to the effect that Mrs Bloch had been shot by men from the State Research Centre, and her corpse dumped in a sugar plantation near the Jinja road, twenty miles from Kampala. One informant had even drawn a map to mark the spot.

Hearing the news that Amin's thugs were almost certainly responsible for Mrs Bloch's death, Crosland called an immediate meeting at the FCO to consider Britain's response. Relations between Britain and Uganda had never properly recovered from Amin's expulsion of Asians holding British passports in 1972, and the expropriation of British-owned companies and tea plantations in the same period. But the fall-out from the Entebbe Raid had brought matters to a head: first Amin ordered the expulsion from Uganda of British diplomat Peter Chandley and his wife for contradicting his claim that Dora Bloch had rejoined the other hostages on 3 July; then Amin made 'serious threats' against the rest of the British community in Uganda; and now there was the news that Bloch had indeed been murdered.

At the meeting, Crosland's deputy Ted Rowlands argued for an immediate break in relations with Uganda, as did most of the under-forties; the over-forties, including the permanent secretary and his deputy, were against such drastic action, not least because there was no precedent for breaking with a Commonwealth country. Crosland had the casting vote. 'I think on this occasion,' he said, after much

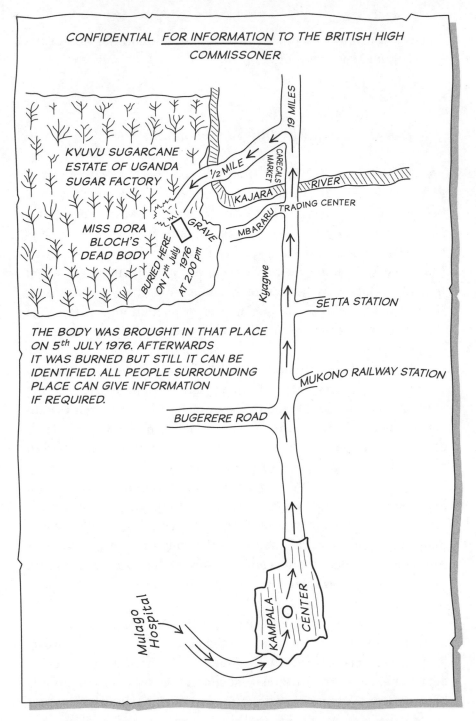

A copy of the hand drawn map of Dora Bloch's grave that was given by a Ugandan informant to the British High Commissioner.

hesitation, 'I'm for youth. We'll take a fortnight to do it. All systems go to warn Britons to get out of Uganda.'

His reasoning seems to have been that the possibility of 'negotiating compensation for the lost assets against the background of a misman-aged Ugandan economy seemed remote', that the number of British expatriates was diminishing by the day, and that the High Commission was 'not being allowed to function as it should'.

By now the location of Bloch's body was public knowledge in Uganda as people came in their hundreds to view the grisly remains: an attempt had been made to burn the corpse, but the white hair 'remained conspicuously identifiable'. Among the eyewitnesses was the famous Ugandan photographer Jimmy Parma who worked for the *Voice of Uganda* newspaper. When word got round that he had taken pictures of the corpse, Parma was picked up in broad daylight by Amin's henchmen and later murdered.

Dora Bloch and Jimmy Parma were far from the only victims of Amin's fury in the wake of Operation Thunderbolt. Blamed for allowing the Israelis to land, the three air traffic controllers on duty at Entebbe on the night of the raid were also murdered on the presi-dent's orders, as were many hundreds of ethnic Kenyans, including the director of civil aviation, and a number Karamajong tribesmen who were seen by Amin as the enemy within because their lands straddled the disputed Ugandan–Kenyan border. On 16 July the Kenyan border police estimated that more than 3,000 Kenyans had fled from Uganda.

The Kenyans responded by expelling several hundred Ugandan railway and airport staff, and by asking Britain to supply arms and ammunition to combat a possible Ugandan attack. Britain 'agreed instantly to the Kenyan request' and 'immediately put in train arrange-ments for flying the equipment to Kenya by the fastest possible route', though the difficulty of 'gaining overflying rights' meant the delivery time was longer than either party had hoped.

Finally, on 28 July, Crosland announced in the House of Commons that 'with deep regret' Britain was severing diplomatic ties with Uganda. It was doing so, he explained, because it was no longer possible for High Commission staff 'effectively to discharge their duties'.

Henceforth France would represent British interests in Uganda. It was the first time Britain had taken such action since breaking with Albania in 1946.

Sunday 18 July 1976, Damascus, Syria

In the two weeks since the raid, Gerd Schnepel and his comrades in the RC had been considering 'brutal' ways to take revenge for the deaths of Böse and Kuhlmann at Entebbe, including the destruction of planes in flight. When nothing came of these plots, Schnepel and Johannes Weinrich flew to Baghdad to meet Wadie Haddad and 'clean up the situation'. 'We went,' said Schnepel, 'to analyse the defeat, make some agreements and work out how to contact each other. Because things were still in danger of being discovered.'

It was after this trip to Baghdad that Schnepel began to reconsider his membership of the RC. About a year later, during a delegate meeting of the various cells, he announced he was leaving the group. He no longer believed that its tactic of conducting joint operations with other international terror groups was likely to succeed. 'I thought it wouldn't bring us success,' he said. 'We would either all be killed, like Boni and Brigitte, or be put into prison. The enemy was too strong to fight in this way. We had to look for different ways of bringing down capitalism or finding an alternative. I eventually went into organic agriculture in Franconia in Germany, then in Washington state in the United States, and finally in Nicaragua.'

For the RC in general, however, Entebbe marked a watershed. 'For most group members,' wrote Katharina Karcher, a historian of German left-wing terrorism, 'the failed kidnapping would lead to a turn away from "anti-Zionist" attacks, which had previously consti-tuted a central field of action for the group.' A few – Weinrich included – felt that, despite Entebbe, they should not limit their activities to West Germany and should 'participate in armed conflicts around the globe'. But this 'international cell' became increasingly isolated from the rest of the RC who avoided further attacks against Israeli targets and focused instead 'on local struggles and new social movements such as the anti-nuclear movement and the women's movement in West Germany'.

The events at Entebbe – particularly the reports of a 'selection' of passengers, 'Jews on one side, non-Jews on the other, with the Jews slated for execution' – had a profound effect on other German left-wing radicals like Joschka Fischer, the future foreign minister, who knew Wilfried Böse and Hans-Joachim Klein, and had himself supported the PLO's anti-Zionist cause in 1969. 'Suddenly,' wrote Paul Berman in his book *Power and the Idealists*, 'the implications of anti-Zionism struck home to him . . . Now he knew what it meant. Fischer seems never to have gotten over the shock of Entebbe . . . He [later] cited the hijacking and especially the "selection" of Jews as part of his *Desillusionierung* with the violent left.'

Berman added:

Entebbe had such an effect on quite a few of West Germany's New Leftists. A new suspicion was dawning on these people . . . It was a worried suspicion that New Left guerilla activity, especially in its German version, was not the struggle against Nazism that everyone on the New Left had always intended. It was a suspicion that, out of some horrible dialectic of history, a substantial number of German leftists had ended up imitating instead of opposing the Nazis – had ended up intoxicating themselves with dreams of a better world to come, while doing nothing more than setting out to murder Jews on a random basis: an old story.

Saturday 1 April 1978, Beirut, Lebanon

Palestinian officials stunned the world by announcing the death of Wadie Haddad, the fifty-year-old 'godfather' of international terrorism, architect of the Entebbe hijackings and Israel's Enemy No. 1. According to three Beirut newspapers, Waddad had expired of an 'incurable disease' – thought to be leukaemia – in an East

Berlin clinic on Tuesday 28 March. But George Habash's PFLP disputed this claim, saying that Haddad had died in an unnamed Arab country and had 'acquired martyrdom', a phrase rarely used for a death from illness. 'I can only say he did not die in Beirut,' said a PFLP spokesman. 'I can't say now where or why he died.' After first stating that Haddad would be buried in Beirut, the PFLP command corrected itself: the body had been flown to Baghdad for interment on Monday 2 April.

Habash travelled to Baghdad to attend the funeral of his former right-hand man, declaring at the airport: 'We came to Baghdad to attend a sad occasion, which is the martyrdom of Dr Wadie Haddad, one of those who fought against imperialism and Zionism.' He said he would 'continue the march of the struggle for the Arab cause for which Haddad died'.

Shigenobu Fusako, the head of the Japanese Red Army and a protégé of Haddad's, added: 'He gave extreme care to each detail. He was a maniac for the most absolute secrecy. With him, the risk of error was eliminated. He duped many secret services, especially the Mossad. He still remains today, even after his death, our master and our model.'

Many at the time suspected Israeli involvement in Haddad's death. This involvement was given added credence in 2006 with the publication of Aaron J. Klein's *Striking Back*. Having discovered Haddad's love of fine chocolate, says Klein, the Mossad arranged for the delivery of a box of Belgian chocolates laced with poison. Haddad died several months later after doctors were unable to diagnose his illness. More detail was provided in a second book by American academic Ami Pedahzur. According to Pedazhur, the Belgian pralines were injected 'with a fatal biological substance' that had been developed at the Research Institute of Biology at Ness Ziona in central Israel. Having eaten them, 'the burly Haddad began to shed pounds' and tests showed that his 'immune system had collapsed'. In great agony he continued to deteriorate and eventually died.

The Mossad had tried and failed many times to kill Haddad, redoubling its efforts after the hijacking of Flight 139. Now, finally, it had got its man.

Wednesday 24 May 1978, Nairobi, Kenya

On a spring morning in 1978, Bruce McKenzie boarded a small twin-engined Piper Aztec light plane at Nairobi's Wilson Airport for the short flight to Entebbe. Accompanied by two businessmen, Keith Savage and Gavin Whitelaw, he was due to meet President Idi Amin at State House to discuss an arms deal and the ongoing poor relations between Kenya and Uganda. Given that McKenzie was partly responsible for those frosty relations – having played a key role in persuading Kenyan security chiefs to let the Israeli planes refuel at Nairobi in 1976 – it seems odd that he was willing to beard the lion in his den.

Yet McKenzie had never confessed to his role in the raid and was convinced that his semi-official status as a trusted adviser of President Jomo Kenyatta, as well as his role in supplying Uganda with military hardware, would protect him from assassination. McKenzie was a director of Wilken Communications Ltd of Nairobi, a company owned by Keith Savage which, among other things, distributed radio equipment for the British telecommunications firm Pye. One of Wilken's biggest customers in Uganda was Amin's feared secret police, the State Research Centre, which in August 1977 had ordered sophisticated Pye radio-telephone systems worth £44,500. More orders for radios, boats and vehicles followed, but by then Uganda's economy was in freefall and Amin was struggling to pay his creditors. It was partly to demand payment of unpaid bills, partly to drum up more business, that McKenzie and Savage flew to Entebbe on 24 May 1978. McKenzie's other motive for going, according to Charles Njonjo, was political: 'He wanted to see what he could get out of Amin in the interests of Kenya. He knew that at that time we were trying to cultivate Amin.'

Shortly before his departure from England to Kenya in May 1978, McKenzie invited journalist and friend Chapman Pincher to his Surrey home and told him about his forthcoming trip to Uganda. Pincher was astonished, and warned McKenzie that 'Amin might take revenge for his part in the Entebbe raid.' But McKenzie would not be put off. He explained that he had already made one trip to Uganda and nothing had happened. 'You don't understand the African mind like I do,' said McKenzie. 'I'm convinced that Amin wants to repair his reputation with the West, which is why you should come with me to interview Amin and report the evidence of his good intentions.'

Pincher shook his head. 'I don't need to remind you,' he told his friend, 'that I'm also on his hit-list because I exposed, with Mossad's help, his monstrous role in the hijacking.'

McKenzie insisted that neither of them was in any danger and, much against his better judgement, Pincher eventually agreed to go along. But at the last minute a British businessman called Gavin Whitelaw persuaded McKenzie that he should go instead because he had a commercial proposition to put to Amin. Pincher's trip was postponed.

After landing at Entebbe on 24 May, McKenzie, Savage and Whitelaw were driven to nearby State House where they had 'friendly' talks with Amin. Back at the airport, however, they were told the plane could not take off until one of Amin's cars had arrived with a gift for McKenzie. So they waited, and McKenzie used the time to call his wife Christina and complain about the delay. She had thought he was 'potty' to return to Uganda, but was not unduly worried.

Eventually a car drove up and McKenzie was handed Amin's present: a mounted lion's head. He carried it on board the Piper Aztec which took off at 4.19 p.m. with a pilot and three passengers. During the next forty minutes the control tower at Nairobi's Wilson Airport was contacted three times by the pilot, the last at 5.58 p.m. It was due to land at 6.15 p.m. but that time came and went. The plane had crashed into the Ngong hills with no survivors. The most likely explanation is that Amin's gift, the lion's head, contained a time bomb. That was the conclusion reached by Kenyan intelligence, by McKenzie's good friends Charles Njonjo and Chapman Pincher, and also by his wife Christina who was left a widow with two young boys.

Letters of condolence came from world leaders across the globe, including Jim Callaghan, the Shah of Iran, the Aga Khan and Yitzhak Rabin. The Israelis had already recognized the service that McKenzie did for them during the raid by awarding him the special medal given to participants of 'Operation Yonatan'. After McKenzie's death, the then head of the Mossad, Meir Amit, arranged for a memorial forest to be planted in Israel in his name.

Wednesday 11 April 1979, Kampala, Uganda

Idi Amin's sins finally caught up with him in the spring of 1979 when his capital fell to Ugandan rebels and troops from the Tanzanian Army, and he was forced to flee by helicopter. He went first to the north of the country, then to Libya, and finally to Jeddah in Saudi Arabia, where King Khaled had offered him sanctuary and a generous pension. He lived in Jeddah with some of his family until his death in 2003 of kidney failure.

The humiliation of the Entebbe Raid had been for Amin the beginning of the end because it shattered the myth of his military prowess. In an attempt to shore up his crumbling authority, he struck out 'at those against whom he has a slight grievance, however slight', like the Anglican archbishop Janan Luwuum and two members of his Cabinet. Their murders in early 1977 – and the persecution of the Langi and Ocholi tribes, both of whom he accused of assisting the Israelis at Entebbe – were the triggers for the defection of Henry Kyemba and several other government ministers. Soon after arriving in England in May 1977, Kyemba published a book about Amin's brutal regime, *A State of Blood*, which accused the dictator of orchestrating the murder of over 100,000 Ugandans. Amin's support was dwindling.

In November 1978, troops loyal to the vice-president, General Mustafa Adrisi, mutinied in the south of the country. The insurrection failed and the survivors fled across the Tanzanian border, prompting Amin to accuse the Tanzanian president Julius Nyerere of inciting his soldiers. This was the pretext for Amin's army to invade Tanzania and annex the disputed region of Kagera. But in January 1979 Nyerere's army counter-attacked and, with the support of several Ugandan rebel groups, drove Amin's troops back to Kampala and beyond.

Six weeks after Amin's flight from the capital, Dora Bloch's remains were exhumed from their shallow grave near the Jinja Road and positively identified by an Israeli forensic pathologist using spinal x-rays. They were flown back to Israel and reinterred in a state funeral attended by President Yitzhak Navon in Jerusalem on 5 June 1979.

Wednesday 31 December 1980, Nairobi, Kenya

As the New Year's Eve celebrations were in full swing in the dining room of the famous Norfolk Hotel in Nairobi, a bomb exploded in a bedroom above, bringing the ceiling down on to the revellers. More than twenty people were killed and eighty injured.

The man responsible for planting the bomb was Qaddura Mohammed Abdel al-Hamid, a thirty-four-year-old Moroccan member of the PFLP, who had checked out of the hotel seven hours earlier and flown to Saudi Arabia. The Norfolk had been targeted not only because it was the most famous hotel in Kenya and a regular stop for foreign tourists; but also because it was part of the Israeli-owned Bloch Group of Hotels (no connection to Dora Bloch). The Norfolk's partial destruction, therefore, was an attack on both Kenya and Israel, and was the final act of revenge for the Entebbe Raid.

POSTSCRIPT

The immediate legacy of Operation Thunderbolt was twofold: it encouraged most Western governments to conclude that the correct political response to a hostage-taking situation was not to negotiate with the terrorists and, instead, to launch a military counter-strike if at all possible; this in turn prompted countries like France and the United States to set up specialist counter-terrorist units. West Germany had already done so, in the wake of the botched attempt to rescue Israeli athletes held hostage during the Munich Olympics of 1972, and this new unit, GSG-9, was inspired by Operation Thunderbolt to storm a hijacked Lufthansa Boeing 737 at Mogadishu Airport in 1977. Three years later, Britain's SAS ended the Iranian Embassy siege by killing five terrorists and rescuing all but one of the hostages.

The Lufthansa hijacking was directly connected to Entebbe in that the four PFLP–EA terrorists – two Palestinians and two Lebanese – called themselves the 'Commando Martyr Halime' in honour of their fallen comrade Brigitte Kuhlmann. In Aden, en route to Somalia, the hijackers shot one of the German pilots. Once they had landed in Somalia they demanded the release of ten Red Army Faktion terrorists (including the leaders Andreas Baader, Gudrun Ensslin and Jan-Carl Raspe) and two Palestinians held in Turkey.

The German government's response was to order its GSG-9 commandos to assault the plane on 18 October. During the attack by the commandos (accompanied, according to some reports, by at least one SAS trooper on attachment to GSG-9), three of the terrorists were killed and the other one was wounded and captured; all eighty-six remaining passengers and crew were rescued, though four were slightly injured. The success of Operation Feuerzauber (Fire Magic) prompted the German government to announce an end to negotiations with terrorists. Now convinced they would never be released from jail, Baader, Ensslin and Raspe all committed suicide.

In both this and the later SAS operation in London, however, the rescue assault teams were not operating in hostile territory (GSG-9, for example, had permission for its raid from the Somali government). When the US Army's Delta Force tried something similar in April 1980 with Operation Eagle Claw – the attempt to rescue the fifty-two hostages in the US Embassy in Teheran, and another mission inspired by the Israeli success at Entebbe – it ended in humiliating failure: the loss of seven aircraft (including one Hercules C-130), eight servicemen killed and not a single hostage rescued. Jimmy Carter, the US president, would later attribute his defeat in that year's presidential election to the aborted mission.

Delta Force had been created in the wake of Entebbe by Vietnam veteran Colonel Charles Beckwith, then commanding the Special Forces School at Fort Bragg, with the aim of raising 'a small handpicked outfit that was highly trained, specially equipped, and capable of engaging and defeating terrorists before they could attack American assets'. Beckwith had been seconded to the British SAS and used it as the inspiration and model for the new unit.

The failure of Operation Eagle Claw was attributed in the after-action report to adverse weather conditions and mechanical failure, and no blame was attached to Beckwith and Delta Force. Despite this setback, most Western governments have continued to refuse to negotiate with terrorists, and no more Palestinian attempts to hijack European, Israeli or US planes were made after Mogadishu. Operation Thunderbolt remains the first, and arguably most successful, counter-strike in the West's long War on Terror.

In his 1995 book on the theory and practice of special operations, Colonel Bill McRaven – later the architect of the successful US mission to kill Osama bin Laden – described the Entebbe Raid as 'the best illustration of the theory of special operations yet presented'. The extraordinary impact of the raid, then and now, was best summed up by Max Hastings, the British military historian and journalist, who wrote in 2000: 'In a world of tragedies and frustrations, few people old enough to notice the event have forgotten the great uplift that day gave us. Terror was not invincible. Outrage could be fought and conquered. But only the Israelis, the world acknowledged, could have displayed the boldness and brilliance to launch and execute such an operation, half a continent from home.' He added:

> I was in New York to report the Bicentennial. I saw the euphoria which reigned on every television network that morning, as the news from Entebbe spilled joy into the exhilaration of American's national celebration . . . With hindsight, that day might also be perceived as the high-water mark of Israel's standing in the world, as a bastion of Western values in the Middle East, and a force for the pursuit of justice and freedom. Thereafter, amid the growing rancour of failed diplomacy, the brutal suppression of Palestinian dissent and the invasion of Lebanon, world sentiment drifted steadily away from support for Israel's policies. But the memory of 4 July 1976 deserves to be preserved, for one of the greatest feats of arms in a humanitarian cause since the Second World War.

In Israel, of course, the raid is remembered as one of the greatest moments in its relatively brief history. In the opinion of Ephraim Sneh, one of those who took part, it restored Israel's 'pride and self-confidence' after the 'trauma of the '73 War'. Such a 'spectacular' military and moral victory enabled Israelis to lift their heads up after the 'huge humiliation' of Yom Kippur. 'We started from minus 10,' he said, 'and finished at plus 20.'

Many of the senior officers who took part in the raid have enjoyed successful military and political careers: Dan Shomron went on to become the IDF's chief of staff and died in 2008; Matan Vilnai was appointed deputy chief of staff, a minister in several Labor governments, including deputy minister of defense, and later Israel's ambassador to China; Ephraim Sneh rose to brigadier-general and was also a member of various Labor governments.

Though he did not participate in the raid itself, Ehud Barak played a central role both in planning the operation and in the secret negotiations with the Kenyans. His career since has been meteoric. First he rose to the top of the IDF, replacing Shomron as chief of staff in 1991. Then, in 1995, he joined Yitzhak Rabin's last Labor government as minister of internal affairs. After Rabin's assassination in November 1995 – by an ultra-nationalist Jew who objected to the prime minister's signing of the Oslo Peace Accords that created the Palestinian Authority in the West Bank and the Gaza Strip – Barak was promoted to defense minister, and later served as minister for foreign affairs and prime minister (1999–2001). He retired from politics in 2012.

Not everyone connected with the raid has prospered. The para-trooper Surin Hershko became a paraplegic as a result of his spinal injury and can only write on a computer by using an elongated straw manipulated by his mouth. In 2001, the twenty-fifth anniversary of the raid, he was presented with a special medal commemorating the raid by Prime Minister Ariel Sharon who declared:

> These days, when we are in the midst of an ongoing battle against terrorism, violence and incitement, and when we are making a joint national effort to return to political negotiations without fire, we must rekindle the spirit of that operation. The secret of our strength lies in such spirit and faith, and if we learn how to renew it we will be able to meet all the challenges that still lie ahead.

For those who lost loved ones during and after the raid – particularly the families of the largely forgotten casualties Jean-Jacques Mimouni, Pasco Cohen and Ida Borochovich – such anniversaries are a painful reminder of their grief. As Jonathan Khayat, Jean-Jacques' nephew, explained in a documentary in 2012: 'This spectacular operation, hailed as one of the most brilliant in military history, put a stop to plane hijacking as a means for Palestinian groups to impose their demands on Israel. But behind the light lies a shadow. This operation also ended the life of my 19-year-old uncle Jean-Jacques Mimouni.'

Kobi Cohen, who was present when his father Pasco was mortally wounded, added: 'Our release caused a great celebration, so everyone was in great euphoria. "How did the IDF do it?" . . . In the midst of such a celebration it's difficult to point and say: "People are dead. We have casualties." It might spoil the joy, taint the atmosphere, and we really got the feeling that my dad had been forgotten, and that Jean-Jacques Mimouni had been forgotten.'

Most Israelis are understandably proud of what their soldiers achieved at Entebbe. But are they aware of the raid's long-term political consequences? Did it make peace with the Palestinian Arabs *less* likely because it convinced Israel's political leaders – and populace in general – that their intelligence services and soldiers could deal with any security threat? Did it make it harder for Israeli politicians to push through the compromises required for peace? And does the extreme pride or confidence that comes with military success always end in hubris, as it did for the US Army in Vietnam and Iraq, and for the Israelis in Lebanon in 2006?

Opinion is divided, even in the same family of former hostages. 'It was double-edged,' argues Claude Rosenkovitch. 'We were saved but it was bad for Israel. It made peace less likely. All the time since we have been talking about Entebbe and how successful it was.'

His wife Emma disagrees. 'We did not think like that,' she says, 'when the Oslo peace process was under way in 1993. Arabs might have been prepared to make peace *because* of Entebbe. What happened after Rabin's death is something else.'

NOTES

Day 1: Sunday 27 June 1976

Page 1   'tried to make a path'. Michel Goldberg, *Namesake* (1982, this paperback edition London, 1984), p. 102. After Entebbe, Michel Cojot reverted to his original Jewish surname Goldberg. His children mostly use the name Cojot-Goldberg.

Page 1   'dismantled. . .the controls'. Ibid.

Pages 1-2   'pretty interesting' . . . 'a pain in the arse'. Author telephone interview with Olivier Cojot-Goldberg, 26 November 2013.

Page 2   unscheduled stopover. Goldberg, *Namesake*, p. 102.

Page 2   'Hey Dad'. Author telephone interview with Olivier Cojot-Goldberg, op. cit.

Page 2   'seemed to offer'. . . 'service plus'. Goldberg, *Namesake*, p. 102.

Pages 2-3   Ilan Hartuv. . .non-stop tickets. Author interview with Ilan Hartuv, Tel Aviv, 9 October 2013.

Page 3   'Let's not go'. Yehuda Ofer, *Operation Thunder: The Entebbe Raid – The Israelis' Own Story* (London, 1976), p. 2.

Page 3   Other passengers . . . fly together. Author interview with Martine Mimouni-Arnold, Tel Aviv, 8 October 2013; Eyal Ben, 'Entebbe's unsung hero', ynetnews.com, 29 April 2012.

Page 3   'Quick'. Moshe Miller, 'Miracles at Entebbe', *Zman Magazine*, No. 126, July 2012, p. 128.

Page 4   'After this' . . . 'retired Americans'. Goldberg, *Namesake*, pp. 102–3.

Page 4   Just after noon . . . squabbling children. Ibid., p. 103.

Page 5   In their place . . . and Turkish. Telegram from US Ambassador to France to US Secretary of State, 1818hrs GMT, 3 July 1976, Declassified/Released US Department of State documents, www.aad.archives.gov/aad.

Page 5   Among them . . . ten day cruise. *Daily Express*, 2 July 1976.

Page 5   The Rabinowitzes . . . to ask. Author skype interview with Nancy Rabinowitz, 10 November 2014; Author skype interview with Peter Rabinowitz, 13 November 2014.

Pages 5-6   Claude Moufflet . . . in his briefcase. Claude Moufflet, *Otages à Kampala* (Paris, 1976, translated from French into English by Rachel Kenyon), p. 11.

Page 6   'systematic' . . . let him continue. Ibid., pp. 11–12.

Page 6   Four of Flight . . . moustache. Louis Williams, 'Combined Operations: Entebbe', in *The Israeli Defense Forces: A People's Army*

(New York, 1996), p. 121; Debrief of Mr Russell and Mr Good by British diplomat Michael Llewellyn-Smith, 'British subjects in the Hi-jacking incident', in a Letter from British Embassy in Paris to FCO, 2 July 1976, The National Archives (TNA), FCO 31/2056.

Page 6   'nobody was on duty'. Williams, *The Israeli Defense Forces*, p. 121.

Page 7   'through which' . . . 'cool flight'. Moufflet, *Otages à Kampala*, p. 12.

Page 7   Ilan Hartuv. . . decided not to. Author interview with Ilan Hartuv, op. cit.

Page 7   'Arabs!' Miller, 'Miracles at Entebbe', p. 128.

Page 7   'Why would'. Lauren Gelfond Feldinger, 'Through the Eyes of Hostages', *Jerusalem Post*, 29 June 2006.

Page 7   Meanwhile Claude. Moufflet, *Otages à Kampala*, p. 13.

Page 8   'Dates for you'. Miller, 'Miracles at Entebbe', p. 129.

Page 8   As if . . . Iraq. Ofer, *Operation Thunder*, p. 1.

Page 8   'aready busy' . . . flight deck. Williams, *The Israeli Defense Forces* , p. 121.

Page 8   'Please don't'. Interview with Michel Bacos, in Laly Derai, 'I owe my life to the IDF', *Hamodia*, No. 11, June 2011.

Pages 8-9   But the crisis . . . discourage him. Simon Dunstan, *Israel's Lightning Strike: The Raid on Entebbe 1976* (Oxford, 2009), p. 11.

Page 9   'a long-haired youth' . . . 'trembling arms'. William Stevenson, *90 Minutes at Entebbe: The First Full Inside Story of Operation Thunderbolt* (New York, 1976), p. 4.

Page 9   'livid' . . . 'Don't move!' Moufflet, *Otages à Kampala*, pp. 13–14.

Pages 9-10   'and saw' . . . flame. Goldberg, *Namesake*, p. 103.

Page 10   'already thinking' . . . shock. Author interview with Olivier Cojot-Goldberg, op. cit.

Page 10   'Sitonzeflor!' Goldberg, *Namesake*, p. 103.

Page 10   'about 25' . . . 'taken out'. Moufflet, *Otages à Kampala*, pp. 14-15.

Page 10   'a short' . . . like a leaf. Stevenson, *90 Minutes at Entebbe*, p. 35.

Page 10   'This plane'. Moufflet, *Otages à Kampala*, p. 15.

Page 11   'ripping off'. Feldinger, 'Through the Eyes of Hostages'.

Pages 11-12   'never achieve' . . . 'justice'. Bassam Abu-Sharif & Uzi Mahnaimi, *Best of Enemies* (New York, 1995), pp. 59-60.

Page 12   'felt like' . . . 'Master'. Ibid.

Page 12   'from this' . . . captured. Ibid., pp. 64-5.

Pages 13-14   'made it very' . . . 'Black September'. Ibid., pp. 88–9.

Page 14   Number 1. Debrief of Mr Russell and Mr Good, op. cit.

Pages 14-15   'become a little' . . . hijacking together. 'Goldberg, *Namesake*, pp. 17–20, 104; author telephone interview with Stépane Cojot-Goldberg, 16 January 2015.

Page 15   'severe' punishment . . . 'not be harmed'. Nancy and Peter Rabinowitz, 'Fifty-two Hundred and Ninety Minutes at Entebbe: The Paradoxes of Terror', *Syracuse Guide*, October 1976, p. 17.

Page 15   'pointed for'. Debrief of Mr Russell and Mr Good, op. cit.
Pages 15-16   'official-looking' . . . 'serious for you'. Moufflet, *Otages à Kampala*, pp. 15–18.
Page 17   pipe cleaner. Ibid., p. 18.
Page 17   'beloved' . . . 'Israeli vigilance'. Goldberg, *Namesake*, p. 104.
Page 17   'intimate parts'. Stevenson, *90 Minutes at Entebbe*, pp. 4–5.
Page 17   'special surgery'. Ofer, *Operation Thunder*, pp. 6–7.
Page 17   'An Air France'. Yitzhak Rabin, *The Rabin Memoirs* (1979, this paperback edition Berkeley, California, 1996), p. 282; Yehuda Avner, *The Prime Ministers: An Intimate Narrative of Israeli Leadership* (New Milford, Connecticut, 2010), p. 303.
Page 17   'Freuka'. Avner, *The Prime Ministers*, p. 303.
Pages 17-18   'banged' . . . 'another Sabena'. Ibid.
Page 19   'windowless' . . . 'meet you there'. Colonel Muki Betser, *Secret Soldier: The Incredible True Story of Israel's Greatest Commando* (1996, this paperback edition London, 1997), pp. 289–90.
Pages 20-1   It was shortly . . . Egyptian territory. Ibid, pp. 25–75.
Pages 21-2   With the war over . . . expect to return. Ibid., pp. 117–32.
Page 22   Arriving back . . . 'other jobs'. Ibid., pp. 136–7.
Pages 22-4   The chance . . . another Ma'alot. Ibid., pp. 267–78.
Page 24   Swerving through . . . Ben-Gurion. Ibid., pp. 290–1.
Pages 24-5   'until some' . . . 'sit down'. Moufflet, *Otages à Kampala*, p. 21.
Page 25   'Here is'. Ibid., p. 22.
Page 25   'allowing a glimpse' . . . 'was gaping'. Goldberg, *Namesake*, p. 105.
Page 25   'no one ever' . . . her buttons. Ibid.
Page 26   'Sit down'. Moufflet, *Otages à Kampala*, p. 24.
Page 26   'less like' . . . 'toilet monitors'. Rabinowitz and Rabinowitz, 'Fifty-two Hundred and Ninety Minutes at Entebbe', p. 17.
Page 26   'I didn't ask'. Moufflet, *Otages à Kampala*, p. 25.
Page 26   Agnès and Maggy. They were not their real names but the pseudonyms given to them by Claude Moufflet to protect their identity in Moufflet's autobiographical account of the hijacking, *Otages à Kampala*.
Page 26   Short and chubby . . . photo identity. Moufflet, *Otages à Kampala*, pp. 26-7.
Page 27   'seconds to spare'. Interview with Sara Davidson, in *Situation Critical: Assault on Entebbe*, National Geographic Channel, 12 June 2007.
Page 27   Mindful . . . 'Israeli passports'. Interview with Claude and Emma Rosenkovitch, in Aviv Lavie, 'Surviving the myth', *Haaretz*, 31 July 2003.
Page 27   reserve soldier. Stevenson, *90 Minutes at Entebbe*, p. 5.
Page 27   'What will they do' . . . 'don't know'. Moufflet, *Otages à Kampala*, p. 27.
Page 27   'reduce tension' . . . 'Palestinians'. Goldberg, *Namesake*, p. 105.
Page 27   'If Israel'. Lavie, 'Surviving the myth'.
Pages 27-8   Twenty-two-year-old . . . was safe. Author interview with Martine Mimouni-Arnold, op. cit.

Page 28	sweets and cakes. Moufflet, *Otages à Kampala*, pp. 27–8.
Page 29	'was a system'. Ibid., p. 28.
Page 29	'Madam, you can't' . . . 'top of it?' Ibid., pp. 28–9.
Page 29	'Sit down please'. Ibid., pp. 29–30.
Page 29	'Land it gently'. Interview with Michel Bacos, in Derai, 'I owe my life to the IDF'.
Page 30	'We knew'. Stevenson, *90 Minutes at Entebbe*, p. 36.
Page 30	'arid landscape'. *New York Times*, 11 July 1976.
Page 30	'read or spoke' . . . 'government'. Moufflet, *Otages à Kampala*, p. 31.
Page 30	'welcoming committee'. Author telephone interview with Olivier Cojot-Goldberg, op. cit.
Page 30	'not without humour'. Goldberg, *Namesake*, p. 106.
Page 30	Arab Republic. Debrief of Mr Russell and Mr Good, op. cit.
Page 30	'What the hell'. Author telephone interview with Olivier Cojot-Goldberg, op. cit.
Page 31	'to try landing' . . . Sinai Peninsula. Betser, *Secret Soldier*, p. 291.
Page 31	'preserved a deep'. Max Hastings, *Yoni: Hero of Entebbe* (1979), p. 22.
Page 31	'natural leader'. Ibid., p. 24.
Page 32	'I feel I belong'. Ibid., p. 26.
Page 32	'physical toughness' . . . prize cadet. Ibid., pp. 37 and 46.
Page 32	'shaggy young men' . . . 'our existence'. Ibid., pp. 87-9.
Page 33	'were a little' . . . 'fighting commander'. Ibid., p. 99-100.
Pages 33-4	'began months' . . . 'queue for hell?' Ibid., p. 208.
Page 34	'You need us?' . . . 'Of course'. Betser, *Secret Soldier*, p. 291; Iddo Netanyahu, *Entebbe: A Defining Moment in the War on Terrorism* (Green Forest, Arkansas, 2003), p. 16.
Pages 34-5	'The only thing' . . . 'demands will be'. Ben-Gurion. Avner, *The Prime Ministers*, p. 304.
Page 35	'We are in deep'. 'Operation Entebbe Protocols revealed', *Ynet Magazine*, 11 May 2010, http://www.ynetnews.com/articles/0,7340,L-3980051,00.html.
Pages 35-6	'full responsibility' . . . 'the hijackers'. Shimon Peres, *Battling for Peace: A Memoir* (New York, 1995), pp. 152–3.
Page 36	'any other women' . . . even teeth. Moufflet, *Otages à Kampala*, p. 31.
Page 36	'Our parents' . . . 'believe us'. Ibid., p. 32.
Page 37	'Shouldn't we' . . . 'for the moment'. Ibid., pp. 33–5.
Page 37	'It was tempting'. Goldberg, *Namesake*, p. 106.
Page 38	'hijacking, and landing'. Cipher telegram from Tony Crosland, Foreign Secretary, to British Embassy in Tripoli, 1459hrs GMT, No. 107 of 27 June 1976, TNA, FCO 93/913/16.
Page 38	His first couple . . . secretary of state. Kevin Jefferys, *Anthony Crosland* (1999), pp. 200–2.
Page 38	'Grateful for any'. Cipher telegram from Crosland to British Embassy in Tripoli, 1459hrs GMT, No. 107 of 27 June 1976, op. cit.
Page 39	'I had to get off'. 'Entebbe Thirty Years On: Mancunian on Board', *Jewish Telegraph Online*, 2006, www.jewishtelegraph.com/enteb_2.html.

Page 39	Her first thought. Patricia Martell in *Cohen on the Bridge* (2012), an award-winning animated short film documentary written and directed by Andrew Wainrib.
Pages 39-40	'screwed up' . . . 'that important'. 'Entebbe Thirty Years On: Mancunian on Board', op. cit.; Yeshayahu Ben-Porat, Eitan Haber and Zeev Schiff, *Entebbe Rescue* (New York, 1976; this paperback edition 1977), pp. 33–5.
Page 40	'All of a sudden'. Author telephone-interview with Olivier Cojot-Goldberg, op. cit.
Page 40	'Good luck'. Goldberg, *Namesake*, p. 106.
Page 41	'I did not consider' . . . 'regret'. Rabin, *The Rabin Memoirs*, p. 241.
Page 41	'served the 1974-77'. Peres, *Battling for Peace*, p. 149.
Pages 41-2	Peres's main priority . . . 'negotiation and preparation'. Ibid., pp. 140 and 155.
Page 43	'Air France Office' . . . 17 June. Cipher telegram from British Embassy in Athens to FCO, 1708hrs GMT, No. 296 of 27 June 1976, TNA, FCO 93/913/16.
Page 43	'keep in close' . . . 'and aircraft'. Cipher telegram from FCO to British Embassies in Tripoli and Paris, 1845hrs GMT, No. 108 of 27 June 1976, ibid.
Page 43	'keeping in close' . . . 'Consulate there'. Cipher telegram from British Embassy in Tripoli to FCO, 1929hrs GMT, No. 147 of 27 June 1976, ibid.
Page 44	'Sit down' . . . 'severely punished'. Moufflet, *Otages à Kampala*, pp. 35–6.
Page 44	'sitting on a hijacked'. Author telephone interview with Akiva Laxer, Tel Aviv, 10 October 2013.
Page 44	Claude Moufflet . . . young Canadians. Moufflet, *Otages à Kampala*, p. 36.
Page 45	'not bad' . . . 'veritable animal'. Diary of Moshe Peretz, in Stevenson, *90 Minutes at Entebbe*, pp. 5–6.
Page 45	An hour later . . . 'local time'. Moufflet, *Otages à Kampala*, p. 37.
Page 45	'At long last'. Diary of Moshe Peretz, in Stevenson, *90 Minutes at Entebbe*, p. 6.
Pages 45-6	Major Muki . . . chief of staff. Betser, *Secret Soldier*, p. 292.
Page 46	'a British subject' . . . 'to do so'. Cipher telegram from British Embassy in Paris to FCO, 2012hrs GMT, No. 638 of 27 June 1976, TNA, FCO 93/913.
Pages 46-7	'Aircraft left'. Cipher telegram from British Embassy in Tripoli to FCO, 2036hrs GMT, No. 148 of 27 June 1976, ibid.
Page 47	'well but still'. Ibid., 1014hrs GMT, No. 150 of 28 June 1976.
Page 47	'pretty stupid'. Entebbe Thirty Years On: Mancunian On Board', op. cit.
Page 47	warm-hearted and jovial . . . bratwurst. Author skype interview with Gerd Schnepel (former boyfriend of Brigitte Kuhlmann and member of the Revolutionary Cells), 3 November 2013.
Page 48	'in the student' . . . RC and RAF. Katharina Karcher, 'Sisters in

Arms? Female Participation in Leftist Political Violence in the Federal Republic of Germany since 1970', unpublished PhD thesis, University of Warwick, 2013, pp. 227–8.

Page 48   Another common . . . political change. Ibid., pp. 229–31.

Page 48   'cruelties'. Author skype interview with Gerd Schnepel, op. cit.

Page 48   'bustling organizational talent'. Karcher, 'Sisters in Arms?', pp. 231–2.

Page 48   'You are not pretty'. Email from Gerd Schnepel to the author, 11 November 2013.

Page 48   'moved within radical' . . . 'resolute and honest'. Karcher, 'Sisters in Arms?', p. 233.

Page 48   'friendly, caring'. Email from Gerd Schnepel to the author, 11 November 2013.

Page 49   Kuhlmann . . . '"typical" behaviour'. Karcher, 'Sisters in Arms?', pp. 234–5.

Page 49   The core beliefs . . . 'mass movement'. Ibid., p. 57.

Page 49   'underground' . . . '*Feierabendterroristen*'. Ibid., p. 237.

Page 49   early terror attacks. Ibid., p. 58.

Page 49   openly feminist agenda. Ibid., p. 221.

Page 49   'strengthen the group'. Author skype interview with Gerd Schnepel, op. cit.

Page 50   'There were a lot'. Ibid.

Page 50   No one felt . . . free them. Ibid. Schnepel told me that Brigitte Kuhlmann 'felt an obligation to participate in the freeing of political prisoners in Germany' for personal reasons. She felt she had left Meinhof down.

Page 50   The first joint . . . right-hand man. John Follain, *Jackal: The Secret Wars of Carlos the Jackal* (1998, this paperback edition London, 2004), pp. 65–7, 140–1.

Pages 50-1   With Weinrich . . . the country. Ibid., pp. 104–30.

Page 51   'none of the' . . . ordered to go. Abu-Sharif and Mahnaimi, *Best of Enemies*, p. 164.

Page 51   'plenty of fascists' . . . 'failed to execute'. Ibid., pp. 164–5.

Page 51   Khaled al-Khalili. Statement by the Popular Front for the Liberation of Palestine regarding the Entebbe Airport incident in Uganda', 4 July 1976, in TNA, FCO 93/914. There is much confusion over the exact identity of the seven terrorists killed at Entebbe. According to the PFLP's own statement (above), the seven 'martyrs' were: 'Haj Faiz Jaber'; 'Adurrazaq Assamurai/Abu Addarda'; 'Jabil Al'Arga'; 'Khaled Al Khalili'; 'Ali Al Ma'ati'; 'Mahmood' (Wilfried Böse); and 'Halima' (Brigitte Kuhlmann). See also the Conclusion to 'Operation Yonatan (Operation Thunderbolt), 3–4 July 1976', Confidential IDF Report, IDF & Defense Establishment Archives, Ministry of Defence, Hakirya, Tel Aviv, pp. 103–4 (translated by Karen Gilbert), which lists six terrorists with similar names (but not Jaber).

Page 52   'We were told' . . . refused to answer. Author skype interview with Gerd Schnepel, op. cit.

Pages 52-3	'Here is the new' . . . any news. Avner, *The Prime Ministers*, p. 305.
Page 53	'mean and full'. Moufflet, *Otages à Kampala*, p. 39.
Page 53	'a blond, chubby' . . . 'diplomatic ties'. Goldberg, *Namesake*, pp. 106–7.
Page 54	'Several of the soldiers'. Peres, *Battling for Peace*, p. 153.
Pages 54-5	'tapping at the airport map'. . . back to base. Betser, *Secret Soldier*, p. 293.

Day 2: Monday 28 June 1976

Page 57	The first that. Interview with Michel Bacos, in Derai, 'I owe my life to the IDF'.
Page 57	'chatting in low voices' . . . 'your seatbelts'. Moufflet, *Otages à Kampala*, p. 41; Diary of Moshe Peretz, in Stevenson, *90 Minutes at Entebbe*, p. 24.
Pages 57-8	'fascinating' . . . approaching the plane. Moufflet, *Otages à Kampala*, pp. 41–3.
Page 58	'totally lost' . . . 'a little bit'. Author telephone interview with Olivier Cojot-Goldberg, op. cit.
Page 58	'dumbfounded' . . . both his hands. Goldberg, *Namesake*, p. 107.
Page 58	'interminable' . . . 'shut up!' Moufflet, *Otages à Kampala*, p. 43.
Page 58	'First the German'. Diary of Julie Oiserant [Aouzerate], in Stevenson, *90 Minutes at Entebbe*, p. 36.
Page 59	'nearly illiterate' . . . 'gang of thugs'. Henry Kyemba, *A State of Blood: The Inside Story of Idi Amin* (New York, 1977), p. 15.
Pages 59-60	'Who is this?' . . . 'back to sleep'. Avner, *The Prime Ministers*, pp. 305–6.
Page 60	'armed soldiers' . . . 'surrounded'. Moufflet, *Otages à Kampala*, pp. 43–4.
Page 60	'the savannah' . . . and Germans. Goldberg, *Namesake*, p. 107.
Pages 60-1	'the yellow-shirted' . . . Palestinian. Diary of Moshe Peretz, in Stevenson, *90 Minutes at Entebbe*, p. 24.
Page 61	Just after 8 a.m. . . . Yasser Arafat. Moufflet, *Otages à Kampala*, pp. 44–5.
Page 61	'freely about'. Translation of interview with Michel Cojot in *Le Monde*, in a cipher telegram from Kissinger to the US Ambassador in London, 0057hrs GMT, 9 July 1976, TNA, FCO 93/914.
Page 61	'Amin was cooperating'. Author skype interview with Gerd Schnepel, op. cit.
Page 61	'for a little breakfast'. Moufflet, *Otages à Kampala*, p. 45.
Pages 61-2	'separated from the other' . . . 'the pilots'. Ofer, *Operation Thunder*, p. 23.
Page 62	'They're going to kill' . . . had left Athens. Moufflet, *Otages à Kampala*, pp. 46–8.
Page 63	'Idi Amin negotiating'. Stevenson, *90 Minutes at Entebbe*, p. 25.
Page 63	'would be closely involved' . . . 'emergency duty'. Kyemba, *A State of Blood*, pp. 166–7.

Pages 63-4   'to report' . . . IDF brass. Peres, *Battling for Peace*, p. 154.

Pages 64-5   With breakfast cleared . . . 'Palestinian enemies'. Moufflet,
                Otages à Kampala, pp. 51–3.

Page 65   'to declare' . . . 'imperialism everywhere'. Text of the PFLP
                Communiqué, Monday 28 June 1976, TNA, FCO 93/913/9.

Pages 65-6   'rather good English' . . . 'first round'. Goldberg, *Namesake*, pp.
                107–8.

Page 66   'only two' . . . game away. Moufflet, *Otages à Kampala*, pp.
                51–2.

Page 66   'I'll now tell you'. Ibid., p. 55.

Page 67   'At least now'. Author interview with Ilan Hartuv, op. cit.

Page 67   'fighting for world' . . . 'being killed'. Author telephone inter-
                view with Akiva Laxer, op. cit.

Pages 67-8   'President' . . . suspect the latter. Betser, *Secret Soldier*, pp.
                295–6.

Page 68   Just after one . . . 'on this airline'. Moufflet, *Otages à Kampala*,
                p. 58.

Pages 68-9   'there was a general' . . . 'now over'. Goldberg, *Namesake*, p.
                108.

Page 69   'On behalf'. Moufflet, *Otages à Kampala*, p. 59.

Page 69   Soon afterwards. Diary of Moshe Peretz, in Stevenson, *90
                Minutes at Entebbe*, p. 25.

Page 69   'very strange' . . . 'under our control'. Ibid.; *New York Times*, 11
                July 1976.

Page 69   'We have arrived'. Ben-Porat, Haber and Schiff, *Entebbe Rescue*,
                p. 118.

Page 70   'We still don't know'. Ofer, *Operation Thunder*, p. 27.

Page 70   'uncomfortable, well-worn'. Goldberg, *Namesake*, p. 108.

Page 70   Even then. Rabinowitz and Rabinowitz, 'Fifty-two Hundred
                and Ninety Minutes at Entebbe', p. 17.

Page 70   'it wouldn't get'. Moufflet, *Otages à Kampala*, p. 61.

Page 70   About 500 yards. *New York Times*, 11 July 1976.

Page 71   '"the Peruvian"'. Goldberg, *Namesake*, p. 109.

Page 71   The Peruvian's superior . . . over him. Ben-Porat, Haber and
                Schiff, *Entebbe Rescue*, pp. 84–5; Moufflet, *Otages à Kampala*, p. 59.

Page 71   The last of the trio . . . 'attacks abroad'. 'Statement by the
                Popular Front for the Liberation of Palestine regarding the
                Entebbe Airport incident in Uganda', 4 July 1976, in TNA, FCO
                93/914/17; Conclusion, 'Operation Yonatan', op. cit., pp. 103–4.

Pages 71-2   While Jaber . . . inspection hall. Section 7: Intelligence for the
                Operation, Chapter B: Battle Procedure for the Operation,
                'Operation Yonatan', op. cit., pp. 18–35; Figure 7, The Old
                Terminal in Entebbe, ibid., p. 32.

Page 72   The only other features. Figure 7, The Old Terminal in
                Entebbe, ibid., p. 32.

Page 72   'Look at that!' . . . 'shrieks and claps'. Moufflet, *Otages à
                Kampala*, pp. 61–3.

Page 72   'A plane will arrive'. Ofer, *Operation Thunder*, p. 36.

Page 73   'refused permission' . . . 'in Kampala'. Cipher telegram from

High Commission in Kampala to FCO, 1200hrs GMT, No. 201 of 28 June 1976, TNA, FCO 47/845.

Page 73   'to leave the aircraft' . . . 'the drama'. Ibid., 1400hrs GMT, No. 202 of 28 June 1976.

Page 73   Other cables. Cipher telegram from British Embassy in Athens to FCO, 1045hrs GMT, No. 298 of 28 June 1976, TNA, FCO 31/2054.

Page 74   'she was not previously'. Cipher telegram from British Embassy in Tel Aviv to FCO, 0905hrs GMT, No. 196 of 28 June 1976, ibid.

Pages 74-5   'It's a strange thing' . . . 'operational plan'. Peres, *Battling for Peace*, p. 154; Williams, *The Israeli Defense Forces*, p. 124..

Page 75   'withdrawn, bashful'. Rabin, *The Rabin Memoirs*, pp. 6–7.

Page 75   'a first but invaluable' . . . 'with Israel'. Ibid., p. 274.

Page 76   'away from events'. Ben-Porat, Haber and Schiff, *Entebbe Rescue*, p. 109.

Page 76   'It might be from giraffes'. Stevenson, *90 Minutes at Entebbe*, p. 25.

Pages 76-7   'many [of the hostages]' . . . 'equator'. Goldberg, *Namesake*, pp. 109–10.

Page 77   While they were eating . . . 'permanent sulk'. Moufflet, *Otages à Kampala*, pp. 64–5.

Page 77   There he got talking . . . Willy. 'Gilles' and 'Willy' are the pseudonyms used in Claude Moufflet's book to hide their true identities.

Pages 77-8   Offering Moufflet . . . wooden bar. Moufflet, *Otages à Kampala*, pp. 65–6.

Page 78   'Everyone jumped'. Feldinger, 'Through the Eyes of Hostages'.

Page 78   'I don't smoke'. Goldberg, *Namesake*, p. 109.

Pages 78-9   'It is not easy' . . . 'friendly territory'. Translation of interview with Michel Cojot in *Le Monde*, op. cit.

Pages 79-80   'officials from' . . . 'few headaches'. Kyemba, *A State of Blood*, pp. 167–8.

Page 80   'hurried and superficial'. Diary of Julie Oiserant [Aouzerate], in Stevenson, *90 Minutes at Entebbe*, pp. 37–8.

Page 80   'heart ailment'. Ben-Porat, Haber and Schiff, *Entebbe Rescue*, p. 120.

Pages 80-1   'The troubles' . . . the answer. Ibid., pp. 120-2.

Page 81   A tall, thickly built . . . the hostages. Diary of Moshe Peretz, in Stevenson, *90 Minutes at Entebbe*, pp. 25–6.

Page 81   'Shalom'. 'Ben-Porat, Haber and Schiff, *Entebbe Rescue*, p. 122; Moufflet, *Otages à Kampala*, p. 69.

Pages 81-2   'shake his hand' . . . 'that way'. Goldberg, *Namesake*, p. 116.

Page 82   'You are lucky'. *New York Times*, 11 July 1976.

Page 82   Tall, blond . . . terrorists. Ben-Porat, Haber and Schiff, *Entebbe Rescue*, p. 128.

Page 82   'private planning'. Dunstan, *Israel's Lightning Strike*, p. 139.

Page 83   Born in Siberia . . . Egypt proper. 'Rescue at Entebbe: An Interview with the Chief Pilot', IDF Blog, 5 July 2012, www.idfblog.com/2012/07/05/rescue-at-entebbe-an-interview-with-the-chief-pilot/.

Page 83	The chief advantages. Dunstan, *Israel's Lightning Strike*, p. 139.
Page 84	Aware that . . . 'their fears'. Goldberg, *Namesake*, p. 110; Author skype interview with Nancy Rabinowitz, op. cit.
Page 84	At 8 p.m. Moufflet, *Otages à Kampala*, p. 70.
Pages 84-5	'finally living' . . . 'educate us'. Goldberg, *Namesake*, pp. 110–13.
Page 85	'I was mistaken' . . . 'Arab planes'. Yossi Melman, 'Setting the record straight: Entebbe was not Auschwitz', *Haaretz*, 8 July 2011.
Page 86	'would not meddle' . . . in his stomach. Goldberg, *Namesake*, pp. 111–15.
Page 86	Cojot had changed . . . pyjamas. Author telephone interview with Stéphane Cojot-Goldberg, 25 November 2013.
Page 86	'British officer'. Moufflet, *Otages à Kampala*, p. 76.
Page 86	'hot as hell'. Diary of Moshe Peretz, in Stevenson, *90 Minutes at Entebbe*, p. 26.
Page 87	'an old Jewish woman' . . . 'was over'. Goldberg, *Namesake*, p. 111.

Day 3: Tuesday 29 June 1976

Page 89	It was barely . . . 'not met'. *New York Times*, 11 July 1976; Stevenson, *90 Minutes at Entebbe*, p. 26.
Page 89	'anxiety' . . . 'get out'. Diary of Moshe Peretz, in Stevenson, *90 Minutes at Entebbe*, p. 26; Ofer, *Operation Thunder*, p. 37.
Pages 89-90	'critical stage' . . . 'We'll cope'. Hastings, *Yoni*, pp. 216-18.
Page 91	Yitzhak Rabin . . . been made. Williams, *The Israeli Defense Forces*, p. 124; Ben-Porat, Haber and Schiff, *Entebbe Rescue*, p. 126.
Page 91	'colour' stories. Peres, *Battling for Peace*, p. 154.
Page 92	'Mr Begin' . . . a handshake. Ben-Porat, Haber and Schiff, *Entebbe Rescue*, p. 127; Williams, *The Israeli Defense Forces*, op. cit., pp. 124-7.
Pages 92-3	Tormented by mosquitoes . . . 'All inside!' Ben-Porat, Haber and Schiff, *Entebbe Rescue*, pp. 127-9
Page 93	'very vociferous' . . . French Embassy. Kyemba, *A State of Blood*, p. 168.
Page 93	'If this lasts'. Goldberg, *Namesake*, p. 112.
Pages 93-4	Cojot's advice . . . do without. Ibid., p. 114; Kyemba, *A State of Blood*, pp. 168–9.
Page 94	'how modern'. Moufflet, *Otages à Kampala*, p. 77.
Page 94	'What a megalomaniac'. Feldinger, 'Through the Eyes of Hostages'.
Pages 94-5	Several volunteers . . . on his heart. Moufflet, *Otages à Kampala*, pp. 77–9.
Pages 95-7	The early-afternoon . . . 'the terrorists'. Avner, *The Prime Ministers*, pp. 306–7.
Page 97	'the whole operation' . . . 'the terms'. Kyemba, *A State of Blood*, p. 169.
Pages 97	'France's responsibility' . . . 'believes it himself'. Avner, *The Prime Ministers*, p. 307

Page 98   'I have just communicated'. Moufflet, *Otages à Kampala*, p. 80.
Page 98   'freedom fighters' . . . 'on Thursday'. Diary of Moshe Peretz, in
            Stevenson, *90 Minutes at Entebbe*, pp. 26–7; Moufflet, *Otages à
            Kampala*, p. 80.
Page 99   'to examine military action' . . . special operations. Section 5:
            Actions at the General Staff Level, Chapter B, 'Operation
            Yonatan', op. cit., pp. 13–16.
Page 99   'Listen, Ehud'. Interview with Ehud Barak, in *Live or Die in
            Entebbe*, (feature-length documentary written and directed by
            Eyal Boers), Dynamic Flash Ltd, 2012.
Pages 99-100 It was obvious . . . Muki Betser. Ibid.; Section 5: Actions at the
            General Staff Level, Chapter B, 'Operation Yonatan', op. cit.
Pages 100-1 When Betser . . . mission began. Betser, *Secret Soldier*, pp.
            296–7.
Page 101   'Motta, does the IDF'. Rabin, *The Rabin Memoirs*, p. 283.
Pages 101-2 'There has been no' . . . 'the hostages'. Avner, *The Prime
            Ministers*, p. 307.
Page 102   'maintain our position' . . . 'meticulous examination'. Peres,
            Battling for Peace, p. 155.
Page 102   'presumably' . . . 'unthinkable alternative'. Avner, *The Prime
            Ministers*, p. 307.
Page 102   'woefully confused' . . . Wadie Haddad. Ben-Porat, Haber and
            Schiff, *Entebbe Rescue*, pp. 131–2; Peres, *Battling for Peace*, p. 155.
Page 102   Hofi, for one. Gordon Thomas, *Gideon's Spies: Mossad's Secret
            Warriors* (London, 1999), p. 129.
Page 103   'These people'. Peres, *Battling for Peace*, p. 155.
Page 103   So desperate . . . no reply. Author interview with Martine
            Mimouni-Arnold, op. cit.; Ben-Porat, Haber and Schiff,
            Entebbe Rescue, pp. 137–8.
Page 103   For much of the afternoon. Translation of interview with
            Michel Cojot in *Le Monde*, op. cit.
Page 104   Night was falling . . . 'with nationality'. Ibid.; Goldberg,
            Namesake, p. 117; Diary of Sara Davidson, in Ofer, *Operation
            Thunder*, p. 46.
Page 104   'special treatment'. Moufflet, *Otages à Kampala*, p. 82.
Page 104   Emma's more immediate concern. Author interview with
            Emma and Claude Rosenkovitch, Jerusalem, 22 May 2014.
Page 104   'The feeling.' Diary of Moshe Peretz in Stevenson, *90 Minutes
            at Entebbe*, p. 27.
Page 104   'the worst feeling'. Interview with Akiva Laxer, in *Live or Die in
            Entebbe*, op. cit.
Page 104   'armed and ready' . . . 'Wicked'. Diary of Sara Davidson in
            Ofer, *Operation Thunder*, pp. 46–7.
Page 105   Even those of dual nationality. Author interview with Ilan
            Hartuv, op. cit; Cipher Telegram from British Consulate-
            General in Jerusalem to FCO, 0955hrs, No. 117 of 5 July, TNA,
            FCO 93/913.
Page 105   Not everyone . . . 'menacing gestures'. Moufflet, *Otages à
            Kampala*, pp. 82 and 117.

Page 105   'It is we'. Goldberg, *Namesake*, p. 117.

Page 106   'appeared very Orthodox'. Confidential telegram from US Embassy in Paris to US Secretary of State, 2024hrs GMT, 3 July 1976, US State Department Archives, www.aad.archives.gov/aad.

Page 106   'I'm American'. Ben-Porat, Haber and Schiff, *Entebbe Rescue*, p. 145.

Page 106   'felt a certain contempt'. Interview with Claude and Emma Rosenkovitch, in Lavie, 'Surviving the myth'.

Pages 106-7   'I want you to swear' . . . embraced in tears. Ben-Porat, Haber and Schiff, *Entebbe Rescue*, p. 146.

Page 107   'The terrorists warn us'. Diary of Moshe Peretz, in Stevenson, *90 Minutes at Entebbe*, p. 27.

Page 107   'It was a terrible scene'. Testimony of Julie Oiserant [Aouzerate], in ibid., p. 39.

Page 107   Appalled by the separation. Author skype interview with Nancy Rabinowitz, op. cit.

Page 107   Claude Moufflet and others. Moufflet, *Otages à Kampala*, p. 82

Page 108   Akiva Laxer was struck. Author interview with Akiva Laxer, op. cit.

Page 108   'not just by hazard'. Moufflet, *Otages à Kampala*, pp. 82–3.

Page 108   'free movement' . . . was lost. Goldberg, *Namesake*, pp. 117–18.

Page 109   'We know' . . . been moved. Author interview with Ilan Hartuv, op. cit.

Pages 109-10   'Shimon' . . . 'including Amin'. Ben-Porat, Haber and Schiff, *Entebbe Rescue*, p. 136.

Page 110   'When it comes to negotiating'. Avner, *The Prime Ministers*, p. 308.

Pages 110-11   'Silence!' . . . permitted to leave. Moufflet, *Otages à Kampala*, pp. 83; Goldberg, *Namesake*, p. 119.

Page 111   'Put my father on the list' . . . leave him. Goldberg, *Namesake*, p. 119.

Pages 111-12   That night . . . Jewish citizens. Author telephone interview with Olivier Cojot-Goldberg, op. cit.; Goldberg, *Namesake*, p. 126; Author telephone interview with Stéphane Cojot-Goldberg, op. cit.

Page 112   He knew, of course. Author telephone interview with Olivier Cojot-Goldberg, op. cit.

Page 112   the Rabinowitzes wrote farewell letters. Rabinowitz and Rabinowitz, *Fifty-two Hundred and Ninety Minutes at Entebbe*, p. 29.

Pages 112-13   'As hijackers' . . . 'the French'. Cipher Telegram from Foreign Secretary Tony Crosland at FCO to James Horrocks, acting British high commissioner in Kampala, 1815hrs GMT, No. 99 of 29 June 1976, TNA, FCO 47/845.

Page 113   'Although the Ugandans'. Cipher Telegram from Horrocks in Kampala to Crosland at FCO, 2300hrs GMT, No. 205 of 29 June 1976, ibid.

Page 113   'If you consider it useful'. Cipher Telegram from Crosland at

FCO to Horrocks in Kampala, 2123hrs GMT, No. 100 of 29 June 1976, ibid.

Page 114 'So, gentlemen' . . . 'thousand paratroops'. Ben-Porat, Haber and Schiff, *Entebbe Rescue*, pp. 141–2; 'Rescue at Entebbe: An Interview with the Chief Pilot', op. cit.

Page 114 'What do you want?' Dunstan, *Israel's Lightning Strike*, p. 18.

Pages 114-15 It all sounded . . . 'they sounded'. Peres, *Battling for Peace*, pp. 155–6.

Page 115 'Jaco! Jaco!' Moufflet, *Otages à Kampala*, p. 86.

Page 115 'I've no strength'. Diary of Sara Davidson, in Ofer, *Operation Thunder*, p. 48.

Page 115 'broken and depressed'. Miller, 'Miracles at Entebbe', p. 143.

Day 4: Wednesday 30 June 1976

Page 117 As the hostages slept . . . Amin's air force. Williams, *The Israeli Defense Forces*, p. 128; Betser, *Secret Soldier*, p. 298.

Pages 117-18 'holes in the intelligence' . . . 'responsibility'. Betser, *Secret Soldier*, pp. 298–300.

Pages 118-19 Unofficially . . . stood trial. Charles Hornby, *Kenya: A History since Independence* (London, 2011), p. 319; Chapman Pincher, *Inside Story: A Documentary of the Pursuit of Power* (1978, this paperback edition London, 1981), pp. 353-4. The existence of this secret deal was confirmed to me by Charles Njonjo, the former attorney-general of Kenya and a member of Kenyatta's inner circle, during an interview in late 2013. Njonjo told me that he asked 'Israel to bring a plane down here, [and] put them in'. He thinks the five terrorists later 'disappeared' and that that was the right thing for Israel to do. (Author interview with Charles Njonjo, London, 23 October 2013.) In fact, after repeated inquiries by their government and parents, the Israelis admitted to holding the two West Germans – Brigitte Schulte and Thomas Reuter – who were both given ten-year prison sentences by a military tribunal in September 1979. They were released in early 1981, after serving five years, and deported from Israel. ('Two West Germans Sentenced for 1976 Plot to Shoot Down Israeli Airliner', *Jewish Telegraph Agency*, 14 September 1979, http://www.jta.org/1979/09/14/archive/two-west-germans-sentenced-for-1976-plot-to-shoot-down-israeli-airliner).

Page 119 The third plan . . . 'anybody noticing'. Betser, *Secret Soldier*, pp. 300-1.

Page 120 'They're booby-trapping' . . . 'in charge'. Ben-Porat, Haber and Schiff, *Entebbe Rescue*, pp. 158–9.

Page 120 'I've asked you here'. Peres, *Battling for Peace*, p. 157.

Page 121 'We don't manufacture Phantoms'. Clive Jones and Tore T. Petersen (eds), *Israel's Clandestine Diplomacies* (New York, 2013), pp. 144–6.

Page 121   'greatly influenced'. Peres, *Battling for Peace*, p. 157

Page 121   Bar Lev explained. Williams, *The Israeli Defense Forces*, p. 129..

Pages 121-2   The second of the three . . . 'at Entebbe'. Peres, *Battling for Peace*, pp. 157–8.

Page 122   'Amin's personal advisor'. Jones and Petersen (eds), *Israel's Clandestine Diplomacies*, p. 143.

Page 122   'close to the top'. Peres, *Battling for Peace*, 158.

Page 123   Peres had no sooner . . . 'on surprise'. Ibid., pp. 158–9.

Pages 123-4   The distinctive whump-whump . . . frustration. Moufflet, *Otages à Kampala*, p. 95; Goldberg, *Namesake*, p. 116.

Pages 124-5   'Good morning' . . . 'Goodbye'. Moufflet, *Otages à Kampala*, pp. 95–7.

Page 125   'president of Africa' . . . 'hung up to dry'. Goldberg, *Namesake*, pp. 116–17.

Page 126   captured for posterity. Moufflet, *Otages à Kampala*, p. 97.

Page 126   'massive round'. Ibid.

Page 126   'fascist Israeli government'. Diary of Moshe Peretz, in Stevenson, *90 Minutes at Entebbe*, p. 27.

Page 126   The man translating . . . Soleh Boneh. Author interview with Ilan Hartuv, op. cit.

Page 126   'repeat the terrorists'. Diary of Moshe Peretz, in Stevenson, *90 Minutes at Entebbe*, pp. 27-8.

Page 126   'You are Field Marshal' . . . 'whole building'. Author interview with Akiva Laxer, op. cit.

Pages 126-7   Once Amin had left . . . his post. Moufflet, *Otages à Kampala*, pp. 97–8.

Page 127   'Gentlemen'. 'Operation Entebbe protocols revealed', op. cit.

Page 127   'Mr Prime Minister'. Ben-Porat, Haber and Schiff, *Entebbe Rescue*, p. 163.

Page 128   'We know' . . . 'pressure on us'. 'Operation Entebbe protocols revealed', op. cit.

Page 128   'Gentlemen'. Ben-Porat, Haber and Schiff, *Entebbe Rescue*, p. 165.

Pages 128-9   'The only danger' . . . 'possible minimum'. Ibid., pp. 165–6.

Pages 129-30   'second hand' . . . 'medical attention'. Cipher Telegram from British High Commission in Kampala to FCO, 0930hrs GMT, No. 208 of 30 June 1976, TNA, FCO 47/845.

Pages 131-2   'Silence!' . . . herded before her. Moufflet, *Otages à Kampala*, pp. 100–1.

Page 132   'Hey, hold on'. Author telephone interview with Olivier Cojot-Goldberg, op. cit.

Page 132   'Papa'. Goldberg, *Namesake*, p. 119.

Page 132   'deliberate sign' . . . 'admirable attitude'. Moufflet, *Otages à Kampala*, p. 101.

Page 132   The father. Ibid.; Goldberg, *Namesake*, p. 119.

Pages 132-3   As the growing crowd . . . forty-seven. 'Moufflet, *Otages à Kampala*, p. 102.

Page 133   'It was soon clear'. Diary of Julie Oiserant [Aouzerate], in Stevenson, *90 Minutes at Entebbe*, p. 39.

Page 133 It included . . . 'stateless'. 'Freed Hostages Tell their Story', *Jewish Telegraphic Agency*, 1 July 1976; Cipher telegram from British High Commission in Kampala to FCO, 1300hrs GMT, No. 211 of 30 June 1976, TNA, FCO 47/485.

Page 133 Once all forty-seven . . . sedation. Moufflet, *Otages à Kampala*, p. 102.

Page 133 'alone and free'. Goldberg, *Namesake*, p. 120.

Pages 133-4 'I called this meeting' . . . 'lots of secrets'. 'Operation Entebbe protocols revealed', op. cit.

Page 134 'What progress'. Ibid.

Page 134 'Anything workable' . . . 'nothing firm yet'. Ben-Porat, Haber and Schiff, *Entebbe Rescue*, p. 166.

Pages 134-5 Now more certain . . . 'catastrophe'. 'Operation Entebbe protocols revealed', op. cit.

Pages 135-7 'Mr President' . . . 'save these people'. Transcript of first phone conversation between Bar-Lev and Amin on 30 June 1976, in Stevenson, *90 Minutes at Entebbe*, pp. 209–11, Ofer, *Operation Thunder*, pp. 62–4, and Ben-Porat, Haber and Schiff, *Entebbe Rescue*, pp. 167–8.

Page 137 'most vulnerable' . . . 'wagging'. Goldberg, *Namesake*, p. 120.

Page 137 'various options'. Diary of Moshe Peretz, in Stevenson, *90 Minutes at Entebbe*, p. 28.

Pages 137-8 'the Yachtsman' . . . 'at the time'. Goldberg, *Namesake*, pp. 120–1.

Page 138 'We have not made' . . . peaceful solution. Diary of a Government Spokesman, 30 June 1976, in Stevenson, *90 Minutes at Entebbe*, p. 29

Pages 138-9 Avineri was called in . . . 'in Mauritius'. Ben-Porat, Haber and Schiff, *Entebbe Rescue*, pp. 174–5.

Page 139 Faiz Jaber . . . kicked and punched. Ibid., pp. 171–2; Author interview with Ilan Hartuv, op. cit.; Interview with Nahum Dahan, in *Live or Die in Entebbe*, op. cit.

Pages 139-40 After what seemed . . . 'we're satisfied'. Moufflet, *Otages à Kampala*, p. 117; *New York Times*, 11 July 1976; Author interview with Ilan Hartuv, op. cit.; Interview with Nahum Dahan, in *Live or Die in Entebbe*, op. cit.

Page 140 'collect together' . . . 'troops in Entebbe'. Section 5: Actions at the General Staff Level, Chapter B, 'Operation Yonatan', op. cit.

Page 141 'We're leaving tonight'. Iddo Netanyahu, *Entebbe*, p. 22.

Page 141 'stealing across' . . . 'something will go wrong'. Betser, *Secret Soldier*, p. 303.

Page 141 'Listen' . . . 'keeping you posted'. Netanyahu, *Entebbe*, p. 22.

Pages 141-2 'gesture of goodwill' . . . 'Gandhi see you'. Betser, *Secret Soldier*, pp. 303–5.

Pages 142-3 'A contact' . . . 'the Israelis'. Confidential Memorandum from David Colvin, British Embassy in Paris, to Frank Wheeler, Head of the Near East and North African Department at FCO, 30 June 1976, TNA, FCO 93/913.

Pages 143-4 'We have to formulate' . . . own hands. Ben-Porat, Haber and Schiff, *Entebbe Rescue*, pp. 174.

Page 144 Faiz Jaber . . . 'until you do'. *New York Times*, 11 July 1976.

Page 145 'There is no way out' . . . 'abomination'. Ben-Porat, Haber and Schiff, *Entebbe Rescue*, pp. 176–7.

Pages 145-6 'There is going to be' . . . 'relatives could apply'. 'Operation Entebbe protocols revealed', op. cit.

Pages 146-7 Following his meeting . . . 9 p.m. Section 5: Actions at the General Staff Level, Chapter B, 'Operation Yonatan', op. cit.

Page 147 There were three men present . . . 'dud of a plan'. Dunstan, *Israel's Lightning Strike*, pp. 20–1.

Page 147 'operational concept' . . . 200 hostages. Netanyahu, *Entebbe*, pp. 23-4; Section 5: Actions at the General Staff Level, Chaoter B, 'Operation Yonatan', op. cit.

Pages 148-9 'Motta, do we have' . . . 'meet at eight-thirty'. Ben-Porat, Haber and Schiff, *Entebbe Rescue*, pp. 178–80.

Page 149 'difficult' . . . hurling insults. Diary of a Government Spokesman, 30 June 1976, in Stevenson, *90 Minutes at Entebbe*, p. 29; Author telephone interview with Amos Eiran, 9 October 2013.

Pages 149-50 Earlier . . . own government. Ofer, *Operation Thunder*, pp. 55–6.

Pages 150-151 The arrival . . . went to sleep. Moufflet, *Otages à Kampala*, pp. 111–12.

Pages 151-3 'I've passed on your advice' . . . 'good night, sir'. Transcript of the second phone conversation between Bar-Lev and Amin, 2305hrs, 30 June 1976, in Stevenson, *90 Minutes at Entebbe*, pp. 211–13, and Ofer, *Operation Thunder*, pp. 64–7.

Page 153 Peres nodded. Peres, *Battling for Peace*, p. 159.

Page 154 Olivier Cojot. Author telephone interview with Olivier Cojot-Goldberg, op. cit.

Page 155 'Ladies and gentlemen' . . . 'the affair'. Ben-Porat, Haber and Schiff, *Entebbe Rescue*, pp. 177–8.

Page 155 'veteran officer'. Betser, *Secret Soldier*, p. 306.

Page 155 Olivier was interviewed . . . 'there's no question'. Ibid.

Page 156 Interviewed later . . . 'show up'. Betser, *Secret Soldier*, p. 306.

Pages 156-7 'articulate and well-educated' . . . she was safe. Cipher telegram from Ambassador Kenneth Rush to US Secretary of State (repeated London and other US embassies), 0245hrs GMT, 1 July 1976, TNA, FCO 93/913/8 and 9. The reason why Dr Bass was keeping such a low profile, according to his fellow hostage Ilan Hartuv, was that the doctor feared the consequences if the hijackers discovered he was also a medical officer in the IDF Reserves. He was travelling on a US passport but had also handed in, at a separate point, his military identity card. (Author interview with Ilan Hartuv, op. cit.)

Pages 157-8 As Ivan Oren . . . 'Yes, sir.' Section 5: Actions at the General Staff Level, Chapter B, 'Operation Yonatan', op. cit.; Netanyahu, *Entebbe*, p. 25.

Pages 158-9 'most important post' . . . 'Israeli cabinet'. Henry Kissinger, *Years of Renewal: The Concluding Volume of his Memoirs* (New York, 1999), p. 447.

Pages 159-60   'Hello' . . . 'Okay, Bye.' Teleconversation between Ambassador Dinitz and Secretary of State Kissinger, 6.40 p.m, 30 June 1976, Declassified US State Department Archives, SI 419, released 28 July 2003, 200102979, aad. archives.gov/aad.

Page 160   Unbeknown . . . come to nothing. Cipher telegrams from Herman Eilts, US Ambassador to Egypt, to US Secretary of State, 1424hrs GMT, 6 July 1976 and 1826hrs, 9 July 1976, Declassified US State Department Archives, Review 04 May 2006, aad.archives.gov/aad.

Day 5: Thursday 1 July 1976

Page 161   Claude Moufflet . . . The men laughed. Moufflet, *Otages à Kampala*, pp. 112–13.

Page 162   'Prime Minister' . . . 'arrive in boxes'. Author telephone interview with Amos Eiran, op. cit.

Pages 162-3   Breakfast arrived . . . good spirits. Moufflet, *Otages à Kampala*, pp. 114–16.

Pages 163-4   'Gentlemen' . . . 'imminent danger'. Avner, *The Prime Ministers*, pp. 308–9.

Pages 164-5   'There is an alternative' . . . Peres followed suit. Peres, *Battling for Peace*, pp. 159–60.

Pages 165-6   'Wake up!' . . . 'live or die?' Author interview with Ilan Hartuv, op. cit.; Interview with Nahum Dahan, in *Live or Die in Entebbe*, op. cit.

Page 166   'Does anyone' . . . 'Arab in "type"'. Goldberg, *Namesake*, p. 118.

Pages 166-7   'Your attitude' . . . pieces of pineapple. Moufflet, *Otages à Kampala*, pp. 117–18; *New York Times*, 11 July 1976; Author interview with Ilan Hartuv, op. cit.; Interview with Nahum Dahan, in *Live or Die in Entebbe*, op. cit.

Page 167   'The IDF'. Rabin, *The Rabin Memoirs*, p. 284.

Pages 168-70   'Yes, Prime Minister' . . . 'Thank you'. 'Operation Entebbe Protocols revealed', op. cit.

Page 170   'Could I just add'. Williams, *The Israel Defense Forces*, p. 132.

Pages 170-71   'So be it' . . . 'measure of relief'. Avner, *The Prime Ministers*, pp. 310–11; Rabin, *The Rabin Memoirs*, p. 285.

Page 171   Once Likud . . . reservations. Diary of a Government Spokesman, 1 July 1976, in Stevenson, *90 Minutes at Entebbe*, p. 31.

Page 171   'It seems'. Avner, *The Prime Ministers*, p. 311.

Pages 171-3   One of them . . . 'few hostages'. Moufflet, *Otages à Kampala*, pp. 119– 22.

Page 173   'fake identities' . . . 'flying out'. Betser, *Secret Soldier*, p. 306.

Page 174   'too limited' . . . 'to Israel'. Section 5: Actions at the General Staff Level, Chapter B, 'Operation Yonatan', op. cit.

Page 174   'dropping everything' ... 'down to details'. Betser, *Secret Soldier*, p. 307.

Pages 175-7   'Inform your government' . . . 'and activity'. Transcript of the third phone conversation between Bar-Lev and Amin, 1000hrs, 1 July 1976, in Stevenson, *90 Minutes at Entebbe*, pp. 213–15.

Page 177   'I've some very important' . . . back in. Moufflet, *Otages à Kampala*, p. 123.

Page 177   'Not the crew!' Goldberg, *Namesake*, p. 121.

Pages 177-78   'Could you bring' . . . their suitcases. Moufflet, *Otages à Kampala*, p. 123-4.

Page 178   A former go-go dancer. Kyemba, *A State of Blood*, pp. 149–63.

Pages 178-9   'Hello. Good Morning' . . . 'Good luck'. Moufflet, *Otages à Kampala*, pp. 123–5; Goldberg, *Namesake*, p. 121.

Page 179   'because of the obstinacy'. Diary of Moshe Peretz, in Stevenson, *90 Minutes at Entebbe*, p. 40.

Page 179   What he did not mention . . . that happened. Kyemba, *A State of Blood*, p. 169.

Page 179   'There is an air'. Diary of Moshe Peretz, in Stevenson, *90 Minutes at Entebbe*, p. 40.

Page 180   'gnawed by a supercharged' . . . 'before then'. Avner, *The Prime Ministers*, p. 311.

Pages 180-181   'I want everyone' . . . 'bus outside'. Moufflet, *Otages à Kampala*, p. 125.

Page 181   Cojot took over. Goldberg, *Namesake*, p. 121.

Page 181   Of the first sixty-three. Cipher cable from US Ambassador in Paris to US Secretary of State, 1818hrs GMT, 03 July 1976, Declassified US State Department Archives, 04 May 2006, 654775, aad.archives.gov/aad.

Page 181   As the young Canadians. Moufflet, *Otages à Kampala*, p. 125.

Page 181   Sanford Freeman . . . box of medicines. Author interview with Emma and Claude Rosenkovitch, op. cit.

Page 181   'very much afraid'. Goldberg, *Namesake*, p. 121.

Pages 181-2   One by one . . . 'almost absolute'. Moufflet, *Otages à Kampala*, pp. 125–7.

Page 182   'mistake had been made' . . . 'having company'. Rabinowitz and Rabinowitz, 'Fifty-two Hundred and Ninety Minutes at Entebbe', p. 29.

Page 182   More names were called. Moufflet, *Otages à Kampala*, p. 127.

Page 183   Cojot, meanwhile. Goldberg, *Namesake*, pp. 124–5.

Page 183   'Let me go' . . . 'Palestinian camps'. Moufflet, *Otages à Kampala*, p. 128.

Page 183   'You have been so useful' . . . Franco-Jewish glory. Goldberg, *Namesake*, pp. 122–4.

Pages 183-184   'the Supreme Court' . . . 'had to kill'. Ibid., pp. 52–4.

Page 184   With the full consent . . . 'powerful reasons'. Ibid., pp. 58–78.

Pages 184-5   'a stool by the Righteous' . . . last visit to the Israelis. Ibid., pp. 125–7.

Page 185   'No, you must go' . . . he had to leave. Author interview with Ilan Hartuv, op. cit.

Page 185   'Because'. Goldberg, *Namesake*, pp. 127–8.

Page 185   Returning to the main hall . . . 'Jewish or not'. Ibid., pp. 123–4.

Captain Michel Bacot later claimed in an interview with the *Jewish Chronicle* that he and the crew had had the option to leave and had not taken it. 'When I was being held hostage and had the possibility of being released,' he said, 'I called the crew together and said: "We have to remain with the passengers until the end – that is our duty." It was an immediate, unhesitating decision. Every member of the crew agreed with me . . . It was, simply put, the right thing to do.' (Jeremy Josephs, 'Michel Bacos: The Air France hero of Entebbe', *Jewish Chronicle*, 15 June 2012.)

Pages 185-6	'Are you an Iranian?' . . . their friends. Moufflet, *Otages à Kampala*, pp. 128–9.
Page 186	'What were they doing there?' Rabinowitz and Rabinowitz, 'Fifty-two Hundred and Ninety Minutes at Entebbe', op. cit., p. 29.
Page 187	All this time . . . abandoning the others. Moufflet, *Otages à Kampala*, pp. 129–30.
Pages 187-8	Yehuda Avner . . . 'show me in the morning'. Avner, *The Prime Ministers*, pp. 311–12.
Page 188	Peres's scheme . . . 'rescue plan'. Peres, *Battling for Peace*, p. 160.
Page 188	'the blackmailer's hand'. Rabin, *The Rabin Memoirs*, p. 285.
Page 188	'to procure more'. Peres, *Battling for Peace*, p. 160.
Pages 188-9	As Cojot, Moufflet . . . 'good journey'. Moufflet, *Otages à Kampala*, p. 129.
Page 189	'regained their tourist'. Goldberg, *Namesake*, p. 127.
Page 189	Moufflet did not have . . . 'not really anything'. Moufflet, *Otages à Kampala*, p. 139.
Pages 189-90	Horrocks, meanwhile . . . 'on this point'. Cipher telegram from British High Commission to FCO, 0830hrs GMT, No. 217 of 2 July 1976, TNA, FCO 31/2054.
Page 190	'You're moving!' . . . 'others left'. Ben-Porat, Haber and Schiff, *Entebbe Rescue*, p. 224.
Page 190	Reunited . . . 'still here?' Moufflet, *Otages à Kampala*, p. 133
Pages 190-191	With enough mattresses . . . demeanour had not changed'. Ibid., pp. 140–1.
Pages 192-3	'on the compromise' . . . security leak. Betser, *Secret Soldier*, pp. 307–9.
Page 193	'to determine the method'. Section 5: Actions at the General Staff Level, Chapter B, 'Operation Yonatan, op. cit.
Page 193	A tall, impressive man . . . Egyptian tanks. 'The 25 Most Intriguing People of 1976', *People*, 27 December 1976–3 January 1977.
Page 193-4	'Dan' . . . 'Let's go'. Betser, *Secret Soldier*, pp. 310–12.
Page 195	Maggy was undressing . . . others laughed. Moufflet, *Otages à Kampala*, p. 141.
Page 195	'as if they were'. Miller, 'Miracles at Entebbe', p. 144.
Page 195	'born anew' . . . 'giving in'. Ben-Porat, Haber and Schiff, *Entebbe Rescue*, p. 224; Stevenson, *90 Minutes at Entebbe*, pp. 40–1.
Page 195	Talking among themselves . . . exchange of prisoners. Moufflet, *Otages à Kampala*, p. 141.

Page 196   'a day or two'. Miller, 'Miracles at Entebbe', p. 144.

Pages 196-7   'I am rather astonished' . . . agreed Kissinger. Teleconversation
                  between Secretary of State Kissinger and Ambassador Dinitz,
                  10.05 a.m. (local time), 1 July 1976, Declassified US State
                  Department Archives, SJ6, released 9 May 2005, 200102979,
                  aad.archives.gov/aad.

Pages 197-8   Two planes . . . 'journey with us'. Moufflet, *Otages à Kampala*,
                  pp. 133-4.

Page 198   'certain New Zealand' . . . 'hostages embarked'. Cipher telegram
                  from British High Commission to FCO, 0830hrs GMT, No. 217
                  of 2 July 1976, op. cit.

Page 198   'working with the hijackers' . . . certainly baseless. Cipher tele-
                  gram from the US Ambassador to France to the US Secretary
                  of State, 2045hrs GMT, 3 July 1976, Paris 19568, Declassified US
                  State Department Archives, 4 May 2006, www.wikileaks.org/
                  plusd/cables/1976PARIS19568_b.html.

Page 198   'one of us had concealed'. Goldberg, *Namesake*, p. 127.

Pages 198-9   'really kind' . . . control tower. Moufflet, *Otages à Kampala*, pp.
                  134–5.

Page 199   'We must ask ourselves' . . . 'not rely on the French'. 'Operation
                  Entebbe protocols revealed', op. cit.

Page 200   'Can you present the plan' . . . 'what you told him'. Betser,
                  Secret Soldier, pp. 309–13; Section 5: Actions at the General
                  Staff Level, Chapter B, 'Operation Yonatan', op. cit.

Pages 200-1   'Any dissenters?' . . . 'Bay of Pigs'. Section 5: Actions at the
                  General Staff Level, Chapter B, 'Operation Yonatan', op. cit.,
                  Para 18; Peres, *Battling for Peace*, p. 160.

Page 201   'Wave of Ash' . . . good omen. Tali Lipkin-Shakhak, 'The
                  Forgotten Hero of Entebbe', *Ma'ariv* Saturday supplement, 16
                  June 2006.

Pages 201-2   'Without you' . . . 'wake up at last'. Goldberg, *Namesake*, pp.
                  127–8.

Pages 202-3   It was dark . . . buzz of mosquitoes. Moufflet, *Otages à
                  Kampala*, pp. 144–5.

Page 203   At 8.30 p.m. . . . Bruce McKenzie. Author interview with
                  Charles Njonjo, op. cit.; author telephone interview with Dany
                  Saadon, 16 December 2013.

Page 204   great improvement. Email to the author from Bruce
                  McKenzie's younger son, 24 November 2014.

Page 204   McKenzie was close . . . 'flowing both ways'. Author interview
                  with Christina McKenzie, Haselbech, Northants, 5 July 2013.

Page 204   'talked with many'. Chapman Pincher, *Dangerous to Know: A
                  Life* (London 2014), p. 99.

Page 205   'the most influential'. David Hebditch and Ken Connor, *How
                  to Stage a Military Coup: From Planning to Execution* (London,
                  2005), p. 128.

Page 205   'chief confidant' . . . 'usurp him'. Pincher, *Dangerous to Know*,
                  p. 99.

Page 205   'like a son'. Author interview with Christina McKenzie, op. cit.

Page 205	'planning something' . . . happy to help. Author interviews with Dany Saadon and Charles Njonjo, op. cit.
Page 205	They still owed the Mossad . . . Uganda. Pincher, *Inside Story*, p. 354.
Page 205	and, crucially. 'John Kamau, 'How Mossad threw Kenya into the line of terrorist fire', *Daily Nation*, 17 January 2014.
Pages 205-6	They had not yet discussed . . . hospital treatment. Author interviews with Dany Saadon and Charles Njonjo, op. cit.
Pages 206-7	When Muki Betser . . . calm professionalism. Betser, *Secret Soldier*, pp. 313–15; Lipkin-Shakhak, 'The Forgotten Hero of Entebbe'.
Pages 208-9	At 9 p.m. . . . 'I'm with you'. Peres, *Battling for Peace*, pp. 160–1; Ben-Porat, Haber and Schiff, *Entebbe Rescue*, pp. 243–4.
Pages 209-10	'We will now' . . . 'military rescue'. Peres, *Battling for Peace*, pp. 161–2; Ben-Porat, Haber and Schiff, *Entebbe Rescue*, p. 244.
Pages 211-12	'C'mon Muki' . . . break-ins. Betser, *Secret Soldier*, pp. 314–17.
Page 212	'I don't see any alternative'. Netanyahu, *Entebbe*, p. 48.
Page 212	Noam Tamir . . . no fear. Author interview with Noam Tamir, London, 15 October 2013.
Pages 212-3	Ephraim Sneh . . . combat troops. Author interview with Ephraim Sneh, Herzliya, Israel, 22 May 2014.
Pages 213-4	Jossy Faktor . . . 'teams and blood'. David E. Kaplan, 'A historic hostage-taking revisited', *Jerusalem Post*, 3 August 2006, http://www.jpost.com/Features/A-historic-hostage-taking-revisited.
Page 214	'A hundred shitting' . . . 'overcome and prevail'. Author interview with Ephraim Sneh, op. cit.
Page 214	'Are we going far?' . . . their lives'. Netanyahu, *Entebbe*, p. 57.
Page 214-5	Tormented . . . could he sleep. 'Entebbe Thirty Years On: Through the Army's Eyes', *Jewish Telegraph Online*, 2006, www.jewishtelegraph.com/enteb_1.html.
Page 215	'Motta' . . . 'hardest of my life'. Peres, *Battling for Peace*, p. 162; Ben-Porat, Haber and Schiff, *Entebbe Rescue*, p. 245.

Day 6: Friday 2 July 1976

Page 217	A spontaneous cheer . . . previous Sunday. Moufflet, *Otages à Kampala*, p. 135.
Page 218	'I'm so relieved'. *Daily Express*, 2 July 1976.
Page 218	'future ex-wife' . . . hours later. Goldberg, *Namesake*, p. 131.
Page 218	The official . . . former hostages. Author interview with Stéphane Cojot-Goldberg, Paris, 16 January 2 015.
Page 218	He told the Israelis . . . separate rooms. Goldberg, *Namesake*, p. 131.
Page 218	Most of the Americans . . . city centre. Cipher cable from US Ambassador in Paris to US Secretary of State, 0441hrs GMT, 02 July 1976, Paris 19371, Declassified US State Department Archives, 04 May 2006, www.archives.gov/aad.
Pages 218-9	'We were expecting' . . . 'diplomatic joke'. Author skype interviews with Nancy and Peter Rabinowitz, op. cit.; Rabinowitz and Rabinowitz, 'Fifty-two Hundred and Ninety Minutes at Entebbe', p. 29.

Pages 219-21	Later that day . . . 'infirm to break'. Cipher cable from US Ambassador in Paris to US Secretary of State, 2045hrs GMT, 3 July 1976, Paris 19568, op. cit.
Page 221	Yoni Netanyahu . . . saying a word. Hastings, *Yoni*, pp. 222-3.
Page 222	'I know I'm not with you'. Netanyahu, *Entebbe*, 48; Hastings, *Yoni*, pp. 217-18.
Page 222	It was still dark . . . Uganda. Moufflet, *Otages à Kampala*, p. 145.
Page 222	'Everybody's possessions'. Diary of Moshe Peretz, in Stevenson, *90 Minutes at Entebbe*, p. 65.
Page 222	'land on its soil'. Peres, *Battling for Peace*, p. 162.
Pages 223-4	'much to be preferred' . . . shook his head. Ibid., pp. 162–3.
Pages 224-5	The hostages . . . reach an agreement. Moufflet, *Otages à Kampala*, p. 145; Diary of Moshe Peretz, in Stevenson, *90 Minutes at Entebbe*, p. 65.
Page 225	'most of the family men'. Diary of Moshe Peretz, in Stevenson, *90 Minutes at Entebbe*, p. 65.
Page 225	'our spirit is not broken'. *New York Times*, 11 July 1976.
Page 225	'Look'. Author interview with Ilan Hartuv, op. cit.
Page 225	'We, all the Israelis'. 'Appeal by the Hostages to the Israeli Government', broadcast on the Kampala home service, 1400hrs GMT, 3 July 1976, in TNA, FCO 31/2055.
Pages 225-6	'It's not what we asked' . . . 'best we can do'. Author interview with Ilan Hartuv, op. cit.
Page 226	It was not broadcast'. 'Appeal by the Hostages to the Israeli Government', op. cit.
Pages 226-7	Sergeant Amir . . . drills began. 'Entebbe Thirty Years On: Through the Army's Eyes', op. cit.; Netanyahu, *Entebbe*, pp. 57–8.
Page 227	'warning orders' . . . redundant. Netanyahu, *Entebbe*, pp. 58–9.
Pages 227-8	'Could everyone' . . . 'It's the wind'. Moufflet, *Otages à Kampala*, pp. 146–7.
Page 228	'The question' . . . 'plan'. Ben-Porat, Haber and Schiff, *Entebbe Rescue*, pp. 253–4.
Pages 229-30	'firm ally' . . . 'on the ground'. Peres, *Battling for Peace*, pp. 163–4; Netanyahu, *Entebbe*, p. 65.
Page 230	'could consider' . . . with explosives. Rabin, *The Rabin Memoirs*, pp. 285-6.
Page 230	'supreme importance'. Peres, *Battling for Peace*, p. 164.
Page 231	'So it's a flight' . . . in Tel Aviv. 'Operation Entebbe protocols revealed', op. cit.
Page 231	'There are'. Peres, *Battling for Peace*, p. 164.
Pages 231-2	'Would you be interested' . . . continued writing. Pincher, *Inside Story*, p. 351.
Pages 232-3	'I actually noticed' . . . 'too worried'. Debrief of Mr Russell and Mr Good, op. cit.
Page 234	Livneh began . . . garrison of troops. Netanyahu, *Entebbe*, pp. 66–7.
Pages 234-5	As Livneh left . . . 'it can fail'. Interview with Ehud Barak, in

Live or Die in Entebbe, op. cit.; Author interview with Ephraim Sneh, op. cit.

Pages 235-6   'Some of the assault teams' . . . 'It can be done'. Netanyahu, *Entebbe*, pp. 70–1.

Page 236   The usual lunch. Moufflet, *Otages à Kampala*, p. 148.

Page 236   'that no one is left'. Diary of Moshe Peretz, in Stevenson, *90 Minutes at Entebbe*, pp. 65–6.

Page 236   'What is it mother?' . . . 'stay here'. Ben-Porat, Haber and Schiff, *Entebbe Rescue*, p. 278; Author interview with Ilan Hartuv, op. cit.; *New York Times*, 11 July 1976.

Page 237   'easily removed'. Kyemba, *A State of Blood*, p. 170.

Pages 237-8   'Ehud's gone' . . . if necessary. Netanyahu, *Entebbe*, pp. 73–4.

Page 238   'It needs a lot of work'. Betser, *Secret Soldier*, p. 317.

Page 238   Dagan began work. Netanyahu, *Entebbe*, pp. 75–7.

Page 238   'When the Ugandans'. Betser, *Secret Soldier*, pp. 317–18.

Page 239   'Begin' . . . 'dramatic day'. Operation Entebbe protocols revealed', op. cit.

Page 240   'Amin on behalf''. Cipher telegram from P. E. Rosling at FCO to British High Commission in Kampala, 2 July 1976, TNA, FCO 93/913/15.

Page 240   'In the event'. Confidential letter from David Goodall, Head of Western European Department at FCO, to Roger Westbrook, Private Secretary to Minister of State at FCO, 2 July 1976, TNA, FCO 93/913/7 and 8.

Pages 240-1   'should read a common' . . . 'freedom of manoeuvre'. Confidential letter from Julian Bullard, Minister at British Embassy in Bonn, to David Goodall at FCO, 7 July 1976, TNA, FCO 31/2056; 'Bonn won't climb down: Terrorists stay imprisoned', *Die Welt*, 1 July 1976, BStU Archive [Federal Commissioner for the Stasi Records], Berlin, Mfs/HA IX/9979; 'Between Bonn and Entebbe', *Frankfurter Rundschau*, 6 July 1976.

Page 242   'Don't worry' . . . total darkness. Netanyahu, *Entebbe*, pp. 77–9.

Pages 242-4   'I told you' . . . joke was about. Moufflet, *Otages à Kampala*, pp. 148–50.

Page 244   'Good news' . . . prisoners and keepers. Ibid., pp. 150–1.

Pages 245-6   'Do it again' . . . 'keep it to yourself'. Netanyahu, *Entebbe*, pp. 88–90.

Page 246   Mike Harari. Yossi Melman, 'Legendary Mossad operative behind some of spy agency's most daring operations dies at 87', *Jerusalem Post*, 22 September 2014.

Pages 246-8   The exact terms . . . icing on the cake. Author interviews with Dany Saadon and Charles Njonjo, op. cit.

Pages 248-9   'Shabbat Shalom' . . . Peres was silent. Peres, *Battling for Peace*, pp. 164–5.

Page 250   'very mysterious' . . . 'off the telephone'. Pincher, *Inside Story*, p. 351.

Pages 250-51   As the evening wore on . . . not working. Moufflet, *Otages à Kampala*, pp. 151-2.

Page 251   As the hostages . . . 'of my life'. Miller, 'Miracles at Entebbe', pp. 146–7; Interview with Ruthie Gross, in *Live or Die in Entebbe*, op. cit.
Pages 251-2 'There's just one problem' . . . 'the APCs will'. Netanyahu, *Entebbe*, p. 92.
Page 252   With the briefing over . . . two jeeps. 'Entebbe Thirty Years On: Through the Army's Eyes', op. cit.
Pages 252-3 'The one thing' . . . 'first plane'. Hastings, *Yoni*, p. 224; 'Entebbe Thirty Years On: Through the Army's Eyes', op. cit.
Page 253   'very bad'. Dunstan, *Israel's Lightning Strike*, p. 32.
Pages 253-4 The final officer . . . 'well done'. Netanyahu, *Entebbe*, pp. 94-6; Hastings, *Yoni*, p. 224.
Page 254   It was after midnight . . . the hostages. Hastings, *Yoni*, p. 225.
Page 254-5 The men . . . biggest failure. Netanyahu, *Entebbe*, pp. 100–2.
Page 255   'In a real rehearsal'. Dunstan, *Israel's Lightning Strike*, p. 32.
Pages 255-6 'The top brass' . . . potential for disaster. Netanyahu, *Entebbe*, pp. 97–100.
Page 256   Peres picked up . . . in the morning. Peres, *Battling for Peace*, p. 165.

Day 7: Saturday 3 July 1976

Page 257   'I bet you haven't eaten' . . . was asleep. Hastings, *Yoni*, p. 225.
Pages 257-8 'I feel terrible' . . . 'I don't think so'. Moufflet, *Otages à Kampala*, p. 153.
Page 258   Also stricken . . . 'around him'. *New York Times*, 11 July 1976.
Pages 258-9 In the large hall . . . Uganda that day. Moufflet, *Otages à Kampala*, pp. 153–4; Author telephone interview with Gerd Schnepel, op. cit.
Pages 259-60 Amos Eiran . . . 'can go wrong'. Author telephone interview with Amos Eiran, op. cit.
Pages 260-1 Israeli Ambassador . . . left the building. Author interview with Uri Lubrani, Tel Aviv, 9 October 2013.
Pages 261-2 Retrieving . . . the real reason. Pincher, *Inside Story*, p. 352; *Daily Express*, 3 July 1976.
Page 262   'I'm late' . . . driving away. Hastings, *Yoni*, pp. 222-3; Netanyahu, *Entebbe*, p. 123.
Page 263   'Motta' . . . 11.20 a.m. Peres, *Battling for Peace*, pp. 165–6.
Pages 264-5 Health Minister . . . 'airport hall'. Kyemba, *A State of Blood*, pp. 170–1.
Pages 265-6 'You've got to tell him' . . . 'excellent meeting'. Netanyahu, *Entebbe*, pp. 124–6.
Page 266   For thirty minutes . . . 'approve the plan'. Ben-Porat, Haber and Schiff, *Entebbe Rescue*, p. 288; Rabin, *The Rabin Memoirs*, p. 286.
Page 266   'Prime Minister' . . . 'an alternative'. Peres, *Battling for Peace*, p. 166.
Page 267   'It is Israel' . . . operation was one. Ibid., p. 166; Williams, *The Israeli Defense Forces*, p. 137.
Pages 267-8 For the sick . . . depressing day. Moufflet, *Otages à Kampala*, p. 155.

Pages 268-9   'What I'm about to say' . . . 'heavy cost'. Avner, *The Prime Ministers*, p. 312; Rabin, *The Rabin Memoirs*, p. 287.

Page 269   'I wholeheartedly'. 'Operation Entebbe Protocols revealed', op. cit.

Pages 269-70   'stealth, caution' . . . their decision. Avner, *The Prime Ministers*, p. 313; *The Rabin Memoirs*, p. 287; 'Operation Entebbe Protocols revealed', op. cit.; Peres, *Battling for Peace*, p. 166.

Page 270   'full webbing' . . . 'holiday jaunt'. Peres, *Battling for Peace*, p. 166.

Page 271   'It's for Brigadier' . . . 'in view'. Betser, *Secret Soldier*, pp. 320–1.

Page 271   included images . . . Old Terminal. Secret Entebbe Photos and Maps in the possession of Dr Colonel (Retd) Zeev Drory.

Page 271   Earlier verbal. Netanyahu, *Entebbe*, p. 132.

Page 271   severe turbulence. Ibid., p. 133.

Page 271   Amir Ofer. 'Entebbe Thirty Years On: Through the Army's Eyes', op. cit.

Page 271   'worst of them'. Netanyahu, *Entebbe*, p. 133.

Page 272   After an hour . . . during the flight. Ibid., p. 134.

Page 272   'You have put us' . . . 'military option'. Rabin, *The Rabin Memoirs*, p. 287.

Page 273   'Mr Prime Minister'. Avner, *The Prime Ministers*, p. 313.

Page 273   'Thank you' . . . go ahead. 'Operation Entebbe Protocols revealed', op. cit.; Hastings, *Yoni*, p. 226.

Page 273   'I've just received'. Avner, *The Prime Ministers*, p. 313.

Pages 273-4   Pilot Joshua Shani . . . all was well. 'Rescue at Entebbe: An Interview with the Chief Pilot', op. cit.

Page 274   As during . . . stop at Ofira. Netanyahu, *Entebbe*, pp. 147–8.

Page 274   'planning the rescue' . . . Bester, *Secret Soldier*, p. 324.

Page 275   Netanyahu pulled . . . 'tonight, eh?' Hastings, *Yoni*, p. 3.

Page 275   All around . . . inches of his limbs. Netanyahu, *Entebbe*, p. 153.

Pages 275-6   'Well' . . . 'Gandhi will kill me'. Ben-Porat, Haber and Schiff, *Entebbe Rescue*, pp. 293–4.

Page 276   'Every detail'. Rabin, *The Rabin Memoirs*, p. 288.

Page 277   'If he's there' . . . fell asleep. Netanyahu, *Entebbe*, pp. 150–3.

Pages 277-9   Uri Lubrani . . . make any difference? Author interview with Uri Lubrani, op. cit.

Pages 279-80   'Shimon' . . . an hour later. Peres, *Battling for Peace*, p. 167; Appendix A: Timeline, 'Operation Yonatan', op. cit.

Pages 280-1   'Israel crisis committee' . . . 'no alternatives'. Cipher cable from the German Embassy in Tel Aviv to the Federal Foreign Ministry in Bonn, 1100hrs GMT, No. 438 of 4 July 1976, Politisches Archiv of the Auswärtiges Amt (Political Archive of the Federal Foreign Office), Berlin, 530.35vs-nfd/108233.

Page 281   'criminals'. Confidential letter from Julian Bullard, Minister at British Embassy in Bonn, to David Goodall, Head of Western European Department at FCO, 7 July 1976, TNA, FCO 31/2056.

Pages 281-2   'Shalom!' . . . good omen. Moufflet, *Otages à Kampala*, p. 156.

Page 282   'laboriously decoded'. Susan Crosland, *Tony Crosland* (1982), pp. 344–5.

Pages 282-3	'cool heads' . . . 'suggesting action'. Cipher cable from Anthony Crosland to the British Embassy in Paris, 1833hrs GMT, No. 344 of 3 July 1976, TNA, FCO 31/2055.
Page 283	Wadie Haddad. Author interview with Gerd Schnepel, op. cit.
Page 283	'It's the president' . . . 'I will see to it'. Kyemba, *A State of Blood*, pp. 170–1.
Page 284	'very satisfied air' . . . neon lights. Moufflet, *Otages à Kampala*, pp. 157–9.
Page 284	'sitting just outside'. Alvin Shuster, 'It's O.K., You're Going Home', *New York Times*, 5 July 1976.
Page 285	The first . . . in the morning. Appendix A: Timeline, 'Operation Yonatan', op. cit., p. 107.
Page 285	Lubrani, meanwhile . . . been informed. Author interviews with Uri Lubrani and Dany Saadon, op. cit.
Page 285	'Njonjo'. Author interview with Charles Njonjo, op. cit.
Page 286	'Wake up'. . . 'speed, speed'. Hastings, *Yoni*, pp. 7-9.
Pages 286-7	'the sky flashed' . . . 'minutes away'. Betser, *Secret Soldier*, pp. 324–5.
Page 287	'Everything all right' . . . 'No problems'. Netanyahu, *Entebbe*, p. 157.
Page 287	'So far, so good' . . . 'It'll be okay'. Hastings, *Yoni*, p. 9.
Page 287	He then . . . combat blouse. Ibid., p. 7-9.
Pages 287-8	His preparations . . . with Galils. Betser, *Secret Soldier*, p. 325.
Page 288	'Don't screw this up!' 'Rescue at Entebbe: An Interview with the Chief Pilot', op. cit.
Page 288	He had judged . . . relief. Betser, *Secret Soldier*, pp. 325–6.
Page 288	It was 11.01 p.m. Netanyahu, *Entebbe*, p. 157.
Pages 288-9	Yitzhak Rabin . . . knife-edge. Peres, *Battling for Peace*, p. 167; Stevenson, *90 Minutes at Entebbe*, p. 107.
Pages 289-90	For the second night . . . 'simply unthinkable'. Pincher, *Inside Story*, p. 352.
Page 290	Reducing power . . . cause suspicion. Netanyahu, *Entebbe*, p. 158; Betser, *Secret Soldier*, p. 326.
Page 290	'approaching quietly'. 'Entebbe Thirty Years On: Through the Army's Eyes', op. cit.; Interview with Amir Ofer, in *Live or Die in Entebbe*, op. cit.
Page 292	'the distant halo' . . . Land Rovers. Betser, *Secret Soldier*, pp. 327–8; Section 15: Penetration of the Old Terminal, Chapter C: The Operation, 'Operation Yonatan', op. cit., pp. 71–8; Netanyahu, *Entebbe*, pp. 164-5.
Page 293	This prompted. Netanyahu, *Entebbe*, p. 165.
Pages 293-4	'in a fireball' . . . incoming fire. Betser, *Secret Soldier*, pp. 328–9.
Page 294	Netanyahu shouted. Netanyahu, *Entebbe*, pp. 167-8.
Page 294	As Betser ran on . . . Amos Goren. Betser, *Secret Soldier*, pp. 329–30; Section 15: Penetration of the Old Terminal, Chapter C, 'Operation Yonatan', op. cit., pp. 71–8.
Page 294	But in the lead now . . . in the process. 'Entebbe Thirty Years On: Through the Army's Eyes', op. cit.; Interview with Amir Ofer, in *Live or Die in Entebbe*, op. cit.

Page 294	Yoni Netanyahu . . . close behind him. Netanyahu, *Entebbe*, p. 169.
Page 296	Ofer was within . . . to make sure. 'Entebbe Thirty Years On: Through the Army's Eyes', op. cit.; Interview with Amir Ofer, in *Live or Die in Entebbe*, op. cit.
Page 296	Akiva Laxer . . . on the ground. Author interview with Akiva Laxer, op. cit.
Page 296	Among those woken . . . killing hostages. Moufflet, *Otages à Kampala*, p. 159.
Page 296	Others feared . . . human shields. Author interview with Emma and Claude Rosenkovitch, op. cit.
Pages 296-7	Also now awake . . . in the other. Moufflet, *Otages à Kampala*, p. 159; Shuster, 'It's O.K., You're Going Home'.
Page 297	Looking from . . . open fire. Author interview with Ilan Hartuv, op. cit.
Page 297	'If any army' Josephs, 'Michel Bacos: The Air France hero of Entebbe'.
Page 297	The German . . . as he did so. Author interviews with Ilan Hartuv and Gerd Schnepel, op. cit.
Page 297	Assuming Böse no sign. Moufflet, *Otages à Kampala*, pp. 160–1.
Page 298	'Amnon, don't advance!' Netanyahu, *Entebbe*, p. 170.
Page 298	'to make sure' . . . 'from the bullets'. Betser, *Secret Soldier*, pp. 330–1.
Page 298	Then a small object . . . a pillar. Moufflet, *Otages à Kampala*, p. 161.
Page 299	Betser and Goren saw him. . . fell to the floor. Betser, *Secret Soldier*, p. 331.
Page 299	Only a minute . . . turn and run. Ibid.
Page 299	When the shooting started . . . was fatal. Moufflet, *Otages à Kampala*, p. 161.
Page 299	'It's important to understand'. Amir Ofer, in *Live or Die in Entebbe*, op. cit.
Page 300	Moments after . . . floor above. Moufflet, *Otages à Kampala*, p. 161.
Page 300	'Lie down'. Interview with Amir Ofer, in *Live or Die in Entebbe*, op. cit.
Page 300	Ofer's words . . . above her. Netanyahu, *Entebbe*, p. 170.
Page 300	'Here's one of ours!' Moufflet, *Otages à Kampala*, p. 161.
Page 300	'They are here!'. Author interview with Emma and Claude Rosenkovitch, op. cit.
Page 300	'They're ours.' Moufflet, *Otages à Kampala*, p. 161.
Page 300	Are there any terrorists' . . . 'back with us'. Author interview with Akiva Laxer, op. cit.; Betser, *Secret Soldier*, p. 331.
Pages 301-2	While Muki . . . taken prisoner. Netanyahu, *Entebbe* , pp. 178–80; Section 15: Penetration of the Old Terminal, Chapter C, 'Operation Yonatan', op. cit., pp. 71–8.
Pages 302-3	With his team . . . in the leg. Netanyahu, *Entebbe*, pp. 176–8; Section 15: Penetration of the Old Terminal, Chapter C, 'Operation Yonatan', op. cit., pp. 71–8.

Page 303   It was not until . . . to survive. Netanyahu, *Entebbe*, pp. 169, 180–1.

Pages 303-4   'Muki! Muki!' . . . 'Okay'. Betser, *Secret Soldier*, pp. 331–2.

Pages 304-5   By now all four planes . . . escaped. Netanyahu, *Entebbe*, pp. 191–2; Interview with Surin Hershko, in *Live or Die in Entebbe*, op. cit.

Page 305   No sooner had . . . reception hall. Netanyahu, *Entebbe*, pp. 184–5; Section 15: Penetration of the Old Terminal, Chapter C, 'Operation Yonatan', op. cit., pp. 71–8.

Pages 305-6   Hercules Four . . . to safety. Netanyahu, *Entebbe*, pp. 87–8.

Page 306   Once on the ground . . . 'the runway'. Section 16: Rescue of the Hostages, Chapter C, 'Operation Yonatan', op. cit.

Page 306   By then . . . 'in a bad way'. Author interviews with Ephraim Sneh and Noam Tamir, op. cit.

Page 306   En route . . . the plane. Author interview with Ephraim Sneh, op. cit.; Netanyahu, *Entebbe*, p. 187.

Pages 306-7   Back at the Old . . . their bags. Betser, *Secret Soldier*, p. 333.

Page 307   'very pale' . . . 'your shoes!' Moufflet, *Otages à Kampala*, p. 163.

Page 307   Outside Betser . . . the building. Betser, *Secret Soldier*, p. 334.

Page 307   The departure . . . for safety. Author interview with Emma and Claude Rosenkovitch, op. cit.

Page 308   'Come on' . . . long grass. Moufflet, *Otages à Kampala*, p. 165.

Pages 308-9   One of the last . . . the hostages. Netanyahu, *Entebbe*, p. 189.

Page 309   Inside Hercules Four . . . like a nappy. Moufflet, *Otages à Kampala*, pp. 165–6.

Page 309   'My mother' . . . 'left alive'. Netanyahu, *Entebbe*, pp. 193–4.

Pages 309-10   By now . . . started weeping. Moufflet, *Otages à Kampala*, p. 166.

Page 310   On the flight deck . . . on the plane. Netanyahu, *Entebbe*, p. 194.

Pages 310-11   Halivni reported . . . 'Okay'. 'Revealed General Yekutiel "Kuti" Adam, Operation Entebbe Commander Voice', https://www.youtube.com/watch?v=ZnCLKX_GSXw (translated from Hebrew by Karen Gilbert); Yuval Azoulay, 'IDF releases audio recordings from famed 1976 Entebbe rescue', *Haaretz*, 5 May 2008.

Pages 312-13   It was shortly after . . . he could leave. Netanyahu, *Entebbe*, pp. 195–6.

Page 313   His destination . . . 'Good'. Azoulay, 'IDF releases audio recordings from famed 1976 Entebbe rescue'.

Page 313   'climbed heavy-hearted' . . . 'protectors'. Betser, *Secret Soldier*, p. 334.

Page 313   Reaching the end . . . Embakasi Airport. Moufflet, *Otages à Kampala*, p. 167.

Page 314   Kuti Adam . . . 'army hangars'. Section 17: Clearing of the Old Terminal, Chapter C, 'Operation Yonatan', op. cit.; 'Revealed General Yekutiel "Kuti" Adam, Operation Entebbe Commander Voice', op. cit.

Pages 314-5   Not long after . . . 'heroes'. Betser, *Secret Soldier*, p. 335.

Page 315   The two rearguard . . . no response. Section 17: Clearing of the Old Terminal, 'Operation Yonatan', op. cit.

Page 315 'The plane looks dark'. Azoulay, 'IDF releases audio recordings from famed 1976 Entebbe rescue', op. cit.

Page 316 'We've begun to load'. Ibid.

Page 316 Biran then dismantled . . . thirty-nine minutes. Netanyahu, *Entebbe*, p. 199.

Pages 316-7 'there was fighting' . . . 'tanks and trucks'. Kyemba, *A State of Blood*, pp. 171–2.

Page 317 'broke down'. Cipher telegram from British High Commission in Kampala to the FCO, No. 224 of 5 July 1976, TNA, FCO 31/2055.

Pages 317-8 'out of concern' . . . denied. Ibid., 2010hrs GMT, No. 232 of 5 July 1976.

Page 318 Henry Kyemba . . . troops. Kyemba, *A State of Blood*, pp. 172–3.

Pages 318-9 Gerd Schnepel . . . feared the worst. Author interview with Gerd Schnepel, op. cit.

Pages 319-20 The ministers . . . gauge his reaction. Peres, *Battling for Peace*, pp. 167–8.

Pages 320-1 When Amin's voice . . . call back. Stevenson, *90 Minutes at Entebbe*, pp. 215–16.

Pages 321-2 'made a little speech'. . . but delighted. Peres, *Battling for Peace*, p. 168.

Page 322 'Tell Mr Rabin'. Author interview with Amos Eiran, op. cit.

Pages 322-3 'laconic statement' . . . 'Yoni's death'. Peres, *Battling for Peace*, pp. 168–9.

Pages 323-4 For much . . . back of the plane. Moufflet, *Otages à Kampala*, p. 167.

Page 324 'What's this?'. Author interview with Ephraim Sneh, op. cit.

Pages 324-5 Informed by the pilot . . . 'in the morning'. Author telephone interview with Dany Saadon, op. cit.

Page 325 Minutes later . . . of the raid. Moufflet, *Otages à Kampala*, p. 167; Stevenson, *90 Minutes at Entebbe*, p. 134; Ben-Porat, Haber and Schiff, *Entebbe Rescue*, p. 328.

Page 325 The other casualties . . . on the C-130. Author interview with Emma and Claude Rosenkovitch, op. cit.

Page 326 'I understand'. Author interview with Ephraim Sneh, op. cit.

Page 326 'white face' . . . in an instant. Netanyahu, *Entebbe*, p. 202.

Page 326 'We did our duty'. Betser, *Secret Soldier*, p. 337.

Page 326 'completely stunned'. Netanyahu, *Entebbe*, p. 202.

Page 326 'The president wants you' . . . 'Tell him yes'. Author interview with Uri Lubrani, op. cit.

Day 8: Sunday 4 July 1976

Pages 327-8 Not that the hostages . . . dead bodies. Moufflet, *Otages à Kampala*, pp. 167–70.

Page 328 By now . . . 5.18 a.m. Appendix A – Timeline, 'Operation Yonatan', op. cit.

Pages 328-30 On hearing . . . 'Yes'. 'Idi: After all I've done for Israel', *Jerusalem Post*, 5 July 1976.

Pages 330-1   While most . . . doing so. Betser, *Secret Soldier*, pp. 7-8.

Page 331   A few hours . . . 'through with it'. Author interview with Gerd
               Schnepel, op. cit.; Email from Gerd Schnepel to the author, 11
               November 2013.

Page 331   Forty-five minutes . . . to end. Moufflet, *Otages à Kampala*, p.
               170.

Pages 331-2   'Ladies and gentlemen' . . . No one laughed. Author interview
               with Ephraim Sneh, op. cit.

Pages 332-3   Having overseen . . . 'solve itself'. Kyemba, *A State of Blood*, pp.
               173–4.

Pages 333-4   Waiting beside . . . Sabra liquer. 'Entebbe hostages coming
               back home – 4 July 1976', live footage by an IDF film crew,
               http://www.liveleak.com/view?i=4ae_1278267624.

Page 334   In the hangar . . . in the room. Moufflet, *Otages à Kampala*,
               pp. 171–2.

Page 334   'Thank you'. Author interview with Emma and Claude
               Rosenkovitch, op. cit.

Pages 334-5   'emptied, washed'. Moufflet, *Otages à Kampala*, p. 172.

Page 335   As the hostages took off . . . side door. Betser, *Secret Soldier*, p. 338

Page 335   'How was Yoni killed?' . . . as possible. Netanyahu, *Entebbe*, p.
               207.

Pages 335-6   Betser and the others . . . 'famous initiative'. Betser, *Secret
               Soldier*, pp. 338–9.

Page 336   During the fifteen-minute . . . families were waiting. Moufflet,
               Otages à Kampala, pp. 172–4.

Page 336   'Men and women'. *New York Times*, 4 July 1976.

Page 337   The Israelis . . . finally over. Moufflet, *Otages à Kampala*, pp.
               174–6.

Pages 337-8   For four Israeli families . . . 'my son is dead'. *Live or Die in
               Entebbe*, op. cit.; Author interview with Martine Mimouni-
               Arnold, op. cit.; Author interviews with Jonathan Khayat, 7
               and 8 October 2013.

Page 339   Robert would never discover . . . 'put aside'. *Live or Die in
               Entebbe*, op. cit.

Page 339   For a time . . . operating table. Ben-Porat, Haber and Schiff,
               Entebbe Rescue, p. 332.

Pages 339-40   The first member . . . 'throughout the country'. Netanyahu,
               Entebbe, pp. 7–8.

Page 340   'ran to the terminal' . . . 'ever had'. 'Operation Entebbe proto-
               cols revealed', op. cit.

Pages 340-1   'Mr Speaker'. . . 'pride to us all'. Statement of Prime Minister
               Yitzhak Rabin in the Knesset on the Liberation of the
               Passengers of the Hijacked Air France Plane in Uganda, 4 July
               1976, TNA, FCO 93/914/20.

Pages 342-3   'Not since the Six-Day' . . . 'message of Entebbe'. Avner, *The
               Prime Ministers*, pp. 314–16.

Page 343   British diplomat . . . via Air France. Cipher telegram from
               British High Commission in Kampala to FCO, 0815hrs GMT,
               No. 225 of 5 July 1976, TNA, FCO 31/2055.

Page 343 — 'hadn't got away'. Crosland, *Tony Crosland*, p. 346.

Page 343 — 'to get Mrs Bloch'. Tony Crosland to the High Commissioner at Kampala, 1730hrs GMT, No. 105 of 4 July 1976, TNA, FCO 93/913/13.

Pages 343-4 — Accompanied by his wife ... Dora Bloch. 'Mrs Dora Bloch, UK/Israeli Dual National', Confidential Report by Peter Chandley, 7 July 1976, TNA, FCO 31/2060.

Page 344 — This was the result ... 'both parties'. Kyemba, *A State of Blood*, p. 174.

Pages 344-5 — 'in the presence' ... 'in tears'. 'Mrs Dora Bloch, UK/Israeli Dual National', op. cit.

Pages 345-6 — 'smarting with humiliation' ... 'This is terrible'. Kyemba, *A State of Blood*, pp. 174–6.

Aftermath

Page 347 — 'This is a harsh land' ... 'pain and mourning'. Marcus Eliason of the Associated Press, 'African Nations Condemn Israel's Hostage Rescue', *Abilene Report-News*, 6 July 1976.

Pages 347-8 — 'Government of Israel' ... 'blackmail'. Yigal Allon to the British Ambassador to Israel, 5 July 1976, in No. 139 of 6 July 1976, TNA, FCO 93/913.

Page 348 — 'personal congratulations'. Record of a telephone conversation between the Minister of State [Hattersley] and the Israeli Ambassador, 6 July 1976, TNA, FCO 93/913.

Page 348 — 'We see no particular need'. R. N. Dales, Private Secretary to Roy Hattersley, to Patrick Wright, Private Secretary to James Callaghan, 5 July 1976, TNA, FCO 93/913/13.

Pages 348-9 — 'to express his relief' ... 'were Jews'. Confidential letter from Julian Bullard, Minister at British Embassy in Bonn, to David Goodall, Head of Western European Department at FCO, 7 July 1976, TNA, FCO 31/2056.

Page 349 — France and Switzerland. *Daily Express*, 5 July 1976; Cipher telegram from British Ambassador in Stockholm to FCO, No. 133 of 5 July 1976, TNA, FCO 31/2055.

Page 349 — 'great satisfaction'. *Daily Express*, 5 July 1976.

Page 349 — 'We will not let Kenya'. Teleconversation between Henry Kissinger and Simcha Dinitz, 1210hrs GMT, declassified State Department Archives, SJ20, released 28 July 2003, 200102979, www.aad.archives.gov/aad..

Page 349 — 'Uganda reserves her right'. Cipher cable from US Ambassador to the UN to State Department, 1437hrs GMT, 6 July 1976, US State Department Archives, www.aad.archives.gov/aad.

Page 350 — 'unprecedented aggression' ... 'the UN'. TNA, FCO 93/913.

Page 350 — 'has not been used' ... 'public stance'. Cipher telegram from British High Commission in Nairobi to FCO, No. 1738 of 5 July 1976, TNA, FCO 31/2055.

Page 350 — 'The Kenyans'. Ibid., No. 1746 of 5 July 1976.

Page 351 — 'only in such a way' ... 'its mistake'. Cipher telegram from

British High Commission in Kampala to FCO, No. 223 of 5 July 1976, ibid.

Page 351   'government terrorism'. Ismail Fahmy, Egyptian Foreign Minister, quoted in cipher cable from British Embassy in Cairo to FCO, No. 653 of 5 July 1976, ibid.

Page 351   'latest act of piracy' . . . 'member state'. *Daily Express*, 5 July 1976.

Pages 351-2 'any inquiries' . . . 'had happened'. Kyemba, *A State of Blood*, pp. 176–7.

Page 352   Amin . . . categorically denied. Cipher telegram from British High Commission in Kampala to FCO, No. 233 of 5 July 1976, TNA, FCO 31/2055.

Page 352   'had been dragged' . . . 'own losses'. Cipher telegram from British High Commission in Kampala to FCO, No. 225 of 5 July 1976, TNA, FCO 93/913.

Page 352   'access to Mrs Bloch'. Draft cipher telegram from FCO to British High Commission in Kampala, 5 July 1976, TNA, FCO 93/913.

Page 352   A day after . . . into the ground. 'Israelis Honor Slain Commander', Associated Press, in *Abilene Reporter-News*, 7 July 1976.

Page 353   'There are times' . . . 'of innocents'. Hastings, *Yoni*, pp. 233–5.

Pages 354-5 'for the sole benefit' . . . 'rejected by France'. Goldberg, *Namesake*, pp. 132–4.

Page 355   'many more hostages' . . . 'same thing'. Author interview with Ilan Hartuv, op. cit.

Page 355   Hartuv's written deposition . . . open court. Ibid.

Page 355   'It's a moral victory'. *New York Times*, 5 July 1981.

Page 356   'the Palestinians' . . . 'the government'. Cipher telegram from British High Commission in Kampala to FCO, No. 263 of 8 July 1976, TNA, FCO 31/2056.

Pages 356-9 Uganda's foreign minister . . . to be adopted. *Maintenance of international peace and security*, Chapter VIII, pp. 286–90, http://www.un.org/en/sc/repertoire/75-80/Chapter%20 8/75-80_08-15-Complaint%20by%20the%20Prime%20 Minister%20of%20Mauritius.pdf.

Page 359   Arriving back . . . had been found. Crosland, *Tony Crosland*, p. 351.

Page 359   The British High Commission . . . mark the spot. Robert Verkaik, 'Revealed: The fate of Idi Amin's hijack victim', *Independent*, 13 February 2007.

Pages 359-61 Hearing the news . . . 'out of Uganda'. Crosland, *Tony Crosland*, p. 351.

Page 361   'negotiating compensation'. G. R. Berridge, 'The British Interests Section in Kampala, 1976–7', January 2012, http:// grberridge.diplomacy.edu.

Page 361   'remained conspicuously' . . . later murdered. Kyemba, *A State of Blood*, p. 177.

Page 361   Dora Bloch . . . fled from Uganda. 'Dispute between Uganda and Kenya', *Keesing's Record of World Events*, vol. 22, August 1976.

Page 361	The Kenyans . . . had hoped. Ibid.; Confidential memo of the meeting between Ted Rowlands, Minister of State at the FCO, and Kenyan High Commissioner, 28 July 1976, TNA, FCO 93/914.
Pages 361-2	'with deep regret' . . . 1946. 'Great Britain severs diplomatic ties with Uganda', *San Bernardino County Sun*, 29 July 1976.
Page 362	'brutal' . . . 'in Nicaragua'. Author skype interview with Gerd Schnepel, op. cit.; Email from Gerd Schnepel to the author, 11 November 2013.
Pages 362-3	'For most group members' . . . 'West Germany'. Karcher, 'Sisters in Arms?', pp. 240–1.
Page 363	The events at Entebbe . . . 'an old story'. Paul Berman, *Power and the Idealists: Or, the Passion of Joschka Fischer and its Aftermath* (New York, 2007), pp. 58–60.
Pages 363-4	'incurable disease' . . . 'Haddad died'. 'Terrorism's Godfather Is Dead', Associated Press report, *Santa Cruz Sentinel*, 2 April 1978.
Page 364	'He gave extreme'. Follain, *Jackal*, p. 144.
Page 364	Many at the time . . . eventually died. Ami Pedahzur, *The Israeli Secret Services and the Struggle against Terrorism* (New York, 2010), pp. 61-2; Aaron J. Klein, *Striking Back: The 1972 Munich Olympics Massacre and Israel's Deadly Response* (New York, 2006), pp. 207-8. After Haddad's death, the PFLP-EA was dissolved, though other splinter groups from the original PFLP continued to operate. Many of Haddad's people joined a new group set up by Carlos the Jackal called the Organisation of Arab Armed Struggle. Its members included former RC terrorists Johannes Weinrich and Magadalena Kopp (who left Weinrich to marry Carlos in 1979). Carlos and Weinrich were finally arrested in the mid-1990s – the former in the Sudan and the latter in Yemen – and are currently serving life sentences for terrorist offences in France and Germany respectively.
Page 365	On a spring morning . . . 24 May 1978. Ed Harriman, 'The British connection', *New Scientist*, 10 May 1979, pp. 432–5.
Page 365	'He wanted to see'. Author interview with Charles Njonjo, op. cit.
Pages 365-6	'Amin might take' . . . trip was postponed. Pincher, *Dangerous to Know*, pp. 105-6.
Page 366	After landing . . . 'potty'. Author interview with Christina McKenzie, op. cit.; Pincher, *Dangerous to Know*, p. 106
Page 366	Eventually a car . . . young boys. Author interview with Christine McKenzie, op. cit.; Pincher, *Dangerous to Know*, p. 106; David Ochami, 'Ugandan agents killed former Cabinet minister, says dossier', *Standard* (Nairobi), 23 January 2013; Hornby, *Kenya*, p. 319.
Page 367	'at those against'. Kyemba, *A State of Blood*, p. 179.
Pages 367-8	Six weeks after . . . spinal x-rays. Cipher telegram from British High Commission in Kampala to FCO, No. 155 of 30 May 1979, TNA, FCO 93/2110.
Page 368	As the New Year's Eve . . . Entebbe Raid. *New York Times*, 9 January 1981.

Postscript

Page 370   'a small handpicked' . . . Delta Force. John C. Frederiksen,
                Fighting Elites: A History of U.S. Special Forces (New York,
                2011), pp. 154–7.

Page 370   'the best illustration'. William H. McRaven, *Spec Ops: Case
                Studies in Special Operations Warfare Theory and Practice* (New
                York, 1995), p. 378.

Pages 370-1   'In a world' . . . 'Second World War'. Max Hastings, *Going to
                the Wars* (London, 2000), p. 250.

Page 371   'pride' . . . 'plus 20'. Author interview with Ephraim Sneh, op.
                cit.

Page 372   'These Days'. Judy Lash Baling, 'Remembering Entebbe', 3 July
                2001, in http://www.jerusalemdiaries com/article/6

Page 372   'This spectacular operation' . . . 'been forgotten'. Jonathan
                Khayat and Kobi Cohen, in *Live or Die in Entebbe*, op. cit.

Page 373   'It was double-edged' . . . 'something else'. Author interview
                with Emma and Claude Rosenkovitch, op. cit.

BIBLIOGRAPHY

Primary Sources

Archives

BStU Archive (Federal Commissioner for the Stasi Records), Berlin, Germany
Politisches Archiv of the Auswärtiges Amt (Political Archive of the Federal
  Foreign Office), Berlin, Germany
IDF & Defense Establishment Archives, Tel Aviv, Israel
The National Archives, London, UK
US State Department Archives, Washington, US

Private Papers

Dr Colonel (Retd.) Zeev Drory

Books

Abu-Sharif, Bassam, and Uzi Mahnaimi, *Best of Enemies* (New York, 1995)
Avner, Yehuda, *The Prime Ministers: An Intimate Narrative of Israeli Leadership*
  (New Milford, Connecticut, 2010)
Benedikt, Linda, *Yitzhak Rabin: The Battle for Peace* (London, 2005)
Ben-Porat, Yeshayahu, Eitan Haber and Zeev Schiff, *Entebbe Rescue* (New
  York, 1976; this paperback edition 1977)
Berman, Paul, *Power and the Idealists: Or, the Passion of Joschka Fischer and
  its Aftermath* (New York, 2007)
Betser, Colonel Muki, *Secret Soldier: The Incredible True Story of Israel's
  Greatest Commando* (1996, this paperback edition London, 1997)
Crosland, Susan, *Tony Crosland* (London, 1982)
Dunstan, Simon, *Israel's Lightning Strike: The Raid on Entebbe 1976* (Oxford,
  2009)

Follain, John, *Jackal: The Secret Wars of Carlos the Jackal* (1998, this paperback edition London, 2004)

Frederiksen, John C., *Fighting Elites: A History of U.S. Special Forces* (New York, 2011)

Goldberg, Michel, *Namesake* (1982, this paperback edition London, 1984)

Hastings, Max, *Going to the Wars* (London, 2000)

Hastings, Max, *Yoni: Hero of Entebbe* (London, 1979)

Hebditch, David, and Ken Connor, *How to Stage a Military Coup: From Planning to Execution* (London, 2005)

Hornby, Charles, *Kenya: A History since Independence* (London, 2011)

Jefferys, Kevin, *Anthony Crosland* (London, 1999)

Jones, Clive, and Tore T. Petersen (eds), *Israel's Clandestine Diplomacies* (New York, 2013)

Kissinger, Henry, *Years of Renewal: The Concluding Volume of his Memoirs* (New York, 1999)

Klein, Aaron J., *Striking Back: The 1972 Munich Olympics Massacre and Israel's Deadly Response* (2006)

Kyemba, Henry, *A State of Blood: The Inside Story of Idi Amin* (New York, 1977)

McRaven, William H., *Spec Ops: Case Studies in Special Operations Warfare Theory and Practice* (New York, 1995)

Moufflet, Claude, *Otages à Kampala* (Paris, 1976, translated from French into English by Rachel Kenyon)

Netanyahu, Iddo, *Yoni's Last Battle: The Rescue at Entebbe, 1976* (Jerusalem, 2013)

Netanyahu, Iddo, *Entebbe: A Defining Moment in the War on Terrorism* (Green Forest, Arkansas, 2003)

Netanyahu, Jonathan, *The Letters of Jonathan Netanyahu* (Jerusalem, 2001)

Ofer, Yehuda, *Operation Thunder: The Entebbe Raid – The Israelis' Own Story* (London, 1976)

Pedahzur, Ami, *The Israeli Secret Services and the Struggle against Terrorism* (New York, 2010)

Peres, Shimon, *Battling for Peace: A Memoir* (New York, 1995)

Pincher, Chapman, *Dangerous to Know: A Life* (London, 2014)

Pincher, Chapman, *Inside Story: A Documentary of the Pursuit of Power* (1978, this paperback edition London, 1981)

Rabin, Yitzhak, *The Rabin Memoirs* (1979, this paperback edition Berkeley, 1996)

Stevenson, William, *90 Minutes at Entebbe: The First Full Inside Story of Operation Thunderbolt* (New York, 1976)

Thomas, Gordon, *Gideon's Spies: Mossad's Secret Warriors* (London, 1999)

Williams, Louis, 'Combined Operations: Entebbe', in *The Israeli Defense Forces: A People's Army* (New York, 1996)

Williamson, Tony, *Counter Strike Entebbe* (London, 1976)

Articles etc

Azoulay, Yuval, 'IDF releases audio recordings from famed 1976 Entebbe rescue', *Haaretz*, 5 May 2008

Baling, Judy Lash, 'Remembering Entebbe', 3 July 2001, in http://www.jerusalemdiaries.com/article/6

Ben, Eyal, 'Entebbe's unsung hero', ynetnews.com, 29 April 2012

Berridge, G. R., 'The British Interests Section in Kampala, 1976–7', January 2012, http://grberridge.diplomacy.edu

'Between Bonn and Entebbe', *Frankfurter Rundschau*, 6 July 1976

'Bonn won't climb down: Terrorists stay imprisoned', *Die Welt*, 1 July 1976, BStU Archive [Federal Commissioner for the Stasi Records], Berlin, Mfs/ HA IX/9979

Cohen on the Bridge (2012), animated short film documentary written and directed by Andrew Wainrib

Derai, Laly, 'I owe my life to the IDF', *Hamodia*, No. 11, June 2011

'Dispute between Uganda and Kenya', *Keesing's Record of World Events*, vol. 22, August 1976

Eliason, Marcus, of the Associated Press, 'African Nations Condemn Israel's Hostage Rescue', *Abilene Reporter-News*, 6 July 1976

'Entebbe hostages coming back home – 4 July 1976', live footage by an IDF film crew, http://www.liveleak.com/view?i=4ae_1278267624

'Entebbe Thirty Years On: Mancunian on Board', *Jewish Telegraph Online*, 2006, www.jewishtelegraph.com/enteb_2.html

'Entebbe Thirty Years On: Through the Army's Eyes', *Jewish Telegraph Online*, 2006, www.jewishtelegraph.com/enteb_1.html

Feldinger, Lauren Gelfond, 'Through the Eyes of Hostages', *Jerusalem Post*, 29 June 2006

'Freed Hostages Tell their Story', *Jewish Telegraphic Agency*, 1 July 1976

'Great Britain severs diplomatic ties with Uganda', *San Bernardino County Sun*, 29 July 1976

Hamerman, Josh, 'Battling against "the falsification of history"', ynetnews.com, 4 February 2007

Harriman, Ed, 'The British connection', *New Scientist*, 10 May 1979, pp. 432–5

'Idi: After all I've done for Israel', *Jerusalem Post*, 5 July 1976

'Israelis Honor Slain Commander', Associated Press, in *Abilene Reporter-News*, 7 July 1976

Josephs, Jeremy, 'Michel Bacos: The Air France hero of Entebbe', *Jewish Chronicle*, 15 June 2012

Kamau, John, 'How Mossad threw Kenya into the line of terrorist fire', *Daily Nation*, 17 January 2014

Kaplan, David E., 'A historic hostage-taking revisited', *Jerusalem Post*, 3 August 2006, http://www.jpost.com/Features/A-historic-hostage-taking-revisited

Karcher, Katharina, 'Sisters in Arms? Female Participation in Leftist Political Violence in the Federal Republic of Germany since 1970', unpublished PhD thesis, University of Warwick, 2013

Lavie, Aviv, 'Surviving the myth', *Haaretz*, 31 July 2003

Lipkin-Shakhak, Tali, 'The Forgotten Hero of Entebbe', *Ma'ariv* Saturday supplement, 16 June 2006

Live or Die in Entebbe, feature-length documentary written and directed by Eyal Boers, Dynamic Flash Ltd, 2012

Melman, Yossi, 'Legendary Mossad operative behind some of spy agency's most daring operations dies at 87', *Jerusalem Post*, 22 September 2014

Melman, Yossi, 'Setting the record straight: Entebbe was not Auschwitz', *Haaretz*, 8 July 2011

Miller, Moshe, 'Miracles at Entebbe', *Zman Magazine*, No. 126, July 2012, p. 128

Ochami, David, 'Ugandan agents killed former Cabinet minister, says dossier', *Standard* (Nairobi), 23 January 2013

'Operation Entebbe Protocols revealed', *Ynet Magazine*, 11 May 2010, http://www.ynetnews.com/articles/0,7340,L-3980051,00.html

Rabinowitz, Nancy and Peter, 'Fifty-two Hundred and Ninety Minutes at Entebbe: The Paradoxes of Terror', *Syracuse Guide*, October 1976, p. 17

'Rescue at Entebbe: An Interview with the Chief Pilot', IDF Blog, 5 July 2012, www. idfblog.com/2012/07/05/rescue-at-entebbe-an-interview-with-the-chief-pilot/

'Revealed General Yekutiel "Kuti" Adam, Operation Entebbe Commander Voice', https://www.youtube.com/watch?v=ZnCLKX_GSXw [translated from Hebrew by Karen Gilbert]

Shuster, Alvin, 'It's O.K., You're Going Home', *New York Times*, 5 July 1976

Situation Critical: Assault on Entebbe, National Geographic Channel, 12 June 2007

'Terrorism's Godfather Is Dead', Associated Press report, *Santa Cruz Sentinel*, 2 April 1978

'Two West Germans Sentenced for 1976 Plot to Shoot Down Israeli Airliner', *Jewish Telegraph Agency*, 14 September 1979, http://www.jta.org/1979/09/14/archive/ two-west-germans-sentenced-for-1976-plot-to-shoot-down-israeli-airliner

Verkaik, Robert, 'Revealed: The fate of Idi Amin's hijack victim', *Independent*, 13 February 2007

ACKNOWLEDGEMENTS

Though only ten-years-old at the time, I remember Saturday 3 July 1976 as if it was yesterday. A keen tennis fan, I sat transfixed as a young and un-fancied Bjorn Borg took on Ilie Nastase, the enfant terrible of the game, and beat him in straight sets to win the first of his five consecutive Gentleman Singles' titles on the sun-baked grass courts of the All England Club at Wimbledon. Consumed by this sporting drama, I was unaware – as was the rest of the world – that the week-long hijack drama at Entebbe Airport in Uganda was about to come to a sudden and violent conclusion as Israeli planes were even then flying south from Sharm el-Sheikh in the Sinai, carrying commandos who would storm the Old Terminal at night, kill all the terrorists and rescue the vast majority of the 100 or so hostages in the most audacious special forces operation in history.

I may have overheard mention of the raid on TV and radio news programmes the following day, along with accounts of a million US citizens on the streets of Washington to celebrate two hundred years of independence from British rule. By Monday 5 July, however, there was only one story that mattered in the British press: 'Israel rejoices at success of raid to free Entebbe hostages', read the front page headline in *The Times*.

It was huge international news and within a few months had inspired three hastily written books – all by journalists – and three feature films, including *Victory at Entebbe* starring Anthony Hopkins, Burt Lancaster and Elizabeth Taylor. More books followed as the years went by, but not a proper history from the perspective of all those involved: hostages, rescuers, terrorists, politicians, diplomats, journalists and terrorists (of whom remarkably little was known). The spark for my own interest in researching and writing such a dramatic anti-terrorist mission – after many years penning more conventional military histories – was a two line email from my agent: '2016 marks 40th anniversary of the Raid on Entebbe. Might this be worth thinking about? Just a thought . . .'

My initial reaction was cautiously positive. 'Yes,' I wrote back, 'not a bad idea. I can go to Israel to i/v the survivors.' The more I read about it, the more my enthusiasm grew. I was looking to try something new and, as far as I could see, the story had not yet been properly told. I decided to write it unfolding in real time, with the narrative shifting from the sweltering Old Terminal at Entebbe, where the hostages were kept, to the cabinet rooms of the governments involved (particularly Israel), the houses of the hostages' families, the head-quarters of the Israeli Defence Force (IDF), the airport in Paris where the released hostages were debriefed, the bases of the soldiers chosen to spearhead the rescue force and, finally, the C-130 Hercules planes that were used to ferry the rescue force to Entebbe. The inten-tion was to convey the unbearable tension felt by all involved as the clock ticked towards the final, bloody denouement. Where possible I have used dialogue that is sourced from diaries, memoirs, biographies and tape recordings. For the occasional bits of the story where no record of the dialogue exists – or has not yet been discovered – I have constructed it myself using more general accounts of that meeting or conversation, and my own assessment of the personalities involved, their motivations and the type of language they typically used. The result is, I hope, an exciting true story that is exhaustively researched yet reads more like a novel than a traditional history.

I'm particularly grateful to the participants – Israeli soldiers and politicians, hostages, a key member of the Kenyan government and a former terrorist – who shared with me their memories of that trau-matic week and its aftermath: Muki Betser, Amnon Biran, Olivier Cojot-Goldberg, Stéphane Cojot-Goldberg, Amos Eiran, Ilan Hartuv, Aliva Laxer, Uri Lubrani, Christina McKenzie, Martine Mimouni-Arnold, Charles Njonjo, Nancy Rabinowitz, Peter Rabinowitz, Emma Rosenkovitch, Claude Rosenkovitch, Dany Saadon, Gerd Schnepel, Ephraim Sneh, Noam Tamir and Louis Williams.

Of the many other people who contributed in vital ways to the book – giving contact details, setting up interviews, finding and translating documents, recommending areas of research, answering questions about the story and the personalities involved, and reading the manuscript – I would like to thank Rachel Kenyon (my wonderful French translator), Hester Abrams, Rebecca Abrams, Massoud Alikhani, Eyal Boers, Tim Butcher, Juliet David, Uri Dromi, Dr Colonel (Retd.) Zeev Drory, Aliza Eshed, Matthew Fox, Karen Gilbert, Holly Harwood, Yaakov Havakook, Jonathan Khayat, Damien Lewis, Kevin Maxwell, S.H. Neumark, Reuven Merhav, Yossi Melman, Jakob Schäfer, Andrew Sharpe, Fiona Sharpe, Dominic Sutherland and Michal Wulkan.

I am grateful to Penguin Random House for permission to quote from Shimon Peres's *Battling for Peace*; Sir Max Hastings for *Yoni: Hero of Entebbe* and *Going to the Wars*; to Louis Williams for *The Israeli Defense Forces*; to Katharina Karcher, for 'Sisters in Arms? Female Participation in Leftist Political Violence in the Federal Republic of Germany since 1970' (her unpublished PhD thesis); and to Olivier, Stéphane, Yael Cojot-Goldberg and David Franck for their father Michel Goldberg's *Namesake*. I am also grateful to Dr Zeev Drory of the Kinneret Center on Peace, Security and Society in Memory of Dan Shomron for permission to use documents and photos in the center's possession and to Eyal Boers for letting me use extracts from his excellent and moving documentary *Live or Die in Entebbe*. I have endeavoured without success to contact other copyright owners for permission to include material from their books. I would urge them to get in touch.

This book was bought as a joint venture by Rupert Lancaster of Hodder UK and Geoff Shandler of Little, Brown in the US. I thank them both for their backing, and Rupert for his perceptive editing. Sadly Geoff was not able to see the book through to publication, but Vanessa Mobley, my Executive Editor at Little, Brown, has stepped into the breach with enthusiasm and expertise. Both Rupert and Vanessa have been assisted by first-class teams: Maddy Price, Leni Lawrence, Juliet Brightmore and Peter James in the UK; and Morgan Moroney, Daniel Jackson and Meghan Deans in the US.

I always have good reason to thank my agent Peter Robinson (and his wonderful assistant Federica Leonardis), but this time more than ever: he came up with the idea; played a key role in shaping both proposal and manuscript; and then had enough faith to pitch it to film agent Matthew Bates who promptly sold an option to the film company StudioCanal (currently developing a script about the Entebbe Raid with Working Title). The only thing Peter didn't do is write the book.

My wife Louise and daughters Nell, Tamar and Natasha have shown more enthusiasm for this book than any previous, even those dedicated to them. I'd like to think it's because the story encapsulates so much that is good about the human spirit – fortitude, grace under pressure and courage (moral and physical) – and because for most of those involved there was a happy ending. But the real reason, I suspect, is because I foolishly mentioned the faint possibility of a red carpet and a film première. More fool me.

PICTURE ACKNOWLEDGEMENTS

© Africa Media Online/Mary Evans Picture Library: 7 above right. © AP/Press Association Images: 3 above right, 4 above/photo Max Nash, 5 above left/photo Bob Daugherty, 5 below/photo Schlagmann, 9 above and below/photos Michael Lipchitz, 13 below, 14 below, 15 above and below. © Associated Newspapers/REX: 11 above. Courtesy of Cojot-Goldberg family: 6 above and below. © Corbis/photo Jim McDonald: 16 above right. Colonel (Retd) Dr Zeev Drory and the Israeli Government Press Office: 10 below, 11 below. © Getty Images/Keystone: 3 below left, 4 below, 8 below, 14 above right. © Getty Images/United News: 7 below right. Doug Griffin/Toronto Star via Getty Images: 5 above right. © Israel Sun/REX: 1 above, 2 above. Courtesy of the McKenzie family: 8 above. Courtesy of the National Photo Collection, Government Press Office, Israel: 1 below, 2 below, 10 above, 12 above, 13 above, 14 above left. Courtesy of Julian Panton: 16 above left. © Ruch/Ullstein bild via Getty Images: 3 above left. © Sipa Press/REX: 16 below. © TopFoto/AP: 7 above left. 12 below.

INDEX

In Arabic names the definite article (al-), used as a prefix, is ignored in the ordering of entries and placed at the end of the name, e.g. al-Kubaisi can be found at Kubaisi, Basil al-.

Air France Boeing 707 flight
from Tel Aviv to Paris 337
Air France Jumbo 'Château de la
Roche-Guyon' 197–8, 201, 217
'Ali' *see* Ma'ati, Ali al- ('red shirt')
Allon, Yigal 18, 35, 52, 75, 102,
128, 134, 138–9, 148–9, 164,
168–9, 170, 209, 210, 228,
231, 241, 347–8
and Rabin 128, 134, 148–9,
165, 168–9, 209, 210
Almog, Ezra 106–7
Almog, Janet 106–7, 219, 225
Altmann, Klaus *see* Barbie, Klaus
Amin, Idi 8, 21, 22, 58–9, 233
and Air Force fighter jets 94,
125
and Bar-Lev 109–10, 135–7,
151–3, 174–7, 179, 320–21, 329
and Betser 67–8
and Dora Bloch's fate 345–6,
351–2, 357–8, 359–61
collaboration question with
PFLP and highjackers 61,
67–8, 70–71, 78–9, 81–2,
83–4, 95, 96–7, 154, 155–6,
163, 173, 176–7, 190, 196,
220, 231–2, 234, 249–50,
261–2, 329–30, 347, 356, 357
and Dan 329–30
and Dayan 21, 109, 136, 153,
187–8
Entebbe Airport visits 81,
123–6, 178–9, 224, 281–2
flight from Tanzanian Army
367

and Haddad 151, 153–4, 175,
283
and Horrocks 240, 318, 352
intelligence gathering about
121–2
and Israel 59, 61, 81, 101,
109–10, 117, 118, 121–2, 124–5,
136, 210, 215, 224, 229, 230,
261–2, 320–21, 322, 329–30
and Kenya 153, 247–8, 349–50,
361
and Kyemba 63, 79, 93–4, 97,
283, 345–6, 351–2
and Libya 22, 58
and Lubrani 133–4, 278–9
and McKenzie's death 365–6
Mimouni's telegram to 103
and Netanyahu 277
and the OAU *see*
Organization of African
Unity (OAU)
and Operation Thunderbolt
316, 317, 318, 320–21
and Peres 109–10, 121–2,
151–4, 174–7
and Renard 356
report of released Americans
220
and the security/welfare of
hostages 69, 81–2, 93–4,
110–11, 117, 123–6, 129–30,
135–7, 175–6, 221, 224, 283
and the security of terrorists
69
threats against British
community in Uganda 359

ABOUT THE AUTHOR

SAUL DAVID is a military historian and broadcaster. He is the author of *The Indian Mutiny*, which was shortlisted for the Duke of Westminster's Medal for Military Literature, *Military Blunders, Zulu: The Heroism and Tragedy of the Zulu War of 1879* (a Waterstone's Military History Book of the Year) and *Victoria's Wars*.